INTERNAL CRISIS IN SOUTH ASIA

INTERNAL CRISIS IN SOUTH ASIA

DR. MADHU KUMARI

KALPAZ

First Published, 2019

Published by

Kalpaz Publications
C-30, Satyawati Nagar,
Delhi – 110052
Ph.: 011-47034999, 9811692060
www.kalpazpublications.com
E-mail: kalpaz@hotmail.com

Printed at: G. Print Process, Delhi

Cataloging in Publication Data—DK
Courtesy: D.K. Agencies (P) Ltd. <docinfo@dkagencies.com>

Kumari, Madhu, *Dr.*, author.
Internal crisis in South Asia / Dr. Madhu Kumari.
pages cm
ISBN 9789353240721

1. Insurgency—India. 2. Insurgency—South Asia. 3. Internal security—India. 4. Internal security—South Asia. 5. India—Politics and government. 6. South Asia—Politics and government. I. Title.

LCC HV6295.S64K86 2019 | DDC 355.02180954 23

Contents

Preface

In today's world, every state is passing through many crises, conflicts and violence. It is an inevitable feature and part human nature and it is more common where the communities encompass diverse socio-cultural and economic disparities. It arises and persist when there is clash of interests, clash of identities and discriminations; there are resources but are not equally and adequately distributed; when there is struggle to gain power and the concerns of human security are neglected.

For the purpose of this discussion, internal conflict is defined as the existence of organized groups within states which enjoy some degree of intra-group legitimacy and coherence and whose demands and interests are not readily reconciled or resolved within existing domestic institutional (political, judicial or economic) mechanisms. This definition suggests that internal conflict within a state is linked to the inability of existing institutional mechanisms at the national, regional or local level to adequately manage or address the concerns of dissatisfied groups, resulting in the resort to violence by members of these groups or by state authorities.

South Asia has earned a status of its own as an important area in conflict studies and why not? South Asia is one of the most crisis prone region in the world with some of the highest levels of contested borders; militarised inter-states disputes which have witnessed five full scale inter-state wars; where adversaries are nuclear armed major powers and some of its states have earned the distinction of becoming a part of the hub of global terrorism; where no country is free from insurgencies and separatists movement; where human life is less significant killing every day many people, forcing them either to migrate or converting in the name of religion.

The potential cost of crises in South Asia are always remain high due to global political strategic and development dynamics including the role of great powers inflicted by the forces and factors from outside the region as in case of Afghanistan. The crisis generated in Afghanistan as a result of first the Soviet intervention and then by the United states to wage a war on terrorism. Some crisis in south Asia are inherited and strategically induced because of the inter-state rivalries. A typical example is the Kashmir crisis between India and Pakistan which has been deepen and sharpen the various regional divides and complicated the problem. The strategic imperatives of the world order dynamics contributed to South Asian crisis while the ideological issues have done so indirectly and gradually stimulating and reinforcing many internal issues.

Insurgencies and ethnic-sectarian-communal crisis have been precipitated and nurtured by the internal political turbulence, socio-cultural fault lines and development distortions in all South Asian States. Like Naxalites or Maoists insurgency in India; Baluchistan, Pashtunistan, Gilgit-Baltistan and Sectarian crisis in Sindh and MQM in Pakistan; Madhesi movement in Nepal and Tamil insurgencies of 1980s and now the anti-Muslims violence in Sri Lanka; Islamic extremism and violence against minorities especially Hindus in Bangladesh. Only in Maldives, it is a political crisis for establishment of democracy. Identity and ownership of the state and the nation-in-the-making bring diverse social groups at daggers drawn. Pakistan's unsettled national identity, accentuated by the dominance of Punjabis over the Sindhi, Baluchi and Pathan social groups, and Sri Lanka's decision in 1959 to carve itself out as a Sinhala-Buddhist State by ignoring the sensitivities of the minority groups of Tamils and Muslims have been at the root of serious internal crises. Displacement of marginalised populations and alienation of cultural (tribal) groups is considered one of the important reasons behind the rise of not only Naxal insurgency but all insurgence movement all over India. Since the past 72 years, democratic evolution in India has been confronting numerous challenges to integrate the marginalised social groups and now the surge of hitherto neglected and discriminated caste and tribal groups are putting huge pressure on the capacities of the state and its political processes. Unequal distribution of the fruits of development and the widening gap between aspirations and acquisitions of the poor people are also aggravating the situation. In Nepal, the 10 years of Maoist insurgency from 1996 to 2006 was sustained by the marginalised tribal and regional groups who are now demanding equal and respectable status in Nepal "New Constitution".

South Asian states crisis have their colonial legacies and turbulence process of state building and nation building and the absurdity of the methods used for transfer of powers that contributing to the persisting sources of tensions and war on the unresolved questions as the Kashmir crisis and Pakistan's problems of Baluchistan ,Pashutinistan, Gilgit – Baltistan and Sindhustan etc.

Many internal crises in South Asia have Cross-borders dimensions. Taliban in Afghanistan obtains significant support from Pakistan's border areas and having link with ISISI of Iraq, Syria Iran. Bangladesh Islamic outfits have links with Pakistan, Afghanistan, Saudi Arabia and ISISI. Sri Lanka Buddhists groups like Bodo Bela Sena have link with Myanmar and Thailand while Muslim fundamentalists/terrorist groups are linked with the ISISI and other Muslim terrorist groups across Asia.

Despite the economic globalization, technological innovation, and population flow which are rapidly transforming the world, this region remains trapped in lingering cycles of conflict and violence, contributing to underdevelopment, poor governance, and instability. In an increasingly inter-connected and porous region, with the stream of people, arms and ammunitions, legal and illegal trade, and ideologies crossing national borders, conflict and violence in one country is severely impacting other countries.

In response of these issues, Internal Crises in South Asia presents a critical overview of the diversity and complexity and nature of crises entrenched in complex historical patterns and current trends. This volume covers all the South Asian States except Bhutan that is fortunately unaffected by any internal crisis. Significantly, this volume contextualizes types of violent conflicts and specifying the predominance in different areas. Each chapter is focused with in-depth knowledge and analysis understanding of local politics and power and political regimes which has profound connections between internal crisis and violence, land and natural resource, borders and boundaries, insurgencies and terrorism.

The best way to attain firm understanding to the problems is to recognize the enduring questions in unfolding the internal crisis and to make connections between the past and present and to view them from different perspectives, this volume is organised into Nine Chapters followed by conclusion and observations. Chapter I serves as introduction to the South Asian Crises and their root causes. It describes how the cluster of Eight states having geographical proximity, historical legacy, social cultural, ethnic and economic similarities are fighting with these internal problems more than 70 years. It focuses many factors which characterize the dynamics and nature of these crises. It provides the basic concepts and elaborate the thematic frame-work and a rationale for recognising acute crises.

Chapter II focuses a comprehensive discussion on India Internal Problems Naxalists / Maoists insurgency. Though India is facing many communal-sectarians- religious- ethnic and regional problem, but the two problems are more alarming that are Naxalists and Kashmir. In this chapter, efforts are made to analyse how a small agrarian movement of 1967 against the local landlord in Naxal Bari West Bengal has developed into full bloom insurgency and spreaded into 20 states killing thousands of people. This chapter tried to examine and evaluate the origin causes and consequences of Naxalists insurgency and why the Indian government both Central and states failed to control it. Recent attacks of Naxalists proved that even the present Modi Government is also failed in its counter insurgency operations.

Kashmir is the gravest internal crisis in India since 1947-48. An armed Insurgency and Separatists movement in Kashmir was started in 1990s by those who lost election under the banner of Jammu and Kashmir Liberation Front with the support of Pakistan. Pakistan has been consistently contesting claims over Kashmir territorial rights and supporting the insurgents and terrorists to attacks on India. In Chapter III, the author examines how militancy continues to grow in Kashmir involving the children's and educated youth in violent militant activities like attacking and pelting stones on security forces. An attempt is also made in this chapter to analyse the counter-insurgency and peace process including military actions and confidence building measures. An approach is also made to understand how the present chaos in Kashmir encapsulate the differing priorities and in the absence of an overarching strategy under various states government unable to reach any successful solution. The main role in this failure is the state political parties- National conference and Peoples Democratic Party who for their own political survival using Kashmir as a tool.

Chapter IV deals with the Islamic fundamentalism and Separatist movements in Pakistan. A process of society-wide Islamization has now reached its full bloom with the wide presence of radical Islamist groups. The rising radicalization in Pakistani society reflects the attitude of politicians, bureaucrats and army and the State who acknowledges Islamic fundamentalists as part of the national political mainstream. The policymakers of Pakistan and security services use religious extremists in regional battlegrounds such as Kashmir and Afghanistan also contribute to their impunity.

In truth, Pakistan is a conflicted state lacking the crucial components needed for nationhood- a strong common identity, mental make-up, a shared sense of history and common goals. The failure so far to has created a cohesive national entity flows from inequalities, absence of effective democracy and dysfunctional Political and legal system. The inter-ethnics and inter-religious violence have plagued Pakistan whether it is the problem of Sindhi and Muhajirs, Pathans and Punjabis, Baloch, inert-Muslims- Shia or Sunni (Ahmadiya) or Hindus, so on. This chapter focuses how Pakistan is afflicted by the separatist sentiments in Gilgit-Baltistan, the Pashtunistan and FATA, the Sindh and the Baluchistan threatening national integrity. Pakistan frontier province facing Afghanistan continues to have strong separatist forces based on Pashtun Identity. All these movements are ethno-national and secessionist born before 1950 around the period of Indian independence from British & the subsequent partition of India. The communal basis of the state kept Pakistan internally uncertain of its national identity and created a potentially volatile and perennial cause of conflict. There is a serious debate among the analysts and policy makers if Pakistan would be able to keep its unity and territorial integrity intact in face of multiple internal challenge.

Afghanistan has been passing through phases of internal crises- civil wars, violence and terrorism but the most devastating challenge is the persisting Taliban insurgency. Chapter V is related with the emergence and resurgence and terrorism of Taliban. With the withdrawal of US NATO forces, Taliban insurgency revives and openly active in 70% of the country, while ISISI has also put its foot in 30 districts of North Afghanistan. This chapter has comprehensively discussed the fragmented and polarized society of Afghanistan ethnic groups those have aggravated the internal struggle and gained support from the different external powers. The problem of Afghanistan in fact is the result of external powers interference and their geo-political interests. In its cold war politics, the united states in collaborations of Pakistan put all the efforts to oust the Soviet forces and gave birth to Taliban. Efforts are also made in this chapter to evaluate the peace process ranging from high level political negotiation to international negotiations but nothing is come out.

Internal crisis in South Asia has also changed regimes and political system and created new states by altering the boundaries as a result of fierce conflict, Bangladesh emerged as a new sovereign state. Chapter VI discusses the rise of Islamic extremism and ethnic violence against minorities in Bangladesh and a new brand of nationalism with an Islamic flavour that has gradually replaced secularism as the basis of nationhood. This Islamic extremism, a new fabric of Bangladesh society has ruined the secular texture and has been posing threat to the democratic forms of state. Genocide against Hindus on the basis of religion which was exemplary earlier in Pakistan, is now a general phenomenon in Bangladesh. Islam is both as the idea of the nation and as an integral part of their identity. This chapter analyses the factors and attitude of political parties and their leaders as well as the Islamic leaders who want to create the state polity solely guided by Islam. Political parties too have risen to prominence that have been implicated in violence against Hindu minority. Human Rights Watch and Amnesty International report that "both the Bangladesh Nationalist Party (BNP) and the opposition parties, led by the Awami [People's] League, have used crude 'cocktail' bombs, knives, and guns against one another and the police, causing scores of casualties", particularly after the elections of 2001 when members of the Hindu community were targeted because of their alleged support for the opposition. The scale, diversity and complexity of these internal conflicts hinder the ability of institutional mechanisms to effectively manage conflict.

Chapter VI also focusses a critical analysis of Rohingya problem which Bangladesh is facing now. The influx of large numbers of Rohingya refugees in Bangladesh has been putting pressure on its internal environment and posing numerous internal problems and challenges. Reluctance of Myanmar to back its citizen, Bangladesh will have to fraught many consequences.

Nepal a beautiful Himalayan kingdom engulfs into political instability and various problems from the monarchial absolutism, Maoist armed rebellion to the present ethnic crisis over the new constitution – Madhesi Movement. Chapter VII illustrate the constitutional deadlock which was persisted since 2006 after the end of Maoists "People's war" and joined the competitive politics. The political bickering delayed the framing of new constitution and took eight years in adopting new constitution. But the promulgation of Nepal New Constitution on 20th September 2015 gave birth to violent demonstrations and protests by the Madhesi and Terai people killed many people.This chapter analyses discriminations and deprivation of migrated Indian population and several tribal groups led to the emergence of resentments and identity-based movement in Madhesi. The new Constitution unfortunately failed to satisfy and give relief from the age-old discriminations to the Madhesi and Terai population. The extensive manipulation in making new constitution compromises with the provisions of demarcation of provinces and state's federal structure, proportional representations, citizenship rights of women and so on. If the demands of marginalized tribal and regional groups are not integrated in equitable and respectable manners, a separatist movement would gain momentum.

Sri Lanka 's present crisis can be viewed in Chapter VIII arising from competition between the national perspectives of two cultural ethnic groups the Sinhalese and the Muslims. Many of the important watersheds in this conflict are closely associated with contests over the cultural patterns and symbols of independent Sri Lanka. Even after the elimination of Tamil insurgency, the ruling regimes failed to sustain peace in the country and engulfs into Anti- Muslims Violence. Sri Lanka is coming closer to the emergence of Islamist terrorism step by step. Recent violence against Muslim in 2018 and serial bombs- blasts in April 2019 in Colombo killing 359 people and injured hundreds of people are the examples. Although Sri Lanka remained formally committed to multiparty democracy through much of this period, significant Sinhala nationalists and left-wing revolutionaries' groups found themselves outside this constitutional framework. A careful observation and analysis of anti- Muslims violence this chapter shows that Sinhala-Buddhist extremism treated Muslims a new enemy and the rise of Islamists fundamentalism and terrorism provided a suitable tool to handle and demonise the community. If the ethnic violence is not resolved politically and amicably, a new insurgency is awaited in Sri Lanka.

Chapter IX is a study of Maldives' Political Crisis which is primarily a struggle for power and demand for Democracy. Since the establishment of Republican state in Maldives, the autocratic rulers and authoritarian regimes adopted the method to sustain in power and end their opponents. This Chapter analyses the political movement started by Mohammad Nasheed and pave the way for democracy but it was short-lived. This chapter comprehensively evaluates how the President Yameen instituted plans to crackdown its opponents and prevents them from contesting Presidential election by using Judiciary. It also evaluates the conditions for a democratic country whether Maldives is fulfilling it or not.

The book is ended with its concluding remarks and observations given in the dynamic natures of all these internal crises. This book will help policymakers, government officials, scholars, development professionals, and security analysts to deeply and effectively understand contemporary conflict and violence in South Asia. I am confident that publication of this book will go long way in understanding the profound influence of approaches discussed in various chapters.

Madhu Kumari

Acknowledgement

First of all, I would like to thanks Almighty God who gave me strength and enable me to work on such current issues of now-days.

Not forgotten my family for providing every support which are most needed for Completion of this work.

The completion of this work could have not been possible without the assistance of my Colleagues who played a crucial role in facilitating my work and guided me at various Points of time.

I thank all my friends who in one way or another gave moral support in various Matters.

Most of all I want to thanks my husband and soul mate who constantly supported and encouraged me in completion of this book.

I thank my publisher and appreciate their efforts for publishing this work and paying Constant attention in publication.

Chapter - 1

South Asia and Internal Crisis: An Introduction

In South Asia, as a whole, there are so many significant developments both external and internal those need special attention. In the contemporary scenario, South Asia has been magnified following the collapse of communism and subsequent regional developments that led the restructuring of great powers priorities. It seems that the region is on the pile of fire, burning and having no peace at all. All the South Asian states whether great powers or small states- India or Pakistan, Afghanistan or Bangladesh, Maldives, Nepal or Sri Lanka facing numerous internal crises so that the very survival of these states comes onto forefront. The existence of states or nations are under numerous serious threats from various groups and factions, religious, regional, communal or ethnic seeking to make demands for their survival upon them.

South Asia has been remained a tension-ridden region because of the internal crises. The legacy of conflicts is deep rooted in historical, socio-cultural, political, religious and ethnic divides that generate violence and defy all attempts of stabilisation the subcontinent more than half century. Simmering separatists and extremists' violent movements or insurgencies in India, Pakistan, Afghanistan, Bangladesh, Nepal, Sri Lanka and Maldives have been threatening peace and security of these states. Although, India's have remained comparatively stable and evolved smoothly but the separatists and insurgency movement in Kashmir, North East and Maoists/ Naxal movement in numbers of districts of India are at presently threatening internal security. Pakistan, belongs to a group of fragile country, is particularly vulnerable in certain aspects of statelessness and wrecked by internal division between provinces and among the forces of modernism and militant radical Islamists and terrorists' outfits. In Bangladesh, the rise of religious fundamentalism and extremism has subsided the democratic values. Being an Islamic country so declared by Gen. H. M. Irshad, it is imposing serious threat to the just and democratic socialist cohesion of society. Since, the political Islamists want to establish an Islamic polity guided solely by Islam. It has giving place for the rise anti-minorities especially anti-Hindus violence targeting to change the social texture of the country into a totally Bengali Muslim country. With the end of the era of Monarchy and Maoist insurgency that undermined Nepal security for a decade, Nepal has transited to democracy but it is still facing the constitutional deadlock and political instability from the Madhesi movement. The ethnic conflicts in Sri Lanka ended after the three decades violent blooded war between LTTE and Sinhalese but still currently giving rise to another violent movement against Muslims. Afghanistan. All these violent internal crises have made the whole region dangerously volatile and a source of serious concern for the World.

South Asia, known as Indian sub-continent, as a region is generally known as the cluster of geographically proximate countries that share common historical bonds, cultural and social identities and economic, political and strategic interests. South Asia has been endowed with disheartening pictures in almost every social, economic and political context. This region is fast emerging as the poorest, most illiterate, malnourished and most deprived segment of the world. Human deprivation in South Asia is colossal in the global scale as it produces only 1.3 percent of the world income. It is the home of 1.5 billion people that is nearly one-fourth of the world and each year it increases the total population of the fifty small member states of the UN. Almost all South Asian Countries are facing endemic corruption, social exclusion, poor governance, inefficient administration and non-pro-people bureaucracies which hinder all programme of progressive development. In contrast to widespread human deprivation, contrast with the large armies, South Asia is the only region where military budget of every year expanding on the purchase of hi-tech arms, modern weapons and large armies. South Asia overall picture is more complex. Besides the conventional and nuclear risk, it has the image of a region of chronic instability. The growing tensions between India and Pakistan and continuous infiltrations and attacks on Indian border increase the probability of a nuclear war in this part of the world. Nuclearization of both countries though has brought a balance of deterrence and stability but it is likely to deter Pakistan from continuing the proxy war as was proved by the Kargil intrusion and subsequent escalation in militancy.

South Asia is also the birth place of several religions namely Hinduism, Jainism, Buddhism and Sikhism. The continental civilisation also nursed other major world religions that came through invaders and occupants like

Islam, Christianity, Judaism, Zoroastrianism and Bahai faiths. The South Asian Countries today have the people of the most of these religious faiths living with together and sustained with of the basic instinct of engagement, absorption and accommodation thus evolving a unique culture. It is the only region where Western political institutions go hand in hand with the non-western traditional culture and religion plays an important active role in every corner of politics.

It is an interesting laboratory where religious traditions have developed a similar variance of democracies with different cultural background from the west. During the 1990s, South Asia was the biggest democratic region after the transition from authoritarian rule in Pakistan, Bangladesh (1990) Nepal (1988, and now after the end of Monarchy (2002) Maldives (2008), Sri Lanka after the end of LTTE insurgency. the only form of Hindu and Islamic democracies is to be found in Nepal and Bangladesh and Buddhism received a foremost place in Sri Lanka.

In plural societies assertion for identity and autonomy on the basis of ethnicity, language, religion and culture has been a common problem. Owing to the majoritarian form of governance, only the majoritarian groups are benefited in the process of modernization and they form the mainstream of the socio-political fabric. The minority groups remain isolated, deprived and at the periphery of the system. However, it has been seen that in the process of socio-economic and political modernization, these groups are also mobilized. Their mobilization makes them conscious about the discrimination that they are faced with and they began to assert in an organized way. This group mobilization and assertion naturally takes place on the basis of their primordial loyalties and sentiments such as race, ethnicity, religion, culture, language and so on.

Acute and latent internal crises are jeopardizing the political stability of South Asian States. There are many factors which characterize the dynamics and nature of these problems:

- First- the rise of sectarian state.
- Second- democratic distortions.
- Third-Majority versus Minority.
- Fourth, National building and dis-integration.
- Fifth, Identity Crisis and Social cohesion.
- Sixth, Equal participations and distribution.
- Seventh, crisis of legitimacy; and
- Last, crisis of good governance and stability.

Rise of Sectarian State

The rise of sectarian states has its root in the multi-religious and multi-ethnic societies which has led to the alienation of the minorities and give rise to seek their rights, aspirations and identity preservations. In India, the social- communal, religious, linguistic, ethnic turmoil and unrests is the clear evidence of failure of even a secular state to integrate its divergent groups. The sharpening of communal tensions in India are the result of the rise of fundamentalists forces that are pursuing the politics of religious segregation. In case of the Pakistan, its founder Mohammad Ali Jinnah's vision of a Muslim Majority secular state, not an Islamic state, was soon shattered after his death. The separation of Bangladesh was also a consequence of the dominance of Punjabi ethnicity of an Islamic state. Similarly, the sense of deprivation in North Western Frontier Provinces, Baluchistan, Gilgit and Sindh as well as the rise of Shia-Sunni sectarian conflict are also the result of unrest and a reflection of Islamic assertions. Bangladesh's secular culture has also succumbed to the political-exigencies of Muslims sectarian forces since 1978. The unrests of minorities especially Hindus is the reflection of Bengali and Islamic assertions. In Nepal, the Tarai movement of the Maoists insurgency of the late 1990s were the manifestation of protest against the dominance of hill people and against a Hindu state respectively. Nepal declared itself a Hindu state under the new constitution in 1962. Sri Lanka unleashed movement for a Sinhalese Buddhists state in 1956. The JVP insurgency in the early 1970s and Tamil insurgency in 1980s were the resulted from the politics of ethnic consolidation of Sinhalese in the political system. Now the anti-Muslims violence is a new challenge for Sri Lanka's secular credentials.

Another factors for the rise of Islamic sectarianism states in south Asia is the influence of Wahhabism. It is a new school of Islam from Saudi Arabia which has been transforming South Asia's religious landscape. Wahhabism, a fundamental Sunni school of Islam originating in Saudi Arabia, entered South Asia in the late 1970s. With public and private Saudi funding, Wahhabism has steadily gained influence among Muslim communities throughout the region. As a result, the nature of South Asian Islam has significantly changed in the last three decades. The result has been an increase in Islamist violence in Pakistan, Indian Kashmir, and Bangladesh.

Democratic Distortion

At the dawn of independence, all countries of South Asia opted for a democratic form of government. Some adopted the system substantially and some superficially. In the course of time, most of them abandoned or suspended the democratic system. In fact, these states were highly influenced by the post-war mood of the West. The United States openly bestowed its favour on the newly born independent states if they presented a democratic appearance and prepared to resist communist challenge. For various reasons, the South Asian states accepted democratic form of government that is parliamentary form of democracy with a prime Minister as a head of government and president as head of the States as in India and Bangladesh or a Governor-General as in Pakistan and in Sri Lanka. Nepal selected a category of their own i.e. the aspiring elites based their bid for power on democratic principles. In Nepal, Democracy served as an instrument for destroying the traditional reserve of power and legitimized the hereditary rules to claim to power.

From the middle of 1950, the liberal faces of South Asia began to change. Democracy was put to severe test which it had not stood before and as it turned out. It could not stand the test on its own, in some countries it collapsed, in others, it just managed to revive because it was supported by the additional devices as in 1975 India declared emergency. The specific factors which were responsible for the collapse of democracy were mainly the undemocratic competition for power and lack of consensus among political elites and the political role of the military. The first factor is the most important and complex and is mainly responsible for the fall of democracy in India. The second factor emerged out of the first and explain the collapse of the system in Pakistan and Bangladesh.

From 1951-1955 and 1959-1960, the Nepal democratic government was torn asunder by the personal ambitions and jealousy of the political leaders. In 1952 the leading nationalist party of the country Nepali Congress split into factions and with the support of King Tribhuvan functioned as PM through-out. It consequently weakened and discredited the role of political parties and at the same time strengthening the hand of king against democracy. In this state of affairs, when the politician seemed to be so grossly involved in preventing each other from holding the reins of power, the king assumed the role of savior. In 1955, King Mahendra, after assuming power, dissolved the National government and promulgating direct rule of the crown. However, in 1959-60 the democratic rule restored in Nepal for a short while. The political parties in opposition united but the framework of democracy again failed as there was no constitution and no general election. The Constitution Assembly failed to draft the constitution thus no substance was put into the frame work of democracy.

Like India, Pakistan inherited a non-political military but in the first decade of its independence, it faced many problems. It was not endowed with a strong party and charismatic leadership committed to democracy but the authoritarian regime and military intervention in every government. Jinnah was a strong leader but autocrat by force of circumstances and temperament. In fact, he ruled the country like a constitutional dictator consequently democracy could not have gained ground in Pakistan. Pakistan was left with no leader of continental status after the death of Jinnah.

For decades, Pakistani Politics has remained highly unstable and unpredictable owing to a multipronged contest between political parties and the military, on the one hand and the dynastic political parties dominated by land owning elites on the other. The role of various power centres and the shadow of civil- military relations has been continued to affect the democratic transition and consolidation of power in Pakistan. In 1956, the adoption of new constitution was dried out when struggle in East Pakistan and west Pakistan resulted in collapse of the civilian government and Martial law was declared in 1958. The constitution was abrogated, legislature dissolved and political parties were banned and general Ayub Khan was appointed chief Martial and Administrator. In oct. 27,1958 he dismissed the president and assumed full control of the government.

The wheel of coup that runs Pakistan stops periodically for rest and relaxation. It is not the people who love coups or are averse to democracy, it is ruling class particularly the army which is uncomfortable with even a simulacrum of democracy even if it remotely appears upsetting the status-quo, the rule of the feudal or warlords. The army ensure that polity will firmly remain in their grip who in turn cede supremacy to the army tacitly even above the constitution. People do not configure in this arrangement nor are they meant to.

The military formally came into in power in 1958 first time as a result of military coup. Iskander Mirza, a bureaucrat turned President used army to usurp power, only to find within days that power was totally taken over by the then Army Chief General Ayub Khan. In 1969, General Yahya Khan imposed Martial law by overthrowing the government of Ayub Khan. Yahya Khan rule in Pakistan was the shortest period of Martial law as Yahya Khan held elections in 1970s and transferred power to Zulfikar Ali Bhutto though only after the debacle in East Pakistan in1971. Bhutto was more of a military man, he subverted constitutional norms and made highhandedness. His guiding principle was from rigging of elections to murders of opponents.

The revolving door of democracy and dictatorship took Pakistan from a rising nation to a reviled one. General Zia-ul-Haqq imprint on society and institutions are run so deep that decades after his death, Pakistanis are still failing to overpower it. In 1977, Gen. Zia-ul-Haqq deposed Prime Minister Bhutto and declared Martial Law. After execution of Bhutto, Zia-ul-Haqq policies fundamentally transformed Pakistan Polity that created an almost entirely theocratic form of government, empowering society's most violent and intolerant impulses and undermining the basis of a plural democratic political structure in Pakistan for decade to come. Zia's ideological project, his education policies envisioned to induce a loyalty to Islam and Pakistan and living consciousness of ideological identity designed a narrow religious and historical pedagogy at all grades levels. Its demonized minorities and vilified secular thought. His cultivation and arming of organized jihadist groups in CIA sponsored Afghan Jihad led to untold death and destruction in the country with an estimate ranging from 60-80,000 dead over the last 15 years turning Pakistan into a hub for global Jihad. The dreaded blasphemy laws he strengthened became a convenient tool for the persecution of minorities and other vulnerable groups.

The political polarization of the 1980s gave chance to Nawaz Sharif a businessman turned politician whose political ambitions fitted well with the political needs of military regime of Gen. Zia-ul-Haq for cultivating anti-Bhutto groups. The divided mandate of 1988 election and with the support of military, he became the Prime Minister for the first time in 1990. With a two third majority in 1997 election, Nawaz Sharif came to power for the second term. He appeared to be high and began to exercise real power as a chief executive, giving up on the caution and care that military regime and a strong praetorian tradition demanded. In forcing the Chief of Army Staff, the President and the Chief Justice of Pakistan to resign within a span of a year, he was unable to appreciate the political logic and reasoning of the consolidating power in a democracy with a complex and painful legacy of subversion of the constitution. He was removed by the military and also humiliated, imprisoned, tortured, convicted and later exiled.

The constitutional amendment of Article 58(2)(b) passed by Parliament in 1985, was repeatedly used to remove three elected government twice headed by the PPP and Musharraf had to directly intervene to sack the second PML-N government in October 1999. General Pervaze Musharraf not only squelching democracy like Zia but also rewarding his Nawaz's Patron with at least political exile. Pervez Musharraf was removed from power in 2007 as a result of internal maneuvering from within his own institution in collaboration with key civilian players. Senior military management saw Musharraf as strategically hazardous, especially with his out of box' suggestions for solving Kashmir and giving a free hand to the US in fighting the war on terror. The legal community came in handy to orchestrate a movement which eventually led to Musharraf's removal since the dictator could not be ousted without first sufficiently de-legitimizing him in December 2007, the assassination of Benazir Bhutto created conditions that made untenable for him to continue for long as President.

In 2008, the election of President, the PPP's Asif Ali Zardari got elected. The PPP also formed government at the centre headed by Prime Minister Yusuf Raza Gillani. In 2013 election, the PML-N and Nawaz Sharif formed the government both at Centre and the Punjab. There were widespread hopes that Nawaz Sharif electoral victory in June 2013 would mark Pakistan's definitive transition towards democracy, expand the weight of civilian governments and improve its further prospects. But hopes had proved wrong with the deepening political instability and verdict of court in corruption charges on Nawaz Sharif. The Supreme Court disqualified him from being prime minister. The Pakistani court has indicted Nawaz Sharif and his wife, daughter and son-in-law on corruption charges stemming from documents leaked from a Panama Law firm.

Pakistan Army is a politically potent force conscious of maintaining its legitimacy and kept the government on edge. The Memogate Scandal, a plan which was probably hatched to force President Asif Ali Zardari to resign, was planned by General Kiyani and Ahamad Shuja Pasha. The Sharif Government just like Zardari government ceded control over many policies to the army and its institutions, especially those pertaining to national security. Over the many decades, Pakistani's military has turned into a parent -guardian type role that may not necessarily seek direct intervention but will exercise indirect control through partnering with critical civilian actors and tailoring a legal/ constitutional frame work that safeguards its role in policy making.

Table 1: Patterns of Rule in Pakistan[1]

Type	*Duration*	*Period*
Direct Military Rule	17 years	1958-62 1969-71 1977-85 1999-2002
Elected Government under a Military President	15 years	1962-69 1985-88 2002-2007
Elected Government under a Civilian President		1988-1999 2008-till date
Supremacy of the Non-Parliamentary Forces under Formal Parliamentary Rule	20 years plus	1947-1959
Civilian Supremacy	6 years	1971-77.

Bangladesh acquired its sovereign status through a war. After independence, Bangladesh adopted moderate and secular Muslim democracy but its policy is far from reality. Indeed, since Bangladesh's independence from Pakistan in 1971, the durability of both secularism and democracy have been undermined by numerous military coups—many of which involved multiple counter-coups before a clear “victor” emerged—in 1974-75, 1977-1980, 1981-82, 1996, and 2007. In January 2012, the military claimed it had thwarted another coup.It began its independent existence with a political army consisting of guerrilla freedom fighters- Mukti Vahini. In 1975, through an army coup, military stepped into power and replaced the Mujib government by the military dictatorship and General Zia-ur-Rahaman who through two further coups succeeded in assuming supreme power of the states. In fact, in 1972, Mujib’s disestablishment of Islam as the state’s religion caused a strong resentment among the orthodox sections of the community and some army officers. Mujib assumed absolute Presidential power, abandoned the parliamentary system and imposed one party rule, left no channel for any future political transitions, the only way was to remove him through assassination.

Sri Lanka in the political process enjoyed the status of a third world "model democracy" after gaining independence in 1948. Universal franchise was granted to Sri Lankans by the British colonial government in 1938. Since then, the broader political process which was fed with anti-colonial and nationalistic feelings by the political leaders reached a milestone when gaining independence in 1948 and matured in electing a strong Sinhalese nationalist government in 1956. Sri Lanka embarked on an "open economic policy" following the change of government from the coalition of Bandaranaike's Sri Lanka Freedom Party (SLFP) to Jayawardena's United National Party (UNP). Signs of democratisation had been faded until 1980s provided by the notion of the decline of liberal democracy". Sri Lanka has been ruled under emergency regulations for much of the 1980s and up to the end of Tamils ethnic crisis. Every month, the parliament extends the emergency rule on the grounds of politically motivated violent activities of the Tamils and Sinhalese. It has become one of the rituals of Sri Lanka's parliamentary procedure. The decline in liberal democracy in Sri Lanka were mainly due to the increasing domination by politicians (associated with the parties in power) over other elements of the state apparatus and over society generally, and a declining regard for legal and procedural formality. The termination of the autonomy of the judiciary; control of mass media through nationalisation or indirect coercion and pressure; the introduction of new constitutions or constitutional amendments for reasons of short-term political expediency were other reasons for disruption of democracy in Sri Lanka.

Maldives’ history is full with the history of one-upmanship. The first president Abdul Gayoom’s rule from 1978 to 2008 was reinforced by a corrupt autocracy, accompanied by his proverbial iron-fist. The first spell of native rule, after its transition from the British colonial yoke, set the tone for future autocrats in the country. Though there was relative calm in the archipelago for 30 long years, Gayoom had to shrug off multiple coup attempts in his long and eventful rule. But being a wily tactician, he managed to survive till the last day of his rule. Despite being a ruthless ruler, he found it difficult to ignore incessant waves of democracy hovering around Maldives. He introduced democratic process in the Constitution that provided a system of multi-party electoral competition. Eventually, this unique provision in the Constitution gave an opportunity to Nasheed, a former political prisoner, to inflict a historic defeat on the longest serving President of the island.

Mohammed Nasheed, a young progressive leader signalled a gradual transition towards a full-fledged democratic Government. However, it was a difficult task for the newcomer to survive in power for long and he could not complete his five-year term as he could not match the political tactics of Gayoom. By 2012, President Nasheed had to resign after a police mutiny and weeks of demonstrations against his Government around the country. His supporters and the Maldives Democratic Party considered it as a coup against the first democratically elected President of the country. Gradually the political scene of the country changed in Gayoom's favour. He won the run-off election against Nasheed in 2013. Later, Nasheed was arrested on terrorism charges and sentenced to 13 years in prison.The transition had been billed as a successful model for Muslim countries to embrace democracy and build credible, democratic institutions. However, the Maldives model has been floundering especially after February 2012 when the police and army forced Nasheed out of office in what he called a putsch by entrenched state interests represented by the PPM and the Gayoom family.

In March 2017, the Maldives faced another power coup when the Opposition lawmakers tried to wrest the control of the Government from Yameen. The Yameen government refused to enforce the court order to release all convicted politicians including ex-President Nasheed and declared a 'State of Emergency'. Subsequently, the Armed Forces arrested two judges and Gayoom, his son Faris Maumoon (a legislator) and son-in-law Mohamed Nadheem were jailed. He curtailed Press freedom in entirety. All these were viewed as cruel attempts by Yameen to stay in power for longer, and he made it clear that he would not tolerate any challenge or Opposition to his rule.

Democracy has been on the retreat in the Maldives for years. It was 10 years ago that the Maldives made transition from dictatorship to democracy. In 2018,the third multi-party election held in the Maldives and the joint opposition presidential candidate Ibrahim Mohamed Solih, defeated President Yameen.

Democratic principles are not new to the Afghan people. The democratic tradition to make decisions jointly on the basis of consensus in tribal councils called "Jirga" was in Afghan culture. Democratic elections in contemporary Afghan politics is something else. After the fall of the Taliban in Afghanistan there was a strong desire from the West to conduct democratic elections quickly, as they said to leave a "light footprint" in the country and let the Afghans lead the process forward. Elections were held quickly in Afghanistan and were regarded successful and as legitimate. Unfortunately, the elections after this has become more and more controversial and problematic. The presidential elections were marked by electoral fraud, corruption and cronyism, and the security situation around the election was disastrous and could not make peace and order.

The democratization process in Afghanistan has various challenges. What democracy and elections are not necessarily perceived positively in Afghanistan? Many equate it with western ideals and culture, which is seen as too free and immoral. One needs both education of the voter and the politician, so people get to see what kind of impact and influence they can have in a democratic system. Afghanistan is a highly centralized state where the President sits on top with almost all of the power, while those elected in districts and provinces have very little influence. This leads to an all or nothing concept where the one who has Kabul, has control of everything. This in turn has a major impact on the security situation and cooperation between tribes and clans in the country. Responding to these challenges in Afghanistan, it need extensive work in the field of democracy. The formation of democratic institutions and political parties are essential for the well-functioning of democracy.

Minority v/s majority

South Asian states have been passing through national integration problems threatened by the minorities v/s majorities issues. The root of the problem lies in the conflict of loyaltiesconflict between traditional or primordial attachment to tribe, region, religion ethnic or race and their loyalty to the civil politics associated with the newly established state. This is an inevitable problem in the process of national integration. It is also potentially dangerous when economic or intellectual dissatisfaction threatens revolution, while disaffection based on race, language or culture threatens partition, irredentism or merger and redrawing the maps of every state many times. The problem looks more severe and chronic because of the age- old traditions to the great extent where the sense bound up in the actualities of blood, race, language, locality and religion.

In South Asia, there are innumerable minorities which can be broadly classified into three categories:

The first Category comprises the minorities which hold no live awareness of their separate identity and have accepted the national norms, ethos and assimilated with the majority community while retaining in some cases their distinct cultural symbols, religious beliefs etc. For example, Buddhist in Nepal; Jain, Buddhist, Parsi, Sikhs and Christians in India. Such Minority communities hardly pose any threat to the process of national integration.

Second Category includes minorities which retain their separate identities and are unassimilated but because of their size and geographical location or both do not hold political option to agitate for separate state of their own. A large number of minority communities fall into this category like Muslims and untouchables in India, Hindus in Bangladesh.

In third category, we may be placed the minorities which have an intense awareness of their separate identities and are unassimilated with others. They have the political option and demand to have separate autonomous or independent states. Such as Naga and Mizo in India, Baluch and Pathan in Pakistan, Tamils in Sri Lanka. All these minorities have one common feature that each predominately populates in a particular region in a state. The threat of separation or recession which such minorities often pose, stem solely from their advantageous geographical position. Their habitation along the border areas of a particular country gives them the additional advantage of obtaining arms and aid from across the border.

Integration is primarily a mental process when people of the country see themselves as vital component, a nation emerges. In India, Muslims and Dalits who are still far from being assimilation. In their case, it is really a matter of social and economic assimilation politically, constitutionally and legally. They have equal rights with Hindus. In the government Jobs, they are more privileged than the members of the majority community but the social intermixing and inter-marriages are still not common and restricted. The causes, thus for persisting communal tension occasionally breaking into Hindu-Muslims or Dalits-Hindu riots are to be traced in the attitudes towards the communities concerned. Now, Hindus have long been discriminated more than the Muslims on political grounds and against their own lower caste or casteless co-religionist- Dalits on political and economic ground. The Muslims too have nourished and asserted their own separate identity for a long time. Dalits have constituted economically the most exploited and socially the worst discriminated against segment of Indian society. Until now they have been the most salient sufferers. From 1975, Dalits stood up for their rights and who by sheer force of education, industry or enterprises have forced their way out of the dungeon of poverty and cultural backwardness. Yet they have not been readily accepted by the Majority Community as its own but have also made their way easily into the core of Indian Establishment. Though exploited by the Hindus, Dalits have never felt alienated from them. The display of assertiveness on their part promises their rapid integration with rather than separation from Indian Society.

Likely in Bangladesh, Hindus constitute an indigenous minority. The Hindu minority became the target of widespread violence before and even after the independence. After partition in 1947, the violence against Hindus in the then Pakistan and after independence in Bangladesh was a continuous phenomenon and followed religiously by the Muslims majority. Hindu Community is passing through the same ordeal as in 1971 till now. All types of atrocities-violent attacks, killing, rapes, slaughter, forcible annexation of properties burning houses, abduction, forced migration and conversion are taking place. These attacks are not only systematically carried out by the hardliner Islamists but also supported by the main stream political parties. Hostilities between the Awami League and BNP have enhanced the ability of Islamist groups to pursue their agenda without repercussion.

Pakistan, a state since 1947, has been still lacking crucial components needed for nationhood: a strong common identity, mental make-up, a shared sense of history and common goals. The failure so far to create a cohesive national entity flows from inequalities of wealth and opportunities, absence of effective democracy and dysfunctional legal system. The inter-ethnic violence has plagued Pakistan whether it is Muhajirs and Punjabis, Sindhi and Pathans, Baloch or any other of the country's ethnic groups. Schools in Baluchistan refuses to hoist Pakistani flag or sing its national anthem. Sindhi' accuses Punjabis of stealing their water, the Muttahida Quami Movement (MQM) runs Karachi on strictly ethnic grounds, and the Pashtun of NWFP successfully had the province officially renamed Khyber Pakhtunkhwa. In getting job, caste and sect matters more than ability and ethnic groups wage pitched battles against each other throughout the country.

Since 1990s, the Muhajirs are demanding the whole Sindh province as a separate state for themselves. This in turn resulted in lot of bloodsheds, violence and loss of lives of muhajirs, local peoples, and army and police personnel. Even after sixty years, the rift between the locals and refugees and their descendants has widened instead of narrowing there is conflicts among inter-Muslims particularly the case between Sunni-Shias. Violence between these two groups has escalated in the last decade to frightening levels, so much so that members of both groups have been attacked in mosque.

Sri Lanka, the ethnic divide between Tamils and Sinhalese was resulted the Tamils insurgency for at least thirty years. The seeds of conflict were existed even before independence in 1948.The British colonial policy of divide and rule sowed the seeds of tensions between the Sinhalese and Tamil communities. Tamil although well-educated were given disproportionate numbers of jobs in the civil services by the British. After independence, the Sinhalese majority held sway and its politician sought to redress the balance with populist but discriminatory policies against Tamils. The attitude of the government and the Sinhalese people who were not inclined to concede the Tamil minority rights which they claimed for themselves.

The Tamil insurgency developed in the late 1970s against the backdrop of repeated refusal by the political elite of the majority Sinhalese community to pay heed to the Tamil demand for regional autonomy. In 1977 during the parliamentary election, the demand for self-determination for Tamils entered a period of mass mobilization. The anti-Tamil riots of 1983 reached a flash point over the killings of just nine soldiers in Jaffna by the Tamil tigers fighting for a separate homeland for Tamils eventually turned a full-blown civil war between Sri Lankan state and a host of Tamil militant groups. Among the Tamil nationalist groups, the LTTE had the strongest and the most uncompromising, commitment to the goal of a separate Tamil state called Eelam.

National Disintegration

The process of nation building has always been challenging in the context of plural societies. In the process of nation building, it is generally assumed that after a certain stage of development the minority cultural groups will assimilate in the mainstream. However, it does not happen in most of the cases due to the cultural impositions as well as the discriminatory policies of the majoritarian governments. As a result, not only that the minority groups remained dissatisfied and isolated but they also began to assert in an organized way on the basis of their primordial loyalties and sentiments. It natural threatened the very process of nation-building and a conflictual situation emerged thereby posing a challenge to the star security of the state.

In all South Asian countries, there is a problem of national integration which simultaneously imposing the crisis of State building and then Nation building to a lesser or greater extent whether it is India, Pakistan, Bangladesh or Afghanistan or Nepal, Sri Lanka or Maldives. The problem of state building and nation building came naturally in the post-colonial era after independence from Britishers. All the governments in South Asia have to cope with violent conflicts that threaten the integrity of their statehood showing the failure of democratic institution to deal with these challenges. However, the state structure came to manifest itself much more strongly with the events taking place within the system. The existing structure and culture of political system are unable to cope with the problem or challenges which confronts it. The problem arises when there is a serious threat coming from the side of a domestic or international environment so that very question of its survival comes into forefront. The problem of Nation building is closely related with the state building while the problem of state building has been solved but nation building has still remained to create threatening posture for the very survival of the political system. People are failed to transfer their commitment and loyalties from smaller tribes, village or pretty principalities to the large political system.

Identity Crisis and Social Cohesion

The South Asian countries provide a unique example of multi layered conflicts animating due to social pluralities and discriminations. It is interesting to note that except Maldives to a large extent, all the South Asian countries have plural societies divided in terms of race, ethnicity, caste, language, religion and culture. There are minority and majority cultural groups. The socio-economic and political dominance have been challenged by the minority cultural groups thereby giving rise to sub-nationalist tendencies in the region. In fact, the sub-nationalist tendencies have given rise to secessionist movements and even actual secession. Thus, ethno-nationalism has become an important feature of the countries of the South Asian region. The assertion of identity and autonomy as the basis of culture, ethnicity, religion and language has been a significant issue and it has led to horizontal and vertical conflicts.

The fact remains that the mainstream approach which seeks to being various ethno-cultural groups into the composite mainstream culture has failed. It has not only been strongly contested by different groups but they have asserted upon their identity. In fact, in the half a century since independence, the stability of the post-colonial state in South Asia has been threatened by recurrent and violent conflict between the central authority and a variety of ethnic minorities. The Muhajir uprising in Pakistan, Tamil separatism in Sri Lanka, tribal insurgency in the Chittagong Hill tracts of Bangladesh, irredentism in various parts of India such as Kashmir, problems in North East, Sikh Separatism, rise of ethno-regional assertions in Nepal, etc are few examples of contemporary movements in South Asia. This demonstrates that a genuine spirit of unity, which is a necessary concomitant of nationalism, and a necessary prerequisite for the initiation of the process of nation building, does not exist in the third world countries in general and South Asia in particular. Therefore, it can safely be said that the process of nation-building and ethno-nationalism has worked at cross-purposes in the post-colonial world countries.

When the ruling elites in South Asian countries embarked upon the twin-projects of state-building, and nation-building simultaneously, they had to face many challenges and hurdles. Their strategies, policies and methods of achieving the task was also fraught with short-sightedness, shortcomings and conflict generating. Thought potentially complementary, but in absence of a balanced approach, these two processes may work in opposition to each other. While state-building is generally followed by creation and concentration of governmental authority, nation-building particularly in multi-ethnic societies requires a participatory and responsive political set-up. In their concern for the state's survival as an independent international entity, the governing elite overemphasizes the process of the state-building, sometimes even at the cost of nation-building.

Meanwhile, both religion and ethnicity have been significant in the construction and reconstruction of group identities in the region. In the process, both were sometimes competing, confronting and/or complimenting each other. From the early part of the twentieth century till 1947, the salient variable for defining national and nationality in South Asia was religion. Particularly, the religion based two-nation theory has been vital in determining the political fate of the Indian sub-continent. In post-1947 era, however, the religion as the basis of nation has often been put to acid test. Where on the one hand, Pakistan has officially upheld and carried forward the religious nationalism while negating the ethnic ground realities, in India on the other hand, religion was implicitly re in forced in the state nationalism. However, at the same time in India, ethnic realities were acknowledged to certain extent, as there was a fundamental reorganization of the states (territory) on the basis of language within an Indian version of federal polity in the decade of fifties. But this recognition and acceptance of the ethnic realities was not always real and genuine. Moreover, in Nepal, Bhutan, Sri Lanka and Pakistan, the state remained negligent to the issues of ethno-nationalism and as a result, identity assertion become a serious issue.

The disturbing social structure and disintegration of society into various minor and major groups have enhanced class and groups consciousness as well as their identities. The people do not identify themselves with their political system nor recognize their national territory as their homeland but identify their own personal identities with their own territorial limits. There is a lot of contradictions between traditional political culture and having its roots in the loyalties of individual towards their community, caste, region and religion and a modern political culture requiring that they should sacrifice their primordial loyalties at the altar of their national commitments. For example, in India, peoples of every region have their identity as Bengali, Marathi, Tamilians, Keralites, Bihari, Rajasthani and so and so but they do not identify as Indian. It is the common feature of every South Asian states. As far as religion is concerned, Islam has been playing an instrumental role as in case of Pakistan, Afghanistan, Maldives and Bangladesh, the best examples.

Islam provided the ideological bases / foundation for the two-nation theory, which claimed the distinctiveness of the Hindus and Muslims and called for separate nation state for Muslims of Indian Sub-continent Pakistan. Later in 1971 due to Bengali ethnic movement, further led to the break-up of Pakistan and gave birth to a new state-Bangladesh. Further, Zia-ul Haqq used religion to provide legitimacy to an illegitimate government and also to mobilise Islamic parties in jihad against Soviet Union in Afghanistan. His reliance on a Sunni version of Islam alienated Shia minority community and since then one finds the prevalence of the Shia-Sunni conflicts in Pakistan.

Crisis of identity is posing a threat to the social cohesion. Social cohesion required the entire polity is organized as a system of interacting relationship among the various groups and in relationship between the state and articulating citizens.

Equal participations and distribution

Socio-economic differences and uneven development has created discriminations, exploitations and inequalities among different groups and dividing the people rich and poor; high castes and low castes; educated and uneducated etc.. This uneven development and unfulfilled aspiration of the people have a sense of deprivation. In absence of just and equitable economic developments and distribution of its benefits, people feel dissatisfy and that derives the affected groups to assert themselves and resulted into violence and conflicts. In such a state of affairs, the articulation of group interests and political mobilization result in confrontations. A problem arises when various political parties and groups operates with a view to influence the decision-making process or when are restricted from becoming anomic organizations. The failure of economic growth made the state more vulnerable.

Liberalization and privatization of economy has resulted in accentuations of economic disparities, as benefits have not reached the masses. This is bound to increase social and economic tensions. For example, in India's backward areas like Bihar, Chhattisgarh, Jharkhand and the North Eastern state etc. both liberalization and privatization are likely to succeed due to the lack of the basic infrastructure and significantly inefficient administrative set up.

It raises the questions how state powers are to be used to influence the distribution of goods, services and values throughout the society. State needs to evolve an adequate system of representation and just and equitable distribution of power and resources in order to maintain social peace and harmony. However, dominance of the state structure, especially the bureaucracy and the military, by one or two ethnic groups tended to augment ethnic tension and violence. In India, Pakistan, Nepal and Sri Lanka and Bangladesh, discrimination with minorities has been tending to create the crises of participation and just and equitable distributions. For instance, the 1972 Constitution of Bangladesh pronounced secularism as a fundamental principal of state policy but the constitutional changes under military rulers compromised the principle of secularism and gave rise to religion based discriminatory politics. Hindus became targets of discrimination by the Central authorities in West Pakistan through string of new laws. None of the Government in Bangladesh since its independence has taken any decisive step to protect Hindus in face of potential threats including the current attacks. It is practice, in Bangladesh, the religious minorities especially Hindu cannot be given highest positions like head of state, chief of armed forces, governor of Bangladesh, Banks, Ambassador, and Secretary in the ministry of defence, Home &Foreign Affairs and finance. They are deliberately discriminated in recruitment in civil and military jobs, business and trade, bank loans and credits. The mainstream political parties are not ready to accept any Hindu.

In India, it is not the problem of participation and distribution but it is the politics of appeasement. Indian politics have remained generally stable and evolved smoothly, in comparison to its neighbours. India continues to swear by its secular credential over the past decade or so, but sectarian forces have raised their heads and threatening secularist structure. It has also led to the alienation of minorities and given rise to ethnic aspirations and separatist's movement to seek their rights and identity preservation. The unrest and ethnic turmoil in the Northeast are the clear evidence of failure of even secular state to integrate its socially divergent groups. Secular state came under threats when the politician manipulating emotional sensitivities of communities, majority and minority formula on communal lines for their votes Bank. The religious denomination has also been introduced and accepted in politics.

The government has failed to prevent communalism, religion and regionalism entering as a key reason in the fragmentation of the society and the nation. In Sri Lanka, Tamil insurgency was also the result of the politics of ethnic consolidation of the Sinhalese in the political system. In Pakistan, the separation of Bangladesh was a consequence of the dominance of the Punjab ethnicity under the grab of an Islamic state. Similarly, the sense of deprivation in North Western was a reflection of Bengali and Islamic assertion. In Nepal, the Maoists insurgency and the Madhesi movement are manifestations of the failure of state and the dominance of hill people respectively. In Bangladesh, the Chakma unrest and now the Islamic assertion gave rise to Islamic extremism.

Crisis of Legitimacy

The crisis of legitimacy refers to the problem of achieving agreement about the legitimate nature of authority and the proper responsibility of government. In search of legitimacy, the authoritarian and sectarian forces are struggling for power by mobilising religion, region, caste and communities both internally and externally. What should be the limits to the executive or bureaucratic authority or what should be the pattern of central and local authority, are some question related to the crisis. It is to be noted that the backward societies ridden with theocratic values where people still cling to the idea that political system should confirm to the percept of their religion.

Crisis of good governance and Political stability

The crises of good governance and stability is the result of democratic distortions and insurgency in South Asia. We have been witnessing an erosion of democratic process and assertion of authoritarian governance in most of the South Asian countries. Democratic institutions nurtured by the people in their respective countries have not contributed much to change and are not at all conducive to the welfare of the people. The hundreds of billions of dollars of financial aid given to the poor people failed to reach them. According to the Human Development Commission Report, South Asia is one of the most poorly governed regions of the world, with the exclusion of a voiceless majority, unstable political regimes and poor economic management. The system of governance has become unresponsive and irrelevant to the needs and concerns of the people. Almost all South Asian countries are facing endemic corruption, social exclusion and inefficient/ non-pro-people bureaucracies, failure of law and order which hinder all programs of development including efforts for a healthy and beneficial open world.

Political disorder and failed states have created a security dilemma among the distinct groups that are often exploited by ambitious and unscrupulous politicians. Weak states in the third world have a higher level of concern with domestically generated threats to its internal security because they have not been able to create domestic, political and social consciousness of sufficient strength to eliminate large scale of such forces as a major element in the political life of the nation. The best example is Pakistan which belongs to a group of fragile country ranked one of the top 20 fragile states and has been vulnerable in certain aspects of statelessness. As Pakistan's inability to control internal conflicts and security challenges by various armed militant groups, the legitimacy of the government continues to erode.

Table –2: Status of South Asian Country in Fragile States Index 2018.

S. No.	*Name of the Country*	*Rank*	*Score*
1.	Afghanistan	09	106.6
2.	Pakistan	20	96.3
3.	Bangladesh	32	90.3
4.	Nepal	39	87.9
5.	Sri Lanka	50	84.9
6.	India	72	76.3
7.	Bhutan	81	74.3
8.	Maldives	89	72.4

Source: Fund for Peace, Washington D.C. 2018.

Conflict is an inevitable feature of every society but may be more common within communities that encompass diverse cultural identities and disparities. Most obviously, the above-mentioned factors are crucial / relevant. The principal content of historical legacy and primordial hatreds are perceived as the traditions and memories of the past religious conflicts. It is also the case with the socio-economic explanation, in which the strain of modernization, is said to produce a revival of religion in order to give people some stable meaning within the turmoil of socio-economic change. In case of political explanation, according to which people seek refuge from the security dilemma in the ruins of failed states by fleeing in protection of a religious community. Religion certainly seems to have been present in a wide range of ethnic conflicts since the decades. It provides overwhelming evidence to these conflicts.

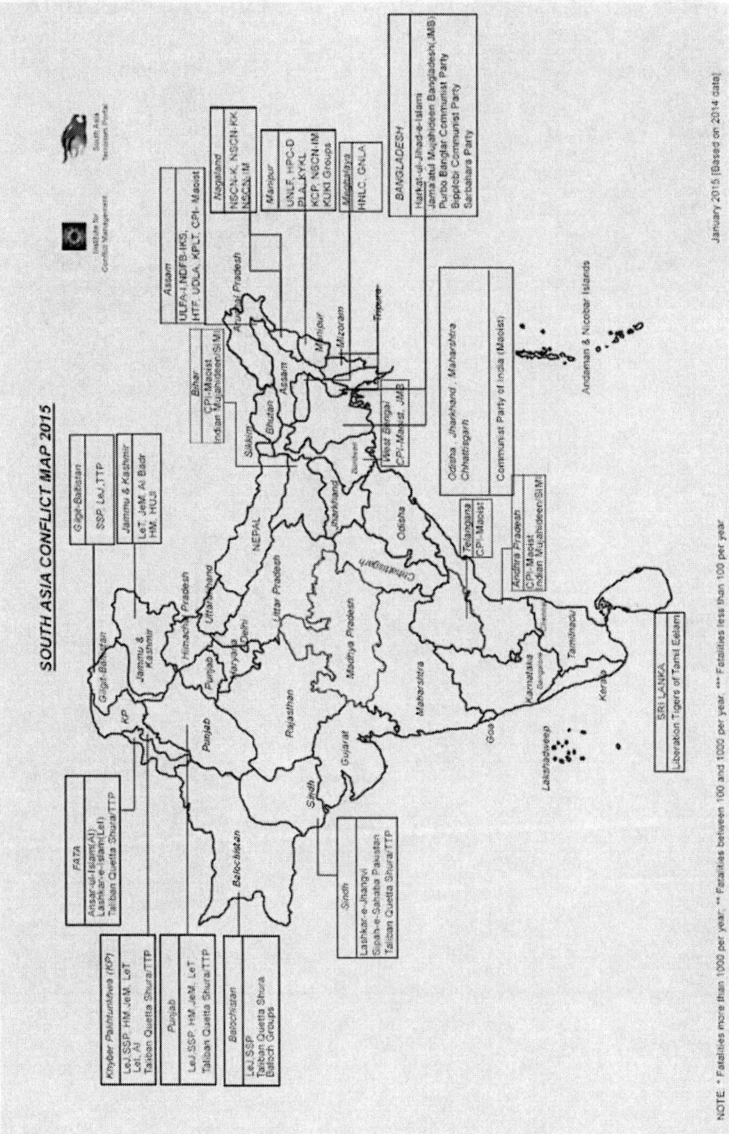

Map-1 South Asia Conflict Map

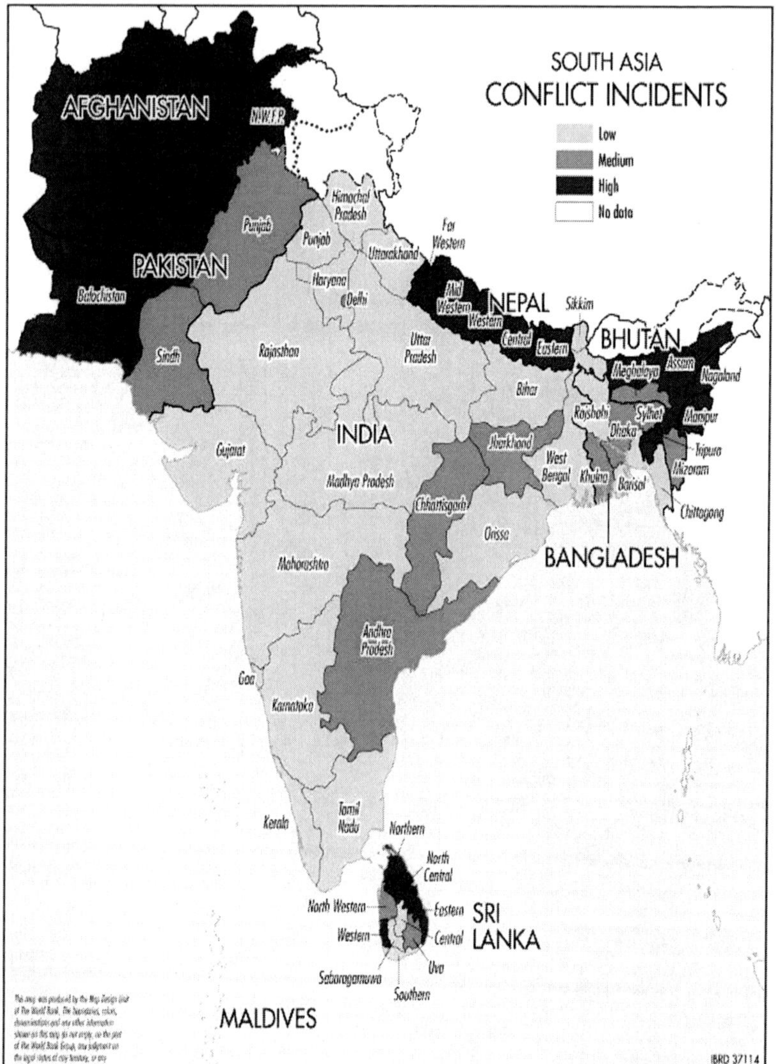
SOUTH ASIA
CONFLICT INCIDENTS
Low
Medium
High
No data
AFGHANISTAN
N.W.F.P.
PAKISTAN
Punjab
Balochistan
Sindh
Himachal Pradesh
Punjab
Uttarakhand
Haryana
Delhi
Rajasthan
Uttar Pradesh
Far Western
Mid Western
Western
Central
Eastern
NEPAL
Sikkim
BHUTAN
Meghalaya
Assam
Nagaland
Bihar
Rajshahi
Sylhet
Manipur
Dhaka
Tripura
Mizoram
INDIA
Gujarat
Jharkhand
West Bengal
Khulna
Barisal
Madhya Pradesh
Chhattisgarh
Chittagong
Orissa
BANGLADESH
Maharashtra
Andhra Pradesh
Goa
Karnataka
Tamil Nadu
Kerala
Northern
North Central
North Western
Eastern
Western
Central
SRI LANKA
Uva
Sabaragamuwa
Southern
MALDIVES
IBRD 37114
FEBRUARY 2010

Table 3 : Major Internal Crisis in South Asia.

Name of the country	*Problem/crisis*	*Religious groups*	*Ethnic groups*
India	Maoistsor Naxal insurgency Kashmir Insurgency andseparatists movement North-East insurgency movements	Hindus 81.3% Muslims 12% Christians 2.3% Sikhs 1.9% Jain, Parsis , Buddhists and others 2.5%	Indo-Aryan 72% Dravidian 25% Magnoliid and others 3%
Pakistan	Islamic fundamentalism Sindh Mujahiir conflict Gilgit, Baluachistan, Pakhunistan Waziristan FATA movements	Muslims 97% (Sunni 77% and Shias 20%) Hindu Christians and others 3%	Punjabi, Sindhi, Baluch, Pathan(Pashtun), and Muhajir
Nepal	Constitutional crisis and Madheshi Movement	Hindu 86.2% Buddhists 7.8% Muslims 3.8% and others2.2%	Brahmin, chetri, Newar, Gurung, Magar, Tamang, Rai, Limbu, Sherpa, Tharu and others.
Bangladesh	Religious Extremism and Islamic Fundamentalism	Muslim 90% Hindu 9% Other groups 1%	Bangali Muslims, Non- Muslims Tribals groups
Afghanistan	Taliban insurgency and Terrorism	Muslims 99% Sunni Islam 90% And Shias7-15% Hindu and Sikhs 1%	Pashtun, Tajik, Hazara, Uzbek Aimak, Turkmen, Baluch, few others Pashayi, Nuristani Pamiri, and Arab etc.
Sri Lanka	Anti-Muslims Violence	Buddhists 70% Hindu 15% Christians 8% Muslims 7%	Sinhalese, Tamils Moors(Muslims) Burgher Malay and vedda.
Maldives	Constitutional crisis	Muslims Sunni) 98.4% Hindus0.111%, Christians 0.4%, Buddhists 0.6%	Dhivehis, indo- Aryan people, Sinhalese and Tamils, Girravaru people.

Sources: SIPRI Yearbook 2000, OxfordUniversity Press 2000; The International Institute for Strategic Studies, Chart for Armed Conflict, The Military Balance2002, London: OxfordUniversity Press, 2002; United Nations Development Programme>www.undp.org/dpa/coweblinks/index.html.

Notes

1. Mahammad Waseem, Civil-Military Relations in Pakistan, in Rajshree Jetly (ed.) Pakistan in Regional and Global Politics, Routledge, New Delhi,2009.

Chapter - 2

India's Major Internal Crisis: Naxalist Insurgency

India's security is vulnerable to threats, tensions, conflicts and violence's originating both from indigenous and exogenous resources. The domestic dynamics of India's internal security are reflected in its socio- political milieu, the main of which is its diversity. It is reflected in the variety of its communities, castes, ethnic groups, language and dialects, religious beliefs, customs and traditions. With different manifestations of culture, all operating in a complex and varied environment.

Indian States after independence inherited only the physical base consisting territory and people-geographical integration of Indian states. Its democratic institutions had to provide social cohesiveness to make India a nation. While India succeeded to some extent but in certain areas, India has reached conflicting situation to a point of violence where various groups contesting, hence resulted into insurgency separatism and terrorism.

India, a secular state, came under direct threat when the politician manipulating emotional sensitivities of communities and words majority and minorities were formally introduced and accepted in political arena. In the politics of votes, the denomination of religions, communities' castes and region become essential identifications. Indian polity failed to prevent these denominating factors entering into as a key reasons and fragmentation of the society, state and nation. Fragmentation of society was added further by reservation.

Electoral politics since 1950s have resulted in diffusion of both state and politics. The institution of governance and democracy have been diluted and politics have lost their ideological and moral moorings. While on the one hand, it has led to the expansion of social base of politics, on the other

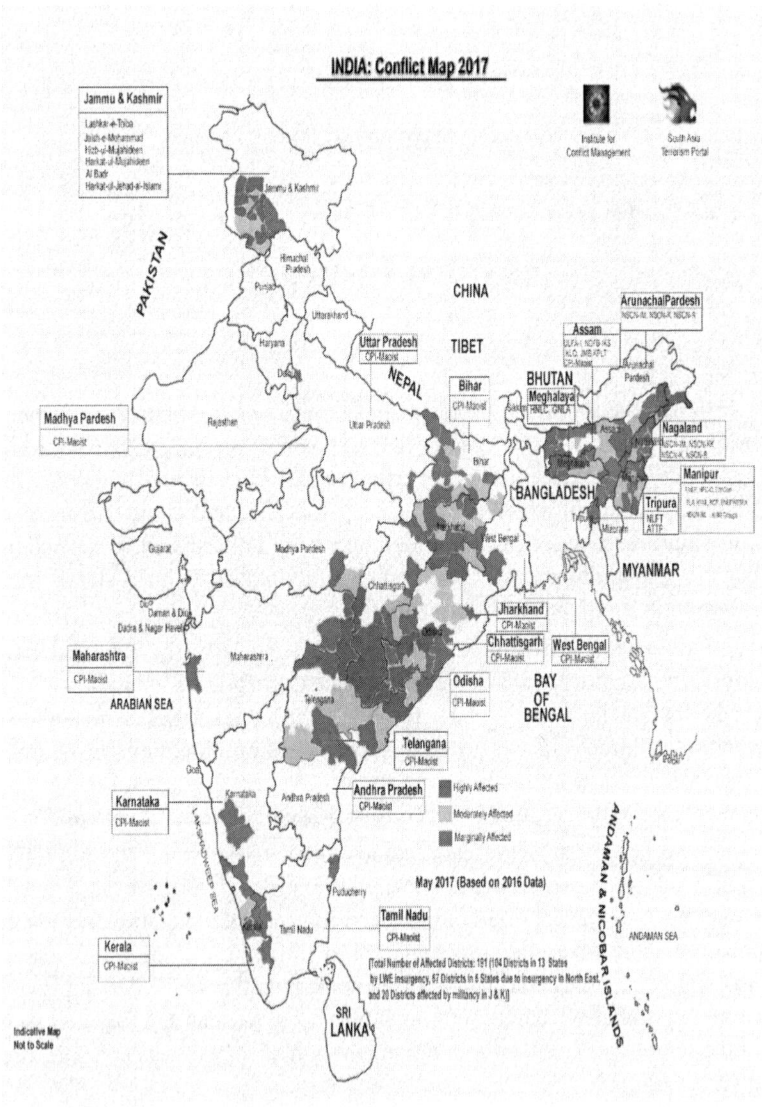

Map-2: India-Conflict Map

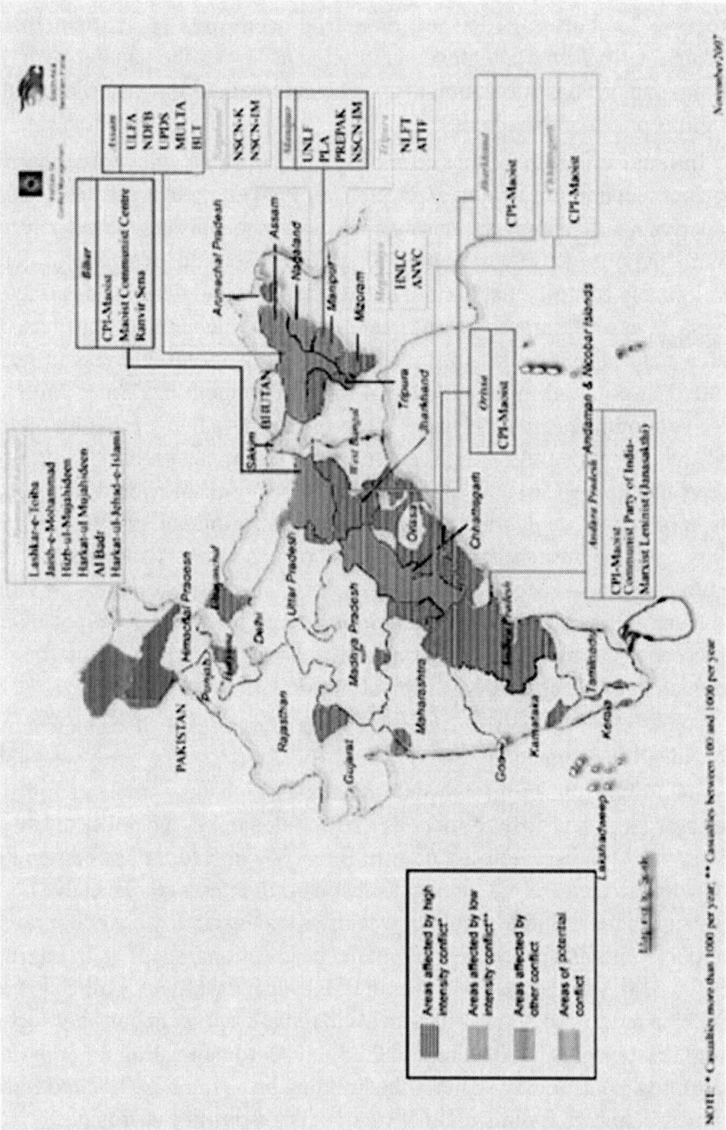

Map-3: India's Conflict Affected Area

hand, due to bad politics, it has resulted in politicization and aggravation of all problems. Political liberty and electoral politics have led to agitation and unrest. More than any other single factors, electoral politics has resulted in breakdown of cohesiveness of society, exploitation of diversities, created insecurity of cultural identity, encourage religious revivalism in its fundamentalist form, heightened ethnicity and widen the gap between the sub-national groups and nationalism. The hall mark of the distortion of the system is political expediency.

Internal crisis in India are mostly the result of uneven economic development and unfulfilled aspirations of the people that creates a sense of deprivation. Economic insecurity and Social inequality are the root causes. It is in the absence of just and equitable distribution of economic and development benefits that people feel dissatisfied and derives the affected groups to assert themselves and resulted into violence and conflicts. In such a state of confrontation, the articulations of group interests in itself resulted in political mobilizations of ethnic communities. Since most of these communities are rural and land resources based, any pressure on the land due to industrialization, development, modernization or migration further increase social and economic pressure. Unemployment is another reason of economic distress and strife. Liberalization and privatization of 1990s has also resulted in accentuation of economic disparities as the benefits have not reached to the poor masses. The backward areas of India like Bihar, Orissa, Chhattisgarh, Jharkhand and North-East are not likely to succeeded due to the lack of basic infrastructure sufficiently and inefficient administrative set up and government inefficiency.

Weak states in the third world have a higher level of concern with domestically generated threats to security because they have not been able to create domestic, political and social consciousness and strength to eliminate large scale use of force as a major element in the political life of the nation. This has been the case in India. Though India has responded adequately to the external threats, its response to internal threats have been totally inadequate. India's internal weakness and instability has encouraged external threats and pose a serious challenge to national security. In internal security field, whether it is in Kashmir or in North East states, both Pakistan and China have been helping insurgents to remain a point of constant focus. Since the late 1960s, both china and Pakistan coordinating training, funding and arming of insurgents. This is the building up of indirect threat to India in which Pakistan, India's main adversary, is a front-line surrogate.

Naxalist or Maoists insurgency

Over the past many decades, India has been coupled with gravest internal security threat – the Maoist or Naxalite insurgency. Maoists insurgency began in May 1967 as a small agrarian rebellion and violent movement against the local landlord at Naxalbari in west Bengal by the poor tribal people. Now it has full blown into full insurgency covering 223 districts across the 20 states and taken lives of 10,000 people and displaced another 15,000 thousand people of these states. The situation has become more grave owing to the recurring attacks by the Maoists against the state apparatus and sheer bloody mindedness killings of peoples, political leaders and elected representatives, security and police personnel, land lords, suspected informers, police stations, armouries, jails, railway stations and trains and train tracks, electricity stations and its transmissions, schools and so on who stand up to rebel their might. On April 25, 2017, 300 Maoist militants attacked on paramilitary forces and killed 55 personnel and injured six in the South Sukma region of Chhattisgarh. This is indeed a threat to our democratic Republic, the UPA PM Manmohan Singh pointed out that left wing extremism is "India's greatest security threats". The increased intensity of violence, coupled with the spatial growth of the movement has added a new dimension to the challenges being faced by the state.

Genesis of movement

The Naxalite movement came into being as a result of prevailing social and economic issues. In fact, while conducting an enquiry into the uprising, the West Bengal State Secretariat of the CPI(M) stated, "Behind the peasant unrest in Naxalbari lies a deep social malady- malafide transfers, evictions and other anti-people actions of tea gardeners and jotedars." These issues were longstanding and there was no dearth of reform legislation. The spirit of the law remained confined to paper and the people were left to languish. Therefore, it recognized that the causes were in essence, socio-economic.

All the regions in which the Naxal movement took hold are ones with alarming levels of poverty. In Telangana, in the districts of Karimnagar, Adilabad and Warangal poverty was 95.8% while in the rest of the state it was between 50 and 60 per cent. After independence, the Indian government pursued agricultural policies focused on massively improving output without doing enough to check economic and social disparity. With the commercialization of agriculture, economic disparities widened. The rich got richer and the poor get poorer. The attempt of the government to abolish zamindari created a class of rich peasants from the backward classes. With the spread of communist ideology, there was greater mobilization of the sharecroppers (bargadars) and landless laborers, who mostly belonged to the so-called lower castes and tribes. This polarized the agrarian classes and created an environment of confrontation.

Mr. Kannabiran, President of the Andhra Pradesh Civil Rights Committee, said that the main objective of land reform was social transformation and it should not be collapsed with the question of immediate productivity impact of land reforms.[3] The failure of land reform was the macro-issue that affected both social and economic conditions of the people.

After independence the Indian government started the protracted and difficult process of abolishing the Zamindari system, to eliminate the role of intermediaries. By the end of the 1950s, the processwas completed[4] 20 million erstwhile tenants became landowners. One rough estimate says that area under tenancy[5] declined from 42% to around 20% by early 1960s. However, to a large extent this was caused due to eviction of tenants by landlords and not by actual reform in the system. The next part of land reform was tenancy reform. Its objectives were to guarantee security of tenure to tenants, to ensure fair rent rates and to gain rights of ownership of land he/she cultivated, subject to some restrictions, at well below market rates.[6] In West Bengal, two major acts for land reform were passed in the 1950s aimed to eliminate intermediaries (zamindars and jotedars) and bring fixed rent tenants into a direct relationship with the state.[7] It gave the state powers to inquire into land transfers and cancel the transfer if it was not bona fide. Abolition of intermediaries was generally successful. However, numerous loopholes and poor implementation meant that the landlords were able to retain control over large tracks of land. It did not protect the rights of Bargadars (sharecroppers), who were the most deprived section of society.

From 1947 to 1969, as part of land reform implementation in West Bengal, only 300,000 acres of above-ceiling land was redistributed, a little less than 3% of the cropped land in the state.[8] The 1961 census estimated that 82 percent of the tenancies in the country were insecure. Bargadars received no protection until 1970, when the government, woken from stupor by the Naxalbari uprising, amended the West Bengal Land Reforms Act to cover them also.[9] The legislations themselves were not strong enough and implementation was extremely ineffective.

Naxalites are a group of far-left radical communists, supportive of Maoists political sentiment and ideology. The Maoists movement built and started by the Communist Party of India (Marxists) leading to the formation of CPI (Marxist- Leninist), People's war group, the People Liberation Guerrilla Army (PLGA) and Agrarian Revolutionary. This movement has evolved through various phases. In the first phase1960-and early 1970s in the wake of Naxalbari uprising, revolutionary came out in numerous groups all over the country and joined forces in the AICCCR (1968) then CPI (ML) 1969) altogether across West Bengal, Andhra Pradesh, Bihar and parts of Uttar Pradesh and Orissa. But the counter-insurgency campaign of the government and the declaration of emergency in 1975 supressed the movement to a larger extent.

Phase second started in 1980s was a prescient. Gradually, the internal differences over the strategy and tactics among the Maoist movement factions led to fragmentation of the original party CPI(ML). In post emergency period, the movement was revived and the CPI(ML) and all major factions of the movement adopted a clear-cut proletarian framework of armed struggle. Charu Majumdar, the founder of CPI(ML) was no advocate of isolated and exclusive armed actions but for him two key phrases were the integration of landless rural people and politics in command. He developed a clear-cut proletarian frame work of armed struggle, exclusively propagate the total politics of seizure of power and build concentrated areas of anti-feudal peasant movement; and established the leadership of landless and poor peasants as the vehicle of proletarian leadership over the struggle and rely on them rather than on party organizers. He encouraged peasants to arm themselves with locally available weapons rather than sophisticated fire arms and combined different forms of struggle as seizure of crops with armed attacks on class enemies and states and so on. "Annihiliation of class enemies" emerged as a new form of class struggle in the Sri Kakulam peasant movement which succeeded to some extent the beginning of armed struggle with broad mass mobilisation.

In some regions, this led to the formation of peasants' squads, mass upsurges and helped to build and sustained armed peasant struggle in Bhojpur and neighbouring region of Central Bihar. But in many areas, annihilation of class enemy formula was wrongly campaigned with a lot of indiscriminate and unnecessary killings diverted from peasants' movement, hence, in the process got isolated from peasant's class struggle.

In 1990s, the Maoists abandoned peasant struggles and organised into squad armed activities mainly in forests and mountainous regions while the original Maoists body remained the main repository of ultra-left and anarchist's activities. Similar trends emerged within and around the CPI (ML).

Since the 1990s, the Maoist movement was renewed because of the neo-liberalisation, globalisation and privatisation of Indian economy. With free, open and competitive market economy, an unplanned and speedy conversion of agricultural lands into real states, setting of special economic zones (SEZ), the takeover and encroachment of the commons and natural resource, all have led to the mass distress following loss of non-market access to the means of subsistence and dispossession through displacement and that was without any legal redress for the victims. Hence, the Maoist insurgency became more violent and spreading to the larger number of most Indian states.

Maoist violence was reached on its highest intensity from 2004 to 2009 with longitudinal growth and added new dimensions to the challenges being faced by the Indian government and the states. A significant factor that contributed to the growing influence of Maoism was the merger of two most important groups- the People's War Group (PWG) and Maoists Communists Centre (MCC) and the formation of a new united group called Communist Party of India (Maoists). It had given combined effect to the new outfit in terms of strength, capability and resources.

The CPI (M) launched its new programme called Democratic Revolution, supports that the revolution will be carried and completed through armed agrarian war and protracted the people's war with seizure of power remaining as its central and principal task called Democratic Revolution affirms that the revolution will be carried out and completed through armed agrarian war and protracted people's war with seizure of power remaining as its central and principal task. It also supports the struggle of sub-nationalities for self-determination, including the right to secession. This programme gave a new impetus and momentum to the Maoists insurgency. A well planned and well conducted attacks were carried out with military efficiency and increased numbers of causalities. To recount a few incidents, in 2007, the Maoists massacred 55 policemen and special police officers and injured 12 others in an attack on a police post at Rani Bodli in Chhattisgarh. Since then numbers of attacks arrived out in Orissa, Jharkhand, Bihar, Chhattisgarh, Maharashtra and West Bengal. (see Tables: 5-6). While 100 police men died in Naxal' s attack in 2004, its numbers increased three-fold in 2009 as 300 security personnel killed by them in ambushes and land mine blasts. (Table-4).

Table- 4: Major Maoists Fatalities

Year	*Total Number of Incidents*	*Killed*					*Injured*					*Initiated By Civilians*	*Initiated By Security Forces*	*Initiated By Militant*	*Initiated By NS*
		C	SF	M	NS	Total	C	SF	M	NS	Total				
2014	28	24	54	68	4	150	18	27	6	8	59	0	1	17	8
2015	15	3	22	45	0	70	0	10	0	0	10	0	4	8	3
2016	35	27	24	123	0	174	12	20	0	0	32	0	10	17	8
2017	20	6	52	64	0	122	4	22	1	0	27	0	4	11	4
2018	28	8	36	113	0	157	0	22	0	0	22	0	15	13	0
2019	6	3	0	22	0	25	0	0	2	0	2	0	2	2	2
Total*	**132**	**71**	**188**	**435**	**4**	**698**	**34**	**101**	**9**	**8**	**152**	**0**	**36**	**68**	**25**

* Data till, March 09, 2019.

Table 5

Year	*Incidents of Killing*	*Civilians*	*Security Forces*	*Terrorists/Insurgents/Extremists*	*Not Specified*	*Total*
2014	185	127	97	121	4	349
2015	170	89	56	110	0	255
2016	262	122	60	250	0	432
2017	199	109	76	150	0	335
2018	217	108	73	231	0	412
2019	27	15	1	32	0	48
Total*	**1060**	**570**	**363**	**894**	**4**	**1831**

*Data till March 09, 2019.
Sources: South Asia Terrorism Portal, 2019.

In 2007, it was estimated that Naxalites were active across "half of the India's 28 states" which constitutes about 40 percent of India's geographical area known as the "Red Corridor". According to estimates, they were active and controlled 92,000 square kilometres area in approximately 180 districts in ten states.[10] In August 2010, Karnataka was removed from the list of

Table 6: NaxalAffected Districts:*

State	**# of Districts in State**	**# of Districts Affected**	**Districts Affected[29]**
Jharkhand	24	18	Hazaribagh, Lohardaga, Palamu, Chatra, Garhwa, Ranch i, Gumla, Simdega, Latehar, Giridih, Koderma, Bokaro, Dhanbad, East Singhbhum, West Singhbhum, SaraikelaKharsawan, Khunti, Ramgarh
Bihar	38	11	Aurangabad, Gaya, Rohtas, Bhojpur, Kaimur, East Champaran, West Champaran, Sitamarhi, Munger, Nawada, Jamui
Chhattisgarh	27	10	Bastar, Bijapur, Dantewada, Kanker, Rajnandgaon, Sarg uja, Jashpur, Koriya, Narayanpur, Sukma
Odisha	30	9	Malkangiri, Ganjam, Koraput, Gajapati, Rayagada, May urbhanj, Sundargarh, Deogarh, Kandhamal
Andhra Pradesh	13	8	Guntur, Prakasam, Anantapur, Kurnool, Visakhapatnam, East Godavari, Srikakulam, Vizianagaram
Telangana	10	8	Warangal, Karimnagar, Adilabad, Khammam, Medak, N algonda, Mahbubnagar, Nizamabad
Maharashtra	36	3	Gadchiroli, Chandrapur, Gondia
Uttar Pradesh	75	3	Sonbhadra, Mirzapur, Chandauli
West Bengal	19	3	Bankura, West Midnapore, Purulia
Madhya Pradesh	50	1	Balaghat
Total	319	**74**	

Note: 44 districts have removed from the list of 126 Naxal-hit districts while eight new districts have included. The number of worst-affected districts has also gone down from 35 to 30, Ministry of Home Affairs, Government of India.

Naxal-affected states[11] In July 2011, the number of Naxal-affected areas was reduced to (including proposed addition of 20 districts) 83 districts across nine states.[12]

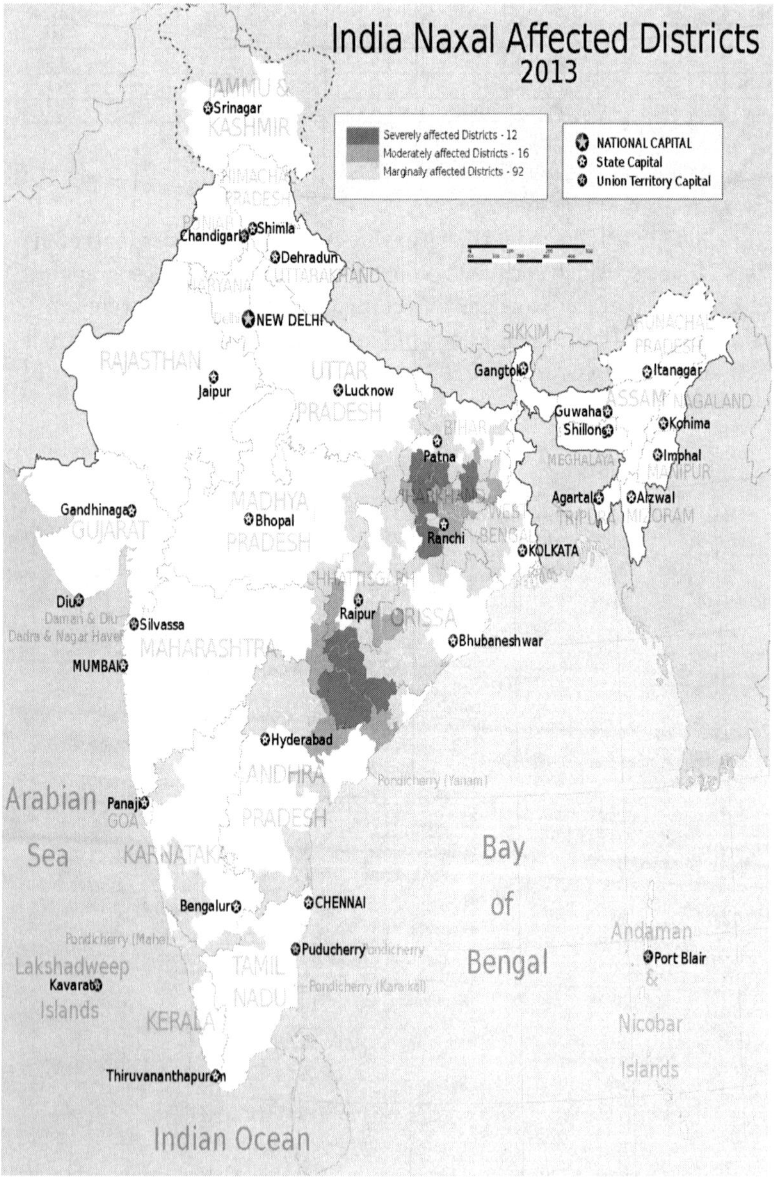

Map-4 India Naxal Affected Districts

The Naxalites operate in 60 districts in India, mainly in the states of Odisha (5 affected districts), Jharkhand (14 affected districts), Bihar (5 affected districts), Andhra Pradesh, Chhattisgarh (ten affected districts), Madhya Pradesh (8 affected districts), Maharashtra (2 affected districts) and Wset Bengal (8 affected district). In West Bengal areas west of Howrah are affected by the insurgency. Chhattisgarh is the epicentre of the conflict (2007).

Strategies and tactics

Maoists states 'from the very beginning our orientation, perspective and the method of building mass organisations and mass struggle should be to serve the war directly or indirectly'. War i.e. partisan armed actions against states and /or ruling party isolated from the natural objective course of peasant movements. Since the beginning, Mao's dictum, power grows out of the barrel of a gun', has been the credo of the Naxalites. The programme of the CPI(M) launched as New Democratic Revolution encourage this objective and want to capture the power of states through force and use of violence. Therefore, the Maoists' movement has been carried out and completed through agrarian revolutionary war that is protected peoples war with the seizure of power remaining as its central and principal task. It also supports the struggle of sub-nationalities for self-determination, including the right to secession. Like peasants in Singur and Nandi gram raised arms against the corporate for their land grab; adivasis in Lalgarh revolted against police atrocities demanding apologies and punishment for guilty officials. As in Nandigram, tens of thousands of women and men with their traditional weapons actively liberated their own lands and earned great support from all corners of India and abroad.

Maoist has adopted typical Maoists features like kidnappings, serial killings often with barbaric features such murdering a teacher in front of school children, compelling the body of a slain CPI(M) cadre to rot under the sun for days together and so on. The Maoist strategy of armed actions and violence, kidnapping, political killings, raid on police stations, destructions and bombardment on police stations railway stations and tracks run only on the strength of guns and vast network of extortions. A huge levy, is regularly collected from contractors, brick kiln owners, Tendu leaf and other businessmen and industrialists, illegal forests produce contracts and coal and iron ore miners corporate houses and bureaucrats. With a many fold increase in the flow of funds in the rural areas for various NGO projects and government projects, Maoists find convenient to share a slice of this development.

Why the Maoist armed struggle has still gained a social base in India? The actual conditions of the tribal rural area where people live in abject poverty, lacking all basic civic amenities and denied their entitlement as a citizen of this country, the Maoist still carry the burden of the peoples hopes. Despite all confusion, violence and the problems peoples still have the hopes for liberation from poverty, discrimination and exploitations. The poor people though economically and socially deprived were not overly concerned about the problem of land acquisition or the issue of development and displacement. The sole issue, the most fundamental one is that of the right to life. Even after 50 years in power, the self-proclaimed pro-poor and labour government continues to announce new schemes for the social and economic upliftment have failed. All democratic forums remain ineffective and insensitive to the demand of the poor peasants and tribal. All this created favourable situation for the rise of radical politics and armed insurgency.

For the theoretical and contextual explanation of terror and violence, it is necessary to understand sources and causes, ways and technique, ideologies and structure of Maoist violence. Poverty, corruption and non-governance increases the opportunity of rebellion. There is a strong link between poverty in India and the operation of Maoist insurgency. Maoist revolutionaries able to recruit the poor tribal people where the states lack the resources to provide basic services and security adequately. Lack of infra structure and basic services like education, health, housing and jobs, no roads and transportation, all are related to a greater number of violence and conflict incidence. All the schemes of pro-poorer like NREGA failed to provide economic security to these people. Maoists insurgents have exploited the government inefficiency and made roads in to develop region as Maoists sanctuary. They have developed a wide base among adivasis / tribal by dint of painstaking work over a long time. The Maoist depicted image of saviours has significantly contributed to the growth of the movement in new areas also. Their efforts to curb the feudal practices and social oppression by confiscating and redistribution of surplus ceiling land, higher agricultural wages, reduction of stranglehold of landlords, moneylenders and contractors, protection from harassment by forest and government officials and the police, among others have been gaining supports from the locals.

Maoism has an appeal especially to the disadvantaged sections of the society including SC/ST. The districts with greater share of SC/ST population support Maoist violence. In fact, where the opportunities to these groups are restricted and discriminated because of traditional caste-based system, it encourages to facilitate mobilization of rebellion violence. Such organised and collective violence garners significant massive support from local people and left- wing intellectuals ranging from Noam Chomsky,

Mahashewta Devi to Ashis Nandy, and human rights community. A few intellectuals given the widespread perception about the effectiveness of a possible totalitarian government that the Maoists intend to form. This sympathetic support of Naxalism also accord some legitimacy to the movement. They also strike a chord of sympathy and support among a section of students with revolutionary leanings. In their main areas of works, they sometime mobilize hundreds and thousands of people in their militant programmes.

Aggressive business and accommodating politics are now the main reason of Maoist sustainability. The government initiative to install industries in the mineral rich areas of Chhattisgarh, Orissa and Jharkhand has led to a displacement of tribals and intensified exploitation of mineral and natural resources, land acquisition and compensations issues. the Maoists have been effectively able to exploit these problems for their own political objectives. The business interests of some big industrialists in India like Tata Group, Arcelor Mittal, Essar Steel, POSCO group, Jindal steels all are engaged in either aggressive planning or execution of a slew of project ranging from mining of iron ore, coal to steel production and the power projects across the conflict areas of Chhattisgarh, Jharkhand, Orissa, Bihar and West Bengal. These industrial activities typically involve the displacement of populations and imperfect exercise that breed resentment and rebel in these regions. Maoists have also taken common cause against special economic Zone (SEZ) and the effect of globalisation. Millions of rural people are being rendered proletarian in the form of casual and contract labour, hungry, malnutrition ridden, homeless and land less paupers, force migrants threatened indigenous peoples and so on. Fundamentally, the Maoists people's war is about the path of development of capitalist class in which poor are the victims of new democratic development where they are supposed to be beneficiary. In Danateware, Bastar and Bijapur district of Chhattisgarh, in context of large-scale acquisition of land by the corporates in mineral rich region, entire village have been forced to evacuate and villagers were forcibly herded into camps.

The State Governments are facilitating many business houses for land procurement and providing paramilitary security to corporate house without understanding the dynamics that operates in areas and inevitably displacement of the tribal people without any resettlement and rehabilitation. Neither the Government nor industrialists have given preference to rehabilitation but only resettlement. Security and para-military forces are engaged directly or indirectly to perpetuate a project and allowing use of company assets for abuse such as overlooking mistreatment of the people. Like in Singur and Nandigram, the people rose in arms against acquisition of land by Tata group; adivasis in Lalgarh revolted against police atrocities. In Nandigram, tens of thousands of women and men with their traditional weapons created their own liberated zone and earned great support from all corners of India and Abroad. Many industrialists namely Arcelor Mittal, The Essar group, Vedanta, Tata steel POSCO, Rio Tinto, BHP Billiton and S Jindal groups gave ultimatum to the concerned states/central government. At last, they had to dump their projects and shifted to other states because of local resistance.

The hills and forests region rich in natural resources as Dandakaranya- land, water, forest and mineral resources- has become one of the main arenas for expropriation of social property by the big Indian and foreign capitalists facilitated by the Central and States governments. Planned mining and industrial projects, development of eco-tourists resorts has spurred the construction of highways, roads, railways, hydro-electricity and underground pipeline. In such circumstances, the pattern of development and industrialisation are benefitting the capitalists instead of the people living in those regions, though it is claimed that it is for the benefit of rural tribal people but not in real sense implemented. Adivasis' livelihood based on agriculture and minor forest produced are in jeopardy. The infra-structure and the mining and industrial projects have led/ are leading to mass displacement and environmental damages.

Maoists groups too have stakes in electoral politics and political parties. They cannot avoid taking part in electoral politics but they do so in their own distorted ways-indirectly, secretively and consiperationaly usually supporting one ruling or other against each other. Rather than fielding its own candidates and contesting independently, they support political parties with an eye to some temporary gain for itself. This strategy was most successfully implemented in Andhra Pradesh Assembly election in 2004. They called for one sided boycott on TDP and BJP and campaigned in favour of congress. In Bihar, during the Lalu Yadav Era, the Maoist were known as Rastriya Janta Dal (RJD) men. In many places, they mobilized votes and managed booth in favour of RJD candidate while changing the prospects of rival candidate of CPI (ML) in 2005. In Jharkhand, Maoist squads allowed themselves to be utilized by the ruling BJP in the 2005 Assembly election. In 2010, the number of Maoists contested on JMM tickets and have helped the JMM party in many areas. In West Bengal, they use their power in Nadigram to clear the ground for the entry of Trinamool Congress (TMC) and subsequently they have trained their guns mainly on CPI(M) cadres. In 2009, the Maoists went beyond this and express his party open preference for Mamta Banerjee. Now that her purpose has been served and she find herself within striking distance from the coveted seat of power in west Bengal, she has step by step distances herself from the Maoists.

To be precise, a number of factors have contributed to the growing influence of the Maoists and their increased intensity of violence and stepped up mass mobilization:

- Most important factor was the merger of the two potent groups PWG and MCC have gave new synergy in term of strength capability and resources both human and material for launching attack son security forces. The combined strength of the CPI(Maoists) increased tremendously. In 2004, the combined strength of Maoist is estimated to be 15,000 armed cadres more than the 3000 Kashmiri militants.
- Merger had provided a large swathe of India- from Bihar to Andhra Pradesh for the Maoist to move both for operation and safe heaven to hide and take shelter. This has been giving them an upper hand and ability to attack across the states whenever they want. While the states police are restricted by law and jurisdictions and lack of coordination, the Maoists are not.
- They have well organised and coordination networks.
- The Maoist has gained a new avatar. In the starting of movement in late 1960s, they used bows, arrows, axes, pistols and small bombs. The Maoists now have new range of modern, sophisticated and lethal weapons which include AK-47s, light machine guns, INSAS rifles, self -loading rifles, grenade, mortars, rocket launchers among others. They have been acquiring these weapons through raids on police armouries and snatching arms of the policemen killed in attacks and incidents, apart from, the Nepalese Maoists, terrorists and other insurgent groups are supplying the weapons. Earlier the LTTE was also the main sources of providing arms to the Naxals.The easy availability of explosive in the Red Corridor has facilitated them to lay the landmines to kill the states troops with more devastating effect. They have R&D units which fabricate and upgrade weaponry, including devices which have added to the strike power of the Maoists. Naxalites acquire most of their weapons by raiding state police facilities. Weapons are also purchased in foreign bazaars and smuggled across India's poorly defended borders with Nepal, Bangladesh, Myanmar, and China. Some sources also report a domestic manufacturing capability. Maoists have admitted that the Indian state severely damaged their political and military intelligence units, and central weapon manufacturing, magazine and supply departments between 2009 and 2012.

- The Maoists had also changed their strategy from guerrilla warfare policy of hit and run to mobile warfare that is attacks in large numbers with a purpose to annihilate security forces and to loot their weapons. To ensure direct participation of the masses in armed activities, Maoists attempted to promote armed mass action as a part of their military campaign. To ensure direct masses in armed activities, the Maoist have also been attempting to promote armed mass action as a part of their strategy.
- The government attempts to install big industries in mineral rich areas of Chhattisgarh, Orissa, Jharkhand and Bihar caused the displacement of larger numbers of tribal and poor people and their exploitation raising the serious issues of land acquisition mechanism, compensation and so on. The Maoists have been effectively able to exploit these problems of the tribal for their own political objectives.
- Lack of consensus and co-ordinations among the states in dealing with the challenges and problems of the Maoists. The Maoist have been taking full advantage of this situation.
- The Human rights of the local people are not respected and that prove counter-productive while carried out the counter-insurgency operations. For instance, in case of Lalgarh where police operation ended up creating more Maoists in the form of Jan- militia.
- As regards finances and their sources, the mineral rich areas of Central India which are also the pockets of the Naxal's influence provide them with the large funds by way of extortion and levies from the contractors, businessmen, transporters, siphoning off of development funds, voluntary contributions and looting of treasuries and banks. These funds, estimated to the tune of Rs. 1000 crore a year, stated the Economic times, April 9, 2009, are being utilized for increasing their cadre strength, procurement of arms R&D work, information and publicity besides running the organisation.
- In several Maoist affected states, natural resources have been expropriated to finance rebel activity. Mining and rough terrain provide material and non-material support to Maoist insurgents groups. This factors which facilitate rebellion are more associated with the grievances related measures. Maoists violence and conflicts are occurring more with greater frequency and severity where mining operations providing opportunities to loot resources to finance their operations.

- The Forest terrain provides cover from the state and Maoists favours remote areas densely forested which lie beyond the reach of the state to enforce the rule of law. Violence is greater in districts sharing borders with other districts themselves experiencing Maoists attacks. Studies indicates that the incidence, frequency and severity of Maoists violence is positively and significantly related to the number of lethal events in neighbouring districts and the cross-border spill over effects are occurring in the six states national as well as sub-national levels. Districts with large shares of forested land are more corelated with the presence of Maoists activity.
- The rebels have bureaus in most states tasked with recruitment, agitation and raising level of cadre strength and awareness. This is how rebellion in several ways a prelude to gain power.
- The Naxalist movement found enormous support among the educated youth.
- The Naxalist movement found enormous support among the educated youth. These young men and women belonged to the petty bourgeoisie.[13] Universities became hotbeds of radical ideology, perpetrating acts of violence in an attempt to overthrow the state. Ironically, they are precisely the section of the students who shunned their politics, disdained going in for the drudgery of mobilizing and organizing fellow students in absence of employment.[14] Their sense of disillusionment and the fiery idealism of youth directed them to Naxalist ideology. The repression of Naxalism during the emergency also attracted a large number of youths to Naxalism as a rebellious reaction to the government's oppression.[15] Naxalism appealed to each of these groups for different reasons.
- Finally, the positive contributions of the Naxalists to the Adivasis and Dalits has given the Maoism an image of saviours from the feudal practices and social oppression, protection of stranglehold of landlords, moneylenders and contractors and protection from harassment from forests police and other government officials. This has significantly contributed the growth of movement into new areas. It appeals to the disadvantaged sections of society, given widespread perception about the effectiveness of a possible totalitarian government that the Maoists intend to form. Sympathetic support of Naxalists from left wing intellectuals and human rights community also accord some legitimacy and glamour to the movement.

States Responses and Counter-Insurgency Initiatives

Indian government over the past many decades have been trying to solve this gravest internal security threat to the country. In 2008, Prime Minister Manmohan Singh warned, "Naxalism is the greatest threat to our internal security." But the credit for the existence of the movement for over 50 years is also go to the Government which has failed abysmally in addressing the causes and conditions that sustain the movement. The problem has been in the Indian state's perception of the causes of the Naxal movement. When the Naxal uprising began in 1967, the Indian government looked at it as a law and order problem. It did not analyse the causes of the movement and the extent of mobilization of people. Hence, it believed that it could and would put an end to it in a short span of time using force. Y. B. Chavan, the then Home Minister in addressing the Lok Sabha on June 13, 1967, said, the Naxalbari armed clashes as mere "lawlessness"– a transgression to be repressed and contained.[16] So, the government launched a massive police operation that drove the movement underground and brought most of its leaders under police custody within four months of the uprising.

The Naxal's movement has continued to grow in spite of the government actions. Strategist has evolved security-centric policy to contain it except in Kerala and West Bengal where during the first phase of the movement in 1960s, progressive land reforms played an important role in dealing with it.

The Governments have enacted several laws to empower themselves to combat Naxals. The West Bengal Government enacted the West Bengal (Prevention of Violent Activities) Act 1970 to arm itself to repress the uprising. No particular National act has been enacted so far specifically to counter the Naxal movement, but various 'anti-terror' acts have been used to curb Naxal violence and too often to target sympathizers by stamping them as Naxalites. This trend was followed in several other states also. For instance, in Andhra Pradesh in 1983, the N.T Rama Rao government even liberalized arms licensing to enable people to 'protect' themselves from Naxal's .[17]

Federalism certainly poses some obstacles to comprehensive strategies but it cannot sufficiently explain current ambivalence. When sufficiently threatened, the central government has deployed coordinated counter-insurgency campaigns across multiple states, as it did with the Army's 1971 Operation Steeplechase (in West Bengal, Bihar, and Orissa) Operation Green Hunt in 2009.

In short, the Central Government's counter insurgency initiatives focused:

- Deal sternly with the Naxalites indulging in violence.
- Address the problem simultaneously on political security and development fronts in holistic manner;
- Ensure interstate coordination in dealing with problem
- Give priority to faster economic development in Naxal's affected prone areas;
- Supplemented the efforts and resources of the affected states on both security and development fronts;
- Promote local resistance groups against Naxallites;
- Use mass media to highlight the futility of Naxal's violence and the consequent loss of life and property;
- Evolve a proper surrender and rehabilitation policy for Naxalites; and
- Discourage affected states from any peace dialogue with the Naxal's groups unless and until they are not agreed to give up violence and arms.

The UPA government has laid down a clear plan to tackle the Maoists extremism. It has formulated a two- pronged strategies, first- Law and order Approach- military and armed actions simultaneously with the air force and special armed forces and second-social integration approach. Upon coming to power in 2014, the Modi Government continued this two-pronged approach.

Law and Order Approach

The government has launched a Police Modernization Scheme in areas affected by Naxal movements. Under this scheme huge sums of money have been provided to the state governments by the central government to modernize their equipment and tactical gear including latest communication, vehicles and infrastructure facility. States have also been told to regulate police stations and outposts that are susceptible to Naxal attacks and have to be fortified. Due to increased use of IED by the Naxalites and the increased number of casualties the government has decided to provide the forces with Mine Protected Vehicles (MPV). Central Para Military Forces have been deployed on a long-term basis by the government to help the state governments to fight against the Naxals. The states have also been relieved from paying the charges involved in deploying these forces for about 3 years which nearly is about Rs.1100 crores.[19]

- The government, to discourage the youth from the path to militancy, has revised the recruiting guidelines to permit 40% recruitment in Central Para Military Forces from areas affected by Naxalism.
- The government has also raised a special force of 14,000 personnel consisting of Central Paramilitary Forces, state police and ex-servicemen from areas affected by Naxalism. At present 36 battalions of Central Para Military Forces are deployed in Naxalite affected areas.
- The government has set-up the Indian Reserve (IR) battalions to strengthen the security networks in the states. These forces along with additional security provide youth with employment opportunities.
- The Centre has also raised the amount provided to each battalion to Rs.20 crores from the previous Rs.13 crores. In April 2006, the government authorized the formation of nine more Indian reserve battalions of 1000 personnel each.
- In order to ensure that the activities by the Nepalese Maoists don't affect India, SSB has been deployed along the Indo-Nepal border. They have been given a massive fund of Rs. 444 crores for their modernization.
- Like insurance scheme for police personnel, community policing, expenditure incurred on publicity to counter propaganda of Naxalites, rehabilitation of the Naxals and raised the level of imbursement from 50% to 100% etc. Presently 76 districts in 9 states which are badly affected by Naxal activities are covered in this scheme.
- Plans for the formation of three to four specialized Anti-Maoist Centres at critically important locations at inter-state boundaries which will be equipped with five helicopters each and would be manned by the CRPF and the pilots would be called from the Army/BSF/Air Force. The use of UAV's for reconnaissance missions and collection of intelligence from Naxal affected areas has been authorized by the Centre. Ex-servicemen have also been called for the formation of an auxiliary force which will primarily be supervising the work of detecting mines and explosives laid by Naxalites. Around 4,800 ex-servicemen have already joined the fight and an expected 5,000 are expected to join. The government of Chhattisgarh started the Counter Terrorism and Jungle Warfare College in Kanker imparts training to counter the well trained and motivated guerrilla force of the Naxals, where police

personnel are given rigorous training in guerrilla warfare and are made to live in the open and taught how to live off the land. Even the Army who as such are not very interested in getting themselves dragged into tackling Naxalists have been training 16 companies of paramilitary and state personnel to counter Naxalists operations.

- States have also established their own special security force like Andhra Pradesh has formed the Greyhounds which are said to be one of the most effective police force to combat the Naxals problem and the government of Uttar Pradesh has also raised a battalion of the Provisional Armed Constabulary consisting of the local youth. Even the Central government has formed the COBRA which is a special force formed to deal with Naxalists in any state.

Special Laws have been made by the Government are:

Rehabilitation and Resettlement Policy, 2007

The Government issued a Rehabilitation and Resettlement policy in 2007 for the displaced people who lose their land for industrial growth. Under this policy land in change for land will be given, job to at least one member of the family, vocational training and housing benefits including houses to people in rural areas and urban areas are some other benefits.[21]

Forest Rights Act, 2006

Forest Rights Act of 2006 recognizes the rights of the scheduled tribes and forest dwellers who have been living in the forests for years but their rights have still not been recognized.[22] The Ministry of Environment and Forests has also allowed use of 1 hectare of land for non-forest purposes and conversion of kutcha roads into pukka roads.

Chhattisgarh Unlawful Activities prevention Act,2006

This bill has provisions defining the unlawful activities, declaring an organisation unlawful and formation of an advisory board wherever the state government feels the need for its establishment.[23]

Social Integration Approach

Social Integration Approach to tackle the Naxal problem is related with Social-Economic-Development. In 2003-2004, Indian government started the Backward Districts initiative and the Backward Regions Grant Fund (BRGF) under which 55 of the worst affected areas in 9 states were to be provided the funds of Rs. 2475 crores to tackle the problem.

Approximately 250 districts have been included the BRGF scheme to accelerate socio-economic development which is to be administered by the Ministry of Panchayati Raj. Various state governments have allocated funds to the affected areas as West Bengal government, Karnataka, Chhattisgarh, Jharkhand and Orissa. West Bengal Government allocated Rs.50 crores for the underdeveloped rural areas of the state and a separate fund of Rs.5 crores were set aside for Paschimanchal comprising of 74 blocks of Bankpura, Purulia, West Midnapore, Burdwan and Birbhum districts. They also created a separate department for Paschimanchal development to expedite the implementation of poverty alleviation programs.[24] Chhattisgarh government has also announced houses worth Rs.1 lakh and employment to the kin of who got killed in the Maoist violence and the Jharkhand government increased the insurance amount to be given to the kin of policemen.[25]

Various schemes launched have been launched by the government like the Pradhan Mantri Gram Sadak Yojana (PMGSY) which offers tremendous opportunities for rural road connectivity. The National Rural Employment Guarantee Programme (NREGP) is implemented in 330 districts affected by Naxalism so as to universalize the demand-driven programme for wage-employment. Other schemes in addition to the above-mentioned schemes are Bharat Nirman, National Rural Health mission (NRHM), Sarva Shiksha Abhiyan (SSA), Integrated Child Development Services (ICDS) and other income generating and social security schemes of the Ministry of Rural Development, Agriculture, Panchayati Raj and Tribal affairs. The central government has also providing assistance in the formation of Ashram, schools and hostels for girls and boys in tribal areas.[26]

States like Jharkhand and Orissa have offered huge incentives to the Naxals who surrender themselves. Further, the government has offered cash equivalent to the price of the weapon surrendered. They will provide them with life insurance cover, vocational training, agricultural land, health and educational facilities for their children.[27]

The government constituted an 'Empowered Group of Ministers' to counter the problem of Naxalism headed by the Home minister and selected chief ministers.[28] The government under the Unlawful Activities Prevention has banned the Communist Party of India (Marxist-Leninist) - People's War and all its associated groups, the Maoist Communist Centre (MCC) and its front organizations. The government has also constituted a Task force which will comprise of Nodal officers from the Naxal affected areas and officers from the IB, SSB and the CRPF. There is also a Coordination Centre that was set up in 1998 headed by the Union home minister with

Chief Secretaries and DGPs of the Naxal affected areas for the coordination of steps taken to control Naxal activities.[29]

Since June 2005, the Government of Chhattisgarh, with the support of the Home Ministry has been waging a counter-insurgency operation against the Naxalites named the Salwa Judum in Dantewada district of Chhattisgarh. In 200 villages, people has mobilized against the Maoists, going on processions and holding meetings. The Salwa Judum 'activists' are armed with guns, lathis, axes, bows and arrows. Up to January 2007, "Special Police Officers" (SPOs) had been appointed by the Government under the Chhattisgarh Police Regulations. They actively participate in the Salwa Judum and are given weapons and military training by the security forces as part of an official plan to create a civil vigilante structure parallel to that of the Naxalites. Salwa Judum 'activists' have become vigilantes who assert the right to control, intimidate and punish anyone they consider to be a suspected Naxalite. However, The Government does not accept responsibility for the actions of the Salwa Judum 'activists', it sponsors, encourages, promotes and assures them full state protections and grants them impunity to operate as an extra-legal authority within the district. The Maoists also retaliate with attacks on camps, SPOs and police. But Salwa Judum has only intensified the violence from both sides and campaign and has backfired badly. The states encouragement of vigilant groups such as Salwa Judum as a part of counter-insurgency strategy has been severely criticised that had led to fratricidal war between the Tribal even the supreme Court.[30]

Modi government initiative

Modi government described Naxalism as a social problem, identify it with the historic mistreatment of Tribals. Modi advocated development and dialogue to "woo them back" by winning their hearts and minds.After the Sukuma Attack in 2017, the Central Government has come up with a fresh plan for combating left wing extremism called SAMADHAN as the new Anti-Naxal doctrine of the NDA government.[31] In fact, SAMADHAN, which means "solution" is actually an action plan which the UPA -II government had explored in the past—developing infrastructure, fast tracking central schemes and asking states to coordinate in joint operations with the central paramilitary forces deployed in the red zone. For Modi government, SAMADHAN means a combination of Smart Leadership to convert failure into success—Aggressive Strategy, Motivation and Training, Actionable Intelligence, Dashboard Based KPIs (Key Performance Indicators) and KRAs (Key Result Areas), Harnessing Technology, Action plan for each Theatre and No access to Financing.

It is a significant indicator that influence of Left-wing extremist are reducing. With three districts in Jharkhand and two districts in Bihar no longer in the list. The new list of LWE-hit areas now includes 90 districts spread across 11 states. The eight newly-added districts include Malappuram, Wayanad and Palakkad in Kerala, all of which border the Maoist-infested trijunction running through Karnataka and Tamil Nadu. This is the first time that Kerala has been included in the list of Maoist-affected states. The other new LWE-hit districts are Mandla in Madhya Pradesh, West Godavari in Andhra Pradesh, Kabir Dham in Chhattisgarh and Angul and Boudh in Orissa. These districts border existing Naxal-hit districts or states have been included in order to pre-empt any spill-over effect. A decision has taken to pre-empt them by extending benefits of Security Related Expenditure (SRE) to the adjoining districts as well.[32] The revised list of districts affected by Maoist violence and activity was approved by the Union home ministry as part of its redrawn security-related expenditure (SRE) schemes norms effective from April 1, 2018. Under the SRE Schemes, the centre reimburses security related expenditure incurred by the state on transportation, communication, hiring of vehicles, stipend to surrender Maoists and construction of infra-structure for forest etc. in left wing extremists affected districts.

Table - 7: Ministry of Home Affairs Data on Naxalites Arrest & Surrender 2005-2018

Year	*Arrests*	*Surrender*
2005	1950	2131
2006	1270	1281
2007	1456	390
2008	1743	400
2009	1981	150
2010	2878	265
2011	2030	394
2012	1901	445
2013	1397	282
2014	1696	676
2015	1668	570
2016	1840	1442
2017	1888	685
2018	755	284

* Data till May 15, 2018.

Table - 8 Nexal deaths and surrenders since 2009

Year	*Naxals killed*	*Naxal Surrendered*
*2018	18	7
2017	149	547
2016	244	2281
2015	101	615
2014	99	656
2013	151	1704
2012	117	403
2011	199	225
2010	277	152
2009	294	73
Total	1649	6663

* Till 11th February.

India over the past decades have been trying to solve this gravest internal security threat in the country but are not successful. The expansion of Maoist net-works and the calibrated extension of their violence suggest a significant strategic failure on the part of the state. Experts admit the Naxalites insurgency receives lower priority compared to other threats. Numerous governments have conserved resources and deployed minimalist strategies against rebels that do not threaten their core. A threatened region of strategic or economic import may compel the costly and sustained inputs that an effective counter-insurgency campaign demands, but in other regions, the costs prove prohibitive for anything more than containment.

In spite of the host of development schemes, Initiatives and plethora of legislations, the conditions of Adivasis in Naxal affected Areas remain terrible. The problem of terrorism-insurgency cannot be addressed through security response or use of force but must be resolved through the implementation of a range of programmes for poverty alleviation, the empowerment of disadvantaged groups, the redressal of grievances and delivery on wider development goal to undercut the recruitment pool of terrorist and violent political groups. The states' capacities to deliver an acceptable level of development to populations in the problem areas are themselves limited by demographics and available natural and financial resource based on the structural infirmities. The development solution has progressively become an alibi for persistent failures to address immediate tasks of response. The time frames of counter-terrorism and developmental policy cannot be reconciled. The counter-terrorism demands immediate responses; development is by definition, a long-drawn out process.

An old, ill-trained and ill-equipped forces in the hit areas and states having no orientation to deal with a full-blown insurgency is another major reason for failures. The police and population ratios of the affected area are very low. As against the international norms of 250 policemen per 100,000 and national average of 143, Bihar is a low 60, Jharkhand 164, Chhattisgarh 134, up 94 and Orissa 100. Worst, these numbers reflect sanctioned strengths and not the actual strengths available on the ground. Policemen in these states operate under abysmal working conditions with little technical support, antiquated weapons and hardly any training in jungle warfare. In many states, there is no new recruitment therefore whenever there is any attack the states have to ask for more central forces and the central forces are at a disadvantage given their ignorance of the terrain and lack of intelligence.

The crisis of leadership is more acute. At the rank of DSP, SSP, fighting leadership at the rank of assistant sub-inspector are severely inadequate. Manpower deficits are of course infinitely compounded by extreme shortfalls in technical, technological and training variables, by irrational and wasteful deployment of forces, and by persistently imprudent political interventions. The outcome is that current capacities of police force in the afflicted states are simply insufficient to design an effective response to the Maoist challenge.The centre operational strategy seeks to concentrate this force in the areas specific Maoists dominance to recover these areas and bring them under civil administration. Maoists simply refuse to confront the state in its areas of strength where the state deployments are heavy, they simply walk away.

Many laws are inefficient and causing problems to Tribal and Scheduled castes by negating the spirit of the various safeguards available to the scheduled tribes under the constitution and other laws in the country.The act providing 'land for land' has become a nightmare for the government and has become a stumbling block for ensuring industrialisation. Likely, the Unlawful activities prevention act (UAPA) which was formulated, only to silence the appropriate discord and dissent brewing in the minds of people, has also failed to make a distinction between the anti-social, anti-national elements from the people. CSPS Bill, 2005 also provides the District Magistrate unconditional powers to notify places which he thinks are being used for unlawful activities without any prior notification and without evidence.

The Government has to do more than counter-insurgency measures to solve the problem of Naxalism. the historical and ideological origin of the movement make it clear that it is thriving on the dissatisfaction of the marginalised and alienates population. The Socio-economic perspective of Naxalism has shaped this rebellious movement due to the failure of the institutional mechanism and frame work to give justice and establish an egalitarian society for the tribal and landless people.The marginalized took up arms only to break down the insensitive establishment. The only solution is to stop the exploitation and must implements employment, poverty alleviation and land reform programmes, counterinsurgency measures cannot achieve much. Incentives provided them under Forest Rights acts must be protects. Government has to instil faith in the people that they will be govern in better manner than by the Naxal. Only with consolidated efforts on the part of the legal,political framework and socio-economic reforms, the problem of Naxalismcan be solved.

Notes

2. India Faces Internal Challenges from Maoists Naxalite, The Financial Express, 3 June 2015.
3. G.R Sahay, Naxalite Movement in India: the State Response, Journal Of Defence studies IDSA, Issue 2, vol.4 April 2010.
4. T. Haque and G. Parthasarthy, "Land Reform and Rural Development: Highlights of a National Seminar",27(8), Economic and Political Weekly, February 1992, at 395. Source: http://www.jstor.org/stable/4397623 (Last Accessed on : 10/01/2010).
5. B.Chandra, India Since Independence, New Delhi Penguin Books ,2000, p.408.
6. Ibid. p. 409
7. Ashook Handoo, Naxal problem Needs Holistic approach, September 8, 2008.
8. West Bengal State Acquisition Act Laws, 1953 See in West Bengal Laws, Vol. 6 at 7.
9. T. Hanstad and J. Brown, Land reform Law and Implementation in West Bengal, Lesson and Recommendation, Dec. 2001. Source: http://www.rdiland.org./PDF/PDF report 112.pdf.
10. Communist Fight in India; Notes and Commentaries, Maccaine.org. archived, 27 July 2011.
11. Uppsala Conflict Data Programme, Conflicted Encyclopaedia Government of India, CPI Maoist Actor Information May 29.2013.
12. Ibid.; Primer: who are the Naxalites? Rediff.com.news, May 4,2009.
13. M.Sen, The Naxalite and Naxalism 6(3/5) Economic and Politically Weekly, Jan. 1971, p.195.
14. 58%in Ap say Naxalism good, Finds Times of India Poll, Times of India.
15. Fatalities in Left Wing Extremism: 1999-2006, Ministry of Home Affairs, October 1, 2017.
16. S.Banerjee, Naxalbari: Between Past and Future,37(22) Economic and Political weekly, June 2002.
17. R. Ravikanti, People's war" and state response: The Naxalite Movement in Telangana", University of British Columbia, September 1995, at 33 Source: https://dspace.library.ubc.ca/handle/2429/3955;S. Banerjee , "Naxalbari: Between Past and Future", 37(22), Economic and Political Weekly, June 2002, 2115.
18. http:/idsa.in/jds/4 2 201. Naxalitemovementinindia.
19. Ajai Sahani, Dreamscape of Solutions, Seminar 607, March 2010, pp.56-60.
20. Status Paper on the Naxal Problem as on March 13, 2006 Ministry of Home Affairs http://www. Satp.org/satporg/countries/india/document/papers/06 march 13; Naxal Conflict in 2006, Asian Centre for Human Rights at 63.

21. S. Dharmadhikary, Resettlement Policy: Promising Start and a letdown" source http://www.indiatogether.org/2007/nov/hrt-randrpol.htm.
22. Forest Rights Act 2006 ,Government of India.
23. Chhattisgarh Special Public Securities Act 2006.
24. Status Repot on Naxal Problem, Ministry of Home Affairs, March 13, 2006.
25. *Ibid.*
26. *Ibid.*
27. *Ibid.*
28. Raman Dixit, Naxalite movement in India: the State's Response, Journal of Defence studies, IDSA. vol.4 issue 2 April 2010.
29. *Ibid.*
30. The Hindu , July 5, 2011.
31. Namrita Biji Ahuja, Modi's Government New Anti-Naxal Mantra, the Week, 8 may 2017.
32. Home Ministry Statement, Times of India, April 16, 2018.

Appendix - 1

Major Maoists Attacks 2005-2018.

Nov.13, 2005	Attack on Jahanabad District jail and police lines and other offices.
March 15,2007	Raided police-post at Rani Bodhi, Chhattisgarh and Police officers.
Februrary15,2008	A massive attack by hundreds of Maoists on Nayagrah Town in Orissa. Overran the district armoury, a training centre and a police station, killed 13 policemen and 2civilian and looted more than 1200 weapons and large quantity of ammunition.
June 29,2008	39 Grey hound commandos of Andhra Pradesh Killed in ambush in Orissa.
July 16,2008	17 people killed in landmine blast in Malkangiri District of Orissa.
July 12, 2009	30 policemen killed in Rajnandangaon in Chhattisgarh.
October 2009	34 policemen killed in Gadchiroli district of Maharastra.
February 14, 2010	Maoists attacked a police camp at Sialda in West Midnapur district of West Bengal and gunned down 24 policemen and set the camp on fire.
April 6, 2010	76 police personnel were killed the Maoists in the jungles of Dantewada, Chhattisgarh.
May 28, 2010	Attacked a Mumbai bound train at Jhargram West Chattisgarh
October 18, 2012	Killed 6 CRPF Jawans and injured 8 police official in Gaya district.
May 25, 2013	25 leaders of Congress Party were killed Darbha valley in Chhattisgarh.
July 2, 2013	SP and 4 other Police officials were killed in Jharkhand and Dumka Areas.
February 28, 2014	Maoists Attacked and killed 6 Police officials in Dantewara Districts.
March 11, 2014	15 security personnel were Killed in Sukuma district.

May 12, 2014	Maoist Blast in Gadchirolli Killed 7 and injured 2 personnel.
April 24, 2017	Sukuma Attack killed 26 persons.
March 13, 2018	Nine CRPF official were killed and six were injured in Sukuma district.
May 20, 2018	7 Jawans Killed in Dantewada, Chhattisgarh.

Sources: Data collected and complied from different sources.

Chapter - 3

Kashmir Insurgency and Separatists Movement

Kashmir is a story of missed opportunities and contested borderlands of hopes and dreams of millions of people. For over six decades, Kashmir has remained a contested land, a battleground over which belligerent states seem to have created their reason d'etre. The Pakistan leadership and Indian leadership whether military or civilian believe that Kashmir is an integral part of their homeland and a loss of Kashmir will mean an end to the idea of nations.The conflicting situation in Jammu and Kashmir has been continued from 1947 which resulted into four Indo-Pakistan War. Also, since 1990s, the state has been engulfed into two situations. First, the existence of separatist militancy/ insurgency/ violence and terrorism and second, the bringing the state into the mainstream of democratic process of governance.

The insurgency in the 1990s was born not out of religious separatism, but a complete denial of room for democratic dissent in the valley after the arrest of Sheikh Abdullah in 1953. From 1957 till 1972, every election in the valley was rigged to ensure a sweeping National Conference victory. The National Conference's victories were not altogether unpopular as the party's main purpose was to ensure the domination of the valley over the politics of the entire state. As a consequence, two successive generations of Kashmiri youths were denied the political space to express their growing frustration and anger with an increasingly corrupt and predatory state government that was being backed uncritically by Central Government and Indian National Congress Party.

In 1987, the National Conference entered into an electoral alliance with the Congress. The elections were allegedly rigged in favour of Abdullah.

The Muslim United Front (MUF), which emerged as a political voice for the youth was denied a reasonable presence in the state assembly through vote manipulation, a large section of the youth became convinced that they would never be allowed to secure the right to dissent, let alone govern, through the Indian democratic system. This led to the rise of an armed insurgency movement by those who lost the elections under the banner of Jammu and Kashmir Liberation Front (JKLF) and supported by Pakistan. Although Pakistan sheltered and supplied these groups with logistical support, arms, recruitments and training. The JKLF's goal was Kashmiri independence and not a merger with Pakistan.

Militant movement was transformed into a mass struggle. With JKLF at forefront large number of militant groups like Allah Tigers, People's League and Hizb-e-Islamia sprung up. Weapons were smuggled on a large scale from Pakistan. In Kashmir, JKLF operated under the leadership of Ashfaq Majid Wani, Yasin Bhat, Hamid Sheikh and Javed Mir and this growing pro-Pakistani sentiments were developed in Kashmir. JKLF used distinctly Islamic themes to mobilise crowds and justify their use of violence. They sought to establish an Islamic democratic state where the rights of minorities would be protected according to Quran and Sunna and economy would be organised on the principles of Islamic socialism.

In the second half of 1989, the alleged assassinations of the Kashmiri people, Indian emissaries and political collaborators by Jammu and Kashmir Liberation Front (JKLF) were intensified. Hundreds of officials were killed to paralyse government's administrative and intelligence apparatus in the state. Farooq Abdullah resigned in January 1990 and the state was placed under the President rule under Article 356 for six years.[1] To control and supress the insurgency, Armed Forces Special Powers Act(AFSPA)[2] and Disturbed Areas Act of Indian constitution were imposed on Kashmir in September 1990 by giving armed forces the powers to arrest and kill without warrant to maintain public order. During this time, the dominant tactics involved killing of prominent figures in public gathering to push forces into action and the public prevented them from capturing these insurgents. This sprouting of sympathisers in Kashmir led to the hard-line approach of Indian army.

Militancy as it was erupted also developed the separatist sentiments of general people in the Kashmir Valley. The spontaneous outburst of the people chanting "Azadi" slogans in streets of Srinagar and other parts of the valley not only created the crisis of legitimacy for the mainstream politics but also a collapse of the political order. The political parties and leaders went into hibernation and gun became the rule of law in the whole Kashmir. Hordes of young, Kalashnikov-wielding men roamed the streets and neighbourhoods of Srinagar, the capital, and the valley's other towns like Baramulla, Anantnag and Sopore. The sound of gunfire and explosions mingled with chants of Azaadi ["freedom"] emanating from demonstrations large and small. People from all strata of society took part in protests against Indian rule. An overwhelming presence of armed forces, thousands of civilians were killed, maimed, tortured, detained, disappeared.The separatist groups and leaders incited the Kashmiri youth to join the insurgency in the name of Jihad while Pakistan Military Inter-Service intelligence supplying deadly weapons and training to Kashmiri Youth and insurgents.

The main militant organisation leading this movement were the Jammu and Kashmir Liberation Front (JKLF), who believes in an independent and sovereign Kashmir from both India and Pakistan. Yasin Malik, chairman of the Jammu & Kashmir Liberation Front was the most prominent face of Kashmiri separatism. Hizbul Mujahedin(HM) another significant organisation with the pro-Pakistan ideology, embarked on a campaign of killing pro-independence fighters and assassinating prominent pro-independence political and religious figures. In its emerging phase of 1980s, Pakistan cut off aid to the JKLF and plotted splits and defections in the pro-independence camp while building up the HM with a programme of all-out support. These two largest insurgent groups, JKLF and HM subscribed to different and conflicting visions of Kashmiri "self-determination". The JKLF's slogan, *Kashmir banega khudmukhtar* ['Kashmir will be sovereign'] stood in contradiction to the HM's - *Kashmir banega Pakistan* ["Kashmir will be part of Pakistan"]. The latent fissure in the Azaadi movement steadily deepened and turned lethal. The JKLF's leaders knew that neither Ladakh nor Jammu would go along with secession. Had religion been their main driving force, JKLF leaders could have espoused the Dixon Plan, proposed by the British in 1947, to hand over the Kashmir valley to Pakistan. But not once in so many years of its existence has the JKLF advocated this "solution".

India-Pakistan and the Kashmir Insurgency

India and Pakistan share a turbulent history in Kashmir. Three of the four wars were fought between India and Pakistan over Kashmir. At the time of independence, the Hindu Ruler of Jammu and Kashmir with 80 % of Muslim population wanted some kind of independence for their state and did not took any firm decision to accede the state either to India or Pakistan.

Tensions between Pakistan and the government of Kashmir grew as the Maharaja's indecision frustrated Pakistan and pro-Pakistani factions within Kashmir. In October 1947 armed Pakistani tribesmen backed by the

Table-9 Main Militant Groups In Jammu and Kashmir.

Name	*Year*	*Leaders*	*Foundation*
Jaish-e-Mohammad	1999	Maulana Masood Azahar	Former Militant Commander and in 1999 hijacking of Indian airplane in 1999.
Lashkar-e Taiba (Let)	Early 1990s. In 2002 it was banned and renamed Jamaat-ud- Dawa	Hafiz Mohammad Masood	Attack on Parliament in 2001 and Bombay Attack in 2008
Hizbul-Mujahadeen	1989	Majeed Dar Syed Salahuddin.	Closely linked with Afghan war Lord and Gulbuddin Hikmatyar and Pakistani Religious party Jamaate-e-Islami.
Harkatul Mujahadeen	Early 1995	Jalalduddin Haqqani Maulana Fazlur Rahman Khalil	Pan Islamic group under the command of Jalaluddin Haqqani based in Pakistan and fought Against US-NATO led forces in Afghanistan.
Jammu and Kashmir Liberation Front (JKLF)	1977 backed by Pakistan	Amanullah Khan, Yasin Malik	Organised resistance against Indian rule with the help of Pakistan military regime of Zia-ul-Haq.

Pakistani state attacked his territory. By October 20th the Pakistani Army entered in the conflict in support of the tribal forces in a multi-pronged effort designed to capture the Jammu and Kashmir. Maharaja Hari Singh appealed to the Indian government for military assistance and fled to India. He signed the Instrument of Accession, ceding Kashmir to India on October 26. Indian Government provided the King military support and intervened into the war.

Indian and Pakistani forces thus fought their first war over Kashmir in 1947-48. India referred the dispute to the United Nations on 1 January. In a resolution dated August 13, 1948, the UN asked Pakistan to remove its troops, after which India was also to withdraw its forces with the provision to held a "free and fair" plebiscite allow the Kashmiri people to decide their future. An emergency government was formed on October 30, 1948 with Sheikh Abdullah as the Prime Minister. Pakistan ignored the UN mandate and continued fighting, holding on to the portion of Kashmir under its control. On January 1, 1949, a ceasefire was agreed, with 65 per cent of the territory under Indian control and the remainder with Pakistan. The ceasefire was intended to be temporary but the Line of Control remains the de facto border between the two countries.

In 1957, Kashmir was formally incorporated into the Indian Union. It was granted a special status under Article 370 of India's constitution, which ensures, among other things, that non-Kashmiri Indians cannot buy property there. Fighting broke out again in 1965, but a ceasefire was declared in September. Indian Prime Minister, Lal Bhadur Shastri, and Pakistani President, M Ayub Khan, signed the Tashkent agreement on January 1, 1966. They tried to resolve the dispute, but the death of Mr Shastri and the rise of Gen Yahya Khan in Pakistan resulted in stalemate.

In 1971 a third war, resulting in the formation of the independent nation of Bangladesh. India declared war on December 3, 1971 after Pakistani Air Force planes struck Indian airfields in the Western sector. Two weeks later, the Indian army marched into Dhaka and the Pakistanis forces surrendered. In the Western sector the Indians managed to blockade the port city of Karachi and were 50 km into Pakistani territory when a ceasefire was reached. In 1972 Indira Gandhi and Zulfikar Ali Bhutto signed the Shimla Agreement, once again agreed to resolve the issue peacefully, as domestic issues dominated.

Since then, Pakistan has been consistently contesting and claiming territorial rights over Kashmir. From the 1980s, Pakistan placed its full weight behind supporting and financing the Kashmir insurgency and taking advantage of growing dissatisfaction among Kashmiri youths. Kashmiri youth frequently opposed the Indian state in moment of severe social unrest blaming Indian Government for mishandling the Kashmir.

The Fedayeen Phase

Since 1999, an atmosphere of acute tension and fear has been prevailed in the Kashmir Valley. The year 1999 marked the high point of a concerted campaign of "*fidayeen*" attacks, targeting a number of Indian official installations in the valley - mostly army and paramilitary camps and police headquarters. Suicide and bombs attacks carried out by fedayeen's insurgents who wanted to force their way into the security premises. The Fedayeen attacks commenced just after the Kargil War. The larger numbers of Fidayeen assaults were carried out by the Lashkar-e-Taiba (LeT), an organisation of religious radicals founded and headquartered in Pakistan and led by Pakistanis and the Jaish-e-Mohammad (JeM), a similar - albeit much smaller - Pakistani group. The LeT entered the Kashmir war in the mid-1990s as part of an ISI strategy to have cadres of trusted Pakistani radical groups in Kashmir. In the early to mid-1990s, the Kashmiri insurgent ranks consisted almost entirely of locals. The Lashkar-e-Taiba recruited local Kashmirisas a Fidayeen cadre. But the large majority of those who executed these attacks were Pakistanis – mostly from Pakistan's Punjab province by crossing the border. Between mid-1999 and the end of 2002, at least 55 such attacks took place and 161 military, paramilitary and police personnel died, as did 90 perpetrators. The relatively small number of fatalities did not capture the psychological impact at the time of the Fedayeen campaign, both on the Indian security establishment and the population at large. The highest number of attacks took place in 2001 in which largest number of causalities and civilian killed. The Fedayeen violence spill all over India. In December 2001, Fidayeen, heavily armed gunmen, attacked the Indian Parliament. They were just prevented by vigilant security staff from entering the parliament building, where hundreds of parliamentarians and ministers were present, and were killed security men in the portico of the building after a 45-minute gunfight. The Indian government alleged that these five men were Pakistani extremists. In November 26,2008, the LeT carried out the famous attack on Mumbai, killing 166 people, using a more indiscriminate variant and the technique.

Kashmir Violence and revival of Insurgeny2007-2018

Throughout 2007, Kashmir reverberated with protest and demonstrations involving a large mass of people, most of these protests were due to growing anger against the state focusing on administrative matters, the atrocities, fake encounters and violation of human rights by the armed forces and security personnel. In June 2008, the government order of transferring land to Shri Amarnath Shrine Board responded agitations (Amarnath Agitation) throughout the Kashmir Valley and Jammu. The Amarnath Agitation was seen as a plan of government to change the religious demography of the Muslims majority state and subsequently the fear of an economic blockade of the valley. This was the time when separatist groups were facing the crisis of relevance. In mere one stroke, the political scenario of the Jammu and Kashmir changed into massive demonstrations resounding with the slogans of Azadi, and once again the separatist's politics was ascended into Kashmir resulted in a breakdown of political order and crumbling mainstream politics. In 2009, the murder and rape of two women in Shopian caused pro-longed protest and made it difficult for newly elected government of National Conference to operate in normal manner. The 2010 stone-pelting upsurge continued for five months claiming 112 lives mostly of youth in police actions resulting in a virtual collapse of political authority and turning national and international spotlight once again on Kashmir.

The demand for self-rule with the slogans of "Le ke rahenge Azadi" was revived by the Hurriyat leaders and "Quit Kashmir" was tag given by Syed Ali Shah Gilani to its protest politics. During the 2008-2010, the killing of the people in the process of mob control accelerated the protests.

Self-determination became the central symbol of agitation. The youths of Kashmir were enraged most at the continued killing of the Kashmiri civilians by the security forces. The killing of two youth in army firing in Bomai in February 2009; killing of carpenter by CRPF in Khaigam in Pulwama district in March 2009, rape and murder of two women in Shophian in May 2009; killing of two civilians in a custody of a special operation group of police in Alochi Bag in May 2009; killing of a man near the security picket in Dangiwachi Camp in North Kashmir, 2009; killing of a teenager by a tear gas shell in Baramulla in October 2009, killing of a civilian from Pulwama allegedly used a human shield by security forces in an encounter with militants; killing of a teenage boy playing cricket hit by a smoke fired by the police in February 2010, these incidents intensified the protest and anger of the Kashmiri peoples. It had and still has been a main cause of protest and a plea for extremist's politics.

There have been major contradictions between the expectation of the people and the response of the state. The desires for normalcy had brought the people back into the democratic politics of governance even while retaining their sympathies with separatists cause and presumably led them to expect change in the ground realities. One most important expectation was the remove of securitized and militarized structures and security checks imposed in the civilian areas and continued since the period of militancy . All political parties in Kashmir though ideologically different, have been demanding the withdrawal of the Armed Forces Special Power Act (AFSPA), and repeal of Disturbed Area Act (DAA), and Public Security Act (PSA).

Kashmir was rocked by violent protests again in July 2016, when Hizbul Mujahideen militant Burhan Wani was killed in a gunfight with security forces. Wani's death plunged the state into deep turmoil, Indian security forces fighting against a large number of disenfranchised Kashmiri youth who concerned to Wani's anti-India resistance movement and calls for jihad. Widespread protests broke out across the Kashmir Valley between angry youth and the security forces that resulted the death of 30 civilian people including police officer and injured more than 2,000 protesters. The police also fired on demonstrators with bullets to the less-lethal pellets. Umar Nazir, a 12-year-old boy's both eyes were hit and injured by the pellet gun with little vision while he was in the courtyard of his home, not protesting. The injuries raised questions about the tactics of security forces all over India while the security forces were struggled to maintain order in Kashmir where the insurgency has roiled the region for decades. Though in previous years, the insurgency has decreased but not disappeared (see the chart). Protests against the security forces had been continued and the rallies over the weekend were unusually widespread. Indian state facing a crisis of governance with no clear plan to prevent escalating violence. In a preventing step, a strict curfew was imposed in the Kashmir Valley during the Eid Celebrations which renewed the fresh cycle of violence between protestors and security force. It killed two protestors and injured several more.[3] The police had tough time to control the situation in rural Kashmir where number of protests were more. "We have detained the provocateurs of violence and those people who were instigating the youth to pelt stones. All these measures are showing the results",[4] said a police official. During the first 50 days of uprising, around 2,000 youth were arrested by the police and another 210 persons were charged under the public Safety Act (PSA). Nearly 9000 people were arrested made at the completion of 100 days of the unrest while 503 persons were booked under the PSA, a law under which a person can be jailed without a trial for up to two year. "Who so ever has taken the law in his hand will be dealt accordingly," a police official said.[5]

In fact, Burhan Wani was a role model and cult figure for the youth of Kashmir. His psychological warfare tactics were aimed at delivering threats to the security forces and attracting more youth into insurgency, partly because 60 percent of the valley's population is below the age of 30. An interpretation of Islam-variously described as "ultra-conservative," "fundamentalist," or "puritanical" – has been steadily gaining ground in many parts of Kashmir, and the jihadist passion is one of major factors for joining the insurgency for new recruits. The attempts to change the worldview and vocabulary of Kashmiris to suit the Wahhabi-Salafi mentality is not only disturbing but also precludes the prospects for peace. The new wave of insurgency speeded primarily in Pulwama, Anantnag, Kulgam and Shopian and were mostly by educated youths and reasonably belong to good socio-economic status.

Stone pelting known locally as *kanie jung* has become a tool of resistance in the hands of young boys of Jammu and Kashmir to express their anger against the security forces and the state. It has been continuously implemented in the years – 2008, 2010 and 2016. Now the stone pelting has been a recurring form of protest in Kashmir.[6] After the death of Burhan wani in July 2016, the tens of thousands of young stone palter came out on street and pelted stones on the security forces and confronted with them. Across all over the valley, during the 2015-2017 total 4799 incidents of stone pelting had been reported.[7] In 2018, 759 cases of stone pelting reported by the Ministry of Home Affairs.[8] Protests were qualitatively different from earlier protests in intensity, scale, number of protestors injured, the rapid mobilization of anti-India supporters, and the sloppy response of the state to deescalate violence. More than one hundred were shot to death in the confrontations, and several thousand were injured. The stone-palters, some of whom used internet-based social media to organise, are predominantly teenage boys and young men in their twenties. In other words, they were either children or not yet born when Kashmir turned into brutal warzone two decades ago, and have grown up in the environment described above. Unlike their previous generation, who picked up the AK-47, this generation's weapon of choice is the stone, but the sense of grievance is equally intense. Militancy continues to grow in Kashmir after security forces gunned down a fourth Jaish-e-Mohammad (JeM) terrorist in Uri town of Baramulla district on 12th March 2018 in an operation. Similarly, on 13th March 2017, the Indian Army foiled an infiltration bid by armed militants in Jammu and Kashmir's Keran sector in Kupwara, aided by Pakistan's Border Action Team (BAT).

Ever since the outbreak of armed insurgency in Jammu and Kashmir in 1989, over 23,300 terrorists have been killed in the state while 6,340 security personnel have been martyred. The SATP website mentions that the number of civilians killed stand at more than 14,790 till November 12, 2017.

Table-10 Yearly Fatalities.

Year	*Incidents of Killing*	*Civilians*	*Security Forces*	*Terrorists/Insurgents/Extremists*	*Not Specified*	*Total*
2014	91	28	47	114	0	189
2015	86	19	41	115	0	175
2016	112	14	88	165	0	267
2017	163	54	83	220	0	357
2018	204	86	95	270	0	451
2019	42	9	57	55	0	121
Total*	698	210	411	939	0	1560

*Data till , March 26, 2019.]

Source: South Asia Terrorist portal 2019.

Each month at least eight to ten new youth are joining the various terror groups such as the Hizbul Mujahideen, Lashkar-e-Taiba (LeT) and the JeM. The youths who are joining are either locals from Kashmir or from Pakistan who cross over into India," said a senior security official.[9] Two of the new recruits are doctorates and eight are post graduates, the army data showed. PTI had reported in December last year that 2017 had seen the highest number of local recruitments to various militant groups in seven years. According to data placed before Parliament in March 2016, there has been a steady increase in the number of youths taking up arms in the Valley from 2014 onwards, as compared to 2011, 2012 and 2013. In 2010, 54 youths joined militancy. This dipped to 23 in 2011 and slipped further to 21 in 2012 and 16 in 2013. According to an Indian Army data – quoted by Reuters – at least 70 young Kashmiris joined the insurgency in the 2014 with most joining the banned group, Lashkar e-Taiba. Data for the number of youths joined militancy were 66 in 2015, 88 in 2016 and 126 in 2017.[10] The spurt in locals joining militancy began after the killing of Hizbul Mujahideen terror group's poster boy Burhan Wani.

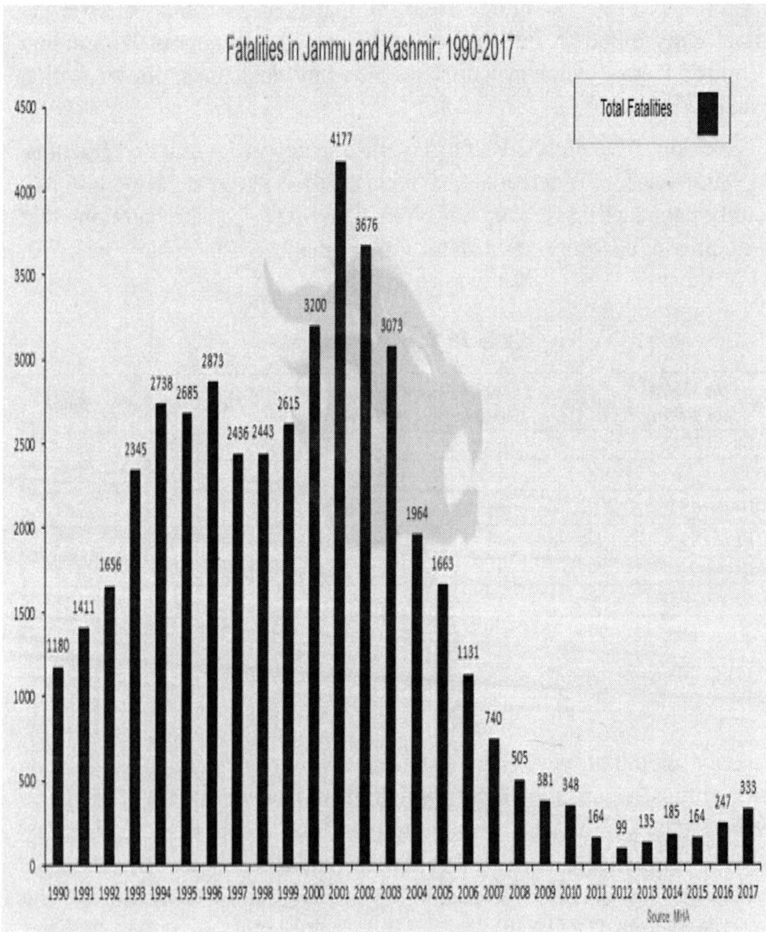

Graph-1

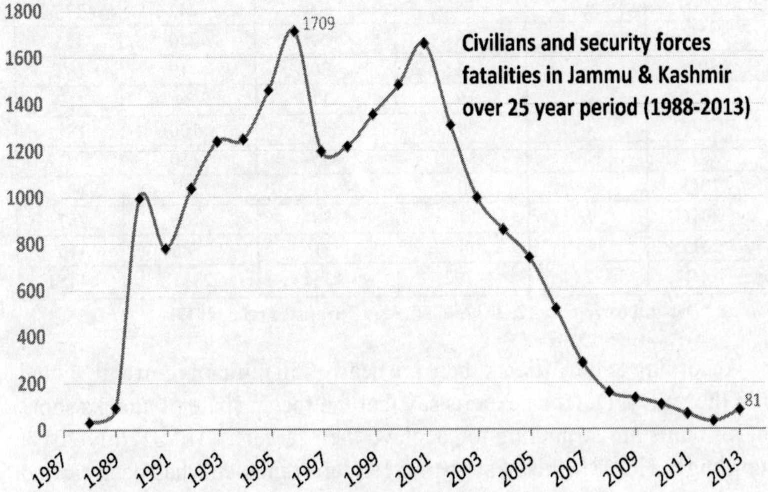

Graph-2

Table-11: Fatalities in Terrorist Violence 1988-2017

Year	*Incidents*	*Civilians*	*Security Force Personnel*	*Terrorists*	*Total*
1988	390	29	1	1	31
1989	2154	79	13	0	92
1990	3905	862	132	183	1177
1991	3122	594	185	614	1393
1992	4971	859	177	873	1909
1993	4457	1023	216	1328	2567
1994	4484	1012	236	1651	2899
1995	4479	1161	297	1338	2796
1996	4224	1333	376	1194	2903
1997	3004	840	355	1177	2372
1998	2993	877	339	1045	2261
1999	2938	799	555	1184	2538
2000	2835	842	638	1808	3288
2001	3278	1067	590	2850	4507
2002	NA	839	469	1714	3022
2003	NA	658	338	1546	2542
2004	NA	534	325	951	1810
2005	NA	521	218	1000	1739
2006	NA	349	168	599	1116
2007	NA	164	121	492	777

(*Contd...*)

2008	NA	69	90	382	541
2009	NA	55	78	242	375
2010	NA	36	69	270	375
2011	NA	34	30	119	183
2012	NA	16	17	84	117
2013	NA	20	61	100	181
2014	NA	32	51	110	193
2015	NA	20	41	113	174
2016	NA	14	88	165	267
2017	NA	54	71	185	310
Total*	47234	14792	6345	23318	44455

Sources: *Data till November 12, 2017, South Asia Terrorists Portal, 2019.

According to the official, there are nearly 250 militants currently holed up in the valley. Defence experts say that the recent spate of attacks show that militants are struggling to "achieve their targets." Till 31 July 2017, according to Home Ministry statistics, 194 terror incidents had been carried out in Jammu and Kashmir in which 39 security personnel and 115 terrorists killed. Infiltration attempts along the LoC were highest in 2012, has seen a further "marked increase" over the previous three years 2014-17. As many as 31 infiltration attempts stopped by the army.[11] The fact that there was a continuing influx of terrorists from Pakistan and emergence of militants within Kashmir. Replying to a written question in Lok Sabha, Union Minister of State for Home Kiren Rijiju said that 515 infiltration cases were reported

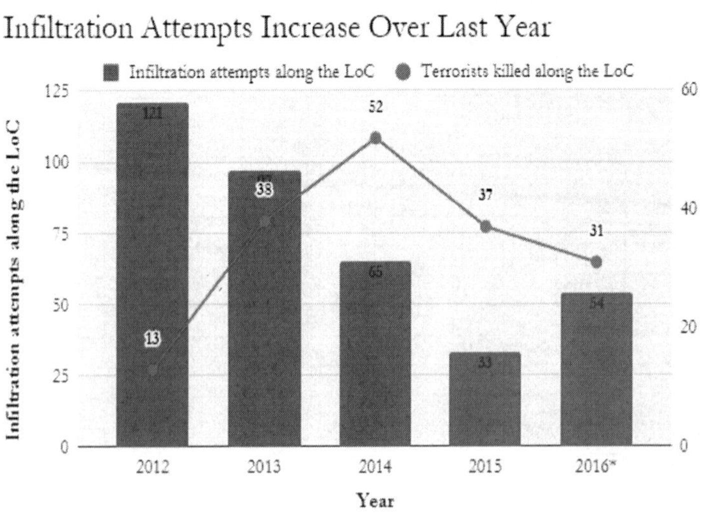

Graph-3

in 2017 in which 75 militants were killed in 2017 in comparison to 454 cases in 2016 in which 45 militants were killed and in 2015, altogether 223 infiltration cases were reported in which 64 militants were killed.[12]

Anger towards Indian authority is deeply rooted in the Kashmir valley, but the credibility of Pakistan is at an all-time low among the population, over more than two decades because of Pakistan's precarious situation as a state. The people of the Kashmir Valley know that their fate is not in their hands; it is in the hands of those who wield power in New Delhi, not in Rawalpindi. Jammu and Kashmir consist of much more than the valley - the regions of Jammu and Ladakh, where the majority of people identify with India, while Pakistani-administered Kashmir's population is vertically split between those who identify with Pakistan and those who aspire to independence. Agha Shahid Ali expressed a hope for genuine peace in Kashmir: "We shall meet again, in Srinagar, by the gates of the villa of peace, our hands blossoming into fists, till the soldiers return the keys and disappear."[13]

Central and State Governments unilateral ceasefire during the Ramzan was failed to bring any positive result. The murder of Shujaat Bukhari, editor of *Rising Kashmir*, with two security guards, as well as the abduction and murder of a soldier of the Rashtriya Rifles, Aurangzeb highlighted the inherent dangers of a blind political gambit, launched in the hope that 'something positive' could emerge. After decades of counter-insurgency experience, and the demonstrable failure of past 'unilateral ceasefires', policy planners continue to ignore the fundamental dynamics of violence

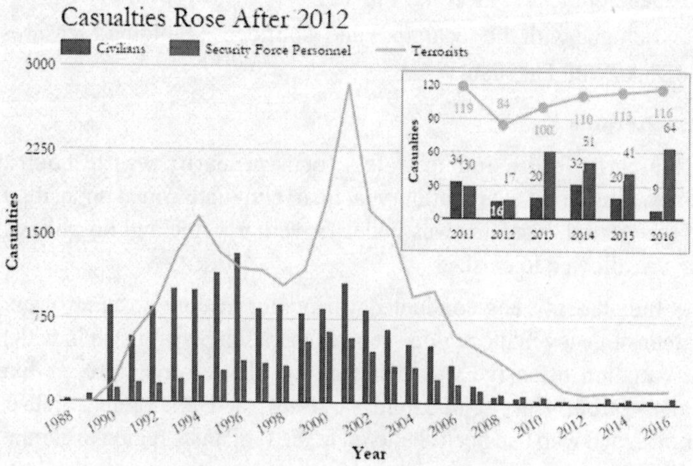

in Jammu & Kashmir (J&K). After the Bukhari and Aurangzeb killings, the Centre abandoned all idea of a 'ceasefire' extension.

There is no decline in incidents. SATP data indicates, there were at least 24 terrorism-related incidents between April 17 and May 16, 2018, resulting in 36 fatalities. Between May 17 and June 17, there were 64 such incidents, with 36 fatalities. Both SF and terrorist fatalities rose, from five to nine in the first category, and from 14 to 23 in the latter. Further, the number of explosions over these periods rose from two to 20. However, fatalities in the civilian category declined significantly, see in graphs. However , Bukhari killing demonstrates the transient and illusory nature of any sense of greater security in Kashmir.

Counter Insurgency Measures and Peace Process

Kashmir is an integral part of India and any demand for Azadi or Self Determination is the violation of Indian's sovereignty. Indian government has used both military and democratic processes to control the insurgency and establish peace in Kashmir. Military forces have been empowered by exemplary laws like AFSPA (Armed Forces Special Powers Act). In the early 1990s, Indian government primarily tried every military tactics to control insurgency and eliminate armed opposition. During this period, Kashmir was under Governor's rule and no political process was allowed to exist. However, when the military action became successful, Indian state tried to revive political institutions to bring democracy and progress in Kashmir. It is under the banner of 'normalcy' that following steps were adopted to establish peace process:

- Military Actions
- Democratic and Electoral Process.
- Dialogue with the separatists and Confidence building Measures
- Talks with Pakistan

Military Actions

In the early 1990s, Indian state's focus primarily was to control insurgency. It has tried every military tactic to eliminate armed opposition. During this period, Kashmir was under Governor's rule and no political process was allowed to exist.

The Indian army has conducted various operations to control and eliminate insurgency in the region such as Operation Sarp Vinash in which a multi-battalion offensive was launched against terrorists groups like Lashkar-e-Taiba, Harkat-ul-Jihad-e-Islami, al-Badar and Jaish-e-Mohammad, and who had been sheltered in the Pir Panjal region of Jammu and Kashmir over several years. The subsequent operations led to the death of 60 terrorists and uncovered the largest network of militant hideouts in the history of insurgency in Jammu and Kashmir covering 100 square kilometres.

The "Operation All Out" was carried out by the security forces working hard to flush out the militants from the Kashmir region when the Amarnath Yatra terror attack took place on July 10, 2017 - in which eight Hindu pilgrims from Gujarat were killed and at least 18 others injured. It has been received success in killing the top guns of key terror groups including Lashkar-e-Taiba's Abu Dujana, and slain Hizbul commander Burhan Wani's successor Sabzar Ahmad Bhat, Khalid of Jaish-e-Mohammed (JeM), and the nephews of JeM chief Masood Azhar and 26/11 mastermind Zakir Ur Rehman Lakhvi. The "Operation All Out" was a landmark of sorts, neutralising a record number of terrorists till date. In 2017, a total 213 militant were eliminated by the security forces.[14] Lt. Gen. Ranbir Singh in a press Release stated that in 2018, more than 250 terrorists were killed and nearly 54 arrested and 4 surrender.[15]

In an aggressive step, the Army has re-introduce Cordon and Search Operations (CASO) as a "permanent feature" of its campaign against militants. Army sources said CASO will be carried out in a major way in militancy-hit areas of Kulgam, Pulwama, Tral, Budgam and Shopian in south Kashmir. "CASO will be a permanent feature as part of counter-terror operations after a gap of 15 years,"[16] sources told. Army had discontinued CASO following stiff opposition from the local population and after 2001 launched cordon and search operations only on specific intelligence-based inputs. The security establishment felt that CASO had alienated the local population from the armed forces due to difficulties people faced during such operations. The decision to re-introduce CASO as a major feature of the counter-terror operations comes against the backdrop of anger over the recent killing of civilians and security forces.[17]

In this operation, 5,000 personnel from the Indian Army, the paramilitary Central Reserve Police Force and the Jammu and Kashmir Police launched the cordon and search operation in Shopian district—one of the biggest in recent times.[18] Experts say that India is signalling a change in tactic on how it deals with the cross-border terror threat emanating from Pakistan. Security personnel closed in on the approximately two dozen villages in the area and began a meticulous combing operation after clearing all civilian residents, a senior security officer familiar with the development close to site of the operation said.

Dialogue with the Separatists and Confidence Building Measures

There have been many efforts to alienate the Hurriyat Conference politically and at the same time there have been intermittent efforts to engage them. In response to this, Hurriyat has also followed the same policy. Within the separatist camp, there are some who have moderated their stand and held dialogue with New Delhi while few have not compromised. The central government started the peace talks with the All Party Hurriyat leaders as well as Pakistan in 2002 to resolve the matter related with the Kashmir and as a part of comprehensive peace process invited the All Party Hurriyat Conference (Mirwaiz Group) for dialogue. Two rounds of talks were held with Atal Bihari Vajpayee and another round of talks with Manmohan Singh government.

During the Vajpayee government significant peace initiatives were made to engage the separatist groups. K.C. Pant was appointed as the chief interlocutor aimed to engage the militant groups and Hurriyat in a dialogue process. The All Party Hurriyat Conference rejected the invitation as they demanded to include Pakistan in the talks. They said, problem of Kashmir is triangle and it cannot be solved without the negotiations of all three- India, Pakistan and the separatist leaders. Hizbul Mujahideen group declared cease fire in July 2000 and agreed to talk with Indian Government and Indian government also reciprocate. Indian government continued with attempts to start a dialogue in the spirit and immediately extended ceasefire during the Ramadan with the hope to restart the process. But the cease fire and dialogue process were impeded by the divisions among militant groups and cease fire was called off on May 2001.

Despite the obstacles, Indian government tried to continue the dialogue process. An eight members Kashmir Committee was also constituted under the Chairman ship of Ram Jethmalani which was dissolved and then PM Vajpai appointed N.N. Vohra as special representative to hold dialogue talks with the separatists. In January 2004, talks were held between the Kashmiri separatist leaders, All Hurriyat Conference (M) and the Indian government and first time Yasin Malik, Shabir Shah, Firdous Sayeed opted for dialogue and political struggle. All party Hurriyat Conference under the leadership of Molvi Abass Ansari and its members including Mirwaiz Omar Farooq, Bilal Gani Lone, Abdul Gani Bhatt, Fazal Haque Qurashi held two rounds of talks in January 22 and 27 March 2004 but major group that had chosen to remain outside the dialogue process was APHC(G) because, according to them, dialogue under Indian constitution and without any proper agenda, is a futile exercise and wastage of time.

In May 2004, UPA government efforts to promote dialogue have been helped by several militants abandoning the armed struggle. On June 2005, a nine- member delegates of AHPC (M) including Mirwaiz and Yasin Malik visited to Azad Kashmir and Pakistan and had talks with the Azad Kashmir and Pakistani leaders. Soon after, APHC (M) welcomed the four-point formula of General Parvez Musharraf but it was strongly rejected by Geelani faction and the United Jihad Council.

The dialogue process was carried forward by the UPA government. In February 2006, Indian Government invited Hurriyat leaders and other political leaders for Round Table Conference. Hurriyat Conference refused to participate but the political parties National Conference and PDP participated. It failed to bring any fruitful or the permanent solution of the Kashmir dispute and agreements between Sri Nagar and New Delhi have failed. However, Indian government set up Working Groups to further the dialogue process in the region.

In 2010, Indian government restarted the peace process and sent an all- party delegation under the Home Minister P. Chidambaram to assess the ground situation in the valley. This delegation invited all the representatives and political leaders of Political parties and Hurriyat Conference. Hurriyat Conference rejected the invitation but the members of delegation met him at his residence and urged to restore normalcy in the valley. He proposed five points formula to restore normalcy. While moderate faction of Hurriyat boycotted to meet the delegation but submitted a memorandum to the delegation. On the basis of suggestions, Cabinet Committee on Security announced Eight Point plan to defuse crisis in Kashmir.

- Appointment of a interlocutors to continue the dialogue process with all sections of people including political parties, youth and students and organisations and civil society organization and alike.
- To withdraw all the charges and release all the students and youth arrested for stone pelting or in other cases.
- To review the cases of all public safety Act détentes and withdraw detention orders.
- To review the deployment of security forces and unified command in the Kashmir valley especially in Sri Nagar and the notification of disturbed areas will be review.
- Appointment of Two special Task Forces one for Sri Nagar and other for Ladakh to examine the development and infrastructure facilities and make recommendations.
- To give ex-gratia relief of Rs. 5 lakhs to the families of deceased person.

Besides this, the UPA government appointed an expert committee under the chairmanship of C. Rangarajan with the purpose to formulate a job plan for Jammu and Kashmir state. Further, they sent a group of interlocutors consisted of Dileep Padgaonkar, Radha Kumar and MM Ansari to hold extensive talks with all sections of society. On October12, 2011, they submitted a report proposing a New Compact Formula suggesting to take confidence building measures. The Report recommended to improve the Centre States relations and devolution of powers; favour the amendments in the Public Safety Act, re-appraisal of application of controversial Armed Forces Special Powers Act. It also suggested to set up a constitutional committee to review all Central Acts and Articles of the Constitution of India extended to the state after 1952 Delhi Agreement. The most important recommendation was to delete the word 'temporary' from the heading of Article 370 and from the title of Part XXI of the constitution and replacing it with the word 'special'. The report also recommended the implementation of recommendations of working groups on Confidence Building measures in particular the return of all Kashmiri pandits, establishing Judicial Commission to look into the matter of human rights violations and the rule of law reforms.

The Mainstream political parties welcomed the peace initiatives of the Central Government but the All Hurriyat Party Conference rejected these initiatives by saying that it is mere wastage of time. These are not solution but mere time buying tactics. Mirwaiz Omar Farooq also repeated its stand that Kashmir issue has to be resolved through tripartite dialogue or through the United Nations resolution.[19]

The Modi government as a shift from its previous policy appointed Dineshwar Sharma as its special representative or new interlocutor for Jammu and Kashmir to start a sustained dialogue process with all stakeholders including separatists. However, the government has granted full independence to decide his own course of action and talk to whoever he wants to and there is no time frame also. It is a very significant move because the BJP government had constantly maintained a tough line on opening talks with the separatists in particularly after the 2016 unrest that had killed 100 civilians. The appointment of new interlocutor in an indication of central government inclination for dialogue. Prime Minister Modi in his speech on independence day 2017 statedthat "the Kashmir problem cannot be resolved through goli ya gali. It can be resolved by embracing all Kashmiris."[20] Modi Government and Security forces have adopted hardlines stance against militancy. Counterinsurgency operations were picked up, militants and their hideout were specifically targeted and destroyed, mass curfews were implemented and internet access in the valley was cut off. It demonstrates that an insurgency could not survive against the might of the state machinery. This move was welcomed by the PDP Chief Mehbooba Mufti and the National Conference leaders. Farooq Abdullah want Pakistan to be brought in; while Congress leaders commented it as failure of Modi

Muscular approach and admission of its blunders.[21] The move comes at a time when some separatist leaders, including close aides of Hurriyat leaders Syed Ali Shah Geelani and Mirwaiz Umar Farooq, are jailed on charges of receiving cash from Pakistan for subversive activities in the Valley. Both the factions of the Hurriyat Conference have in recent months become increasingly open to dialogue and have hinted their willingness in their statements.

India-Pakistan Talks

In 1999, a short-lived talk in the stormy relations of India and Pakistan was started when the Prime Minister Atal Bihari Vajpai took a bus to Lahore and met his Pakistani counterpart Nawaz Sharif leaving an endearing image that symbolised hope in bilateral ties. Lahore Declaration was signed and under which it was agreed upon that the two sides were fully committed to undertaking measures to reduce risks of accidental or unauthorised use of nuclear weapons. The peace process further strengthened by opening the Uri-Muzaffarabad road, providing free mobility of people across the line of control. Other than opening the road for trade, it held out the possibility of resolving the Kashmir tangle through introducing a fresh perspective on the irrelevance of borders. However, the bonhomie between India and Pakistan did not last long as just months after the visit, the Pakistan Army undertook a covert operation to send its troops into Kargil in Jammu & Kashmir that led to a Kargil War.

The momentum of the peace process reflected not only in such confidence building measures but also the progress of Indo-Pak relations further provided stimulus to the process. General Musharraf emphasised "out of Box solution" and subsequently proposed four-point formula engaging Kashmiris like self-rule demilitarisation. But the peace process got setback due to internal problem of Pakistan in 2007, the forward movement in India-Pakistan peace process started stalling. Internal Dialogue with separatists also holdup as the Manmohan Singh government substituted the policy of direct dialogue with the separatists with round table conferences involving the main stream political parties and organisation of Jammu & Kashmir.

Democratic/Electoral Process as Confidence Building Measures

Nevertheless, the persistence of separatist sentiment does not undermine the simultaneous extension of democratic space. The conflict situation that marked political responses during the last decade continues to impact the internal politics of state. Both separatists and democratic politics exist side by side. In 1996 the government made efforts to restore mainstream political process by holding Assembly election under the supervision of Security forces and with active support of counter-insurgents. As a prelude to this, the government released top political activists including Shabir Shah, Syed Ali Geelani and Abdul Gani Lone and many extremists leaders were also released to gain the confidence of the people. Farooq Abdullah's National Conference emerged as the key player among all parties and formed the government. No doubt, this provided space for elected government to pacify the crisis of legitimacy which continued till 2002 despite the ascendancy of the separatist's sentiment. This was mainly due to the popular disillusionment with militancy and violence on the one hand and a heightened urge for normalcy on the other.

In 2002 Assembly election, a free and fair election was the part of confidence building measures which the then Prime Minister Atal Bihari Vajpayee had initiated to ease the feelings of Kashmiris. For the first time in electoral history of Kashmir, the people participated in spite of the separatists call for the boycott of elections and militant's violence. Though participation of people was uneven in Kashmir but the 2002 elections provided great credibility and confidence of people to the elected government.

Democratic politics which had been totally delegitimised in the early period of militancy started gaining credibility after 2002 Assembly election, seen as not only fair and transparent but also genuinely competitive. The formation of People's Democratic Party (PDP) was a landmark development in the politics of Kashmir which changed the character of power politics and identified itself with Kashmiri identity politics. The party became a new political player in 2002 assemble election and emerged as a coalition partner of the Congress. The PDP located its politics in the context of the conflict situation specially responding to the common people's sensitivities. The PDP's 'healing touch' provided succour to the people troubled by prolonged insurgency and violence and helped it to gain popularity and facilitated the process of making power politics relevant in the given situation. Instead of denying its role and relevance, the PDP acknowledged the popular basis of separatists' politics and define it as a sphere distinct from the politics of governance dealing with larger issues of an ultimate resolution of the conflict. This helped the people associate with the mainstream politics without the fear of separatists 'politics. The PDP's manifesto defined its vision of conflict resolutions on the principle of Self-Rule signalling its readiness to agree to any other formula of conflict resolution acceptable to the people of state. This created a sense of crisis among the separatist's leaders, even Pakistan. The separatist's issues not only challenged the exclusivity of separatist's politics, it positioned mainstream politicians as legitimate stakeholders in the politics of the state.

The PDP rule saw a new wave of resistance and demonstrations over many incidents and issues such Amarnath Land Transfer and violation of Human rights by the armed forces. This provided opportunities to revive the defunct and divided Hurriyat in particular Geelani's factions. Geelani faction emerged as a formidable representative of the Kashmir separatist movement.

The expansion of mainstream politics in the Kashmir Valley has been taking place at the cost of separatist politics. An overlap has been developed between the two kinds of politics. In the fact, the political parties recognized the relevance of separatists' politics and thus sought to attain legitimacy by borrowing heavily from it and separatists also recognised it as a politics of governance. As a result, a distinction being made in Kashmir between the politics for governance pursued by the main stream parties as different from the politics for resolution of Kashmir conflict pursued by the separatists.

In the Kashmir 2014 Assembly election, PDP and BJP Coalition government was formed but it is ended in June 2018 due to ideological differences. PDP-BJP differences over the killing of Burhan Wani as it led to violent protests resulting in the death of over 85 people and PDP decision of ceasefire during the Ramadan. Rajnath Singh, Minister of Home Affairs,unilaterally ended the ceasefire and resumed the counter-terrorism operations in the valley in the stir of increasing militancy incidents during the ceasefire period.

Indian government has adopted two broad approaches to deal with an insurgency till now. One is the conventional military approach, also called anti-insurgency or enemy-centric approach, which focuses on targeting the insurgents. These strategies have sometimes been labelled as counter-terrorism. The other is a population-centric counter-insurgency (COIN) approach, which is aimed at cutting off the insurgents' supply lines by either providing incentives to the population for supporting the counter insurgent forces, or by imposing costs on the population for supporting the insurgents. The general bias of the population-centric COIN perspectives is to give prominence to winning the hearts and minds of the population, which essentially means convincing the people that the advantages of supporting the government against the insurgents outweigh the advantages of supporting the insurgents.

The ultimate goal of both the approaches is to restore stability and the population's support for the government and army forces, however, the means are different. "Iron fist" anti-insurgency operations are the need to maintain a large military presence just to create a sense of safety and stability. Although the risks of implementing and using anti-insurgency tools are too many. The problem of a population-centric approach is that it causes the soft target population to suffer retribution when insurgents begin to view the people to be conspiring with the counter-insurgency forces. The terrifying scenario for population-centric approach is when the insurgents are the local population. In such cases, the government forces are seen as occupiers and are rarely able to gain the trust of the civilian population. The religious beliefs are wrongly shaped and used by the insurgents to obtain support and trust among the community then the countering insurgency becomes even more burdensome.

The conflicting situation in the Kashmir raises many questions for the centre as well as the state governments: Why is the rhetoric of terrorist groups such as Hizb-ul-Mujahideen gaining alarming popularity among Kashmiri youths and mobilizing them in thousands to join the militancy? Can a larger military presence bring stability and return the Kashmir valley to normalcy? Answers to these questions require rethinking on India's counter-insurgency approach in Kashmir. These dangerous turns of events and the cyclical waves of violence affecting the Kashmiri state indicate that the Indian counter-insurgency approach in Kashmir is failing. The Central government must conduct a fundamental reappraisal of its counter-insurgency strategy in Kashmir that is predominantly a military approach is unlikely to mitigate future violence.

The present chaos in Kashmir encapsulates the differing priorities. The fresh violence in Kashmir has jolted the central government, which was gradually receding into complacency. In the absence of an overarching strategy under the People's Democratic Party (PDP)- Bharatiya Janata Party (BJP) coalition government in Jammu and Kashmir, there seems to be confusion at the highest echelon as to which policy tools should be accorded primacy. The result has been a stalemate in counter-insurgency strategy, unable to fully succeed in reaching the desired objectives.

Notes

1. President Rule was imposed on 19 January 1990 till 9 October 1996 completely for 6 years 264 days.
2. AFSPA (Armed Forces Special Powers Act) was introduced in Kashmir in 1990. It provides security forces extraordinary powers to shoot, search and arrest without warrant, all under immunity from prosecution in respect of anything done or purported to be done in exercise of powers conferred by this Act.
3. Ieshan Wani, Age, Gender, Culpability No Bar: Pellets Are Cruel and Unusual Punishment for Kashmir, August 16, 2016 https://medium.com.
4. Mudasir Ahmad, In Kashmir, No Body Is Buying Parrikar's Link Between Demonetisation and Fall in Stone Pelting, the Wire, November 16, 2016.
5. *Ibid.*

6. In 2008 Amarnath Shrine Land transfer incidents.
7. Ministry of Home Affairs, PTI March 7, 2018.
8. Ministry of Home Affairs, december 12, 2018. source: http://www. times now news. com.
9. Militancy growing in J&K as terrorist influx continues, warn officials, Live Mint, March 14, 2018.
10. The Chief Minister said while replying to a written question by National Conference leader Ali Mohammed Sagar.
11. Abhishek Waghmare, India's army's 2016 Death Toll of 64 highest in Six years, India Spend. sept. 21, 2016.
12. TheEconomicTimes>//economictimes.indiatimes.com/articleshow/61123607.cms? utm_source=contentofinterest&utm_medium=text&utm_campaign=cppst
13. Sumantra Bose,The evolution of Kashmiri resistance, Aljazeera, August 2, 2011.
14. India Today, October 13, 2018.
15. Economic Times Jan 17, 2019.
16. Kashmir:Army Reintroduces Cordon and Search as part of Counter-terror, Live mint, May 11, 2017.
17. The Economic

    Times//economictimes.indiatimes.com/articleshow/58632117. cms? utm_ source = conten to finterest & utm_medium=text&utm_campaign=cppst.
18. Shaswati Das& Elizabeth Roche, Army carries out combing operations in south Kashmir's Shopian, Live Mint, 4 May 2017.

Appendix - 2

Notable terrorist attacks in J&K

- July and August 1989 – 3 CRPF personnel and politician Mohd. Yusuf Halwai of NC/F were killed.
- 1989 kidnapping of Rubaiya Sayeed daughter of the then Home Minister of India Mufti Sayeed.
- 1995 kidnapping of western tourists in Jammu and Kashmir– Six foreign trekkers from Anantnag district were kidnapped by Al Faran. One was beheaded later, one escaped, and the other four remain missing, presumably killed.
- 1997 Sangrapora massacre – On 22 March 1997, seven Kashmiri Pandits were killed in Sangrampora village in the Budgam district.
- Wandhama Massacre- In January 1998, 24, Kashmiri Pandit living in the village of Wandhama were massacred by Pakistani militants. According to the testimony of one of the survivors, the militants dressed themselves as officers of the, Indian Army entered their houses and then started firing blindly.
- 1998 Prankote Massacre 26 Hindu villagers of Udhampur district were killed by militants.
- 1998 Champanari massacre 25 Hindu villagers killed on 19 June 1998 by Islamic militants.
- 2000 Amarnath Pilgrimage massacre-30 Hindu pilgrims massacred by militants.
- Chittisinghpura massacre-36 Sikhs massacred by LET militants.
- 2001 terrorist attacks on Jammu and Kashmir legislative assembly-On 1 October 2001, a bombing at the Legislative Assembly in Srinagar killed 38.
- 2002 Raghunath temple Attack-First attack occurred on 30 March 2002 when two suicide bombers attacked the temple. Eleven persons including three security forces personnel were killed and 20 were injured. In second attack, the fidayeen suicide squad attacked the temple second time on 24 November 2002 when two suicide bombers stormed the temple and killed fourteen devotees and injured 45 others.
- 2002 Qasim Nagar Massacre-On 13 July 2002, armed militants believed to be a part of the Lashkar-e-Taiba threw hand grenades at the Qasim Nagar market in Srinagar and then fired on civilians standing nearby killing 27 and injuring many more.

- 2003 Nandi Massacre– 24 Hindus killed in Nadimarg, Kashmir on 23 March 2003 by Lashkar-e-Taiba militants.
- 20 July 2005 Srinagar Bombing – A car bomb exploded near an armoured Indian Army vehicle in the famous Church Lane area in Srinagar killing 4 Indian Army personnel, one civilian and the suicide bomber. Militant group Hizbul Mujahideen, claimed responsibility for the attack.
- Budshah Chowk attack – A militant attack on 29 July 2005 at Srinagar 's city centre, Budshah Chowk, killed 2 and left more than 17 people injured. Most of those injured were media journalists.
- Assassination of Ghulam Nabi Lone – On 18 October 2005, suspected Kashmiri militants killed Jammu and Kashmir's then education minister Ghulam Nabi Lone. Militant group called Al Mansurin claimed responsibility for the attack. Abdul Ghani Lone, a prominent All Party Hurriyat Conference leader, was assassinated by unidentified gunmen during a memorial rally in Srinagar. The assassination resulted in wide-scale demonstrations against the Indian forces for failing to provide enough security cover for Lone.
- 2006 Doda massacre- On 3 May 2006, militants massacred 35 Hindus in Doda and Udhampur districts in Jammu and Kashmir.
- On 12 June 2006, one person was killed and 31 were wounded when terrorists hurled three grenades on Vaishno devi shrine-bound buses at the general bus stand.
- 2014 Kashmir valley attacks-There were four attacks on 5 December 2014 on army, police and civilians resulted in 21 deaths and several injured. Their motive was to disrupt the ongoing assembly elections.
- 2016 Uri Attack- Four armed terrorists sneaked into an army camp and lobbed grenades onto tents causing massive fire culminating in the death of 19 military personnel.
- 2018 Sunjunwan attack-On 10 February 2018, Jaish-e-Mohammad terrorists attacked Sunjuwan Army Camp in Jammu and Kashmir. 6 Indian army soldiers, 4 terrorists, 1 civilian died and 11 were injured.
- 2019 Pulwama Attack- on 14th February 2019 Jaish-e Mohammad attacked the CRPF convoy killed 44 military Officials.

Appendix - 3

Working Group on Confidence Building Measures (CBMs)

This group under the Chairmanship of Mohammad Hamid Ansari was formed to look into certain problems in Kashmir and also provide the remedies for those problems. It was established after the announcement made by Manmohan Singh (PM) in the Round Table Conference held in Srinagar on 24 and 25 May, 2006. The Working Group submitted its report in January, 2007.

Agenda

The group had the following agenda before it:

1. Measures to improve the condition of the people affected by militancy.
2. Schemes to rehabilitate all orphans and widows affected by militancy.
3. Issues relating to the relaxation of conditions for those who have foresworn militancy.
4. An effective rehabilitation policy including employment for Kashmiri Pandit migrants.
5. An approach concerning issues relating to the return of Kashmiri youth from areas controlled by Pakistan.
6. Measures to preserve and protect the unique cultural and religious heritage of the State.

Recommendations of the Working Group

In the light of its agenda, following were the recommendations made by the Working Group:

A. Following measures are needed to improve the conditions of people affected by militancy:

(1) The necessity of curbing human rights violations. Prime Minister's commitment for 'zero tolerance' of human rights violation was appreciated. The need to strengthen the State Human Rights Commission (SHRC) and revitalize its functioning was asserted. The state Human Rights Commission shall be strengthened on the lines of National Human Rights Commission (NHRC) and it shall be provided with investigative machinery. Also, its recommendations shall be obligatory and in case of non-acceptance of its recommendations, the reasons for a speaking order shall be given. An empowered committee shall be established to report regularly

on the action taken by the Government on the recommendations of the commission.

(2) All the victims of the militants shall be provided relief and assistance. An order of preference was given to the affected in terms of their loyalty and proximity to the state. For example, the first beneficiaries of relief were considered to those victims who are associated with military, paramilitary or police. Then, those who were not connected with militancy.

(3) Termination of exceptional laws and maintenance of law and order through normal laws. It was recommended that laws like AFSPA and Disturbed Areas Act violate the fundamental rights of citizens and adversely affect the public and hence, these shall be scrapped.

B. Following schemes and measures were recommended for the rehabilitation of the orphans and widows affected by militancy:

1. Complete data of widows and orphans affected by militancy shall be collected for making their rehabilitation effective. A social cell shall be set up for the identification and rehabilitation of widows and orphans.
2. Relief to victims shall be speedy and reach them directly.
3. Administrative delays and malpractices in reaching relief to the concerned shall be curbed.

C. Measures relating to rehabilitation of militants who have given up militancy consisted of providing them a hope of a dignified life and a general amnesty to those who are languishing in jails.

D. For rehabilitation of Kashmiri Pandits, following measures were recommended:

1. The right of the migrant Pandits to return to their original place of in habitance.
2. Besides, job opportunities for Pandits, safety of Pandit property from illegal occupation and other necessary measures for their safe return.

E. The approach for the return of the youth from the Pakistan controlled Kashmir shall involve the classification of their infiltration and their identification which may involve their numbers and other criteria for their return.

F. A comprehensive policy on the preservation of the cultural and religious heritage shall be made. For this, comprehensive plans and autonomous institutions shall be made.

Besides these, there were other recommendations of the Group. As this group was the result of the Round-Table Conferences, its recommendation has very less meaning for the Hurriyat Conference. However, it was a positive development in the sense as it somehow got the attention of the Moderate faction.of the Hurriyat. But the recommendations of this group mostly remained on paper. Also, there were other groups which looked at different aspects: some focused on the economic development of Kashmir, some on the Confidence Building Measures (CBMs) across Line of Control (LOC) and so on. All this dialogue process flourished in an era where militancy had waned down and when there was a change in the electoral politics in Kashmir. The dialogue process happened in the era of PDP rule.

Chapter - 4

Pakistan: Islamic Fundamentalism and Separatists Movements

Pakistan founded in 1947 on the religious identity carved out of Hindus majority on the premise that two people could not live together peacefully within one nation state. Decades after the horrific bloodbath of partition, Pakistan is still lacking the crucial components needed for the nationhood, a strong common identity, mental make-up, a shared sense of history and common goals. The failure so far to create a cohesive national entity flows from the absence of effective democracy, dysfunctional legal system and from inequalities of opportunity. Internal divisions between provinces and the forces of militant and radical Islam have created political uncertainty and failure of state machinery in Pakistan. The country has also been facing secessionist movements from tribal and militant groups. The security situation has deteriorated to such an extent that the capital area of Islamabad, Rawalpindi and Karachi are no longer immune from terrorist attacks by the cadres of the Taliban and its Pakistan allies the Al Qaeda. Form violence to assassinations and murders of minorities leaders both the religious and ethnic minorities; attack on churches and temples; forceful conversions in name of purifying the Islam, discriminations in job. Castes and sects matter more than ability. Blasphemy laws has given right to kill anyone.[1] Muslims and non-Muslim minorities such as Christians, Hindus and Sikhs have been the targets of suicide bomb attacks and their community members converted to Islam against their will. The assassination of Salman Taseer, Governor of Punjab and Pakistan's Minister for Religious Minorities and massive demonstration of support for the assassin and intimidation underlined the alarming spread of the Taliban brand of fundamentalist Islam in the country. It has also triggered intro-inspection and discourses on social, religious and national identity and shrinking space for liberal discourses. Ansar

Abbasi, Journalist with the Urdu Newspaper Jung, legitimise Salman Taseer's murder by stating that "the court of the people had the right to kill any "blasphemer". This is the picture of Pakistan, the people demonstrate their adherence and loyalty to Islam. What the Quran says or does not say; it is immaterial. Islam became accepted as the basis of the state and any suggestion to the contrary continues to evoke a fierce public reaction.

Pakistan which has 96 % Muslims population, one of the most hostile nations for religious minorities and placed the country among the top five overall for restrictions on religion, singling out its anti-blasphemy statutes.[2] Courts frequently use such laws to give death or lifetime-jail sentences to minorities accused of insulting Islam. Often, their crime is as simple as openly professing their own faiths. A study on Pakistan from the United States Commission for International Religious Freedom counted more than 200 attacks among religious groups and 1,800 casualties resulting from religion-related violence between 2012 and mid-2013, one of the highest rates in the world. Though Pakistan's constitution guarantees freedom of religion, reports of forced conversions to Islam, kidnappings of non-Muslims, job discrimination, blasphemy arrests and razzings of minority houses of worship are frequent. According to the Human Rights Commission of Pakistan, 34 people were charged with blasphemy in 2013. The US Based Human Rights Watch[3] reports that at least 16 people are on death row in the country for blasphemy, and 20 are serving life sentences. All religious minorities in Pakistan face daily reminders of their plight even Muslim minority such as Shiites and Ahmadis. According to human rights groups, public school textbooks regularly demonize minorities[4] and emphasize the nation's Islamic roots over contributions from people of other faiths. Labour Studies[5] have shown minorities stuck on the lower rung of the economy, often working as servants, sweepers and day laborers. Newspapers occasionally report on businesses that deny non-Muslim customers.

Social fabric of Pakistani society: Pakistan's social structure is consisted up of religious minorities total just 9 million among 183 million Pakistanis. The biggest groups are Christians and Hindus, each of which accounts for less than 2 percent of the population. Smaller are the numbers of Sikhs, Zoroastrians, Buddhists, Bahá'ís, Jews and Ahmadi Muslims. Shiite Muslims make up about a quarter of Pakistanis, but they, too, find themselves increasingly persecuted by dominating Sunni factions. In 1947, almost 23 percent of Pakistan's population was comprised of non-Muslim citizens but nowadays, the proportion of non-Muslims has declined to approximately 3 percent. The distinctions among Muslim denominations have also become far more accentuated over the years. Muslim groups such as the Shias who account for approximately 20-25 percent of Pakistan's Muslim population, Ahmadis who have been declared non-Muslim by the writ of the state.

Ethnic minorities include Sindhis ,Pathans or Pakhtuns (2006 Census of Afghans in Pakistan), Mohajirs, Baluchis. Religious Minorities include Christians, Ahmadiyas, Hindus, Shi'as, Isma'ilis, Bohra and Parsis. Historically, there was also a small contingent of Jews in Pakistan who emigrated to Israel in 1948. According to the Government of Pakistan's National Database and Registration Authority (NADRA), 2012, the population of registered religious minorities in Pakistan was as shown in Table -12.

Table-12: Minorities in Pakistan

	Minorities	*Percentage*	*No.of Populations*
1.	Hindu	1.6	1,414,527
2.	Christians	1.59	1,270,051
3.	Shia's	10-12	900,000
4.	Ahmaddiyas	0.22	125,681
5.	Bahai's		33,734
6.	Parisis		4020
7.	Sikhs		6,146
8.	Sindhis	14.1	
9.	Pathans/Pakhtuns	15.42	
10.	Mohajirs	7.57	
11.	Baluchis	3.57	

Genesis of Islamic Fundamentalism

When Pakistan was founded in 1947, Mohammad Ali Jinnah wanted to create a homeland for South Asia's Muslims, not an Islamic state. He clearly declared that non-Muslims would be equal citizens in the new country. But Pakistan's trajectory after independence has been very different. After the death of Jinnah, the Objective Resolution of 12 March 1949 was the first step towards the transformation of Pakistan from Muslim State into an Islamic state. The resolution started with the statement that sovereignty rest with Allah. Other consequences were the grudging concession that adequate provision shall be made for minorities to freely profess and practice their religions and develop their cultures. This created the concept of minorities in Pakistan's polity and denied the right to equality- a basic requirement of democracy.

Soon after the seize of the power in 1978, General Zia-ul-Haqq, started the process of Islamization. He began long state sponsored project. Democracy was demonised and declared un-Islamic, culture was purified of Hindu contamination, urdu was cleansed of Hindi words, capital punishment was freely used, dress codes were introduced and religion was introduced in every aspect of public and private life. Education was the key weapon for Zia's strategy. In 1981, he ordered the education authorities to rewrite the history of Pakistan. He pushed to convert secular laws into religious ones, installing Sharia courts and enacting anti-blasphemy statutes. Through the 1990s and 2000s, conservative Islamic movements gained cultural and political sway[7] subverting the region's historically more open approach to faith, including non-Islamic traditions.

The blueprint to transform Pakistan into an Islamic State was prepared by Abul Ala Maududi, founder of the Jamaat-e-Islami (JI), the South Asian analogue of the Arab Muslim Brotherhood. According to Maududi, the future constitution of Pakistan had to be based on the underlying assumption that sovereignty rested with Allah and the state's function was solely to administer the country. According to him, Sharia was the law of the land and no man-made law could contravene the Sharia. From Maududi's point of view, Non-Muslim culture had a negative impact on Muslim life. "It destroys its inner vitality, blurs its vision, befogs its critical faculties, breeds inferiority complexes, and gradually but assuredly saps all the springs of culture and sounds its death-knell," he wrote. According to him, "the Holy Prophet has positively and forcefully forbidden the Muslims to assume the culture and mode of life of the non-Muslims."[8]

Over the years, the Islamist rejection of "non-Muslim" culture took the form of attempts to define a limited "Muslim" culture and limiting the freedom of non-Muslims and Muslims alike to embrace diversity. While non-Muslims were easily defined as "the other," a struggle also started to determine who among Muslims were pure Muslims and who had allowed Persian or Indian culture and practices to taint their faith. Over the decades, Pakistan transformation from a moderate Muslim Majority country into the one where majority of the citizens wanted Islam to play a key role in politics, the effects of indoctrination is now clearly visible where fundamentalist are busy blowing up schools, youths are becoming jihadist and militant extremists. The post Zia generation- which believes to solve the country problems through fundamentals of Islam leads to nowhere. The adherence to true Islam has been leading to conflicting society in many ways and violent political forces favouring the Pakistani Taliban's to impose its version of sharia through the Kalashnikov and suicide bombing.

Separatists Movements/ Conflicts

Pakistan, a state since 1947, has been failed to create a cohesive national entity flows from the absence of effective democracy and discrimination and dysfunctional Political and legal system. The inter-ethnics and inter-religious violence has plagued Pakistan whether it is the problem of Sindhi and Muhajirs, Pakhtuns (pathan) and Punjabis, Baloch, inter Muslims- Shia or Sunni (Ahmadiya) or Hindus, Gilgit and Baltistan and so on. Schools in Balochistan refuses to hoist Pakistani flag or sing its national anthem;

Sindhi's accuses Punjabis of stealing their water, the Muttahida Quami Movement (MQM) runs Karachi on strictly ethnic grounds. In getting job, caste and sect matters more than ability and ethnic groups wage pitched battles against each other throughout the country.

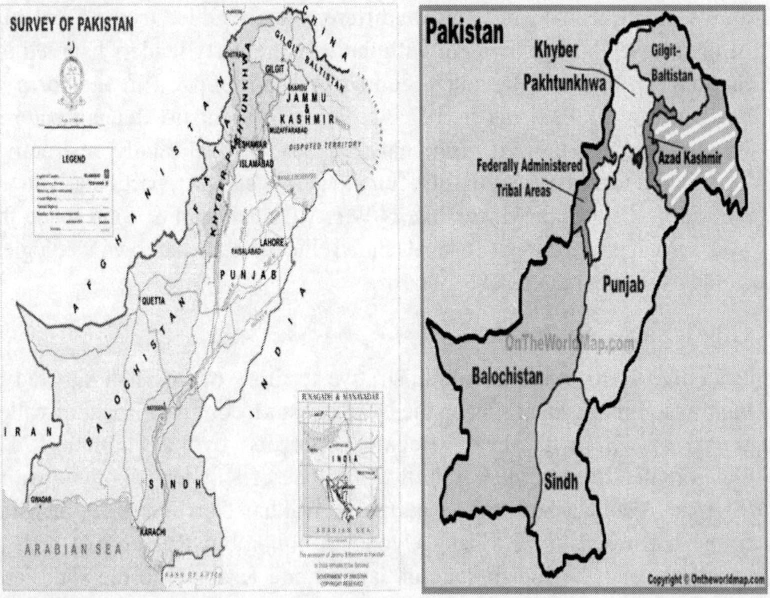

Map-5 Provinces of Pakistan

The most important movements those threatening the national integrity of Pakistan are the Pashtunistan movement, the Sindhi movement and the Baluchistan movement, Gilgit Balitistan and FATA. All these movements were ethno-national and secessionist born before the period of independence and the subsequent partition of India. Except Pashtunistan movement, other two movements turned irredentist immediately after the formation of Pakistan.

The formation of these irredentist movements can be attributed to the basic anomalies in the Pakistan movement itself. The Pakistan movement led by Muslim league under the leadership of Mohammad Ali Jinnah who was able to win Pakistan on the basis of Muslim nationalism but there were a number of weaknesses that affected the later developments within Pakistan. The three most significant weaknesses included the lack of consensus on the structure of the new nation; lack of a proper mechanism to deal with regionalism, and the inherent weakness in the organizational structure of the party itself. The educated Muslim class was deeply divided on the question of the future of Pakistan. The liberals wanted it to be a secular state, the Islamists, represented by Mullahs wanted an Islamic state and the leftists wanted a socialist Pakistan. These differences, initially dormant, manifested afterwards creating room for dissent & frustration. The lack of an effective mechanism to tackle different issues added to the perplexity of the party. This was evident with the way the party leaders handled the language issue. The language controversy epitomized in the form of the partition of Pakistan in 1971, creating a linguistic Bengali state in its East. Finally, the organisational weakness proved fatally destructive. The lack of an organisational structure to garner support, particularly in the culturally distinct provinces like N.W.F.P, Baluchistan & Sind made the Muslim league dependent on local landed elite that had their own ideological & socio-political agenda.

Gilgit-Baltistan Problem

Gilgit-Baltistan is an administrative territory of Pakistan situated in the trans-Himalayan region on the North western corner of Kashmir valley a part of which has been illegally occupied by Pakistan in 1947. Geographically, it borders with the province of Khyber Pakhtunkhwa to the west, Azad Kashmir to the southwest, Wakhan Corridor of Afghanistan to the northwest, the Xinjiang Uyghur Autonomous Region of China to the north, and the Indian state of Jammu and Kashmir to the south and southeast.

Map-6 -7:Gilgit Baltistan

At the time of the Partition, the region had been a remote and nearly inaccessible part of the Dogra-ruled state of Kashmir. It was in 1842 that one of the local chieftains sought the help of a Sikh army from Kashmir against his opponent. The area soon came under British control who then ceded it to the Kashmir state under the Treaty of Amritsar. It was forcibly made a part of Kashmir by the British and sold to the Dogra ruler Gulab Singh in 1846.

Gilgit-Baltistan, under the Maharaja of Jammu and Kashmir, consisted of five regions- Jammu, Kashmir, Ladakh, Gilgit Wazarat, and Gilgit Agency. It took a long time for the Maharajahs Gulab Singh and Ranbir Singh to extend their writ over Gilgit, Hunza and Nagar, and not until 1870 did they assert their authority over Gilgit town. The Indian government undertook administrative reforms in 1885 and created Gilgit Agency in 1889 for the British to secure the region as a buffer from the Russians. As a result of this Great Game between Britain and Russia, Gilgit Agency was expanded by the Maharajah Hari Singh in 1935 leasing the Gilgit Wazarat to the government of India for a period of sixty years. This gave the British government complete control of defence, communications and foreign relations while the Kashmiri state retained civil administration.[9] In 1947, Mountbatten terminated the lease agreement of Gilgit within 15 days after India attained independence. It gave the princely states the right to merge with either of the two provided their territory had geographical continuity with the nation they wished to accede to.Gilgit again came under the direct rule of the Maharaja as a legal part of his state.

After independence, both India and Pakistan went for territorial consolidation. The Maharaja of Jammu and Kashmir decided not to accede to either India or Pakistan. The situation soon changed as Pakistan invaded the princely state in October 1947 and Maharaja Hari Singh acceded to India. Pakistan captured the entire Gilgit region - generally called Gilgit-Baltistan - by the treachery of British military officer of the Maharaja. Under lease, Gilgit-Baltistan was protected by a British-controlled force called the Gilgit Scouts. After the British terminated the lease, they allowed two of their officers - Major W A Brown and Captain A S Mathieson - to the Maharaja for the purpose of looking after the defence of Gilgit-Baltistan till an alternative arrangement was found. Major Brown revolted and captured King's governor Brigadier Ghansara Singh. On November 2, 1947, he hoisted the Pakistani flag and declared that Gilgit part of Pakistan. Pakistani forces occupied Gilgit-Baltistan on November 4. Since then, Gilgit-Baltistan has been under Pakistan's administrative control.[10]

Current Status of Gilgit-Baltistan

GB is loosely defined as a centrally-administered, partially-empowered and economically-dependent part of Pakistan. After gaining control of the region, Pakistan renamed the Gilgit Wazarat and Gilgit Agency as the Northern Areas of Pakistan. Since then, Gilgit-Baltistan has been treated as a separate geographical entity by successive Pakistani governments, covers 85,793 sq. km. It is surrounded by the Hindu Kush and the Karakoram. In 1970, Gilgit Agency, Baltistan district of Ladakh and hill states of Hunza and Nagar amalgamated to form Federally Administered Northern Areas. Gilgit Baltistan was further divided into two separate administrative divisions: Mirpur-Muzaffarabad (which Pakistan calls Azad Jammu and Kashmir, or AJK) and the Federally Administered Gilgit-Baltistan.

The plight of million people of Gilgit-Baltistan (GB), who live in a fragile environment at the mercy of nature. Gilgit-Baltistan is a multi-lingual region with socio-cultural and ethnic diversity. According to the Pakistani census of 1998, the population of Gilgit-Baltistan was 870,347. Based on this figure, the current population is projected at 1,387,106. Amongst them, the Shias constitute 39 percent, Sunnis 27 percent, Ismailis 18 percent, and Noorbakshis 16 percent. According to the same 1998 Pakistan census, the population of so-called Azad Kashmir was 2,973 million. Based on this, the current population could be 4.59 million. Besides, the language barrier was another divisive factor. The languages spoken by the vast majority in Gilgit-Baltistan included Shina, Burushaski, Khowar, Wakhi and Balti while those living in Jammu and Kashmir spoke Kashmiri, Gojri, Pahari and Hindko.[11]

While administratively controlled by Pakistan since 1947, Gilgit Baltistan has not yet been formally integrated into Pakistan federal state and does not participate in constitutional political affairs. On 16 November

1947, Gilgit Baltistan came under de facto control of Pakistan government, though the nature of its administration has been rather loose and alterable over time. Gilgit-Baltistan does not find any mention in Pakistan's Constitution.The Government of Pakistan decided to keep Gilgit-Baltistan as part of the disputed Kashmir. While proper administrative and legislative set ups were established in Indian controlled Kashmir and AJK, the political and administrative affairs of this region known as the Northern Areas were managed under the law called Frontier Crimes Regulations (FCR).[12] The FCR empowered the Political Agent to act both as the chief executive and the final court of appeal. The local population was denied a democratic setup, a representative government, independent judiciary and the rights provided by the constitution. The population continued to be deprived of the rights and privileges enjoyed by citizens of the Azad Jammu and Kashmir. It is directly administered by the federal government of Pakistan.In 1975, under the prime ministership of Zulfikar Ali Bhutto, the territory was given an Advisory Council.

The Supreme Court took notice of the absence of basic human rights in the Northern Areas while hearing a petition in May 1999. The court gave the government six months to establish an elected administration, independent judiciary and to provide all basic rights enshrined in the Constitution of Pakistan. Following the verdict, half-hearted steps were taken to devolve power to the local level and the Advisory council was renamed as the Northern Areas Legislative council. But the demand for a politically empowered body has been consistently denied to the people.

In 2007, the territory was renamed Gilgit Baltistan and it was given self- government status and autonomous territory. On 29 August 2009, Pakistan government passed the Gilgit-Baltistan Empowerment and Self-Governance Order. It granted self-rule and autonomous status power to the people Gilgit Baltistan. Its powers and structures were set out in the provisions of 1973 Constitution. It replaced the Northern Areas Legislative Council and created an elected Gilgit Baltistan Legislative Assembly and a legislative Council. Gilgit-Baltistan gained de facto province-like status but did not become the constitutional part of Pakistan. The reforms were unsatisfactory as it is continued to be administered by the Ministry of Kashmir Affairs and Northern Areas (Kana) and Gilgit-Baltistan Legislative Assembly (GBLA) remained powerless. Gilgit-Baltistan had an elected Assembly with limited powers to frame laws. In September 2012 the Gilgit Baltistan legislative Assembly approved a resolution demanding provincial status for Gilgit-Baltistan, which was immediately opposed by AJK government.

Pakistan is planning to declare Gilgit-Baltistan region as the fifth province, a move that may raise concerns in India as it borders the disputed Pakistan-occupied Kashmir. A committee headed by Sartaj Aziz, Foreign Affairs Advisor to Prime Minister Nawaz Sharif, recommended that Gilgit-Baltistan be officially recognised as the fifth province of Pakistan in addition to Punjab, Sindh, Balochistan and Khyber Pakhtunkhwa.[13] The Constitutional amendment would be made to change the status of the region.

Gilgit-Baltistan Order-2018, replaces the GB Empowerment and Self-Governance Order of 2009. The new order changes the nomenclature of Gilgit-Baltistan Legislative Assembly to Gilgit-Baltistan Assembly. And, all powers exercised by the four provincial assemblies under Schedule IV of the Constitution of Pakistan have been entrusted to the GB Assembly. The assembly shall have the right to pass legislation regarding mineral, hydropower and tourism sectors. These powers were previously exercised by GB council.[14]

Gilgit-Baltistan Order-2018 has also made some changes in judiciary too. The nomenclature of the chief court has changed to the High Court with a bench of two judges. The chief judge of GB Supreme Appellate Court would be a retired judge of the Supreme Court of Pakistan. A five-member committee has been slated to depoliticise appointment of judges of the GB Supreme Appellate Court and High Court. The prime minister would appoint judges in apex courts on its recommendations. The 2018 order shows changes vis-à-vis rights also. While the empowerment order (2009) guaranteed only 17 basic rights limited to GB territory, as per order-2018, GB citizens could demand his or her rights at any corner of Pakistan with access to all apex courts of the country. In fact, the Pakistan government initiative to give some permanency to Gilgit Baltistan 's political status is the subtle pressure of China. It has been in the news over a considerable period of time that Chinese with their massive investment are not comfortable with the unsettled political status of the region.

Indian protested over constitutional change in the status of GB in view of her concern over Pak administered Kashmir. Gilgit Baltistan Order of 2018 has been subjected to much debate for obvious reasons. Strategically a sensitive region of erstwhile JK state, it has always been treated differently from rest of the state. In fact, it is a shared pain of all regions of erstwhile JK state, GB is no exception. The clamour for a change is understandable. The permanence in political status across LoC could only be ensured by Indians and Pakistanis coming to a comprehensive agreement. Over the last six decades Kashmiri nationalists have failed to make inroads in the region because they have never raised their voice against the injustice being done to the region nor sought to bring Gilgit-Baltistan even to the level of

AJK. This indicated a lack of interest in the region. Kashmiri political parties have therefore failed to strike root here. The Kashmiri nationalists are however vociferously opposing the demand to upgrade the status of the region. Yasin Malik has opposed the move on the ground that it will jeopardise Kashmir cause. "Delhi will then have a political and moral right to integrate Kashmir with India," he argues.[15] The move has raise concerns in India because of the disputed region and borders Pakistan-occupied Kashmir (PoK). It is believed that China's concerns about the unsettled status of Gilgit-Baltistan prompted Pakistan to change its status. According to an earlier report in Dawn newspaper, Pakistan was mulling to elevate the constitutional status of the region in a bid to provide legal cover to the CPEC. The move could signal a historic shift in the country's position on the future of the wider Kashmir region.

The UK Parliament has also acceptedthat Gilgit-Baltistan belongs to India as an integral part of the state of Jammu and Kashmir after legally acceded to Union in 1947. The British parliament on March 23, 2018 passed a motion condemning Pakistan's announcement for declaring Gilgit-Baltistan as its fifth frontier.[16] The motion headed by British Conservative leader Bob Blackman stated that Gilgit-Baltistan, being part of the state of Jammu and Kashmir, has been illegally occupied by Pakistan, denying the people of the region basic fundamental rights.

Challenges

Pakistan has been using colonial tactics of Divide and Rule in the Gilgit Baltistan or can be termed as the Interstate colonialism. While Pakistan has all administrative rights in the regions but people have no rights. The people of Baltistan are forced to pay all the taxes yet they are not acquiring benefits from the government socio-economic policies. No local elite has been employed to rule in the region but the government creating divisions between Shias and Sunnis so as to curtail their demands and rights. People of Baltistan feelings towards Pakistan are quite divided. Nirupama Subramanian says that there are three broad political sentiments prevalent in Gilgit Baltistan. The most vociferous is demand to merge with Pakistan, second is to merger with Azad Kashmir and now, thirdly, they are demanding independence from Pakistan. Gilgit Baltistan feeling no political connection with India.[17] On the other hand, the feelings towards Pakistan are quite divided.

For over more than 70 years, Pakistan has been continued to maintain the status quo in the Gilgit Baltistan denied basic rights and facilities of a modern state.

- With all its natural endowments and potentials for prosperity, GB is spoiled by a rent-seeking, corrupt and inept political system that runs through an inflated bureaucracy and a disempowered local legislative assembly. The Empowerment and Self-Governance Order 2009 replaced by 2018 Order, defines the legislative, administrative and legal functions of governance in GB – including the principle of separation of powers among the local parliament, judiciary and bureaucracy. Although it gives authority of legislation to the local assembly on key subjects of economic, political, cultural and legal affairs, it does not define the processes which could determine the relationship with the federation vis-à-vis financial planning.

- Gilgit Baltistan is not eligible for the National Finance Commission (NFC) award because it is not having provincial status within the constitutional framework. Therefore, there is no plan for resource allocation and distribution based on the planning and recommendation of local legislative assembly. Since budgetary allocations are predetermined and top down, they neutralise the impact of local legislation.
- There is a serious disconnection between the Gilgit Baltistan government and the federal government on important matters regarding regional development. All the budgetary allocations are predetermined by the federal government and top down approach. The local Assembly legislation have no impact because of political control which has reduced the capacity, power, will and commitment of the GB government to devise a developmental roadmap for the region.
- Gilgit Baltistan is not governed under the Constitution, hence it has no power, place and benefits in the national development policy. Under the 18th Constitutional Amendment, this region has not been empowered more importantly even after the devolution of powers to provinces. The federal government does not seem to have any inclusive political strategy of integrating GB into this devolved mode of political governance.
- In Gilgit Baltistan government and administrative set up, the federal government have their own officers. The 2009 order provided an elaborate formula of functional distribution of administrative powers between federal and local bureaucracy. It allows posting of 25 percent, 50 percent, 60 percent and 70 percent of federal officers in GB's administrative setup and all key positions like home secretary, secretary planning, and development and secretary finance are assigned to federal officers. This is an overly centralised power structure and more

disempowering as the federal government have interpretations of role and responsibilities even after the 18th Amendment.

- The centrally-controlled bureaucratic structure is the main impediment to the timely execution of public services. The current political and administrative setup lacks the institutional arrangement of accountability, transparency and inclusivity on important matters of public interest – ranging from financial planning to merit-based hiring of staff on development projects. There has been political appointment on all the key position of foreign development projects which resulted into inefficiency, corruption and collusion for evading monitoring and accountability. Due to lack of coordination, incompetent management and political and bureaucratic interference, the development projects are suffered.
- Gilgit Baltistan has not only self-sufficient but the natural potential endowments with the gemstones, and mineral and water resources, the area is one of the best tourist destinations of the world that can generate biggest revenue in the country. The untapped development potential of this region is an opportunity for investor in tourism, energy and border trade. It has potential of producing 70,000 thousand-megawatt renewable energy from its water resources. According to an estimate, GB has the potential to generate annual revenue of $1 billion from its natural resources and tourism, and fetch the annual revenue of $10 billion through renewable energy. But the delays and irregularities in implementation of the projects, fund allocations, lack of infrastructure and communication roads and lack of government support and responsibility has not been able to meet the development targets and improve the living standard of people.
- Sectarianism has seeped into everyday life and activities in Gilgit. In Gilgit till the 1980s, there was no basis of kinship that could enable people with same racial stock and linguistic group to empathise with each other. To aggravate the situation, the new version of religion tended to demonise the 'other'. Ultimately, it led to the incessant sectarian strife that destroyed the economy, polarised the administration and divided settlements and educational institutions on sectarian lines. Now This is evident from the fact that Gilgit now has no-go areas for both Sunnis and Shias. The situation gave rise to separate transport facilities, schools, hospitals and offices that are based on sectarian lines. Currently, business in Gilgit is factually divided on sectarian

lines.[18] Even new economic opportunities and initiatives cannot save themselves from sectarianism.

- The tourism industry is the backbone of the economy in Gilgit-Baltistan. The unabated violence in the region has badly affected tourism. In 2012, Gilgit-Baltistan witnessed the killing of passengers along the Karakoram Highway (KKH). Owing to the violent events in Hunza, Nagar, Gilgit, Chilas and Skardu, hundreds of foreign tourists have been stranded in these areas in 2016. They were later evacuated by Pakistan Air Force (PAF). This also caused the cancellation of hundreds of trekking and expedition tours to the region. Though nature offers mesmerising sceneries to the tourists, its beauty is marred by sectarian violence.
- Education is also the worst affected by sectarian violence in Gilgit. Historically, schools have played an important role in providing a common space for interaction between students from diverse regional, religious, linguistic and ethnic backgrounds. They helped to create cross-sectarian solidarities among students and provided social cohesion. Since 1990s, it witnessed the mushrooming of schools run by faith-based organisations. Today, even government schools in a locality that belongs to a particular sect are virtually a no-go area for the students of the opposing sect. Private schools feed themselves on the catchment area of their respective sects.

China-Pakistan and India

Sino-Pak bonhomie was borne out of contentious state of affairs with India. China has been an important player in the region. As during the British Raj, Russia and China were the powers to be watched, Pakistan had mostly China to take care of, particularly after the 1962 Indo- China post war situation. Sino-Indian war changed the strategic equation. In the mid-1960s, China constructed the Karakoram Highway linking Kashghar in Xinjiang with Gilgit and Abbottabad through the Khunjerab Pass. In 1963, in an agreement, the Pakistan transferred the Shaksgam Valley (about 5000 to 8000 sq.km. areas) to China to construct the China-Pakistan Economic Corridor (CPEC).

Though, this region is prone to landslides, efforts are on to upgrade Karakoram highway and make it an axis of China's Silk Road Initiative which will link Xinjiang to Gwadar port in Baluchistan through the highway, a possible railroad and oil and gas pipeline. China has invested in a number of projects in the Gilgit-Baltistan region and the Chinese connection is an important element of the region's economy. During his recent visit, President Xi Jinping committed some $46 billion to projects in Pakistan.

Gilgit Baltistan bordering with China is becoming a highly prized territory. China was having far-reaching global designs. In the midst of these diplomatic changes, the people of GB desires for a settled political status. Non-resolution of Kashmir dispute has also left its permanent political status in quandary. The China Pakistan Corridor Project has been subjected to the final settlement of Kashmir dispute as it was included in the agreement. since the legal title of the region through which the China-Pakistan Economic Corridor will run through vests with India. It is the reason the Indian side has protested Chinese activity in POK in the past and again recently.[19] However, this is only a subtext of the larger Indian complaint about the Sino-Pak nexus.

However, India cannot take that at face value. For long years, indeed, beginning in 1947 itself, India had leaned down its own legal claim over Gilgit Baltistan. As a result, the world assumed the 'Kashmir problem' only pertained to the Kashmir Valley which was in India's possession. From the outset, India was less than categorical about its desire to resume control of the Gilgit-Baltistan area, though Nehru did insist that as part of the UN resolution requiring the removal of Pakistani forces from J&K, the Pakistani regulars and irregulars ought to be removed from Gilgit-Baltistan as well. In 2009 and 2010, India opposed sharply to the presence of Chinese soldiers and workers in the region. "India believes that Pakistan has been in illegal occupation of parts of the Indian State of Jammu and Kashmir since 1947. The Chinese side is fully aware of India's position and its concerns about Chinese activities in Pakistan-occupied Kashmir".[20] India also objected the election to be held in the Gilgit Baltistan as an attempt of Pakistan "to camouflage its forcible and illegal occupation of the regions" and to deny its people their political rights; it is being held under a belated effort by Islamabad to give the region a figment of self-rule".[21] India's MEA said, the proposed election in Gilgit and Baltistan under the so-called 'Gilgit Baltistan Empowerment and Self Government Order' of 2009 is an attempt by Pakistan to absorb these territories. India is concerned at the continued efforts of Pakistan to deny the people of the region their political rights, and the efforts being made to absorb these territories.

In his 2016 Independence Day speech, Indian Prime Minister Modi raised the question of Gilgit Baltistan, Balochistan and Pak occupied Kashmir. Modi remarked that the people of Gilgit had thanked him. Now it's time to reach out to them. In raising his voice against Pakistan, agitating for the state to grant political and economic rights to the people of Gilgit-Baltistan as per the United Nations Commission for India and Pakistan

(UNCIP) resolutions on Kashmir. He said, the people of Balochistan, the people of Gilgit, the of Pak occupied Kashmir have thanked me in such a manner from places that I have never been and never had a chance to meet, they have sent wishes to the people of India and thanked us. I am grateful to them.[22] It has been considered as a strong signal of shifting in India's foreign policy. National Security Adviser Ajit Doval has also commented that "we also have a 106-km-long non-contiguous border with Afghanistan that we need to factor in," a clear reference to Gilgit Baltistan's Afghan frontier.[23] Similarly, Vikas Swarup, the spokesman for the external affairs ministry, said: "India's position is well known. The entire state of Jammu and Kashmir, which includes the regions of Gilgit and Baltistan, is an integral part of India."[24]

The question is how to deal with the problem. Gilgit-Baltistan peoples have the options: either remaining part of Pakistan or joining India or want an independent country through referendumIndia is not willing to hold a referendum and Pakistan has no fear of it.

Pakistan's role in the region has been particularly responsible. Pakistan has been trying to change the demography of Gilgit-Baltistan for decades. In 1970s, former Pakistan Prime Minister Zulfiqar Ali Bhutto had abrogated the State Subject Rule to allow Sunni Muslims to settle down in the Shia-dominated Gilgit-Baltistan. Zia-ul-Haqq also followed the same efforts to alter the sectarian balance in the region. In 1988, a huge Lashkar of Sunni extremists was sent in to chastise the Shia population, triggering sectarian strife which has now recurred regularly over the years. This has worked in Pakistan's favour. According to estimates, some 70 per cent of the population are Shias of various denominations and only 30 per cent or so are Sunnis. Currently, the general climate of violence against Shias in Pakistan has taken a toll in the Gilgit-Baltistan region as well. Indian Ministry of Foreign Affairs made a reference to these issues too, said "Unfortunately in recent times the people of the region have also become victims of sectarian conflict, terrorism and extreme economic hardship due to Pakistan's occupationary policies."[25]

Ethnic Crisis: Sindh and Muhajir

Sindh is the most diverse, urbanized, richest and most unevenly developed province of Pakistan.Of all the provinces of Pakistan, Sindh has been facing the most challenging internal ethnic problems. Sindh is the third largest province of Pakistan with an area of approximately 54,407 square miles. It borders with the province of Punjab in the north, India to its east, Baluchistan province and the Arabian Sea and the Rann of Kutch in the South. Sindhi and Muhajirs are two large ethnic communities living in Sindh province. Both Sindhi and the Muhajirs regard themselves as a distinct nation and contest each other's account of recent history and current situation. The ethnic differences among Muslims have proved to be more tenacious in comparison to religion in Pakistan. The people supporting a strong Muslim identity themselves refused to assimilate with ethnically and culturally different people of Pakistan.

Both communities also differ radically on their respective numerical strength. According to Sindhi sources, Sindhi are approximately 50 million and descend from the original Dravidian inhabitants of Sindh. According to their own estimate, some 30 million people, Muhajirs claim to outnumber Sindhi and to be Pakistan's most numerous minorities, constituting more than half the population of Sindh. They are concentrated mainly in Karachi and other urban centres. Muhajir nationhood has always been denied, in contrast to that of other nationalities (Punjabis, Baluchis, Pathans and Sindhis).

Sindh has the second highest Human Development Index out of all of Pakistan's provinces. According to the Census of Pakistan 2017, total Sindh population is 47.9 million. Sindhi of Balochi origins consists of 30% of the total Sindhi Population while Urdu speaking Muhajirs is 19% and Punjabis stand 10% and Pashtuns represents 7% only.[26] In 1947, before the partition of India, the total population of Sindh was 38,87,070 out of which 28,32,000 were Muslims and 10,15,000 were Hindus.[27]

In the colonial period, Aga Khan helped the British in the conquest of Sindh and was granted a pension as a result. Sind was made part of British India's Bombay Presidency as a prize to Aga Khan who help Britishers in the Conquest of Sindh and in 1936 it became a separate province. The British ruled the area for a century and Sindh was home to many prominent Muslim leaders including Muhammad Ali Jinnah. In 1947, required by Britain to join India or Pakistan, Sindhis joined Pakistan in hope to safeguard their autonomy.

With the creation of Pakistan, large numbers of Urdu-speaking Muslims from India were encouraged to settle in Sindh, while Sindhi Hindus were forced by state-sponsored persecution to flee to India. Property vacated by Sindhi Hindus was allocated to the migrated Muhajirs while local Sindhis were not allowed to buy the evacuated property. Later local Sindhis have resented the influx of Pashtun and Punjabis immigrants to Karachi.

The Sindh Conflict is an ethnic conflict between the Sindhi Nationalists and the migrated Muhajirs in the Sindh Province. Before partition, Sindh was a relative peaceful province, with communal violence only erupting sporadically and during partition. In post partition period, communal hatred had multiplied because the migrants to Sindh were angry at the "non-co-operation" in the killing of Hindus.

Sindh Movement

In post- independence Pakistan, the manoeuvrings of the Pakistani state convinced the Sindhis that their community would be marginalised in the set- up.[28] Therefore, Movement for a separate Sindhi State called Sindhuesh was started by Sindh Nationalists and political leader G.M.Syed.In 1967, a Sindhi literary movement was developed under the leadership of G.M.Syed and Pir Ali Mohammad Rashdi against the One Unit policy and the imposition of Urdu by the central government; and to the presence of a large number of Muhajir (Indian Muslim refugees) settled in the province. Later on, Syed openly demanding Separation from Pakistan and an independent state Sindhudesh. In 1972, G.M.Syed further proposed the formation of an independent nation for the Sindhis inspired by the Bangladesh independent movement. The demand of Sindhudesh was also supported by the Sindhi Diaspora[29] including Sindhis in India who had left Sindh after Partition, leaving behind their property as evacuee trusts under reciprocal government supervision.

After the death of the former Prime Minister of Pakistan Benazir Bhutto, the Sindhudesh movement has increased an increase in popularity. Sindhi nationalists alleged that Sindh has been used to the advantage of people

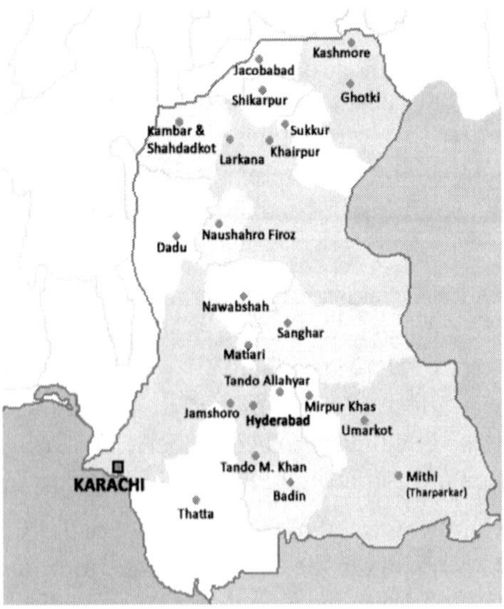

Map-8-9: Sindh Province of Pakistan

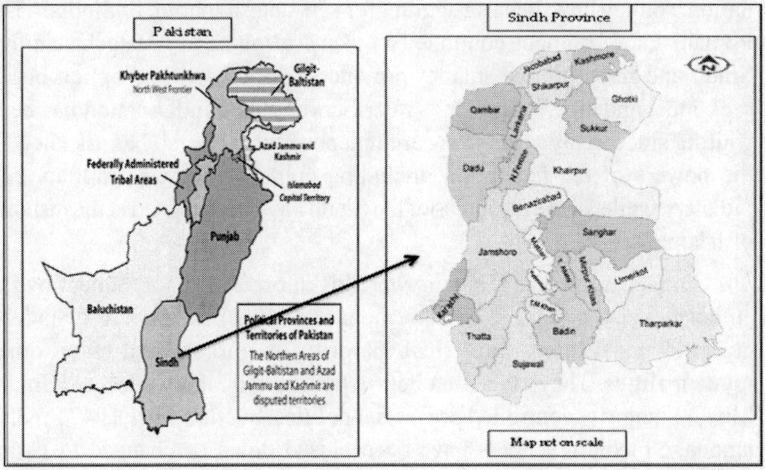

from non-Sindhi ethnic groups specially Muhajir people in key areas of Sindh including Karachi. Large scale migration to Sindh from other regions of Pakistan including Khyber Pakhtunkhwa have increased the Punjabi dominance in the defence sector and the movement of Taliban as well as terrorist attacks on the region.[30] and this is the main cause of recent troubles in Sindh. Pro-Sindhudesh organisations such as the Jeay Sindh Quami Mahaz (JSQM) and World Sindhi Congress have gained a wider support base.

Sindhi separatists totally reject the parliamentary methods of struggle for getting freedom and rights. Therefore, no Sindhi nationalist party has been ever voted into power in Sindh at any level of government.[31] Some nationalist parties and associations are banned for "terrorist, anti-state and sabotage" activities by the Pakistani government. On March 23, 2012, a Sindhudesh rally was organised in Karachi, followed by a freedom march by the pro-separatist Jeay Sindh Quami Mahaz (JSQM) which, according to sources, gathered hundreds of thousands of people to demand independence for Sindhudesh. Hundreds of thousands of leaders, activists and supporters of the Jeay Sindh Qaumi Mahaz attended a freedom march denouncing the Lahore Resolution of 1940.[32] The Daily Times reported that processions occurred in many other cities and towns in Sindh. JSQM Chairman Basir Khan Qureshi expressed his desire for the Urdu-speaking community to integrate with Sindh, calling them "brethren and part of Sindhi nation".

A strike called by the JSMM on 25 January 2014, resulted in a complete strike in the province, excluding some areas of Hyedrabad, Tando, Allahyar, Maitiari and Ghotki. Sindhi feel that they are a separate and full-fledged nation, so they have been struggling for self-determination of Sindh. "The Punjabi Establishment continued to usurp resources of Balochistan and Sindh and now the two smaller provinces are left with no option but to seek independence," said Dr. Safdar Sarki.[33] The Sindhi nation has been waiting since many years to secure independence. Punjab has assumed all the powers of the federation, including civil bureaucracy, military and judiciary while all the resources of the Sindh have been placed at the disposal of Islamabad.

Sindhis argue that Muhajirs were given preferential treatment by the authorities. Despite the growth of the urban Muhajir population, Sindhi's claim to constitute a numerical majority in Karachi and many other municipalities. They argue that before partition, a highly educated Sindhi Muslim majority controlled provincial politics, but that since 1947 Sindhi-language-medium schools have been closed down or changed to Urdu-medium by the authorities, and Karachi University, formerly a major Sindhi educational institution, is now controlled by the Muhajir provincial administration, with Sindhi students denied entry.

On independence, Pakistan made Urdu the national language, denying Sindhi its traditional status in Sindh. In 1972 Sindhi efforts to regain official status for their language resulted in ethnic disturbances provoked by their opponents. They blame tensions with Muhajirs on continuing illegal population transfers and on Muhajir demands for a separate homeland and accompanying violence. Sindhis accuse Muhajir militants of numerous killings and other outrages, including a wave of attacks launched in 1992, with the involvement of Pakistani army.

Sindhis see themselves as threatened by the continued immigration and urban settlement of Muhajirs, and by the influx of Punjabis, many of them military personnel, who, they claim, obtained ancestral Sindhi lands unlawfully. Numerous Sindhi activists and intellectuals are reportedly in prison, some detained without trial, many tortured and denied legal or medical aid. Sindhi also consider that they are deprived of their share of irrigation water and that the province's fossil fuels are being exploited by outsiders for commercial gain, while many Sindhi suffer unemployment and poverty. The opposition to the construction of Kala Bagh dam (1999-2006) reflects Sindhi concern.

Muhajirs Movement

Ethnic differences among Muslims has been a more persistent problem in Pakistan than the religion. The people supporting a strong Muslim identity themselves refused to assimilate with the ethnically and culturally different people of Pakistan. The ethnic identities are so rooted in 'territory' that the

Urdu-speaking migrants has become excluded and exclusively out-group with no territorial base. Muhajirs, means migrants who initially constituted the ruling community having a single, homogeneous, religious, identity. Soon lost the 'sons of the soil' status both at the central and provincial level. They reorganized themselves as a separate ethnic entity in the social universe of Pakistan. Pakistan which was propounded on the principle of the two-nation theory could not accommodated the Muslims who had left out India. Even the Bihari Muslims in Bangladesh, who had supported the Pakistani forces in suppressing nationalist movement in East Pakistan in 1971, have not been incorporated and repatriated to the country. Refusal to accept them has not only negated the two-nation theory but has endorsed the ethnic reality of the polity as immigration of any more Urdu-speaking Muslims from the subcontinent will add to the numbers and clout of the Muhajirs, who now claim to be a separate nationality. The plank of Pakistan-Islam-Urdu failed to established a homogeneous ethnic integrated nation. People claimed to belong to one or the other ethnic community, Muhajirs had no option rather than to assimilated with the local Sindhi groups. They resisted by even refusing to learn local Sindhi language, or constructing their own ethnic group and they opted the second one. The ethnic groups in Pakistan have also linked with politico-economic interests. Therefore, Muhajirs as other ethnic groups, is also fighting for a political space and clout in the country.

Muhajirs claimed that they had struggled and helped to found the state of Pakistan in 1947 leaving the Indian provinces where as in new country they had been in minority. They claim to have brought considerable educational attainment, skills and expertise to the new state and quickly rose to positions of prominence in commerce and the administration. Muhajirs state that their prominence had antagonized the existing feudal social order and led to the deployment of various forms of discrimination against them.

In the face of continuing discrimination and deprivation, the rise of ethno-nationalism was a set-back to Pakistan. In response to the revival of Sindhi nationalism in 1970s, Muhajirs developed a sub-nationalist movement of their own seeking a territorial base so that they can claim sons of the soil to be secured emotionally and politically in Pakistan. Muhajirs did not have these ties, however, as the migrant community, they identified themselves as economic sons of soil of Sindh, particularly Karachi.[34]

In post-1971 era, these territorial associations became a political realities. Secession of East Pakistan and resurgence of ethnic-nationalisms of Sindhis and Balochis movements, encouraged Muhajirs to organize themselves and became more assertive of their demands. Muhajirs which was an 'in between group' with no historic territorial motherland in Pakistan now longing for a territory and get a rightful space in the province of Sindh. This became evident to them with the plight of Bihari Muslims in Bangladesh, consequently a sense of Diaspora generated within the community. They felt insecure in the aftermath of one-unit scheme when there was influx of circular immigrants from Punjab and NWFP. Similarly, after dissolution of one-unit scheme, migration of Sindhis in Karachi invited wrath of Muhajirs. Meanwhile, in the decade of 1980s, Sindhis joined with the Muhajirs to defend their province from onslaught of upcountry migrants, who drain the wealth of Sindh in the province and sending back the wealth of Sindh by earning in their respective home.

In the initial phase, Muhajir dominance in civil bureaucracy was an asset to them. But with the rise of military dictatorship and the increasing role of military in politics the importance of Muhajirs detuned. However, in the post-Zia phase MQM succeeded in increasing its electoral success and succeeded on many occasions in the politics of bargaining. MQM joined civil and military governments. During the Musharraf phase, Muhajirs gained got Political significance. However, in the post Musharraf phase, they were again struggle to preserve their interests. Their position was demoted to junior partners of Punjabis in power structures and subsequently, Pashtun and Sindhi started to replace Muhajirs in important position. Their representation at various levels of government jobs has reduced over the years, due to quota system and partial policies of the government towards the Muhajir community at different points of time. This led to the sense of 'relative deprivation' in the community and caused alienation among Muhajirs. The community which had sacrificed their hearts and home while migrating to new country and provided much needed political leadership, skilled human resource, expertise as well as capital to the nascent polity and economy of the country just aftermath of independence got disillusioned and experienced great deprivation. They had high expectations for the rewards in return to their contributions. But as their representation in the state structures started shrinking, they got disillusioned and experienced 'relative deprivation'.

Rise of MQM

Muhajirs lack common geographical and other objective criteria, therefore, the Muhajir movement was not led by elites traditionally associated with a land or territory rather its leaders were drawn from an urban middle-class background. Muhajir community, which was experiencing 'relative deprivation' at that time, redefined their political identity in terms of ethnicity. It also demonstrates the failure of the state in dealing with the macro-level issues of state-formation, federal-provincial relations, balanced economic development, defining the role of Islam, egalitarian power-sharing mechanism, etc., has compelled the people to articulate their micro-level demands and compete for the limited socio-economic goods, in terms of ethnicity.

In 1984, Muhajirs founded the Muhajir Quami Movement (MQM), led by Altaf Hussain, to assert their rights. In order to evolve a new socio-political identity based on ethnicity, a political outfit – Muhajirs Qaumi Movement was started to overcome the initial inhibition of identifying themselves in ethnic terms. Muhajir Qaumi Movement (MQM) played a crucial role in consolidating Muhajirs society and providing a political organization to the community.[35] It catered and articulated the demands of Muhajirs as a group, in specific terms and stood for interests particularly to deal with Sindhi. Muhajirs codified their particular interests as national interests of Pakistan and Islam and tried to secure them at the cost of the people of Pakistan. During various army operations when the members of the community and MQM were being persecuted, there has been demand of separate Jinnhapur for the Mohajirs[36] as a final abode. Though over the years the they have realized that a separate province for the community is not easy and the demand has faded away.But there still persists a desire among the migrants and implicit sense of having a separate province of its own.

Emergence of MQM as a major political force was not merely a matter of Muhajirs getting organized as such but it marked a sea change in their political attitudes. MQM has consolidated ethnic and communal politics in Pakistan. Amidst continued ethnic clashes with different ethnic groups in urban Sindh and the growing sense of alienation in Muhajirs, MQM emerged as a defender of the community and strengthened the cohesiveness of the community. The charismatic leadership of Altaf Hussain brought disparate people under one organization. He became a symbol of Muhajirs nation. Whenever the activists of the party were assaulted and targeted by members of other groups or the security agencies, Muhajirs felt persecuted and rallied behind their own political organization. So much so that in Pakistan, MQM is the only political party which is confident of its support base and invariably wins all the elections and by elections from the constituencies it decides to contest. The MQM claims to have won major victories in urban Sindh in every election held since 1987.[37] This success, Muhajirs argue, led to the launching of a military/police operation against them in June 1992 resulting in the unlawful killing and torture of thousands of Muhajirs. MQM offices throughout Pakistan were forcibly closed, and MQM's elected parliamentarians were in jail, in hiding or in exile.

The MQM participated in the general election of 1997, achieving the third largest share of the vote. In 1997, MQM(A) officially changed its name from Muhajir Qaumi Movement to Muttahida Qaumi Movement in order to broaden its base from an ethnic party to social reform movement. Muttahida Qaumi Movement boycotted the municipal elections that took place in 2001, but nevertheless participated in the national elections of October 2002, securing most of the urban area seats in Sindh province.

Although, the conflict damaged the MQM's reputation but it led the party to provincial government. The events in 2007 had shown how, in a profound turnabout, Muhajir violence had been directed at preserving the power of military.

Split in MQM

Pakistani governments have waged a propaganda war against the MQM and branding them separatists and terrorists. The state law enforcement agencies have continued their efforts to eliminate the MQM's supporters and leadership. In 1992 the MQM divided into two factions – one led by Altaf Hussain, MQM(A) and the other known as MQM (Haqiqi).

Violence constitutes an important aspect and an integral feature MQM identity, popularity and influence. But in the subsequent years, the party attempted to correct its image and adopted parliamentary methods. It has restructured itself a Muttahida Qaumi Movement in 1988 (meaning United National Movement) and has tried to get rid itself of the Muhajir ethnic tag. The MQM leadership realized the futility of the separatist polity and tried to win back the confidence of the centrist forces, particularly the army. It had restructured itself as a party of the middle and lower class of the country as opposed to the predominantly feudal parties. Due to electoral compulsions and aspiration to become a national party, MQM had tended to broaden its support base by distributing party tickets to the members of other ethnic groups and fighting elections in other provinces also. This has led to the distancing of certain radicals in the community from the party, but nevertheless hold of Altaf Hussain in the party and on the loyalties of the Muhajirs towards his leadership has not weakened. It is evident from the fact that even the Sindhis have won in the recent elections from the Muhajir-dominated localities. In the ensuing conflict and violence in Karachi during 1991, MQM(A) fled the country for London and has not returned.

The party (MQM) has emerged as an exclusive urban middle-class movement. Unlike, the Bengali, Sindhi, or Baluchi nationalist movements, which are rooted in territorial ethnicity, MQM has mixed ethnicity with a migrant ethos. It has secularized the policy and tended to bring forth common issues that directly affect and influence the lives of the individuals and groups. It has particularly been popular amongst youth and its cadre constitutes mostly of the young men. The young, urban and educated leaders and members of the party movement have successfully resisted all the attempts by the central government to dismantle their organization and have been successful in maintaining a high level of legitimacy among their constituency as proved in all levels of elections.[38] However, despite proving its credentials amongst Muhajir community, party has not been able to hold power either in the province much less in the centre independently rather it has to remain content with the position of an ally only. With its separatist rhetoric, militant methods and claims of being a separate nationality it has annoyed almost all the ethnic groups in the country who seldom sympathize with it.

However, MQM remains to be a Muhajir party as long as the party structure is dominated and led predominantly by Muhajirs. Altaf Hussain has been in touch with PONM leaders like Attaullah Mengal and Mehamud Khan Achakzai. MQM organized 'Sindh Solidarity Convention' at Nishtar Park in Karachi in April 2002, where Altaf demanded a new constitution in accordance with the Lahore resolution of 1940. He declared that if people of Sindh are denied their right to self-determination, they will not hesitate to approach United Nations. In March 2000, the party aligned itself with a separatist Sindhi group in a London rally. All these developments indicate that the party is now concentrating more on provincial autonomy as its major demand.

Different positions of Muhajirs and Sindhis

There are also considerable differences between the indigenous Sindhis and the immigrant Muhajirs on several key issues. These are:

- This polarization of the two communities increased during the decades of 1980's.
- Second issue concerns with the affirmative actions and policies of the government which favour Sindhis.Sindhis demanded a greater share of jobs in the provincial services and institutions of higher education while Muhajirs oppose this and want to have preferential treatment in the bureaucracy and in higher educational institutions.
- Finally, there is the controversial issue of further repatriation of Biharis from Bangladesh. The Muhajirs claim that nearly all of the 250,000 Biharis have a right to be settled in Pakistan. This is unacceptable to native Sindhis, who believe that an influx of Biharis into Sindh province would results in the complete loss

of their cultural and linguistic identity. In fact, the issue of the Biharis – which has been a sticking point in efforts to reach any agreement between the political parties of Pakistan – contributed to the downfall of Benazir Bhutto's government (1993-96) and Nawaz Sharif government (1997-99). In the early 1990s, less than 1,000 Bihari were settled in Punjab (Okara).

Common Issues

There are common issues related to both Sindhis and Muhajirs Sindhis and Muhajirs. Sindh has been facing many problems including the weak and unstable economy, poverty, unemployment, corruption and terrorism. The lack of regional and provincial autonomy and continuous interference from Islamabad in the affairs of Sindh is one of the major concerns of both communities. In recent years, Sindhi dissatisfaction has grown over the construction of large dams, perceived discrimination in military/government jobs, provincial autonomy, and overall revenue shares. Both Sindhis and the Muhajirs have made substantial allegations of discrimination and persecution against the government. The past decade 1996-2006 had witnessed an increasing number of targeted killings and kidnapping in urban Sindh, particularly in Karachi, which has affected both Muhajirs and Sindhis. (see Table 13-14). They are largely affected by the influx of Punjabis who dominate the bureaucracy and the armed forces. The persistent bias towards the Punjabis has exacerbated provincial tensions. Sindhis and Muhajirs are also demanding ban on further settlements of Punjabis and Pashtuns in the Sindh province and restrictions on the sale of properties and allotment of businesses to those not domiciled in the province.

Issue of Sindh Local Bodies

The Sindh People Local Government Ordinance 2011 was passed by the Provincial Assembly of Sindh which repealed the Sindh Local Government Ordinance 2001 and revived the Sindh Local Government Ordinance of 1979.[39] The act restored the three tires of government outlined in the 1979 Ordinance. The governor of Sindh argued that Sindh Local Government Ordinance of 2001 was passed by General Musharraf without the consent of the people. Both the MQM and the Sindh leaders protested the act. Further the Sindh people local Government Act, passed by the Sindh Assembly on October 2012,[40] had been a major source of contention between the PPP-led Coalition government and various nationalist groups in Sindh. Sindh Nationalist leaders opposed its dual system which would create greater ethnic divides in Sindh. In 2013, the Sindh Assembly passed a bill by majority approving amendments in the Sindh Local Government act. It included an expansion in the population base used for town and

Municipal committees, and electing mayors and deputy mayors through an open show-of-hand rather than a secret ballot.[41] The amendment bill was opposed by the MQM, Pakistan Muslim League-Functional, Pakistan Muslim League-Nawaz and Pakistan Tehreek-e-Insaf, contended that the amendment was not discussed with them.

There are differences on the structure and bodies of local Sindh government. It is necessary that broad-based ethical principles are agreed upon between the two leading communities to determine the future structure of local government in Sindh. If this does not happen, the issue will resurface with every political crisis, repercussion and fragmentation of the province further. There are many reasons. Karachi contains 62 per cent of Sindh's urban population; 30 per cent of Sindh's total population; and 22 per cent of Pakistan's urban population.[42] Lahore, the second largest city in Pakistan, on the other hand, contains only 22 per cent of Punjab's urban population; seven per cent of Punjab's total population; and 12 per cent of Pakistan's urban population. Individually, the other major cities are a very small fraction of Karachi and Lahore.

Karachi's large-scale industrial sector employees make up 71.6 per cent of the total industrial labour force in Sindh; 74.8 per cent of the total industrial output of the province that is produced in Karachi; and 78 per cent of formal private sector jobs of the province are located in Karachi. Pakistan federal government has dominated industrial interests, in the form of the Karachi Port Trust, Port Qasim, Customs, Railways, Civil Aviation Authority and the armed forces and their various industrial and real estate activities. The city contains 32 per cent of the total industrial establishment of the country; generates 15 per cent of the national GDP, 25 per cent of federal revenues and 62 per cent of income tax.[43] Health, education, recreation, entertainment and media-related institutions and provincial headquarters are located in the city. Therefore, federal and state government always have conflicts as the state feels that the city and its assets do not belong to them.

The second issue is related to the changing linguistic demography of Sindh state. There is a fear among the Sindhi-speaking population (which include Balochi, Seraiki and Brahvi speakers as well) that they are being converted into a minority in their province. In 1941,73 per cent of Karachi's population mother tongue was one of the local provincial languages, 6.2 per cent was Urdu/Hindi, and 2.8 per cent was Punjabi. Pashtu at that time was non-existent.

The 2017 Census claimed the decline of the local provincial languages as their mother tongue to 61.6 per cent while the Urdu speakers increased to 18.2 per cent and remaining are other languages as Pashto, Punajbi,

Baloch and Saraiki.[44] In urban Sindh, the Urdu speakers increased to 42 per cent, mainly because of their large numbers in Karachi and Hyderabad. While in other provinces of Pakistan, Local languages are the mother tongue of 94 per cent of the population of Punjab, 92 per cent of Khyber-Pakhtunkhwa and 82 per cent of Baluchistan.

Migration patterns between 1981 and 1998 show that Punjab, after Sindh, received the largest number of migrants from other provinces. But Punjab received 365,000 migrants from other provinces, while Sindh, with a much smaller population, received 1.1 million.[45] So, their fear is justified as Sindh's politics increasingly revolve around issues of identity, culture and history and miss out on issues of reform, development and deprivation.

Other issue is related with the position of the Sindhi and the MQM. The Sindhi speakers control the bureaucracy and have a majority in the provincial assembly. Thus, through the old bureaucratic system, they can have a major role in the governance of Karachi and Hyderabad and other towns where non-Sindhi speakers live in substantial numbers. The MQM's strength lies in the large Urdu-speaking pockets in Karachi and in the major cities of Sindh but not in the bureaucratic set-up. If the system is more decentralised and autonomous, the more they can exercise power in these pockets and negotiate benefits for their constituencies. This exercise of power also provides them with a role in provincial and national politics.

There are two more issues related to land. First, the devolved system has made the loot and plunder of both rural and urban land possible, leading to ecological disasters, environmental degradation, inappropriate urban land-use, increasing landlessness and oppression. The second issue is related to local commerce, trade and real estate development, which is developing, in spite of official negligence and persecution, in both the urban and rural areas of the province. For the socio-economic development of the province, this sector needs support and protection local government system. But the local government has not even considering it.

While Sindh continues to have difference with MQM in regard to its shares in the development, financial resources and irrigation water, land allotments, migration and employment and because of its internal ethnic problems. Sindh cannot live up to its potential if it is unable to achieve peace, tolerance and cooperation among its residents, especially the two major communities-the Sindhis and the Muhajirs. Both communities have to coexist for safeguarding the vital interests of the Sindh province.[46]

Table- 13: Sectarian Violence in Pakistan: 2001-2010.

Year	*Incidents*	*Killed*	*Injured*
2001	154	261	495
2002	63	121	257
2003	22	102	103
2004	19	187	619
2005	62	160	354
2006	38	201	394
2007	341	441	630
2008	97	306	505
2009	106	190	398
2010	56	504	1167

Sources: Figures are compiled from News reports and are provisional.

Table-14: Violence in Sindh.

Year	*Incidents of Killing*	*Civilians*	*Security Forces*
2012	1182	1161	121
2013	1191	1046	148
2014	811	565	121
2015	344	311	59
2016	153	76	23
2017	55	112	26
2018	23	12	7
2019	10	9	3
Total*	3769	3292	508

Balochis Separatist's' movement:

Baluchistan is the largest of all provinces of modern-day Pakistan, making up nearly two-fifths of the entire country or is half of the Pakistan, covering 44 % of the total area and divided into four princely states. Its location is extremely strategic as the province shares borders with Punjab Sindh, FATA as well as Afghanistan. The province is rich in natural resources like oil, gas, copper and gold and the economy is dominated by its natural gas fields. Even then it is most backward region in Pakistan. Baloch people are ethnically, culturally and socially different from the rest of Pakistan and feel expiated as the hands of the dominant Punjabis.

The Baloch society historically has evolved from tribal structure of 17 major tribal groups and 400 tribal sub groups. Each group is headed by a Sardar (tribal chief) chosen from a tradition Sardar Khel branch of tribe. These tribal groups are not a homogeneous group, but a heterogenous groups

Map-10, Map of Baluchistan

branching out as the Makrani or Western Balochis in Pakistan and south-western Afghanistan, the Sulemani or Eastern Balochis in Iran, and the Brahuis of the Central Kalat plateau of Pakistani Baluchistan. The latter speak the Brahui language, which, though not related to Baluchi, has certain resonances with that language. Balochis are largely Sunni Muslims, followers of the Hanafi school.

The majority of the Baluch people reside in the Baluchistan province of Pakistan. According to the Pakistan's Population Census of 2006, the total population of Baluchistan estimated as 8.2 million out of the total Pakistani population. The Baluch population thus approximates to around 5 per cent of the total population of the country. Baluch nationalists claim that deliberate government policies have resulted in underestimation of the numbers of indigenous peoples. It is also the case that indigenous Balochis have been swamped by 'outsiders', even within their own homelands. The socio-economic conditions of the Balochis are abysmal, with over 50 per cent living below the poverty line.

As regards the origin of Baloch, they are migrated Kurd tribes from around Aleppo in Syria over some 1500 years. Whereas Kurd majority settled in Iraq, Turkey and Iran, the Baloch moved to southern reaches of the Caspian Sea, later migrated into Iranian and then to Pakistani Baluchistan from the sixth century up to 14th centuries. Having settled in what is now their home land, the Baloch have successfully preserved a distinctive identity in the face of stronger cultures surrounding them. Despite the isolation of their scattered pastoral communities, the diverse Baloch tribes have found a strong common denominator in the Balochi language and a uniform folklore traditions and value system. This vitality of their ancient culture heritage explains the tenacity of the continuing demand for the political recognition of the Baloch identity.

The Baloch resistance is historically deep rooted against the any attempt to annex or conquer any part of their land since the last Baloch ruler Nasir Khan. Nasir Khan strongly unified the major Baloch tribes into an agreed system of military organisation and relatively centralised administration. Nadir Shah who conquered Afghanistan helped Nasir Khan with paramount power in Kalat.[47] After the assassination of Nadir Shah, Iranian power declined and Nasir Khan was freed from tributary status. Later on, Nasir Khan accepted Afghan suzerainty in Ahmad Shah Durani. After 1758, Kalat remained a military ally of Afghanistan but enjoyed sovereign status until the arrival of British.

Baluchistan, as a key access to Afghanistan, acquired a new strategic importance with the arrival of British in the 19th century. The contentious relationship between the British and Russia made Afghanistan an important factor as Afghanistan was more inclined towards Russia because of its regional proximity with Central Asia. Britain, to counter Russian push south towards warm water ports, the British adopted the forward policy, designed to halt the Russian advancement by subjugating Afghanistan. The Afghan war of 1939-42 was the beginning of political annexation of Baluchistan by the British colonial power. British concluded treaty with Afghanistan and extended support to the Khan of Kalat. Britishers converted Afghanistan and Baluchistan into a buffer state to provide a shield for their Indian Empire against Russia.

Seeking the direct control over the access routes, the British fought a series of bloody wars with the Baloch for more than four decades. They obtained the right to station troops in Kalat and along the logistical route to Afghanistan through military actions, subsidies and guaranteeing internal tribal autonomy. British followed its policy of divide and rule and divided the original Baloch homeland into several parts-one part went to Iran, a small strip was ceded to Afghanistan, a centrally administered area named

British Baluchistan separated from the Kalat confederacy and three small principalities.[48] This was the first step of alien domination which paved the way for the rise of present crisis and Baloch nationalism.

So long as tribal leaders did not interfere with the British access to Afghanistan and strategic control of the frontier, the Balochis leaders had complete control of internal tribal affairs. By reinforcing power and autonomy of the tribal chiefs under the Sandman System,[49] the British laid the foundations of subsequent conflict between Baloch and the central authority in Pakistan.

Pakistan's government tried to reverse the Sandman policy of internal tribal autonomy to make a strong centralised state and tried to merge the Baloch identity into an overarching Pakistani Identity. Pakistan continued assaults on the Baloch tribal social organization and its rhetoric of a monolithic Pakistani nationalism have come to constitute a fundamental challenge to Baloch's traditional norms and values.

Baluchistan Accession

When British withdrew from India, the Baloch nationalist wanted an independent state. Under the British policy princely states got autonomous status. In August 1947, an agreement was signed between the British Government and the representative of Kalat Muhammad Ali Jinnah and Liaquat Ali Khan signed the agreement which gave Baluchistan the original status of 1838. On the same day, Kalat state and Pakistan signed an agreement[50] which provided that Kalat State will have an independent status while Pakistan shall be the legal, constitutional and political heir of the

British. As an independent state, the Baloch parliament declared Baluchistan independence on August 11, 1947 three days before Pakistan came into existence.

After the formation of Pakistan, all Muslim states-Sindh, Punjab and the then Frontier states merged with Pakistan. Baluchistan, as per agreement, offered special relations in the areas of defence, foreign affairs and communication. The crisis of Baluchistan was started in 1948 when Pakistan demanded the merger with Pakistan. The forcible incorporation of Baluchistan into Pakistan caused fierce nationalist anger.[51] The Kalat National Party resisted the unconditional annexation by Pakistan. Despite this, on. 1 April 1948, the Pakistan Army marched into Kalat and arrested the Khan who surrender but his brother, Prince Abdul Karim declared a revolt proclaiming the independence of Kalat and issued a manifesto in the name of the Baloch National Liberation Committee rejecting the accession agreement signed by the Khan. The Khan of Kalat was forced to sign the document of accession in Karachi in March 1948 hence the independent status was ended. Pakistan controlled the administrative powers and the forcible accession of Baluchistan led to many rebellion and guerrilla resistance in 1948-52, 1958-60, 1962-69, 1973-77 and now from 2003 till date.

Baloch Crisis

The present-day insurgency in Baluchistan is a continuum of the intermittent guerrilla struggle against the Pakistani state that has characterized Baluchistan since 1948. The causes, the issues, the demands and the goal continue to be the same.Kalat's independent status had been affirmed several times by the Muslim League and by the Kalat National Assembly.

The first revolt in Baluchistan was led by Prince Aga Abdul Karim against the Pakistan army in the Jhalawan area in 1950. Khan's younger brother threatened with reprisal by the Pakistan army persuaded Abdul Karim to surrender with assurance of safe conduct agreement and amnesty from Pakistani army. But Pakistani forces dishonoured the agreement by arresting Agha Abdul Karim and his 102 comrades when they came to negotiate on the promise of safe conduct and were sentenced to long prison terms. This revolt was the starting point which became rallying symbol for the Baloch Liberation movement and they did not accept the accession of its state with Pakistan.

The second revolt was led by Nauroz Khan in 1958. This was the direct result of the centralising policies pursued by the Pakistani leaders. The 1956 Constitution of Pakistan merged the four provinces into one province of West Pakistan which created great unrest amongst Baloch nationalist circles. This One Unit plan was resisted by the Baloch nationalist leaders urged Iskander Mirza to exempt the Kalat from one Unit scheme. Abdul Karim who had completed his prison term in 1955 and the Khan who mobilised wide spread demonstrations through tribal chieftains. General Ayyub Khan imposed Martial Law against the Baloch resistance and Pakistani army entered into the Kalat state. Kalat was assaulted and Khan was arrested with his 350 leaders all over Baluchistan. The arrest caused a strong reaction of violence and counter violence with the government which continued for over a year. Again, on the broken promise of Pakistani government, Nauroz Khan and his followers were arrested, tortured and hanged in 1960.

The third revolt took place in 1962 against the atrocities of Pakistan's army, killing the people under the commandership of General Tikka Khan. It was wide spreaded from the Mari and Bugti tribal areas of Baluchistan to Mengal tribal areas of Jhalawan. On the other side, the Baloch also attacking the government forces by ambushing convoys bombing trains, sniping and raids on military camps. In retaliation, the army staged a series of air bombardments. Atrocities by the army were wide spread killed numbers of people.This fighting continued till 1969 when general Yahya Khan withdrew the One Unit Plan and agreed to cease fire with the Pararis.

Pakistan's history is marked by the fourth Major Baloch rebellion of 1973-77 against the government of Pakistan. Despite numerous assurances of devolution set out in the new Pakistani Constitution of 1973 which was drafted after the secession of East Pakistan. The new constitution contained numerous guarantees of the rights to ethnic minorities, reaffirming their separate legal status and right to their own language and culture. But, the Bhutto government disregarded these guarantees and the provinces became increasingly subordinate to central authority. The crisis erupted when Bhutto dismissed the elected Baloch government in February 1973 on the grounds of its alleged encouragement of a secessionist movement, smuggling and opposition to modernization.Bhutto alleged that the government had repeatedly exceeded its constitutional authority and alleged that this had been done in collusion with Iraq and the Soviet Union as part of a plot to dismember both Pakistan and Iran. Following the dismissal of their government, Baloch guerrillas began to ambush army convoys from April 1973.In retaliation, Bhutto launched a major military operation against Baloch people and jailed Baloch leaders- Khair Bux Marri, the chief Minister Attaullah Mengal and the governor Ghaus Bux Bizeno with numbers of their political cadres and activists.[52] The armed struggle continued over the next four years with varying degrees of severity deploying 80,000 Pakistani troops in the province. The fighting was more wide-spread than it had been in 1950s and 1960s. The guerrillas succeeded by July 1974 to cut off most of the main roads linking Baluchistan with surrounding provinces and to periodically disrupt the Sibi-Harnai rail link thereby blocking coal shipments from the Baloch areas to the Punjab. Additionally, attacks on drilling and survey operations stymied oil exploration activities.

Meanwhile the war had escalated; It is estimated that over 5,000 insurgents and 3,000 government troops were killed, and large quantities of livestock were destroyed, while the interruption of food supplies to civilians in insurgent-controlled areas caused great suffering. Some Baluchi rebels surrendered under a general amnesty; others fled to Afghanistan, where they were housed in government camps.

In 1976 the sardari 'tribal chief' system was abolished. The insurgency continued until the fall of the Bhutto government in 1977 and the subsequent release of jailed leaders of the region.

Most of the Balochi leaders left Pakistan and went into exile in Afghanistan, the UK and other places outside Pakistan. Several Baloch groups migrated to Afghanistan where they were permitted to set up camps by Mohd Daud. The Pararis evolved into the Baluchistan Peoples Liberation Front (BPLF) in 1976 led by Mir Hazar Khan Marri, who broke away from Baloch Students Organisation (BSO) led by Sher MuhammadMarri. The anti-Bhutto sentiments of the Baloch nationalists were well manipulated by Zia ul Haq after he seized power in 1977 and his show of clemency was received well by many Baloch leaders including the Baloch triumvirate: Ghaus Bux Bizenzo, Ataullah Mengal and Akbar Khan Bugti.

Tension in Baluchistan was further started building up after General Pervez Musharraf seized power in 1999 and the military started building new cantonments in Baluchistan. It was considered by radical nationalist leaders as a bid by the Army to tighten control over the region. The fifth wave of insurgency that broke out in this context is still on. There are several separatist groups in the province. The strongest among them is the Baluchistan Liberation Army (BLA), designated as a terrorist group by Pakistan and the U.K. Islamabad has claimed that India is backing the BLA.

The heavy-handed tactics were deployed by the Musharraf government under the pretext of the 'war on terror' has resulted in enormous human suffering in Baluchistan and the Tribal belt surrounding the province. In December 2005, the Pakistan military has launched full-fledged operations in Kohlu and Dera Bugti. The military used reportedly jet fighters and helicopter gunships in its operations to attack the suspected hideouts of combatant Marri and Bugti tribesmen in Kolhu and Dera Bugti respectively. According to the Human Rights Commission of Pakistan (HRCP), as many as 53 people were killed and 132 injured in military operations in Dera Bugti in the period of December 2005 till 8 January 2006. Eighteen people, including 12 suspected members of the Balochi armed opposition groups and six security personnel, reportedly were killed during 11-13 January 2006.[53] There were also reports of extra-judicial killings of the detainees by the law enforcement agencies. The military government claims that Baluch and Pakhtun tribesmen are harbouring Al Qaeda militants in the Tribal areas of south Waziristan.

The Baloch Nationalist movement was radicalised by the five years guerrilla warfare. The Baloch People Liberation Front (BPLF) introduce revolutionary ideas into the movement that transcends family clan, sectional and tribal loyalties and saw the Baloch nationalist struggle as part of national liberation struggle in the third world. The BPLF manifesto stressed that it was not fighting a secessionist war for the Baloch alone but a war of National liberation for all the nationalities of Pakistan. It committed to a wide revolution as a reliable base area for the liberation struggle of other oppressed nationalities, classes and democratic forces in Pakistan.

Baluchi demands centred around political and economic autonomy. They are demanding readjustment of power with the federal government not only in defence and foreign affairs, but also in the province having unfettered authority over provincial matters. The continuing denials of provincial autonomy and the enforcement of military rule in October 1999 resulted in armed insurrection led by the Bugti and Marri tribes. Considerable violence erupted after the disclosure of the rape of Dr Shazia Khalid in Sui in January 2005.[54] Since that period the unrestrained use of force by the Frontier Core and the military has resulted in significant bloodshed, extra-judicial killings, torture and arbitrary arrests.

Main Demands/Issues:

The nature of Baloch crisis has various aspects:

- The main issue of Baloch Separatist movement is provincial autonomy and the question of ethnic identity and their rights. Their main demands are the Confederation, maximum autonomy within the federation, and change in the provincial boundaries to create a homogeneous province. Though Baluchistan got the status of a province but it has never been treated as a uniting part of federation. All the governments, whether civilian or military, focused on centralization of power. Their refusal to give provincial autonomy is primarily responsible for the rise of ethnic conflict.
- The issue of Greater Baluchistan: The demographic location of the Baluchistan includes the boundaries of three countries-

Pakistan, Afghanistan and Iran. They considered themselves a nation having proper territory and culture not an ethnic group. But in fact, these Baloch tribes struggling for identity in not integrated with each other. Their internal cleavages within numerous tribes further complicated the issue. Different areas are occupied by different tribes which are also not cohesive to each other. The historical narrative of the Baloch is supportive for the notion of greater Baluchistan. It stresses that before partition the areas which were given to Afghanistan and Iran by British government should be included in greater Baluchistan.

- Issue of Representation in Politics: their demand is to have proper representation in civil bureaucracy and in military. They compare their province with the rest of the three units especially Punjab. About 70% belong to Punjab and rest of the 30% belong to Pathan, Muhajir, Sindhi and Baloch people. There is hardly any Baloch on the top ranks both in civil and military posts. Even the quota for recruitment has not benefited them as the appointment and recruitment are done on the provincial basis, hence mostly Pathans settlers in Baluchistan benefited not the Balochi with their ethnic origin.[55] The gulf between centre and province remained unabridged. They still feel that Punjabi dominance in both the institution has made them alien to the system.
- Economic deprivations and exploitations are another cause of Baloch movement. Baloch Nationalist accuses Pakistani government keeping the mineral rich province poor while Pakistan government say the pace of development is slow due to insurgency. Baluchistan has enormous economic resources which the successive federal governments have exploited without either due acknowledgement of Baluchistan's contribution to the national economy or recompense in monetary or financial measures. Natural gas deposits were found in the Sui area in 1953 and in Pirkoh in 1982. The natural gas deposits of Baluchistan cater in a very large measure to the running of industries, factories, businesses and domestic usage in all of the provinces of Pakistan. The Baluch nationalists claim that the royalties received from these projects are negligible.
- The geo-strategic location of Baluchistan has given its regional as well as international importance in politics since centuries. Its geo-strategic importance compelled the colonial British rulers to make special policies for this region. For Pakistan, the province is now holding greater importance. It is one of the important

location in economic corridor, China has proposed to build at the investment of 46 billion dollar and liking with the development of the Deep Seaport in Gwadar with city of Kashgar, a trading hub in the western Chinses region of Xinjiang. The construction of road links with Afghanistan, and Central Asia, and the Reckodeck project. The Iran Pakistan gas pipe line is also planned to go through Baluchistan.

The war on terror in Afghanistan and regional dynamic of politics in South Asia have forced the Pakistan federal government to control this province. The increased military presence and influx of foreign workers has sparked the Baloch nationalist to believe that they are only subject to subjugation and the Federal government are exploiting their resources for the benefit of Punjab elite group. The federal government's claim that these developments will bring greater prosperity to the Baluchis are refuted by the Baluch tribal leaders who consider this as new variant of economic and political exploitation." The international community supports Pakistan in the war against terror but is not fully aware of the fact that its government and army are involved in promoting Islamic terrorism on its own soil and in other parts of the world," Naubat Mari, a UK resident and march participant, told DW.

- In common with other indigenous peoples, the Baluch also feel that their land and territory have been taken over by outsiders who are politically and economically more powerful.

The most important problem in the province is the large-scale violation of Human rights by both the army and militants. Whenever there is unrest in the province, the Pakistani army used brute force to retain order even the Air force was used against civilian population. The Pakistan atrocities in the province has also attracted the international condemnation. Brad Adams, Asia Director at Human Rights Watch said, "the surge in unlawful killings of suspected militants and opposition figures in Baluchistan has taken the brutality in the province to an unprecedented level."[56] According to Amnesty International Annual Report on Pakistan 2015-16 stated "enforced disappearances continued with impunity. The EU parliament's delegation for relations with the countries of Southeast Asia and ASEAN wrote that EU can not ignore the dire human rights situation in Baluchistan. The main victims of this violence are the people of Baluchistan who are being systematically targeted by paramilitary groups, allegedly sponsored by the Pakistani authorities, Extra judicial killings and enforced disappearance are the most common practices."[57] Indian Prime Minister Modi in his independence day speech highlighted the human rights violation in the region. Pakistani security forces are accused of illegally detaining 19,000 men, women and children in Balochistan. Many of them have been raped and killed.[58]

Baloch militants themselves stand accused of Human rights abuses. Human rights activists have accused nationalist militants and the Government of Pakistan of human rights abuses. Human Rights Watch report criticised Baloch Nationalist of killings, threatening and harassing teachers.[59] The Baluchistan Liberation Army has been branded by the Pakistan and the Britain as terrorist organisation. Pakistan alleged that Since 2000 BLA has conducted numerous deadly attacks on Pakistani troops, police, and civilians and has led inter-communal violence targeted minority communities such as Hazara, Shia and moderate Sunnis who follow Sufis in Baluchistan on the basis of their religious beliefs.[60] An attack on Sufis in Baluchistan was the attack on the shrine of Shah Noorani in which 52 people, including women and children, were killed.[61]

As far as the dominant facet is concerned, the issue of ethnic identity has eclipsed all the other controversies. Baluchi nationalists point to their largely independent history over several centuries.

In order to enquire into the grievances and claims advanced by Baluch leaders, the former Prime Minister Chaudhary Shujaat Hussain on 23 September 2004 set up a special Parliamentary Committee with three sub-committees (unanimously approved by both Houses of Parliament).

- One sub-committee, headed by Senator Wasim Sajjad, was given the task of reaching Constitutional consensus and reforms package to take account of the persistent demand of provincial autonomy. It failed to reach the decision.
- Second committee headed by Senator Mushahid Hussain looked into the measures to extend greater employment to the Baloch youths both in government services and in the mega projects launched by the Central government and foreign country in the province. But the problems remain formidable especially in Projects built and operated by the Chinese contractor such as the copper extraction Plat in Saindak and Gwadar port, hardly any local people is employed.
- Third sub-committee was related with the matter of royalty of the Sui gas field in Baluchistan. In fact, Baluchistan's gas field Sui was getting less royalty in comparison to gas field in Sindh and Punjab. The committee recommended an increase in royalty and gas development surcharge that go to the province.

The Parliamentary committee presented a number of recommendations in March 2005, including greater investment to alleviate unemployment, poverty and underdevelopment in the province; the withdrawal of Frontier constabulary from the interior of Baluchistan; and the shifting of the head office of the Gwadar Port Authority (GPA) from Karachi to Gwadar. None of these recommendations have been taken further by the federal government – instead, coercive means has been adopted such as arrests and detentions of dissident Baluchi nationalists. The Musharraf regime planned to use the historical Pashtun-Baloch divide in the province to counter balance the Baloch Nationalist movement. During the anti-Soviet resistance in Afghan War, numbers of Afghan refugees flooded into Baluchistan and later internecine Mujahdeen civil wars. These Afghan refugees were allowed to acquire Pakistan's nationality and brought properties and strengthened the demographic weight of Pashtun in the province.

In determining the Baloch identity, much importance is given to tribes and clans but the inter and intra tribal conflicts have created factions among the tribal society. Through decades the Baloch are used to live under tribal confederacy and tribal affairs were conducted by their tribal traditions and Sardar hold all the powers.[62] However, infighting between nationalist insurgent groups as of late 2014 has weakened the movement. The Baloch themselves are divided into two rival camps -one having anti-state sentiments and promoting the voice of "Azad Baluchistan" and the other group is known as moderate Baloch, claiming maximum autonomy under 1973 constitution. In a survey conducted by a Gallup for Department of International development in 2012[63] revealed that majority of the Baloch do not support independence from Pakistan but want greater autonomy. Only 37 percent Baloch were in favour of Independence.

Some of the tribes have also formed their political parties to show their presence in main- stream politics. For instance, Baluchistan National party Mengal Group (BNP.M). The Jamhoori Watan Party (JWP) of Bugti tribe and Baloch Haq Talwar was organized by Nawab Khair Bukhsh Murri. Despite the fact that these Baloch Tribes are struggling for Baloch identity and rights yet their tribal system is not integrated with each other. Among the tribal Sardars, the Mengal tribe which have BNP.M and JWP of Bugti tribe is in favour to work within political system. There are some other Sardars or tribes who have joined hands with the main stream National Parties like PPP and PML (N) and (Q). Other Than these tribes, there are activists representing the Baloch middle class like the National Party (NP). Its main stream leadership including Dr. Abdul Hayee Baloch and Dr. Abdul Malik Baloch are also in favour of finding political resolution of the dispute. Baloch group known as militant groups like Baloch Liberation Army (BLA) and the Baloch Haq Talwar believed to have full control over their territory (Nation, 2006). The ideological differences of two factions about independence and political autonomy is another source of destabilization of Baloch society. Consequently, all these factors have limited the intensity of the Baloch separatist movement.

The Baloch militants began killing of their own commanders. The murder of important personalities on the basis of support caused more problems. Nawab Akbar Bugti who was the minister of state for defence during 1958, killed his elder brother Haibat Khan. On this charge Nawab Bugti was put behind the bar. During the imprisonment, he was removed from the office of tribal chief. Attaullah Mengal was also accused of murdering of his uncle and sent into jail.[64] The insurgency has begun to weaken because the Baloch nationalist have taken some reconciliation offers from the government and offer to hand in their weapons. In April 2016, four militant commanders surrendered under reconciliation. 600 rebels were killed and 1025 surrender in August 2016; in April 2017, another 500 Baloch rebels surrendered to the State including the members of BRA, UBA, and LeB.[65]

The Baloch nationalists are also facing strong resistance from the other nationalist groups, notwithstanding participating in the political process. It is being said that their voices are being silenced for the cause of Baluchistan. Although they are convinced of their political alienation and antagonism yet they believe in making struggle within the system.

Pashtun Crisis

The demand for independence and now demands for the provincial autonomy for Pashtun people has generated internal crisis in Pakistan. It is the oldest and most powerful ethno-national movement since the infantile years of Pakistan. From the beginning, the Pashtun movement was anti-imperialist and sympathetic towards the Afghans primarily because of the homogeneous ethnic bonds and aspirations of the Pashtun community. Pashtuns have an ancient history, culture and tradition often identified with the 'Pakti' kingdom as described in the writing of the classical historian Herodotus. Pathan culture and tradition were established between the twelfth and fifteenth centuries, and Pashtu folklore was ingrained the Pathan nationalism which was subsequently reinvigorated by the lyrics of Khushal Khan Khattack.

The Pashtun have a political history beset with internal strife and intrigue. Long before the British arrival, the Pashtun were struggling against the onslaught of advancing Moghul empire however, the Pashtuns were politically united until the colonial rule. Internal feuds in the Pashtun-dominated Afghan regimes of the nineteenth century provided an opportunity to many outsiders, and finally the British to interfere and seized the Pashtun territory between the Indus river and Khyber pass and subsequently divide the half of Pashto peoples by imposing the Durand line in 1893. Pashto nationalist refused to accept this boundary, argued that it will divides a 'people' with a common tradition and history, and continues to deprive Afghanistan of an access to the open sea.

As the ethnic balance changed, the Pashtuns in Afghanistan have intermittently attempted to forge some form of political unity with the Pashtuns in Pakistan that would make possible a restoration of unchallenged Pashtun dominance in Kabul. Anti-British sentiment during the 1920s and 1930s sparked the emergence of a Pashtun nationalist movement on what was to become the Pakistan side of the Durand Line.

The Pashto movement was started before the partition of India. The movement for independent state called Pashtunistan was closely related to Indian National Congress due to its charismatic leader Abdul Ghaffar Khan, popularly known as 'Frontier Gandhi'. Abdul Ghaffar Khan founded the Khudai Khidmatgar (servants of God) movement, designated by Britishers as 'Red shirt' movement, in 1929.[66] It was a Pashtun Social Reformist movement with four major objectives: Intense Pashtun Nationalism, Reform of the Pashtun society, staunch belief in Non-Violence and upholding Islam. In 1931 it allied with All India national congress and increasingly became influenced by the Congress Nationalist Socialist Programme.

During its formative years the movement demand was the provincial autonomy only and not the independent state for Pashtuns. This development took place later. Due to its organizational structure and mass following, it won both the provincial elections held in 1937 and 1946. It was the only Muslim majority province where Muslim league lost in 1946 Assembly elections. During the events of partition, the British government decided to hold a referendum to determine if the N.W.F.P wanted to join India or Pakistan and rationale for handing over the North-West Frontier Province and the adjacent tribal areas, known as the Federally Administered Tribal Areas (FATA) to the new Pakistani state. The Khudai Khidmatgars boycotted the referendum objected that the referendum was not needed because they had already won the elections by clear majority and the referendum had no option for independent Pashtunistan or acceding to Afghanistan. In Ghaffar Khan's Bannu Declaration of 22 June 1947, he demanded that the Pashtuns be given a choice between joining Pakistan and establishing an independent Pashtunistan, rather than to join Pakistan or India.[67] Other Pashtun nationalists also objected that referendum could not be regarded as conclusive and argued that the referendum did not give Pashtuns the option of union with Afghanistan being limited to join either India or Pakistan.

The creation of the Pakistan state was opposed by the Afghans as well as Pashto nationalists who consorted with the Indian National Congress before partition and were led to believe they would gain the port of Karachi if the Pakistan movement failed. Ghaffar Khan's Khudai Khidmatgar wanted a homeland for Pakhtuns, to be named 'Pakhtunistan'. The Afghan leaders appealed to the ethnic sensitivities of the Afghans and urged the inhabitants of the NWFP to join Afghanistan when it became clear that the British departure was imminent. Furthermore the 'support rendered to the movement by Afghanistan' deepened the crisis for Pakistan. This had its origins in the resentment and objection of general Pashto public and the Afghan state to the Durand line drawn in 1893 to separate India from Afghanistan.

About 40-45 million Pashtuns population live in both Afghanistan and Pakistan, but they are divided and engaged in internal feuds. The CIA world Facebook estimate that Afghanistan population was 31.05 million in which 13.39 million were Pashtuns.In Pakistan, Census Data 2005 indicate, approximately 28 million population is Pashtu (who are known as Pathans or Pakhtuns), to this must be included some 2.5 million refugees in Pakistan.[68] The vast majority inhabit the plains of the North West Frontier Province, while a minority of 2.2 million live in the highlands of the semi-autonomous Federally Administered Tribal Areas (FATA). Substantial numbers of Pathans have settled in Baluchistan; up to 20 per cent of the total population of that province is comprised of Pathans. Due to migration to urban areas there are probably over 1 million Pathans living in greater Karachi. Nearly one-third of the population of the current population of NWFP is non-Pakhtun. The non-Pakhtun population consists largely of landless artisans and peasants who are mainly Gujars and Awans by caste. About 68 per cent of the households in the NWFP speak Pashto as their first language, 18 per cent are Hindko speakers, while Seraiki is the mother tongue of just 4 per cent. while Urdu-speaking and Punjabi-speaking migrants account for only 2 per cent of the households.[69] With the exception of Sindh, Islam came to the NWFP earlier than to any other part of South Asia. Since Pakhtuns received their religious instruction from Sunni Turk dynasties, the majority are Sunni Muslims of the Hanafi School. Non-Muslim minorities form less than 0.5 per cent of the population.

There are two to three dozen Pashtun tribes generally divided into four major groupings- the Durranis and Ghilzais concentrated in Afghanistan and several tribes such as Khattaks and Bannuchis centred on the North West Frontier province of Pakistan. The Pashtun society and culture has an egalitarian aura with its hierarchical structures and all powerful sardars.

After the formation of Pakistan, the Pashtun nationalists were continuously doubted by the Pakistan government and continuously persecuted for the movement. The nationalist leaders also accepted the establishment of Pakistan as a reality and confined their demand to regional autonomy. However, in the changed political scenario, the Pashtunistan movement continued its influence and maintained its political legitimacy on two grounds: first, trans-border ethnic and cultural contiguity and linkage with Pashtuns in Afghanistan and second, the fear of a socio-economic and cultural subjugation and submergence at the hands of the dominant Punjabi-

Map-12: Khyber Pakhtunkhwa.

Muhajir elite in the state structure. This fear of the dominance by the non-Pashtun elite to the hold up of cultural heritage in the guise of Muslim nationalism led the strong provincial autonomy movement to guarantee cultural, social and economic rights. This fear was almost common in all the major provinces, therefore this led to the unification of all the ethno-cultural movements from East Pakistan, Sind, NWFP and Baluchistan in 1957. National Awami Party was also formed by the all regional parties of East Pakistan, Sind, N.W.F.P and Baluchistan and its programme was strictly anti-imperialist and demanded autonomy to all the major provinces. But the NAP was banned in 1975 by the Pakistan government blaming that it was working against the integrity of the country by 'preaching a four-nation theory',[70] proclaiming that four provinces in Pakistan were actually for nations and had a right to self-determination. Its senior leaders were banned and its chief Pashtun leader, Wali Khan, son of Ghaffar Khan was arrested.

After, the ban on NAP, the Pashtun leaders formed the National Democratic Party (NDP) in 1976. Its leaders initially maintained that the question of autonomy was a settled matter in the 1973 constitution and there was little room for reopening the issue. But they remained ambivalent throughout till the Soviet invasion of Afghanistan and the subsequent war that severely damaged their credibility and social base.

Federal Administrative Tribal Areas (FATA)

Pashtun Nationalist proposes the restructuring of Pakistan state and demanded to unite all Pashtun regions in FATA, Pakistan's North West Frontier province and Northern Baluchistan in a new province of Pakhtoonkhwa that would have greater autonomy. This demand of Pashtun nationalist was the significant development that conflicted directly to the Pakistan's plan to bring of FATA autonomous areas under federal control. Pakistan has been using this area as protection tract to give shelter for al-Qaeda and Taliban militants since 9/11.

After creation of Pakistan, although the princely states of the NWFP area were abolished, there continue to be eleven designated 'tribal' areas called Federally Administered Tribal Areas (FATA). FATA is a semi-autonomous tribal region and are partly controlled by the Pakistan's Federal government. FATA, in north western Pakistan, consists with seven tribal districts and six frontier regions bordering along-side the Afghanistan province of Kunar, Nangarhar, Patika, Khost, and Paktika to the west and the north; and in the North western Pakistan's provinces of Khyber Pakhtunkhwa and Baluchistan to the east and south. These are Pakistan's Pashtun majority territories who also live in the neighbouring provinces of Khyber Pakhtunkhwa areas and Northern Baluchistan. These 'tribal' areas retain considerable ethnic autonomy. Pakistan govern the FATA areas through the 1901 British Regulation; central and provincial laws do not apply neither the Pakistan's Supreme Court has any jurisdiction. They are ruled by customary laws and a special set of Laws - the Frontier Crimes Regulations. These areas have complete different political and electoral system than rest of the Pakistan.

Pakistan's government control over the Tribal areas was increased since the soviet Occupation of Afghanistan in 1985-86. The continued insurgency in Afghanistan and the sudden deterioration of the situation in Pakistan's North-West Frontier Province make the Pashtun tribes the prime target in the war against terror. The use of FATA as a place for the hide and staging area by al-Qaeda and Taliban forces since the 9/11 has destabilized the areas. The US invasion of Afghanistan in 2001 forced al-Qaeda and Taliban militants to flee to FATA and moved freely across the border. The Taliban and the Mujahedin militant forces operated from Pakistan against the US forces. Pakistani government did not have direct control over these areas and Pakistan allows many militants to launch terror attacks on Afghanistan territory. Until the fall of the Taliban regime in Afghanistan, FATA had cordial ties with Islamabad, but since 2001 a deep mistrust has developed towards Pakistan's federal government. Apart from the humanitarian and economic considerations, the refugees posed a security dilemma because of the presence of large number of refugees from Afghanistan mainly Pashtuns. Over 3 million Afghan refugees came to Pakistan where one out of three of the population were refugees.

The political conditions in the NWFP remained fluid. Continuing political instability, and dissatisfaction with the administration and government policy were reflected in the incident of the Pathan Islamists revolt in Malakand in November 1994 in which at least 200 people died.[71] The Musharraf government favourable policies towards the United States and military support to war on terror annoyed the population of NWFP to such an extent that a pro-Taliban religious coalition, the Muttahida Majlis-e-Amal (MMA) came into power in the province. This has brought about greater orthodoxy and repression of the rights of women and religious and ethnic minorities in NWFP. The US bombings of Afghanistan in October 2001 meant a further influx of refugees, who continue to reside in the province.

From the Soviet invasion of Afghanistan in the 1980s, Pashtuns were tools in the hands of Pakistan and were the direct victims of the "war on terror". Young Pashtuns have become involved in suicide bombings and radicalised the Pashtun Areas which go against their tribal and religious values. A new breed of extremist Islamic sect is taking shape and both the Afghanistan and Pakistan Border have intensified the Islamist zealotry and Pashtun Nationalism. The success and presence of Taliban which have local support bases in KPK and FATA is not simply the result of the inherent predisposition of Pashtuns and Pashtun Society towards violence and extreme social conservatism instead the longer-term patronage by Pakistani military and intelligence services to Taliban.

One of the most controversial actions undertaken by the MMA-led government in NWFP was the adoption of the Hisba bill in 2005. The bill proposed to establish a strict religious regime within the social and legal framework and safeguarding the 'Islamic values. Its provisions were highly ambiguous and were perceived by minority groups as an attempt by the religious orthodoxy to repress all forms of human rights and civil liberties under the guise of 'Islamization'. The proposed legislation was declared unconstitutional and against the provisions of Islam by the Supreme court.

The Court cancellation of the Bill led to political agitation and unrest by the MMA and those who support religious orthodoxy.

In January 2017, Pakistan's federal government under Nawaz Sharif decided to merge FATA with Khyber Pakhtunkhwa and repeal of the Frontier Crimes Regulations after approval from the Cabinet. In 2016, the FATA Reforms Committee proposed a set of "parallel and concurrent" political, administrative, judicial and security reforms, as well as a massive reconstruction and rehabilitation programme for the FATA and recommended to prepare a plan for merger of FATA with Khyber Pakhtunkhwa. Under the plan, FATA would be put under the control of the provincial government through amendments to the Frontier Crimes Regulation (FCR). An annual grant of Rs. 100 billion has been proposed for FATA's development under the proposed merger and the amount will be given from the Federal Divisible Pool. The proposal was finalised and the Prime minister gave approval and on March 2017 the Federal Cabinet approved the merger plan. This proposal has not yet been passed by the parliament.[72]

Although all the political parties supported this move including Pakistan Tahreek-e-Insaf, Awami National Party (ANP), Pakistan People's Party (PPP), Qaumi Watan Party (QWP) and Jamaat-e-Islami, but the JUI- a major ally of the ruling Nawaz Sharif party opposed this move. Pakistan recommendation to merge FATA with Pakhtunkhwa have many reasons. The special status for areas is the reason behind its backwardness that has blocked the developments and paved the way for extremist groups to increase their influence. FATA locals criticised that Pakistan government has deliberately kept the British system in place so that it could use the areas as a buffer region against Afghanistan and intended to control the area in an ever-changing geopolitical situation. However, many experts believe that changing the status of FATA bringing it to Pakistan's mainstream political and legal system will not be effective in tackling the insurgency issue. Pashtun nationalist leaders opposes the merger, saying that the FATA people have the right to remain independent from Pakistan. "FATA is not the only place where terrorists have their safe havens. The new measures are just an excuse for Islamabad to undermine the independence of FATA's people," said Usman Kakar, a Pakistani senator belonging to the Pakhtunkhwa Milli Awami Party.[73]

The Afghan government also opposed the Pakistan move. Pakistan did not consult Afghanistan government on this matter and unilaterally imposed its decision. Afghanistan has bigger claim than Pakistan due to its historical ties with FATA. Afghanistan does not recognize the Durand Line as the official border between Afghanistan and Pakistan, nor do they recognize

FATA as part of Pakistan. The Pashtuns people can easily travel back and forth across the border. But the deteriorating political ties between the two countries are now causing them problems. "FATA and other areas across the Durand Line are unstable and any political change in this situation will further destabilize them."[74] The presence of the Pakistani military in the FATA region will force militants to move their bases to the other side of the Durand line and operate from Afghan soil. Pakistan has already been targeting the groups those posing threats to its interests. Experts view that there is a lack of will on Pakistan's part to stop Islamists from launching attacks from the tribal areas into Afghanistan. Afghan's government believe that in the existing conflicting situation, Pakistan has no intention to involve the local of FATA people in this decision-making process.

Main Issues

The main issues and problems of the Pashtun people are:

- About 30 million to 35 million Pashtuns live in both Afghanistan and Pakistan and since 1947 Pakistan, Pakistan has been following the colonial system and deliberately kept the Pashtun people ignorant, illiterate and uneducated. Only selected families got modern education and had appointed on the top military position. Pakistan's military rulers have an interest in keeping the masses of Pashtun people ignorant.
- The Colonial British rulers and then the Pakistan rulers have followed the old British policy of divide-and-rule till now to play off local Pashtun leaders and in exchange require their loyalty. Pakistan has been using the Pashtuns to dominate other minority groups in other provinces of the state. For instance, the settlement of Pashtuns in the Baluchistan and appointment of Pashtun in the Pakistani military was intended to dominate Balochs, who have been struggling to gain their autonomy since the creation of Pakistan. Without the support of the Pashtun tribes, the Pakistan Army would be unable to control a widespread Baloch insurgency.
- Pashtuns are divided and engaged in internal feuds. Ever since British rule in India, Pashtun tribes have been in conflict either against foreign intruders or among themselves. There has also been severe class conflict between landlords and tenants among Pathans.
- They have deliberately been kept away from modern social and economic development. The economy of the NWFP is still weak. Economic development is not welcomed by some Pathan leaders who have attempted to impede the development as the road

construction in fear that this would erode their own autonomy. Large amounts of opium are produced and consumed in Pathan areas and are an important economic factor.

- Pashtun elites and middle-classes have been historically been, a crucial backbone in the military and intelligence services in Pakistan. In recent years have increased their numbers in the civil service and bureaucracy. It increased indicate the change of Punjabi and Muhajir dominance.
- Geographically, the Pashtun areas are better integrated into Pakistani economy but this is not advantageous for Pashtuns as it is excessively dependent on Punjab province and are dominated by big business interests of in Karachi and Lahore. Pashtun resented towards Punjabi domination focuses and alleged discrimination against the North West Frontier Province in allocation of development expenditure in industrial and agriculture. Pakistan Central government deliberately disrupting the electrification of the Pashtun regions because it does not want them to become industrialised and most of the electricity produce in the region goes to Punjab specifically. Pakistan has been discriminating it in agriculture development even the funds for irrigations primarily use for Punjab and other regions.
- There are vast disparities in the infrastructural and institutional capacities of cities in term of political, institutional, and economic developments in comparison of Punjab. Pashtun who are loyal and strongmen, are employed in daily wages labour in the urban centres like Karachi, Islamabad, and Lahore. The structural conditions that have, over a number of years, pushed Pashtuns into migrations and wage labour in these cities because of the military operations, FCR laws and the uneven distribution of resources and violence and war of terror.
- Pashtuns people are also dissatisfied with Pakistan government resistance to use the Pashto language as the medium of instruction in education. Urdu is the medium of education in state schools with Pashto taught as the optional subject up to eight standards. Pashtun children not only attend the classes conducted in urdu but also use textbook written in Urdu though English is permitted in civil examinations and university and graduate school entrance examination.[75]
- Today they are the direct victims of the "war on terror". The majority of Pashtuns have fallen prey to Arab and Pakistani propaganda against the West. During the Soviet invasion of

Afghanistan in the 1980s, they were tools in the hands of Pakistan and Saudi Arabia. They have lived in poverty and become the proxy soldiers in the confrontation between the West and the Islamic extremists. The young Pashtuns have been radicalised since almost three decades in madrassas (seminaries) for financed by Saudi Arabia and Gulf Countries. The young Pashtuns have become involved in suicide bombing, menaces to cohesion of Pashtun tribal structure and religious values.

- Pashtun peoples are exploited for the benefit of Central of power and the ruling classes that inhabit them. KPK, FATA, and Baluchistan, have borne the brunt of conflicts in the region for the benefit of the Pakistan Central power and its ruling classes because they say the Taliban is an "internal [Pashtun] problem", absolving the ruling classes from any responsibility or creating the conditions of violence in the first place.
- The Pakistani military particularly since the 1980s has been used the areas bordering Afghanistan – Baluchistan, KPK, and most intensely FATA, Afghanistan itself has been a playground for its own geopolitical agenda combined with the US imperial interests in the Global war on terror. General Musharraf sought the co-operation of religious leaders to radicalised the Pashtuns tribes. In fact, extremist religious groups and local Taliban have become an excuse for Musharraf to continue his military rule. Instead, Pakistan's ISI and military services were able to persuade the United States to accept their ill-conceived tribal policies of promoting radical extremist leaders to detriment of more traditional moderate Pashtun leaders.
- Pashtuns are identified as "terrorists", or are blamed as a group for bombings, the drug trade, or criminality by Pakistan's political, military and other officials.
- Pakistan looks at the problem of terrorism as, somehow, a Pashtun problem. "It's their ("tribal") people, and their ("tribal") region, they understand this violence".[76] The issue of armed religious militancy is reduced to a "cultural" one. The success and presence of the Taliban, which does have local support bases in KPK and FATA, is not simply as a result of this assumed inherent predisposition of Pashtuns and Pashtun society towards violence and extreme social conservatism. Instead, the story of the Taliban, which is itself comprised of different and changing units, is made possible by the longer-term patronage by Pakistani military and intelligence services of different Taliban factions. The fact that

the Taliban is also have strong base in Punjab and drawn from ethnic Punjabis. Moreover, when local populations do join the Taliban ranks, there are complex regional, historical, political, social, and economic factors that shape these decisions.

- Pakistan Military interests are neither in the interestsof the west nor of the Pashtuns. Keeping Pashtuns tribes divided and backward might serve the short and long-term militaristic interests of Pakistan.

Pakistan of today is standing at a critical juncture. With the radical Islam on rise, there is a serious concern about the growing nuclear arsenal and if they are fall into the hand of radical militants. The fundamentalists have long standing support from the State with the help of a section of the military and Inter Service Intelligence, both have close link with the country's Islamist terrorist groups beside the Taliban and Al Qaeda. This was the consideration behind Pakistan's initial support of the Taliban regime because after the cold war, there were six or seven countries in support of the Northern alliance and Pakistan's only option was support of the southern faction in pursuit of its interests. Contrary to popular opinion, Pakistan's change of policy in Afghanistan post 9/11 was not a sharp turn as it is made out to be-it was a long curve because Pakistan was aware of the fact that the Taliban were being financed and controlled by external actors with their own agenda. The role of Pakistan as frontline state serving American interests in the war against communist Soviet Union, led to a major fall out for Pakistan and its society.

Dynamics of existing current internal crisis in Pakistan are very complex and deep rooted in its history and politics for many decades. Motives of politics, sectarianism, separatism and fundamentalism are overlapping with the forces of migration, identity, doctrinal disputes and legacy of violent exclusionary political culture. Despite the ideological agenda, these crises are socio-ethnic and economic. A sense of belonging to the territory together with religious and linguistic distinction, these conflicts have created problems of Gilgit-Baltistan, Baluchistan, Pashutnistan or Sindh vs Muhajirs-a fight against outsider. They are further complicated and antagonised over the flux in socio- economic structures and distribution and exploitation of economic and natural resources of one region of Pakistan for the benefit of others region, one ethnic community to the others ethnic community.

Notes

1. The blasphemy law was foisted by the Gen. Zia-ul-Haqin 1986. Since then more than 500 Muslims, 340 Ahmadis, 119 Christians, 14 Hindus and 10 others have been charged under the Laws , Pioneer, March 6, 2011.

2. Global Restriction on Religion, Pew Research Centre, June 21, 2018.
3. Human Rights Watch World Report 2013.
4. http://tribune.com.pk/story/289063 pakistan-educationalsystem-fuels-religious-discrimination-rport/.
5. http://eprints.lse.ac.uk/2900/1/ dealing with dirt and disorder -lser 0version.pdf.
6. National Database and Registration Authority, Pakistan, 2012.
7. http://www.the guardian.com/world/2014/jan/15.
8. Maulana Maududi, Towards Understanding Islam, p. 131; Farahnaz Ispahani, Cleansing Pakistan of Minorities, Hudson Institute, July 31, 2013> https// www.hudson.org/research/9781.
9. Yaqoob Khan Bangash, Three Forgotten Accessions-Gilgit, Hunza , Nagar, the Journal of Imperial and Commonwealth History, 38:1, pp. 125-126.
10. Adrija Roy Chowdhary, Gilgit Baltistan: A Bumpy History, Indian Express. March 27, 2017.
11. Aziz-ud-din Ahmad, Status of Gilgit -Baltistan, Jan.16, 2016.
12. Government of Gilgit Baltistan, Indian Express.
13. Prabhas K Dutta, Gilgit Baltistan: Story of How Region 6 Times the Size of POK passed on to Pakistan, India Today , March 25 ,2017.
14. Dr. Javed Iqbal. Gilgit Baltistan Order 2018, Greater Kashmir, June 4,2018.
15. Aziz-ud-din Ahmad, Status of Gilgit Baltistan, Jan. 16, 2016.
16. The Huffpost India, March 25, 2017.
17. Nirupama Subramanian, Gilgit-Baltistan: Alienation is an Issue but No Connect to India, Indian Express, March 17, 2019; Amir Hussain, Development challenges in Gilgit Baltistan, the international News CN, March, 23, 2018.
18. Aziz Ali Dad,The Sectarian Spectre in Gilgit Baltistan, Siasat Pakistan, June 2013.
19. India Protest Chinas plans for the POK investments.html http://www.livemint.com/ politics/nx9251by bqexgibm in 9ch551/.
20. Pok leaders justify India objection to Chinese projects http://www.theaindian.com/ newsportal feature/100260698.
21. *Ibid.*
22. Prateek Joshi, India Should Reach out To the People of Gilgit Baltistan, the Diplomate, sept. 1, 2016.
23. The Times of India> thetimesofindia.com/ india/need-to-factor-in-our-106km-border-with-afghanistan-nsa/articlesnow/47391553.
24. *Ibid.*
25. Manoj Bajpai, Why India Insist on Keeping Gilgit Baltistan Firmly in Kashmir, the Wire, June 2, 2015.
26. Population Census of Pakistan, 2017.
27. Demographic of Sindh, Wikipedia.
28. Farhan Hanif,Hanif Siddiqi, the Politics Of Ethnicity in Pakistan: Baloch, Sindh and Mohajir Ethnic Movement, Routledge 2012, p.88.
29. Agha Gul, Should Pakistan Be BrokenUp? World Sindhi Congress, 2014.
30. Orla Guerin, Karachi faces Growing Taliban Menaces, BBC News June 5,2012.
31. *Ibid.*
32. Global Voice>https://globalvoiceonline.org/2012/03/28/pakistan.

33. JST demands Sindh's Independence, Dawn Newspaper, March 18, 2012 https://www.dawn.com/news/70341.

34. Mohd. Waseem, Ethnic Conflict in Pakistan : the Case of MQM, the Pakistan Development review , 35:4 part II(Winter 1996) pp.617-692.

35. Aisha Shahzad, Ethnic Politics of Mohajir Quomi Movement from 1983-1993, Journal Of South Asian Studies, 01(02) 2013, pp.105-121.

36. Dr. Sonam Dixit, Identity Politis and Conflict in Pakistan: the Case of Mohajir Community, Justice (Legal Affairs Council) IPC India, June 15, 2015 https://www.linkedin.com.

37. Pakistan- Sindh and Mohajirs, Minority Rights Group international, updated Jnue 2018.; Farhat Haq, Rise of MQM in Pakistan , Politics of Ethnic Mobilization, Asian survey , Vol.35, No.11, Nov. 1995, pp. 990-1004.

38. Noman Baig, From Mohallah to Mainstream : the MQM"s Transformation from an Ethnic to a Catch -All Party, (A thesis) University of Central Oklahoma, 2005.

39. The Express tribune, Karachi Pakistan, 21-2-2013.

40. The Government Repeal Sindh Local Government Act, the Express Tribune, Pakistan, February 21, 2013.

41. Sindh Assembly Approved Amendment in Local Government Act, the Express Tribune Pakistan, October 13, 2013.

42. Arif Hasan, Karachi:The Transport City, The project financed by the IIED, UK, 2015; Karachi Population, world Population Review 2019.

43. *Ibid.*

44. Census of 2017.

45. This figure does not include migration from other countries.

46. *Arif Hasan,* Sindh Local Government: The Real Issues,The Express Tribune, January 11, 2012.

47. Kalat was the Baloch confederacy established in 1666 by Ahmadzias.

48. Khan, A., Baloch Ethnic Nationalism in Pakistan: From Guerrilla war to nowhere? (PP.281-293). Asian Ethnicity: 4:2. 2003, P.284; Rehman, R. (2005). The Crisis in Balochistan. In South Asian journal. April-June 2005, pp.1-8>http;//www. south asian media. net/magazine/journal/8_balochistan.htm.

59. Awan, A,B., Balochistan: historical and Political Process. London : New Century Publishers. 1985, p. 120.

50. See Articles-1 and IV of the Agreement, Khan 1975, pp. 147-149.

51. How Balochistan Became a Part of Pakistan-a Historical Perspective, the Nation, Dec.5,2015. Baloch 2009, p. 352.

52. Selig S. Harrison, Shadow Baluchistan: Baluch Nationalism and SovietTemptations, 1981, New York / Washington: Carnegie Endowment for International Peace.

53. Pakistan/ Balochistan-1947-Present>https://uca.edu/politicalscience /dadm project.

54. Another Face of Terror, the New York Times, July 31, 2005.

55. Kurkreeja, V. Contemporary Pakistan: Political Processes, Conflicts and Crisis. New Delhi: Sage,2003 p. 133.

56. Human Rights Watch Report July, 2011.

57. Satenly Johny, Improvished Balochistan Bleeds through a thousand Cuts, the Hindu, August 16, 2016.

58. http://www.aljazeera/com/indepth/features/2014/2.

59. "The Future is at Stake" Attacks on Teachers Schools in Pakistan's Balochistan Province, Human Rights Watch, 2010.
60. Pakistan: World Report 2016, Human Rights Watch.
61. Aljazeera world News-Balochistan: Pakistan's Other War, November 16, 2016.
62. Jetly, R. Baloch ethnicity and Nationalism (1971-81): an assessment, Asian ethnicity, 5:1, (PP7-26) 2004, p.10; Daily Dawn, Disarming of Militants needed for Peace: President Denies Army Action. (Editorial). Feb 4. Dawn, 2006.
63. 37% Baloch favour Independence, UK survey, The International News, August 13, 2012.
64. Malik Siraj Akbar, the end of Pakistan's Baloch Insurgency, world Post, November 3, 2014.
65. The Dawn, April 18, 2016; Second tire, Third Tire Baloch Militant surrender or Killed , Geo.tv. august 29, 2016.
66. Lester Kurtz, The Khudi Khidmatgar (Servants of God) Movement: Badhshah Khan and The Northwest Frontier in British India 1933-37, International Centre on Nonviolent conflict, July 2009.
67. The Pashtunistan Issue, The US Library of Congress>countryside.us/ Afghanistan/23.
68. Pashtun People, New World Encyclopedia>www.newworldencylopedia.org/entry/ Pashtun people; UNHCR Statistical Summary Report 2006; Afghanistan CIA world Facebook, 2006.
69. Afghanistan Census of Population and Housing: Phase one Household Listing, UNFPA Projects in Afghanistan, 18 February 2007.
70. B.M. Kutty, In Search of Solution: The Autobiography of Mir Ghaus Busksh Bizenjo, Karachi, 2009, p. 20.
71. Pashtuns-Minority Rights Groups https://minorityrights.org/monories/Pashtun.
72. Masood Saifullah, Riaz Sayed, Shamil Shams, Pakistan Struggle to Bring Tribal Areas into Mainstreams, March 23/3/2017 DW/http://p.dw.com/p/2ZpWC.
73. *Ibid.*
74. *Ibid.*
75. Selig S Harrison 'Pashtunistan': The Challenge to Pakistan and Afghanistan, Centre for International Policy Area: Security & Defence - ARI 37/2008 Date: 2/4/2008 2.
76. Sanaa Alimia, On Discrimination Against Pashtun: Reflections from Peshawar, August 2015.

Appendix-4

Separatist Movements of Pakistan

Balochistan

- Ethnic group: Baloch
- Proposed state: Balochistan
- Political party: Baloch National Movement, Baloch Republican Party (member of the Unrepresented Nations and Peoples Organization)
- Militant organisations: Baloch Liberation Army, Baloch Liberation Front, Baloch Republican Army

Sindh

- Ethnic group: Sindhi
- Proposed state: Sindhudesh
- Political party: Jeay Sindh Qaumi Mahaz
- Militant organizations: Sindhudesh Liberation Army

Gilgit-Baltistan

- Ethnic group: Balti people
- Proposed state: Balawaristan or Republic of Gilgit-Baltistan
- Political party: Balawaristan National Front, Gilgit-Baltistan United Movement

Khyber Pakhtunkhwa

Ethinic group:Pashtu

Proposed state: Pashutinistan

Political Party: Awami National party and PPP

Table-15: Pakistan - Terrorist, insurgent and extremist groups

Proscribed Terrorist/Extremist Groups	***Active Terrorist/Insurgent Groups***	***Inactive Terrorist/Insurgent Groups***
1. Sipah-e- Sahaba Pakistan (SSP) 2. Tehreek-e- Nafaz-e- Shariat-e-Mohammadi (TNSM) 3. Lashkar-e- Jhangvi (LeJ) 4. Sipah-e- Muhammad Pakistan (SMP) 5. Tehreek-e- Jaferia Pakistan (TJP) 6. Lashkar-e- Toiba (LeT) 7. Jaish-e- Mohammad Mujahideen E-Tanzeem 8. Rabita Trust 9. Al-Rashid Trust 10. Al-Akhtar Trust 11. Tehrik-e- Jehad-e- Islami 12. Tehrik-e- Nifaz-e- Fiqar Jafaria 13. Islamic State/Islamic State of Iraq and Levant /Islamic State of Iraq and Syria/Daish (ISIS) 14. Al Qaeda	1. Tehreek-e-Taliban Pakistan (TTP) 2. Hizb-ul- Mujahideen (HM) 3. Harkat-ul- Ansar (HuA, presently known as Harkat-ul Mujahideen) 4. Harkat-ul Mujahideen (HuM, previously known as Harkat-ul-Ansar) 5. Al Badr 6. Jamait-ul- Mujahideen (JuM) 7. Lashkar-e- Jabbar (LeJ) 8. Harkat-ul- Jehad-al- Islami (HUJI) 9. Muttahida Jehad Council (MJC) 10. Al Barq 11. Tehrik-ul- Mujahideen 12. Jammu & Kashmir National Liberation Army 13. People's League 14. Muslim Janbaz Force 15. Kashmir Jehad Force 16. Al Jehad Force (combines Muslim Janbaz Force and Kashmir Jehad Force 17. Al Umar Mujahideen 18. Mahaz-e- Azadi 19. Islami Jamaat-e- Tulba 20. Jammu & Kashmir Students Liberation Front 21. Ikhwan-ul- Mujahideen 22. Islamic Students League 23. Tehrik-e- Hurriat-e- Kashmir 24. Muslim Mujahideen 25. Al Mujahid Force 26. Baloch Republican Army (BRA) 27. Jamaat-ul-Ahrar (JuA) 28. Lashkar-e-Islam (LI) 29. Haqqani Network (HN) 30. Balochistan Liberation Front (BLF) 31. Hizb-ut-Tahrir (HuT) 32. Tariq Gidar Group (TGG) 33. Jama'at-ul-Dawa al-Quran (JDQ) 34. United Baloch Army (UBA) 35. Baloch Liberation Army (BLA) 36. Tanzeem-ul-Islami-ul-Furqan (TIF) 37. Taliban 38. Baloch Republican Guards (BRG) 39. Baloch Liberation United Front (BLUF)	1. Lashkar-e- Omar (LeO) 2. Jamaat-ul- Fuqra 3. Nadeem Commando 4. Popular Front for Armed Resistance 5. Muslim United Army 6. Harkat-ul- Mujahideen Al-alami (HuMA) 7. Al Jehad 8. Ummah Tamir-e- Nau 9. Islami Inquilabi Mahaz 10. Al Mustafa Liberation Fighters 11. Ahrar-ul-Hind (AH) 12. Ansarul Islam (AI) 13. Lashkar-e-Balochistan (LeB) 14. Sindhudesh Liberation Army (SLA) 15. Sunni Tehreek (ST) 16. Ghazi Force (GF)

Source: South Asia Terrorist Portal 2019.

Appendix - 5

Pakistan

A chronology of key events:

Muhammed Ali Jinnah - founding father of Pakistan,Born in Karachi, 1876. Pakistan's first head of state until his death in 1948.

Screening the life of Jinnah

1906 - Muslim League founded as forum for Indian Muslim separatism.

1940 - Muslim League endorses idea of separate state for India's Muslims.

1947 - Muslim state of East and West Pakistan created out of partition of India at the end of British rule. Hundreds of thousands die in widespread communal violence, and millions are made homeless.

1948 - Muhammed Ali Jinnah, founding leader of Pakistan, dies. First war with India over disputed territory of Kashmir.

Military rule

1951 - Jinnah's successor Liaquat Ali Khan is assassinated.

1956 - Constitution proclaims Pakistan an Islamic republic.

1958 - Martial law declared and General Ayyub Khan takes over.

War and secession

1965 - Second war with India over Kashmir.

1969 - General Ayyub Khan resigns and General Yahya Khan takes over.

1970 - Victory in East Pakistan election for breakaway Awami League, leading to rising tension with West Pakistan.

1971 - East Pakistan attempts to secede, leading to civil war. India intervenes in support of East Pakistan, which eventually breaks away to become Bangladesh.

General Zia's death in 1988 ended 11-year military rule

Echoes of General Zia

1972 - Simla peace agreement with India sets new frontline in Kashmir.

1973 - Populist Zulfiqar Ali Bhutto becomes prime minister.

Zia takes charge

1977 - Riots erupt over allegations of vote-rigging by Zulfiqar Ali Bhutto's Pakistan People's Party (PPP). General Zia ul-Haq launches military coup.

1978 - General Zia becomes president, ushers in Islamic legal system.

1979 - Zulfiqar Ali Bhutto hanged amid international protests.

1980 - US pledges military assistance to Pakistan following Soviet intervention in Afghanistan.

1985 - Martial law and political parties ban lifted.

1986 - Zulfiqar Ali Bhutto's daughter Benazir returns from exile to lead PPP in campaign for fresh elections.

1988 August - General Zia, US ambassador, and top army brass die in air crash.

Bhutto comeback

1988 November - Benazir Bhutto's PPP wins general election.

1990 - Benazir Bhutto dismissed as prime minister on charges of incompetence and corruption.

1991 - Conservative Prime Minister Nawaz Sharif begins economic liberalisation programme. Islamic Sharia law formally incorporated into legal code.

1992 - Government launches campaign to stamp out violence by Urdu-speaking supporters of the Mohajir Quami Movement.

1993 - Prime Minister Sharif resigns under pressure from military. General election brings Benazir Bhutto back to power.

Nuclear tests

1996 - President Leghari dismisses Bhutto government amid corruption allegations.

1997 - Nawaz Sharif returns as prime minister after Muslim League wins elections.

1998 - Pakistan conducts its own nuclear tests after India explodes several nuclear devices.

1999 April - Benazir Bhutto and husband convicted of corruption and given jail sentences. Ms Bhutto stays out of the country.

1999 May - Kargil conflict: Pakistan-backed forces clash with the Indian military in the icy heights around Kargil in Indian-held Kashmir. More than 1,000 people are killed on both sides.

Musharraf coup

1999 October - General Pervez Musharraf seizes power in coup.

2000 April - Nawaz Sharif sentenced to life imprisonment on hijacking and terrorism charges over his actions to prevent the 1999 coup. Goes into exile in Saudi Arabia later in the year after being pardoned by military authorities.

2001 June - Gen Musharraf names himself president while remaining head of the army.

2001 September - President Musharraf backs the US in its fight against terrorism and supports attacks on the Taliban and al-Qaeda in Afghanistan. US lifts some sanctions imposed after Pakistan's nuclear tests in 1998.

2002 January - President Musharraf bans two militant groups - Lashkar-e-Toiba and Jaish-e-Mohammad-and takes steps to curb religious extremism.

2002 April - President Musharraf wins another five years in office in a controversial referendum.

Thaw with India

2003 November - Pakistan declares a Kashmir ceasefire; India follows suit.

2003 December - Pakistan and India agree to resume direct air links and to allow overflights of each other's planes from beginning of 2004, after a two-year ban.

2004 February - Nuclear scientist Abdul Qadeer Khan admits to having leaked nuclear weapons secrets, reportedly to Libya, North Korea and Iran.

2004 June - Pakistan mounts first military offensive against suspected al-Qaeda militants and their supporters in tribal areas near Afghan border. US begins using drone strikes to target al-Qaeda leaders in the area.

2004 April - Parliament approves creation of military-led National Security Council, institutionalising role of armed forces in civilian affairs.

2005 April - Bus services, the first in 60 years, operate between Muzaffarabad in Pakistani-administered Kashmir and Srinagar in Indian-controlled Kashmir.

2005 August - Pakistan tests its first nuclear-capable cruise missile.

Kashmir quake

2005 October - Earthquake kills tens of thousands of people in Pakistani-administered Kashmir.

2007 February - Pakistan and India sign an agreement aimed at reducing the risk of accidental nuclear war.

Musharraf targets judiciary

2007 March - President Musharraf suspends Chief Justice Iftikhar Mohammed Chaudhry, triggering a wave of protests across the country.

2007 July - Security forces storm the jihadist-occupied Red Mosque complex in Islamabad following a week-long siege.

2007 October - Ex-prime minister Benazir Bhutto returns from exile. Dozens of people die in a suicide bomb targeting her homecoming parade in Karachi.

2007 October-November - Musharraf wins presidential election but is challenged by Supreme Court. He declares emergency rule, dismisses Chief Justice Chaudhry and appoints new Supreme Court, which confirms his re-election.

2007 November - Former prime minister Nawaz Sharif returns from exile.

Bhutto killed, Musharraf resigns

2007 December - Benazir Bhutto assassinated at political rally at election campaign rally in Rawalpindi.

2008 February-March - Pakistan People's Party (PPP) nominee Yusuf Raza Gilani becomes PM at head of coalition with Nawaz Sharif's Muslim League party following parliamentary elections in February.

2008 August - President Musharraf resigns after the two main governing parties agree to launch impeachment proceedings against him.

Nawaz Sharif pulls his PML-N out of the coalition, accusing the PPP of breaking its promise to reinstate all judges sacked by President Musharraf.

2008 September - MPs elect Pakistan People's Party's (PPP) Asif Ali Zardari - the widower of assassinated former PM Benazir Bhutto - president.

Suicide bombing on Marriott Hotel in Islamabad kills 53 people. Soon after, government launches major offensive in Bajaur tribal area, killing more than 1,000 militants.

2008 November-The government borrows billions of dollars from the International Monetary Fund to overcome its spiralling debt crisis.

Tribal areas turmoil

2008 December - India blames Mumbai attacks in November on Pakistani-based militants, and demands Pakistan take action. Islamabad denies involvement but promises to co-operate with the Indian investigation.

2009 March - After days of protests, government yields to demands for reinstatement of judges dismissed by former President Musharraf.

2009 August - The leader of Pakistan's Taliban, Baitullah Mehsud, is killed in US drone attack in South Waziristan. He is succeeded by Hakimullah Mehsud.

Suicide bombing in northwestern city of Peshawar kills 120 people.

Reform efforts

2010 April-Parliament approves package of wide-ranging constitutional reforms. Measures include transferring key powers from president to prime minister.

2010 August - Worst floods in 80 years kill at least 1,600 people and affect more than 20 million. Government response widely criticised.

Al-Qaeda leader Osama Bin Laden was found hiding in a suburban compound in Pakistan

2011 January - A campaign to reform Pakistan's blasphemy law leads to the killing of two prominent supporters, Punjab Governor Salman Taseer in January, and Minorities Minister Shahbaz Bhatti in March.

2011 April - The founder of al-Qaeda, Osama bin Laden, is killed by American special forces in Abbottabad.

"Memogate"

2011 December - Government comes under pressure over a leaked memo alleging senior officials sought US aid against a military coup after the killing of Osama bin Laden in April.

2012 January - Amid growing tension between government and military over "memogate" scandal, army chief Gen Pervez Kayani warns of "unpredictable consequences" after PM Yousuf Raza Gilani criticises army leaders and sacks top defence official.

2012 May - A US Senate panel cuts $33m in aid to Pakistan over the jailing of Pakistani doctor Shakil Afridi who helped the CIA find Osama Bin Laden.

2012 June - Supreme Court disqualifies Prime Minister Gilani from holding office after he declines to appeal against a token sentence in President Zardari corruption row. Parliament approves Water and Power Minister Raja Pervez Ashraf as his successor.

2012 July - Pakistan agrees to reopen Nato supply routes to Afghanistan after the US apologises for killing Pakistani soldiers in November.

Sunni extremist violence increases

2012 September - Muslim cleric Khalid Chishti is arrested on suspicion of planting burnt pages of the Koran on a Christian girl briefly detained for blasphemy. Amid widespread condemnation of the case against the girl at home and abroad, a court dropped it November.

2012 October - Taliban gunmen seriously injure 14-year-old campaigner for girls' rights Malala Yousafzai, whom they accused of "promoting secularism". The shooting sparked a brief upsurge of anger in Pakistan against the militants.

2012 November - Taliban suicide bomber kills at least 23 people at a Shia Muslim procession in the Rawalpindi.

2013 June - Parliament approves Nawaz Sharif as prime minister after his Muslim League-N wins parliamentary elections in May.

2014 June - A deadly assault on Karachi's international airport leaves dozens dead. Uzbek militants fighting with the Pakistani Taliban say they carried out the attack. Peace talks with the Taliban collapse and the army launches a major offensive on Islamist hideouts in north-west Pakistan.

2014 October - Teenager Malala Yousafzai, who was shot in the head by the Taliban but survived to become a campaigner for girls' education, becomes the youngest person ever to win the Nobel Peace Prize.

Peshawar school attack

2014 December - Taliban kills nearly 150 people - mostly children - in an attack on a school in Peshawar.Government responds to the massacre by lifting a moratorium on the death penalty and launching round-up of terror suspects, although critics complain major terror organisers are left alone.

2015 April - India protests over Pakistan court release on bail of suspected mastermind of 2008 Mumbai terror attacks, Zakiur Rehman Lakhvi. Human rights activist Sabeen Mehmud shot dead in Karachi.

2015 April - China and Pakistan sign agreements worth billions of dollars to boost infrastructure. They are designed to end Pakistan's chronic energy crisis and transform the country into a regional economic hub.

2015 June - Pakistan acknowledges that eight out of ten Taliban members allegedly jailed for the gun attack on teenage education activist and Nobel Prize laureate Malala Yousafzai were secretly acquitted at their trial in April.

2016 November - Gen Qamar Javed Bajwa is named as new army chief. The position is arguably the most powerful in the country.

2017 February - The Islamic State group takes responsibility for a suicide bombing at a major Sufi shrine in Sindh which killed nearly 90 people. Pakistan closes border with Afghanistan.

2017 March - Parliament passes a law allowing the country's Hindu minority to register their marriages for the first time since partition from India in 1947.

Rise of Imran Khan

2017 August - Prime Minister Nawaz Sharif is forced to resign after being disqualified by the Supreme Court over corruption charges. He is convicted and given a jail sentence.

2018 August - Former international cricket star Imran Khan becomes prime minister on a pledge to end corruption and dynastic politics, after his Pakistan Tehreek-e-Insaf (PTI) becomes the largest party in the July general election.

2018 November - Asia Bibi, a Christian woman acquitted of blasphemy after eight years on death row, is freed from prison, prompting violent protests by Islamists.

2019 February - Clashes with India follow an attack by the Pakistan-based Jaish-e Mohammad jihadist group on security forces' convoy in Indian-controlled Kashmir.

Chapter - 5

Afghanistan: Resurgence of Taliban and Terrorism

Insurgency, violence, war and terror is another name of Afghanistan. Since the last fifty years Afghanistan has been constantly involving in internal crisis and civil wars and has gone through several phases. The structure of power has collapsed. Inter-ethnic and sectarian tensions are more pronounced with Wahhabi fundamentalist Islam which has established wider and deeper roots in the country. Regional cleavages are very much deep rooted. The framework of political discourse and processes has increasingly grounded in Islamist ideology. Afghan periphery has become heavily weaponized. The insurgent movements, weapons and money from and to various regions of Afghanistan across international borders whether from Iran, Pakistan, Iraq, Syria, Tajikistan, Uzbekistan, Turkmenistan and China has intensified internal crisis. Not only the regional powers but the world powers have fought in this country and committed many mistakes that have great consequences for Afghanistan as well as for the whole South Asia. Whom to blame? Afghanistan itself, Russia, the United States, Britain Pakistan or the Arabs? Currently, the persistence of the Taliban insurgency is the most devastating challenge that Afghanistan is facing. In the wake of horrific killings and attacks of innocent peoples by Taliban, there is no end of the violence and War, only for the dead, it is the end of war not for living human beings.

Taliban is predominantly a group of Pashtun Islamic extremists and a faction of Mujahedeen who emerged to resist the Soviet Occupation (1979-89) with the covert backing of the United States Central Intelligence Agency and its Pakistan counter part of the Inter service Intelligence. They were joined by younger Pashtun tribesmen who studied in Pakistani madrassas, or seminaries; Pashtuns comprise a plurality in Afghanistan and are the predominant ethnic group in much of the country's south and east. During the period 1989-1992 after the withdrawal of Soviet Russia from the region, an anarchy was followed by the collapse of the Afghan central government. Taliban in fact was emerged as a political and religious force which supposedly opposed the tyrannical rule of the local governor and began to instil greater order in the area. The group, led by Mohammed Omar, had the support of many Afghan refugees from Pakistan and gained increasing recognition, power, and support as it began to take control of much of southern and central Afghanistan. The United States funded the Afghans Mujahideen and Pakistan intelligence service trained and protected this group. The United States provided ammunitions and gave billions of dollars to build this Islamic group to fight against Soviet Russia. It has been said that the U.S. was responsible for providing the Taliban with logistical and military advice, along with military hardware.

The movement attracted popular support in the initial Post-Soviet Era by promising to impose stability and rule of law after four years of conflict (1992–1996) among rival mujahideen groups. Talibs entered Kandahar in November 1994 to pacify the crime-ridden southern city, and by September 1996 seized the capital, Kabul, from President Burhanuddin Rabbani, an ethnic Tajik whom they viewed as anti-Pashtun and corrupt. The Taliban regime controlled some 90 percent of the country before its 2001 overthrow. Taliban imposed its brand of justice as it consolidated territorial control. Taliban jurisprudence was drawn from the Pashtuns' pre-Islamic tribal code and interpretations of Sharia[1] coloured by the austere Saudi' Wahhabi doctrines of the madrassas. The regime neglected social services and other basic state functions even as its Ministry for the Promotion of Virtue and Prevention of Vice enforced prohibitions on behaviour the Taliban deemed un-Islamic, requiring women to wear the head-to-toe burqa, or chadri; banning music and television; and jailing men whose beards it deemed too short.

The Taliban ruled Afghanistan from 1996 until 2001, when a U.S.-led invasion toppled the regime for providing refuge to al-Qaeda and Osama bin Laden. The Taliban regrouped across the border in Pakistan, where its central leadership, headed by Mullah Mohammed Omar, leads an insurgency against the Western-backed government in Kabul. Both the United States and Afghanistan have pursued a negotiated settlement with the Taliban but talks have little momentum as international forces prepare to conclude combat operations in December 2014 and withdraw by the end of 2016.

After the withdrawal of NATO forces in 2014, Taliban insurgency has revived with the rise anti-American and anti-Western sentiments among Afghan warlords due to the abuse by the US forces with prisoners in detention, widespread corruption in the Afghan government and civilian casualties caused by U.S. and NATO bombings and slow pace of reconstruction of Afghanistan. Talibans, whom US-led forces spent billions of dollars to build, trying to defeat by providing provided ammunitions, which they forgot to keep track of after the Soviet war. Thus, the U.S. was taken aback when the weapons that they had provided were now being used against them. Since the Taliban was a creation of the Pakistani intelligence agency. Pakistan has been reluctant to fight them and Pakistani military and other personal are now siding with the Taliban.

The regime was internationally isolated from its inception. Two UN Security Council resolutions passed in 1998 urged the Taliban to end its abusive treatment of women. The following year the council imposed sanctions on the regime for harbouring al-Qaeda. Only Saudi Arabia, the United Arab Emirates, and Pakistan recognized the government. Many analysts say Islamabad supported the Taliban as a force that could unify and stabilize Afghanistan while staving off Indian, Iranian, and Russian influence.

Talibans are now openly active in 70% of Afghanistan territory and control much more territory than when NATO troops left in 2014. Taliban are now in full control of 14 districts (that's 4% of the country) and have an active and open physical presence in a further 263 (66%), significantly higher than previous estimates of Taliban strength. Only in 122 districts (just over 30% of the country) Taliban do not have an open presence.[2] These areas are ranked as under government control, but they are free of violence. Kabul and other major cities, for example, suffered major attacks - launched from adjacent areas, or by sleeper cells. About 15 million people - half the population - are living in areas that are either controlled by the Taliban or where the Taliban are openly present and regularly mount attacks. The Taliban, which had imposed its extremist version of Islam on the entire country, also perpetrated countless human rights abuses against its people, especially women, girls and ethnic group Hazaras. During their rule, large numbers of Afghans lived in utter poverty, and as many as 4 million Afghans are suffered from starvation.

Taliban have their stronghold into eastern, western and northern parts of the country and the areas which have fallen to the Taliban since 2014 include places in Helmand province like Sangin, Musa Qala and Nad-e Ali. In these areas, the militants conduct frequent attacks against Afghan government positions from on military bases to sporadic attacks and ambushes against military convoys and police checkpoints , the BBC study reported.Even ISISI are also more active in Afghanistan than ever before, although it remains far less powerful than the Taliban.

Afghan's Ethnic Structure

The fragmented and polarised nature of Afghan society consisted of many different ethnic groups[3] have multiple internal struggles and gained support from the different external powers. Afghanistan is a country known for the multitude of ethnic groups that live inside its borders, like Pashtun, Tajik, Hazara, Baluchis, Uzbek, Aimak, and Turkmen. The majority of the people have a very low quality of life due to the poor development of the country's economy. In Afghan society, the division between Pashtun who have always been dominant and non-Pashtun, is fragmented among the various other tribes. Two major Pashtun tribes, the Durrani and Ghazali has been struggling to form a united Afghanistan. The non-Pashtun ethnic tribes too remain divided. At religious level too, there is divide between Sunni and Shia which corresponds to the ethnic divide between Hazara and non-Hazara. There are also division among the Sunni between Deobandi of Hanafi sect and those influenced by Wahhabism of Saudi Arabia. So, successive Afghan rulers always tried to unite the different tribe and ethnic and sectarian groups.

The regional cleavages are also very deep in autonomous region. The gulf between the Afghan centre and periphery is also continues to widen, producing degrees of regional political and economic autonomy in Afghanistan. So far six such autonomous regions can be identified: the North-Northeast, predominated by Uzbek, Turkman, Tajik, and other Farsi-speaking groups; the Northwest, in which Farsi speakers predominate; the Central highlands, where Farsi-speaking Shi'a Hazaras predominate; the East-Southeast, where Ghalzi Pashtuns predominate; the Southwest, where Durani Pashtuns predominate; and the West, which is populated by a mix of Ghalzi and Durani Pashtuns and Farsi speakers. In each region, political leadership is provided by former members of the American-sponsored "Freedom Fighters," now labelled "Warlords." The Taliban are the ethnic group composed mainly of Pashtuns belonging to the Ghilzai tribes of eastern Afghanistan, and they began to rise under the leadership of Mullah Muhammad Omar. In the 1990s, the predominately Pashtun Taliban movement encountered a hostile population in the North Afghanistan where the majority of people are not Pashtun. The Taliban fought fierce battles and underwent heavy casualties in wresting[4] control of the region from ethnic Hazara, Tajik, and Uzbek warlords and militia groups, often committing violent atrocities and alienating the local population. These non- Pashtuns' leaders and chiefs later on joined the Taliban because they could not rely on the government for protection, according to Barnett Rubin, a former U.S. State Department official and leading specialist on

Afghanistan. Others had joined Taliban because they feel marginalized by the government in terms of money or political representation.

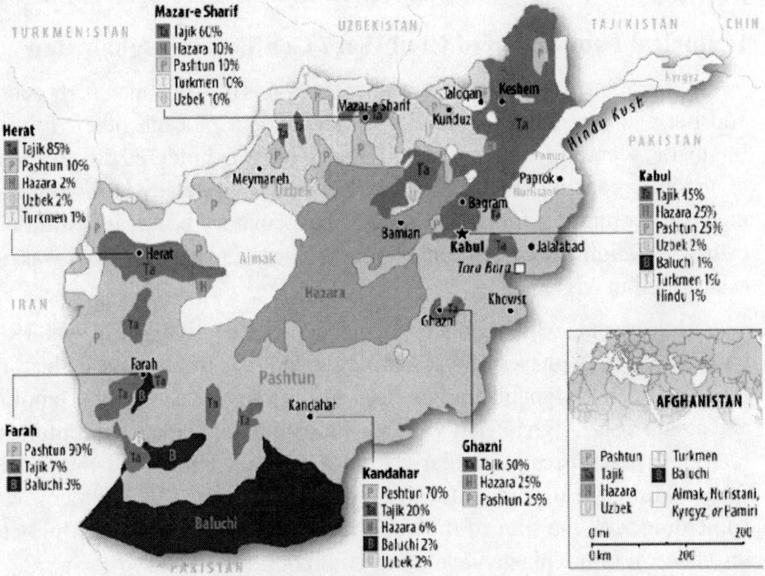

Maps-13: Ethnic Groups in Afghanistan:

The Taliban, though ethnically mainly the Pashto, they had recruited the resented and disgruntled members of other non- Pashtuns groups -Tajiks, Turkmen and Uzbeks who were willing to fight under the flag of the Taliban's Islamic Emirate. With these new recruitments, Taliban's militants had been able to seize the areas outside the Pashtun majority in the south and east of Afghanistan. They had recruited ethnic Tajiks in north eastern Badakhshan Province, and Turkmen and Uzbeks in north western Faryab Province and in the northern province of Jowzjan.[5] It was a clear shift of attitude of Taliban towards recruiting from other ethnic groups and other ethnic groups assumed positions in the Taliban leadership council and key posts in the provinces. Non-Pashtuns makeup around one-quarter of the Taliban leadership council.[6] In Faryab, the Taliban also gave operational command to foreign Uzbek militants of the Islamic Movement of Uzbekistan (IMU), which attracted the local ethnic Uzbeks to their cause.[7] Taliban's ranks have also been supported by hundreds of foreign fighters — including Central Asians, Chechens, and Chinese Uighurs — who resettled in northern Afghanistan after they were flushed out of the Pakistan's tribal regions by a Pakistani military. The Taliban sends cadres to villages to identify and negotiate with tribal chiefs and ethnic leaders susceptible to recruitment, offering power, status, or money, according to Ted Callahan, a western security expert based in Afghanistan.[8] The militant group also sends preachers and established religious school officials to propagate its message.

Historical Foundation of Civil War / Conflicts in Afghanistan

Throughout the history of the state apparatus of Afghanistan, its centre and periphery remained essentially independent of each other. Ethnic, linguistic, sectarian, and regional idioms of identity hindered the prospects of nation, nationality, and nationalism. The poverty, illiteracy, lack of modern means of communications and lack of participatory political institutions caused isolation among the centre and periphery and a nation state was not established in Afghanistan.

Afghanistan, which gained independence after first world war-1919 has passed many phases of wars and internal crisis throughout its history. Geographically Afghanistan has been at the crossroad of many empires and conquerors. Afghanistan's strategic location has made it susceptible to foreign interferences particularly from the Soviet Union and the United States After world war II, the United States emerged as a superpower coinciding with the start of the cold war. because of the strong American influence in Iran, Pakistan and other Gulf countries.

- First Phase -Anglo-Afghan wars.
- Second phase -civil war of 1973
- Third phase 1979-1989-Soviet intervention
- Fourth phase-1992-96- Emergence of Taliban
- Fifth phase 2001-2005-US war against terrorism.
- Sixth phase-Re-emergence of Taliban at present.

The first phase: Anglo-Afghan Wars

Afghanistan had a period of stability which turned immediately into war in the 19th century when Great Britain attacked the country in order to establish their influence in the area. In 1816, Dost Mohammad Khan became the ruler of Afghanistan. Great Britain and Russia manoeuvring for influence in Afghanistan. The British feeling that Dost Mohammad was unable to resist Russian penetration, British forces invaded Afghanistan and appointed King Shah Shujah the chief of the country in 1838. The Afghans could not tolerate neither foreign occupation nor the king imposed upon them, therefore, revolts broke out. In a battle at Parwan on November 1840, Dost Mohammad surrender to the British but the outbreaks continued. In 1842, the king Shuja was assassinated and the country was entered into the phase of unstable peace again when British and Indian troops were massacred during their retreat from Kabul. The situation of war continued till the second Afghan-British war. A Peace Treaty was signed with the British, which gave them the control over the external affairs of Afghanistan.

In November 1875 the British government was concerned primarily with India's relations with Afghanistan. Russian influence was growing in Afghanistan and the British to secure its frontier Sher Ali Khan, Afghan Amir refused the British mission to enter Afghanistan while allowed Russian. British forces invaded Afghanistan on November 1878 and second Anglo-Afghan War took place. Sher Ali fled from the country and the British army occupied Kabul. A treaty was signed at Gandamak (Gandomak) on May 26, 1879, crowning Yaqub Khan as Amir of Afghanistan. Under the treaty, a permanent British embassy at Kabul was established and agreed to conduct country foreign relations with other states in accordance "with the wishes and advice" of the British government. In September 1879, the British forces occupied Kabul on the murdered of British envoy.

With the outbreak World War I, Afghanistan widely supported Ottoman Turkey against Britain. In February 1919, Amanullah Khan took possession of the throne. At that time Britain still exercised an important influence on Afghan affairs. In his coronation address Amanullah declared total independence from Great Britain. This declaration launched the inconclusive Third Anglo-Afghan War in May 1919. A peace treaty recognizing the independence of Afghanistan was signed at Rawalpindi, Pakistan on August 8, 1919, and was amended in 1921. Before signing the final document with the British, the Afghans concluded a treaty of friendship with the new Bolshevik regime in the Soviet Union. Afghanistan thereby became one of the first states to recognize the Soviet government, and a "special relationship" evolved between the two governments that lasted until December 1979, when the Soviet Union intervened in Afghanistan.

The state structure of modern Afghanistan emerged during the colonial period of 1890s. From the starting, the state apparatus of Afghanistan at the centre was heavily subsidized by the British colonial government of India to build its monopoly and exert the political influence over the non-tribal population in the periphery and maintain a strategic distance between the centre and the Pashtun tribal groups on both side of the eastern and southern borders. The British subsidies continued till the year 1919. When Amanullah Khan tried to westernized and introduced social and civil reforms, the Islamists and ethnic tribal groups opposed the state hence, developed social and civil unrest. This culminated in the collapse of the Afghan monarchy in 1929. The monarchy was restored in 1930 with the assistance of the British Government and continued till 1933 when Shah became the king and

Afghanistan remained a monarchy for the following four decades. The country was in a relatively stable period with Great Britain, maintaining its influence till Pakistan and India gained Independence. The most peaceful and stable period in Afghanistan history is from 1933 to 1973 even during the first three decades of the Cold War. Both the United States and USSR provided substantial amounts of economic and military assistance to Afghanistan as a part their cold war politics.

Second Phase: Civil Crisis

Afghanistan again turned into an unstable country in the mid-1970s. The contentious situation arose in Afghanistan in 1973 when Mohammed Daoud overthrew King Zahir Shah, abolished the monarchy and proclaimed himself president of the republic. Political parties were banned and the political activists, specifically of the Islamic Movement, faced severe suppression, most of its leaders were jailed, a few of them escaped to Pakistan. Soviet Union provided support to the government and leaders of Peoples Democratic Party of Afghanistan (PDPA)from the government's crackdown.Butthe deposed king, tribal leaders, representatives of leftist forces and Islamic fundamentalists and their supporters started opposition against Mohammed Daoud.[9] Ultimately, in 1978, a military coup called "the Sour Revolution" was carried the out by the People's Democratic Party of Afghanistan (Marxists) and overthrew the existing government of Mohammed Daoud. President Mohammad Daoud Khan along with 17 members of his family were killed the coup, while many members of the traditional elite, the religious establishment and the intelligentsia were imprisoned, tortured or killed. Five years of presidency of Mohammed Daoud, is a classic example of political exclusion where the state perpetually failed to politically accommodate the collective interests" of other groups seeking participation.

With the help of Soviet Union, new government was formed in Afghanistan by the People's Democratic Party of Afghanistan (Marxists) under the leadership of Noor Mohammad Taraki. Although the Soviet Union was not directly involved in the revolution but it appeared to Soviet representatives in Kabul like "a bolt from the blue".[10] Such a turn of events was welcomed by the USSR even more so since the members of the PDPA proclaimed a policy of establishing socialism in the country. This, in fact, set the tone for overall aid and support to the new regime from the Soviet leadership. From the beginning, the Taraki' government received significant amounts of aid from the Communist Soviet Union in the form of military equipment and Soviet advisors. Nur Mohammad Taraki government began to implement the Communist policies on a nation with a deep Islamic religious culture but it was resisted by the Mujahedeen. It was resulted in armed uprisings and harsh-bloody government repression. Mujahedeen, a loosely-aligned opposition groups of Pashtun tribesmen and other left-wing groups began attacks aimed at overthrowing the Marxist-Leninist government of President Taraki.

From that moment Afghanistan found itself drawn into the orbit of the fierce confrontation of the "Cold War" between two different socio-political systems which made Afghanistan important to both the US and USSR. On the other hand, the PDPA party itself was divided into two rival factions which actually fought each other for control of the government as the same time battling with the Islamic rebels. The one group was led by presidents Nur Mohammad Taraki and Hafizullah Amin and Second group by Babrak Karmal and Dr. Najibullah. The situation in the country deteriorated with a possible armed conflict between the two sides. The Afghan army failed in fighting the Mujahedeen resistance and removing the other left-wing opposition. Consequently, the ruling party requested the Soviet Union army support in order to prevent the Mujahedeen from taking over power. There was a massive initial deployment of Soviet Army troops into Afghanistan in 1979.

Third Phase – Soviet Invasion

On December 24, 1979, the soviet forces moved in Afghanistan and occupied the country. Hafiz ullah Amin was killed and the Soviet Union installed the new government under Babrak Karmal. the Soviet Invasion got strong reaction from world community. The Soviet invasion brought the conflict into the realm of Cold War politics. The US saw this as a prime opportunity to weaken and resist the Soviet Union as part of its cold war strategy and they began to provide training and arms to the Mujahedeen resistance groups, along with extra support from other countries such as Pakistan, Saudi Arabia and the UK, China. The Soviet invasion, coupled with the revolution in neighbouring Iran, also provoked a large response from the Islamic world to resist the Communists. The Islamic Republic of Iran, along with many other Muslim nations and groups, gave aid and sent volunteers to support the Mujahideen. Among these Islamic volunteer fighters was a Saudi millionaire fundamentalist Osama Bin Laden and the other volunteers came to be known as "Afghan Arabs," and they later played significant roles in Islamic guerrilla wars in Algeria, Egypt, Bosnia, Tajikistan, Chechnya and in attacks on American and other Western targets.

The Soviet Forces continued in Afghanistan facing opposition from the international community. In 1988, due to the dragging war and changes in Soviet internal political situations, Moscow signed the Geneva Accords

1988 in which the Soviet government agreed to withdraw its army from Afghanistan by February of 1989. By this time, nearly five million Afghans had fled to Iran or Pakistan and lived as refugees. The war in Afghanistan was over for the Russians, but not for the Afghans, as internal strife continued. This unforeseen defeat caused the Soviets to lose billions of Dollars, and led to the collapse of the Soviet Union.

The political conditions during the period 1979-89 was responsible for the emergence and creation of Taliban. In fact, the Soviet Union intervention resented the Mujahedeen (from whom the Taliban evolved from). At the same time, in a cold war matrix, the U.S. was interested in countering the power of the Soviet Union as a part of its policy of containment of communism in South Asia and Central Asia. Thus, Soviet Union entrance in Afghanistan was definitely increased the communist powers, influence and ideology in the region. Hence, the United States intervened and funded the Mujahedeen troops to fight against the Soviet Union. The Mujahedeen were armed and supported by the U.S., Pakistan and Saudi Arabia and other countries also. Under Reagan's presidency, Congress Democrats formed a partnership with the Pakistan's ISI to recruit and train the Mujahideen to fight ferociously against the Soviet Union. After the withdrawal of Soviet Union, Pakistan was left alone to deal with the problems associated with the post-Russian Era.

Fourth Phase: Emergence of Taliban and Formation of Islamic state

After 1989, the situation in Afghanistan went back again to civil war with the Islamist groups fighting among themselves and turned their gun on each other. Though radicalization of Islam in Afghanistan was started long before the armed forces of the Soviet Union intervention. The post-1978 social and political instability allowed millions of Afghan radicals Islamist to participate in various forms of opposition to the state and demanded to create a secular state following the traditional norms and customs of Islam. Radicalization of Islam was more aggravated in early 1988 when the United States sponsored the mujahidin. The United States open supports and sponsorship to the Mujahedeen divided the country many ethnic-sectarian groups who were vigorously competing for the economic and political benefits of the Western States. The large quantities of weapons and funds given to them intensified historical ethno-linguistic, sectarian, and regional divisions and encouraged alternative social and political structures in the local and regional periphery.

Most important factions in this conflict were led by Mohammad Najibullah, Abdul Rashid Dostum, Ahmed Shah Massoud, Burhanuddin

Rabbani, and Gulbuddin Hekmatyar. In 1992, Abdul Rashid Dostum alongside Uzbek militia force managed to take over the control of Kabul, which consolidated the power for his side. But this was not the end. The Peshawar Accord , March 1992, set the grounds for the future Islamic State of Afghanistan. In 1992, Burhanuddin Rabbani was elected president of the state and he ruled until 1996 even though fight for Kabul continued so the situation of unstable peace continued.

Soviet withdrawal and the corresponding termination of the US subsidies for the Mujahedeen are events that, ipso facto, have led to the emergence of Taliban, and the infiltration of the country by al-Qa'ida. During the period of unstable peace, the situation escalated to crisis. Taliban was able to oust the weakened incumbent government under the leadership of Mullah Muhammad Omar. Taliban captured Kandahar in 1994, followed by Ghazni and Herat in 1995, and finally take over Kabul in September 1996. Taliban established a new regime under the name of Islamic Emirate of Afghanistan. Beginning from this period, the situation in the country got worse after the Taliban disbanded various militias and ruled according to the "Pashtun approach to Sharia law," imposing rigid and fundamental beliefs to the country. Many of the Taliban's leaders followed a fundamentalist version of Deobandi and Wahhabi Islam and a strict interpretation of Afghan social and cultural norms. They enforced the most extreme version of Sharia law ever encountered in the modern Islamic world. The crisis was obvious when they began to commit atrocities against women, girls, and minority groups particularly Shi'a Hazaras. These actions contributed negatively to a state of economic deprivation and malnourishment inside the country. In order to oppose the Taliban regime and their actions, leaders of other ethnic groups joined their forces and formed the Northern Alliance or The United Front by Dostum, Rabbani, and Massoud). They even began to represent Afghanistan at the United Nations, but the conflicts continued with the Northern Alliance succeeding in limiting Taliban progress northward in 1997. In 1998 the city of Mazar-i-Sharif fell to the Taliban, marking their dominance across over 90 percent of the country. This event forced Abdul Rashid Dostum to find refuge in the neighbouring Uzbekistan. Many Pakistani nationals joined the Taliban to fight against the United Front's forces while Osama bin Laden channelled more money in support, citing it as the only true Islamic State. Bin Laden had been involved in the Soviet War, providing money to different militia groups to fight the Soviet forces. He returned to Afghanistan in 1996 after having to flee Sudan and Saudi Arabia, and allegedly used the country as a base to plan and finance attacks internationally.

Fifth Phase-US War Against Terror

Following the 9/11 attacks, the U.S. declared a war against Afghanistan. At this point, the U.S. realized the seeds they had sown. The root cause of the US War on Terror was the insecure situation of the country, and more importantly the threats posed by the terrorist organization Al-Qaeda that had a privileged status in the country and protected by the Taliban in power. The Taliban was harbouring him and refusing to hand over him. The al-Qaeda attacks at the twin tower of the World Trade Centre by some of the 19 hijackers trained in Afghanistan in which more than 3000 people killed, was the trigger cause of the US war against terror. The United States government quickly identified Osama bin Laden the main offender and demanded Afghanistan to hand over him and all other terrorist leaders. On 7th October 2001, the US coalition and NATO forces attacked on Taliban-controlled Afghanistan under the operation Enduring Freedom. Logistical support was provided by other nations including France, Germany, Australia and Canada. On the other side, the Afghanistan local forces that participated in the conflict were the Taliban, Al-Qaeda, as the most important ones, and some small networks or factions like HI-Gulbuddin, HI-Khalis, the Haqqani network, and Lashkar-e-Taiba. The invasion of Afghanistan was intended to target terrorist Osama bin Laden's al-Qaida organization, which was based in the country, as well as the extreme fundamentalist Taliban organization that had ruled most of the country since 1996.The Taliban called the US actions "an attack on Islam, and attack on all Muslim Countries.

They launched a series of aerial attacks on the al-Qaida and Taliban bases in Kabul, Kandahar, Jalalabad, Konduz and Mazar-e-Sharif. They were supported by the Northern Alliance to bring down the Taliban including Tajik leader Mohammed Fahim and Uzbek leader Abdul Rashid Dostum. Thecoalition forces began a ground invasion with Northern Alliance which gave the U.S. and other nations troops air and ground support. The coalition forces also teamed with anti-Taliban forces in southern Afghanistan under the leadership of Hamid Karzai. They capture the northern city of Mazar-e-Sharif on 9 November 2001 from Taliban control. The Taliban regime collapsed with the capture of Kabul in November 2001 and Kandahar in December 6, 2001. It had been besieged by a force led by Karzai that moved in from the north and one commanded by Gul Agha Sherzai that advanced from the south. Though, the Taliban regime collapsed, but the Al-Qaeda organization were able to maintain its positions in Afghanistan. The Taliban and Al-Qaida leaders and their forces took safe hide into Afghanistan's rural areas, mountainous Tora Bora region and across the border of Pakistan. Mullah Mohammed Omar went into hiding rather than surrender. In fact,

Taliban's allowed Osama bin Laden and other key al-Qaida members time to escape into neighbouring Pakistan. By mid-December, the bunker and cave complex used by al-Qaida at Tora Bora had been captured, but there was no sign of bin Laden.

After the fall of Taliban, peacekeeping process were started by the international community at the UNO sponsored Bonn Conference in Germany. In Bonn Conference, various Afghan faction leaders were agreed to cooperated in the political reconstruction of Afghanistan, framing of a new constitution, election for President and National Assembly. The UN Security Council endorsed the Bonn Agreements on December 6, 2001, in Resolution no. 1383 (2001). The agreements established an Afghan Interim Authority with Hamid Karzai as Chairman on December 22nd, 2001. As agreed, UN-mandated International Security Assistance Forces (ISAF) were deployed in Afghanistan in 2002. NATO assumed the control of ISAF forces on August 2003. In 2004, Hamid Karzai was re-elected as president of Afghanistan, and a new democratic constitution was adopted.

The 2004 constitution provided Afghanistan with a powerful central government and weak regional and local authorities—a structure that was in opposition to the country's long-standing traditions. Despite, the vast powers provided under the constitution, Karzai was proved as a weak leader and increasingly isolated due to the ethnic differences and inadequate international support. Karzai's government was also beset by corruption and efforts to build a national army and a police force were affected.

Re-Emergence of Taliban

After 2001, the situation in Afghanistan was not stable and peaceful. The Taliban forces began to regroup and re-organised in the mountainous regions along the Afghanistan and Pakistan borders. They continued to engage U.S. and Afghan forces in guerrilla warfare. The US-Coalition mission was expanded throughout the whole country to eliminate terrorist heads and to provide Afghanistan a secure and democratic future. In 2006, NATO forces took control of security in the whole country in order to eliminate the Taliban and Al-Qaeda groups. In 2008, the NATO troops were provided with 17,000 additional troops from the international allies, with the numbers continuing to rise over the years. In March 2009, the US President Barack Obama followed new strategy for Afghanistan and Pakistan, with the decision to deploy 4,000 US personnel and 30,000 additional troops to train and strengthen the Afghan army and police and providing support for civilians by 2010. By December 2012, there were about 120,000 troops from 50 contributing nations in the International Security and Assistance Force, of which about 68,000 were US troops.

Crisis escalated when about 500 Taliban prisoners escaped from a prison in 2011, and in the same year the president's half-brother and Kandahar governor Ahmad Wali Karzai was killed in the Taliban campaign.

The war continued and many other states joined the NATO force but it was hard guerrillas war where the Taliban engaged in low level skirmishes making use of the rough mountain terrain in order to take shelter from the allied attack. The spontaneous and suicidal attacks over allied convoys and bases resulted in a large scale casualties to the US and NATO forces. Thousands of Afghan civilians, government officials and foreign workers were killed and kidnapped. The United States forces bore heaviest losses by 2010 more than 1,000 US troops were killed in Afghanistan, while 300 British troops and 150 Canadian troops were killed.

Table 16: Number of Fatalities among Western Coalition soldiers from Operation Enduring Freedom 2001-2013.

*Total**	*U.S.*	*UK*	*Canada*	*Germany*	*France*	
2001	12	12	0	0	0	0
2002	70	49	3	4	10	0
2003	58	48	0	2	6	0
2004	60	52	1	1	0	3
2005	131	99	1	1	4	2
2006	191	98	39	36	0	6
2007	232	117	42	30	7	3
2008	295	155	51	32	3	11
2009	521	317	108	32	7	11
2010	711	499	103	16	9	16
2011	566	418	46	4	7	26
2012	402	310	44	0	0	8
2013	161	127	9	0	1	0

Sources: the Statista Portal, 2017.

More than 20 other countries also lost troops during the war. As the fighting dragged on and casualties escalated, the war lost popularity in many Western countries, creating domestic political pressure to keep troops out of harm's or to pull them out altogether. Therefore, an agreement was reached among the participating countries at NATO Summit held in Lisbon in November 2010. All the allied countries agreed over a timetable to withdraw their troops and hand over the control of the country to the Afghan forces by the end of 2014 and the participating countries would gradually departure their forces based on a well-set timeline. In 2012, after Francois Hollande was elected as the new president of France, he decided to withdrew its forces back home, signalling the beginning of the departure of other forces as well, as the conflict seemed to settle down in some areas.

After so many years of conflict, Afghanistan still passing through problems that need to be addressed by the Afghan leaders and international community. The United States have agreed to support Afghanistan even after their withdrawal to solve their internal problems. On May 2nd, 2012, the United States and Afghanistan signed the Enduring Strategic Partnership Agreement, a 10-year strategic partnership agreement (SPA) that stipulated the United States commitment to strengthen Afghanistan's sovereignty, stability, and prosperity, and continue cooperation to defeat Al-Qaeda and its affiliates. This agreement also signals the U.S. intention to designate Afghanistan as a major non-NATO ally in an important peacekeeping attempt. The newly formed Afghan military forces were trained by NATO soldiers in order to prepare them for the handover of Afghan in 2014. Allied forces have also been helping the police forces in their training. In 2012, the Taliban agreed to open an overseas office as a move towards peace talks with the US and the Afghan government, though Taliban's attacks and encounters were still taking place causing causalities to allied and Afghans official and civilians tin the country.

Current Situation

The persistence of the Taliban insurgency is still the most devastating challenge facing the country despite the expensive and concerted efforts of the United States, its international allies, and the Afghan government themselves, it is far from being ending. Taliban fighters are now openly active in 70% of Afghanistan, says a BBC study report, and now control much more territory after the US allied forces left in 2014. The BBC study says, the Taliban's are now in full control of 14 districts (that's 4% of the country) and have an active and open physical presence in a further 263 districts (66%),[11] significantly higher than previous estimates of Taliban strength. Taliban forces have made inroads in areas where they are not in ethnic advantage and are in superior military position. Taliban and other insurgent groups are working against U.S.-backed Afghan security forces and pose a serious threat in 116 out of the country's 384 districts, said Timor Sharan, senior Afghanistan analyst for International Crisis Group. "This gives a clear indication of the growing insurgency that is seriously challenging the Afghan government in many different parts of the country," he commented.[12] General John W. Nicholson, commander of the U.S.-NATO mission in Afghanistan, testified before the Senate Armed Services Committee that the conflict in Afghanistan reflected a "stalemate".[13] Afghanistan is experiencing a continuing downturn in security with more than 40 percent of its districts either under Taliban control or influence.

According to the U.S. Special Inspector General for Afghanistan Reconstruction (SIGAR) only 57.2 per cent of 375 districts were under government control up to February 1, 2017, an almost 15 per cent decline since end-2015. It reported that the Afghan security forces had registered a significant decline in their numbers, while the Taliban and other militant groups had increased their control or influence over Afghanistan since late 2015. Approximately 6,785 Afghan forces were killed and another 11,777 wounded from January to November 2016, significant losses at a time when security forces are struggling with personnel retention. The UN Mission in Afghanistan (UNAMA) also reported a 3 per cent increase in civilian casualties (3,498 killed 7,920 wounded) in 2016 over the previous year.[14] The number of high-profile attacks in Kabul was also higher during the first three months of 2017 as compared to equivalent periods in previous years. The 2017 fighting season began with one of the most lethal attacks in the war, when ten Taliban fighters killed more than 150 Afghan soldiers and civilians after infiltrating an army base near Mazar-e-Sharif.[15] On 21 April, Taliban gunmen and suicide bombers attacked an Afghan army base in the northern Balkh province, killing over 100 military and other personnel and injuring more. The army chief and defence minister both resigned the following day. Two attacks in March targeted police stations and a military hospital, killing 73 and wounding over 240 people. More civilians were killed in the Afghan conflict in comparison to last year. According to a United Nations report released by the UN Assistance Mission in Afghanistan (UNAMA) and the UN Human Rights Office. The report documented 3,804 civilian deaths in 2018. Among the dead were 927 children, the highest recorded number of boys and girls killed in the conflict during a single year.[16] In total, UNAMA documented, 10,993 civilian casualties (3,804 deaths and 7,189 injured), representing a five per cent increase in overall civilian casualties and an 11 per cent increase in civilian deaths compared to 2017.

Table 17: Civilian casualties in Afghanistan from 2007 to 2016.

year	*Civilian Causalities*	*Deaths*
2007	1523	1952
2008	2118	1997
2009	2412	2779
2010	2794	3205
2011	3133	3353
2012	2769	2632
2013	2969	3111
2014	3701	4507

(Contd...)

2015	3565	5312
2016	3510	4561
2017	3438	3498
2018*	1076	0
2019*	105	0

Source: The Statista Portal, 2017.

*Data for the year 2018 and 2019 are based on South Asia Terrorism Portal, March 29, 2019.

Afghanistan suffers from one of the most protracted humanitarian crises of refugee and internally displaced people in the world. The devastation caused by the conflict left an estimated 2 million people dead and 1.5 million people disabled, in part due to the massive urban carpet-bombing campaigns and the large areas of land mines that still exist today. Two million people were internally displaced, and one third of the country's pre-war population fled into neighbouring Pakistan, Iran and further afield.[17]

The 2016 year was the most violent year after 2001 which witnessed, 646,698 persons were internally displaced due to conflict, compared to 70,000 in 2010, this added to the roughly one million conflict-displaced in previous years.[18] In 2016, one million Afghan refugees and migrants forced to return home from Pakistan and Iran. The EU's plan to deport back home some 80,000 Afghans whose request for asylum was rejected has further strain Afghanistan's internal situation. More broadly, the humanitarian community, including UN agencies, estimate that 9.3 million people, or almost one-third of Afghanistan's population need humanitarian assistance as security continues to deteriorate and both Pakistan and Iran force more refugees and migrants to return.

Any new internal displacement in Afghanistan would exacerbate an already serious internal displacement crisis. According to the Internal Displacement Monitoring Centre, over 100,000 people were displaced by conflict in Afghanistan in 2012 and a further 32,000 by natural disasters. In the first six months of 2013 an additional 60,000 people were displaced internally, according to the UN Office for the Coordination of Humanitarian Affairs.[19] The number of people internally displaced due to the conflict surged as fighting intensified in mid-year. More than 300,000 new internally displaced persons (IDPs) in 2016 brought the nationwide total to at least 1.3 million people.[20] Humanitarian organizations reported that many IDPs were living in informal settlements where they lacked access to safe water, sanitation, health care, and education. Many returning refugees and migrants, most from Pakistan, joined the ranks of the IDPs.

Civilian casualties from ANSF operations during ground offensives were also increased due to indiscriminate mortar and rocket fire in civilian-populated areas. Aerial strikes, most from attack helicopters, resulted in the increase in civilian casualties. Mostly victims were women and children. The Taliban and ISISI stepped up their recruitment of child soldiers, particularly in north-eastern Afghanistan. Government forces, including the Afghan National Army (ANA), Afghan National Police (ANP), and ALP increasingly occupied or used schools for military purposes in contested areas.The United Nations also reported a significant increase in attacks against schools by both Taliban and groups affiliating themselves with ISIS. In Faryab, Kunduz, and other provinces, these militia forces were accused of killing and assaulting civilians. These attacks on civilians have taken their toll on the population's mental health. Health experts have voiced concern about the high prevalence of mental health conditions among Afghans, and the lack of community-based mental health services for those with psychosocial disabilities. The overall humanitarian crisis is putting enormous pressure on Afghanistan's public services and infrastructure, especially in urban centres, where 70-80 per cent of internally displaced and returning refugees tend to settle; most are jobless or under-employed, with little or no access to health care or education. Countrywide, as many as 1.57 million people are facing severe food insecurity. Women and girls are often the worst off given the country's socially conservative nature.

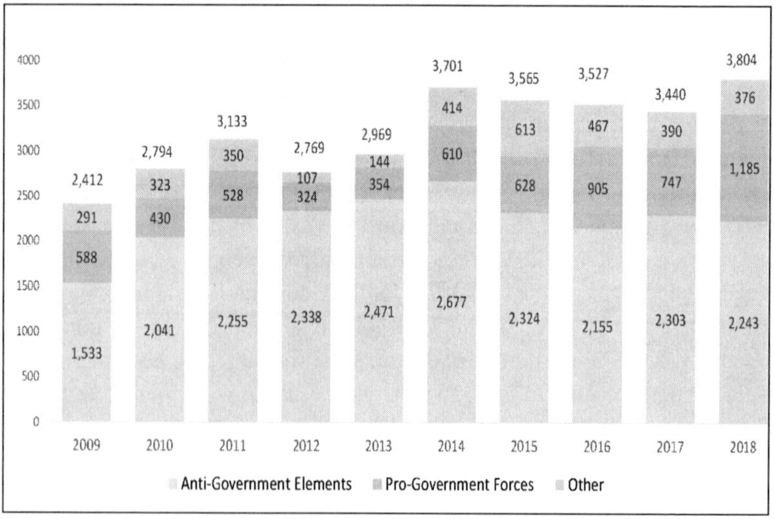

Graph 4 : Civilian Deaths by Parties to the Conflict-2009-2018.

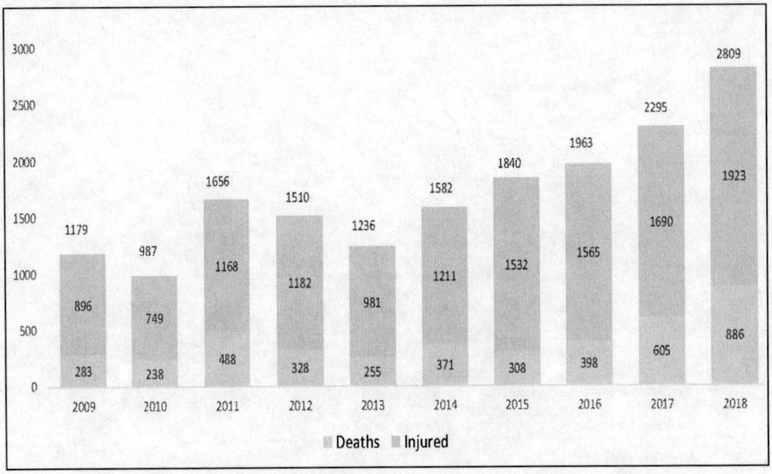

Graph 5: Civilian Death & Injured-Suicide & Complex Attacks 2009-2018.

The United Nations Assistance Mission in Afghanistan (UNAMA), in its Annual Report released on February 15, 2018, documented a total of 10,453 civilian casualties (3,438 deaths and 7,015 injured) in 2017 as against 11,418 civilian casualties (3,498 civilian deaths and 7,920 injured) in 2016. The UNAMA reported the high number of casualties caused by suicide bombings and other attacks using improvised explosive devices (IEDs). The combined use of suicide bombings and non-suicide IEDs caused 4,151 civilian casualties (1,229 deaths and 2,922 injured) comprising 40 per cent of all civilian casualties in 2017.[21]

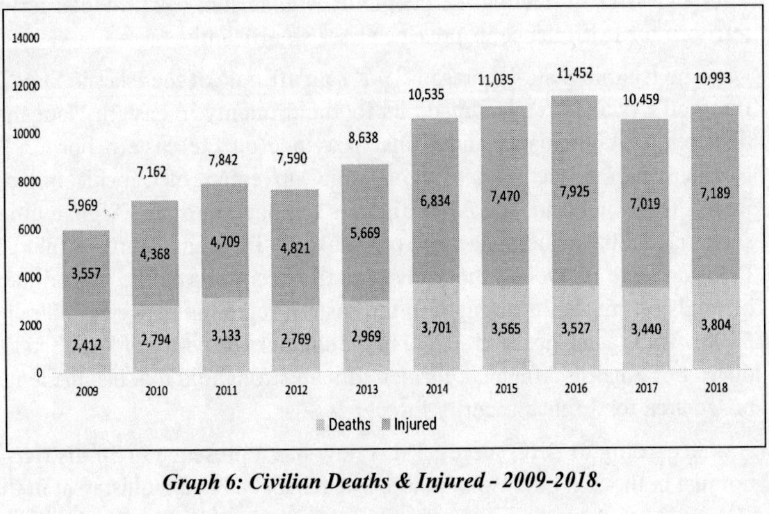

Graph 6: Civilian Deaths & Injured - 2009-2018.

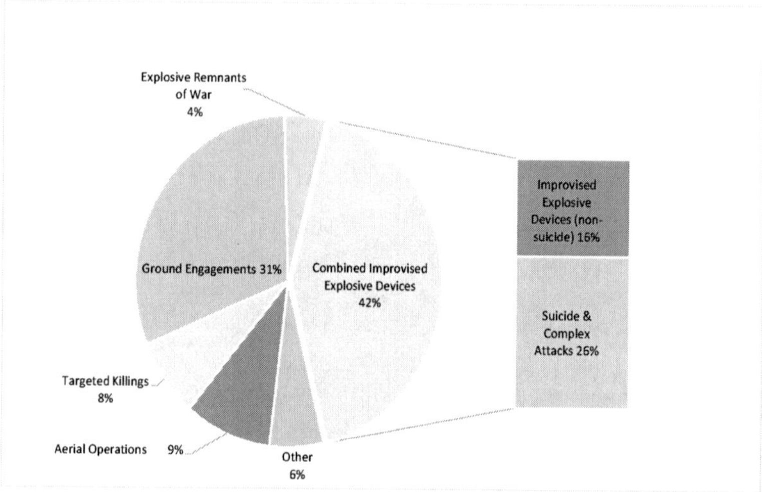

Source: UN Mission in Afghanistan Report, February 24, 2019.

Graph 7:Civilian casualties by Incident Type - 2018.

Other Insurgents Groups- ISISI

ISISI has been rising in Afghanistan for more than a year and expanding its presence rapidly inspite of Taliban's insurgency. The Islamic State in Afghanistan is not a Middle East export to the country rather it consists of several splinter groups and elements expelled from the Taliban, including too sectarian even for the mainstream Taliban. Thousands of ISIS-affiliated fighters hiding in isolated desert or mountain retreats from where they continue to mount terror attacks against security forces and civilians. The lawlessness affecting the people of Afghanistan has provided fertile territory for ISISI hence its presence rises significantly.

The Islamic State-Khorasan (IS-K), an affiliate of the Islamic State in Iraq and Syria (ISIS), has made its foothold mainly in eastern Nangahar districts of Afghanistan and Kunar province on the eastern border. In Northern region, members of the Islamic Movement of Uzbekistan have joined forces with local Taliban fighters to attack northern Afghan cities such as Kunduz including factions of Lashkar-e-Taiba and Tehrik-e-Taliban-Pakistan have relabelled themselves as IS. According to the US military officials estimates, its strength in the eastern region is between 3000 and 5000. Arabs and Chechens settled in the southern province of Zabul, in the district of Khak-e-Afghan, a former Taliban stronghold that has made it a no-go area for Afghan security forces.[22]

According to BBC survey, ISISI now has a presence in 30 districts - not just in the east but also in places like Khanabad and Kohistan at in the north but does not fully control any district at present. The group is fighting with both the Afghan military and the Taliban for territorial control. During 2017 the number of attacks attributed to the group increased, with many targeting urban centres and often Shia Muslims in sectarian attacks almost never seen before in Afghanistan's 40-year conflict. While Islamic State has been targeting in places like Kabul.

The ISISI has established headquarters in the district for recruitment and training camp in a restive southern province bordering Pakistan because of the direct control over a number of districts near the Pakistan border and links with the Pakistani leadership and terrorists' outfits. They are actively recruiting and training locals to join the group as gunmen. "They have a lot of money. People here are very poor, and that makes them very easy targets for these foreigners," said Atta Mohammad Haqbayan, the director of Zabul's provincial council.[23] Zabul's provincial police chief, Mirwais Noorzai, said the ISIS operatives in Khak-e-Afghan are well-equipped with satellite communications technology.

During the period 23 August to 21 November 2017 at least 50 people were assassinated in the provincial capital, Jalalabad. Some of the victims were shot dead and others blown up. Three were beheaded, a hallmark of

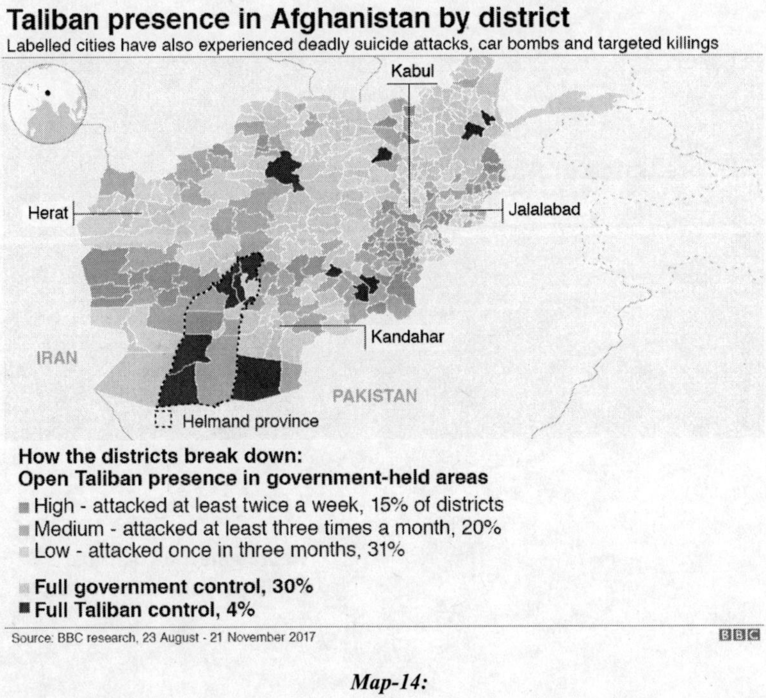

Map-14:

killings by ISISI.[24] ISISI was quick to claim responsibility for the twin bombings in Kabul which killed 25 people, including nine reporters, saying that they were directed at Afghanistan's intelligence headquarters. Afghanistan's security forces struggling to cope[25] with the continued threat

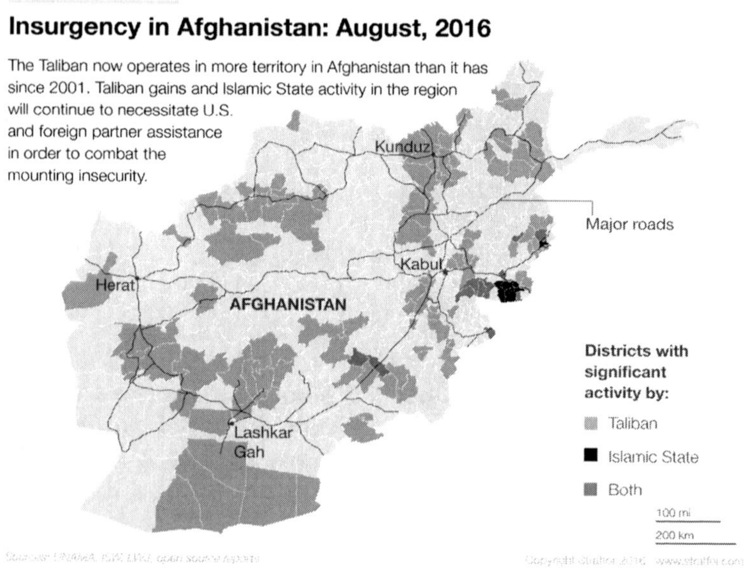

Map-15

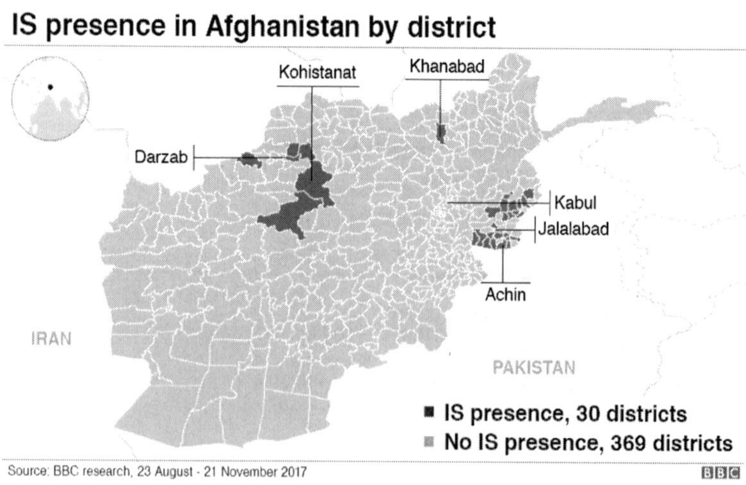

Map-16

posed by the Taliban, are also facing great security threat and mounting pressure of ISISI terror attacks. The US coalition commanders believe that ISIS will continue to remain a threat in these countries so long as key figures in ISISI' leadership remain at large, including Abu Bakr Al Baghdadi, the movement's charismatic leader who established the so-called caliphate in the first place. Like the Taliban, ISIS is committed to driving the remnants of the 15,000-strong NATO mission out of the country and establishing a harsh form of Islamic rule throughout the country.

Table 18: Afghanistan -Terrorists Insurgents and Extremists Groups.

Numbers	*Proscribed Terrorists/ Extremist groups*	*Active Terrorists /Insurgents groups*
1.	Al-Qaeda	Taliban
2.	Lashkare-e-Toiba(LeT)	Islamic State (ISISI)
3.	Islamic State/Islamic State of Iraq and Levant/ Islamic State of Iraq and Syria/Daish (ISIS)	Tahreak-e-Taliban Pakistan (TTP)
		Haqqani Network (HN)

Sources: South Asia Terrorists Portal (STAP) 2018.

The terror attacks and atrocities carried out in Afghanistan by the Taliban and ISISI have many the purposes:

First: due to recent setbacks it has suffered in Syria, the organisation has lost its ability to wreak carnage around the world. After the defeat in Syria and Iraq at the hands of the US-led coalition, the ISIS has to find out its base so that they could survive. This is a question- how to deal with their defeat either they would simply disband or revived its terror influence in the region. Its defeat in Iraq and Syria has certainly had a negative impact on the morale of ISIS recruits. Having seen thousands of their co-fighters perish under the coalition's merciless military assault, many of the survivors have simply decided that jihad is not for them, and returned to their home countries. Analysts believe that there remains a core of adherents to the ISISI creed who have simply melted away with the intention of regrouping[26] and launching a fresh wave of terror attacks in the future.

Secondly, in recent months, the majority of terror attacks carried out against the Afghan government have been the work of the Taliban, that is seeking to reassert its influence in the country following the removal of the bulk of NATO forces that have been trying to destroy the organisation since the September 11 attacks and to counter the ISISI.

Thirdly, the attacks are essential to judge its strength and influence how much of a threat ISIS remains, despite the humiliating defeat where its so-called caliphate has been reduced to rubble. ISIS' arrival in Afghanistan has not gone unchallenged by the Taliban, which resents the introduction of a rival Islamist group that has large numbers of foreign fighters, unlike the Taliban, which is mainly drawn from the indigenous Pashtun community. This has resulted in a number of clashes between the two groups, particularly in Nangarhar province.

Finally, one of the reasons that how ISIS came into existence in the first place is the Obama administration's decision to turn its back on its long-standing commitments to safeguarding the security and well-being of the Middle East.

Rising insurgency and a fraught political transition are exacerbating an already pervasive sense of insecurity about Afghanistan's future. After the transition to Afghan security forces in 2014, the ANDSF has been battling a growing insurgency on several fronts. The presence of ISISI, rival group to the Taliban, is certainly difficult to the Afghan President Ashraf Ghani to revive peace talks with the Taliban leadership. ISIS is opposed to any form of deal and has managed to attract a number of Taliban fighters to its ranks who take the same view.

The increasingly complex and fraught situation that is developing on the ground in Afghanistan is certainly something that the West and its regional allies cannot ignore. An ISISI growth in Afghanistan faces substantial obstacles: The ISISIs brutality is greater than even the brutality of Taliban, the Afghans have been subjected to for decades, it will generate resentment. The Taliban has been better able to calibrate brutality and hide or excuse the violence it perpetrates against civilians. At times, the Taliban has even temporarily reduced violence and overly-restrictive edits to generate acceptance by local populations. By contrast, like ISISI in the Middle East, ISISI in Afghanistan has chosen to rule by sheer brutality. The Taliban has also sponsored opium poppy cultivation in Afghanistan and the jobs and income it provides for ordinary Afghans, thus generating political capital. ISISI in Afghanistan, on the other hand, has prohibited opium poppy cultivation both on grounds of ideological purity the strategic goal of ensuring that the only employment available to local men is as ISISI foot soldiers.

The ISISI in Afghanistan has also drawn the attention of international actors, and the Taliban has been able to capitalize on being seen as a lesser threat by outside powers. For Russia and Iran, the Islamic State is an even greater threat than the Taliban. Both countries have provided support to the Taliban in order to fight ISISI but also as part of their anti-American efforts.

The stability of Afghanistan and the long-term success of counter-terrorism efforts in the country is affected by fractious and polarized politics in Afghanistan. The National Unity Government (created in the wake of the highly contested presidential elections of 2014) has not yet really found its feet. The weakness of the NUG, its political dependencies, priorities and entanglements have limited and undermined its ability to strongly tackle the grasping criminality, illicit economies and organized crime that have become so intermeshed with Afghanistan's political system and international counter-insurgency operations. The country's illicit economies such as illegal mining, logging and drug trafficking have financed and stimulated the violence and conflict. The usurpation of land, taxes and customs, generalized extortion, thuggish monopolistic domination of international contracts and local economic markets, and usurpation of international aid have even more severely undermined the reconstruction efforts and stability in the country. Combined with the impulsive and greedy rule by Afghan power-brokers, these crimes allow the Taliban to present itself as less corrupt ruler and gives the insurgency power and bounciness despite its brutality.

Since 1970s, failure of the Afghan state, poor control and lack of security that has grown in the country has been providing conditions to develop and sustain the Taliban insurgency till now. Most of the people is pro-Taliban so they are joining the Taliban militia even after the fall of Taliban in 2009 and helping the organization of improvised attacks over the US and Afghan security forces. Moreover, the Taliban discourse over this conflict became radical, in an attempt to attract more followers. They have tried to turn the conflict into some kind of sacred war in which the US would want to eliminate the Islamic culture from Afghanistan. In fact, much of the Taliban resilience and growing capacity comes from mis-governance, weak and poor performance, power abuse, capriciousness, corruption, tribal discrimination and predatory behaviour from government official and power-brokers closely aligned with the state. The Taliban has gained power and support from Afghans people because the post-Taliban regime in Kabul failed to build up state capacity to deliver good governance and act against predatory criminality. The new state under former President Hamid Karzai (2001-2014) failed not only to meet the expectations of the population for economic development and service delivery but also to maintain elemental security. Karzai sought to govern by co-option and payoffs, such as appointments, to the country's powerbrokers. The persistent inability to establish good governance, even in areas repeatedly cleared by ISAF and ANSF forces, has often made any security gains highly ephemeral. The current President Ashraf Ghani sought to bring efficiency and technocratic skills to governance, but in doing so reduced the numbers and layers of those having a stake in reform to a much narrower clique of supporters.

The most important factor is the building of bases and training camps in the rocky and mountainous hilly areas provide safe havens for the terrorist and Taliban extremists. The hard terrain of the country mostly dominated by high altitudes and mountains with a great number of caves and areas which the Taliban are using as hiding spots. Though US security forces are more technologically expert but they are not familiar with the local topography. The Taliban developed its military capabilities by taking advantage of sanctuaries in Pakistan's Federally Administered Tribal Areas and the Khyber-Pakhtunkhwa and Baluchistan provinces even in places far from border areas, such as Karachi. Pakistan has provided direct military and intelligence support to the Taliban and its affiliate branches such as the Haqqani group responsible for the most atrocious terrorist attacks in Afghanistan. Although Pakistan receiving very large U.S. counter-terrorism assistance in the form of financial aid and military equipment and facing intense U.S. pressure for almost two decades, yet Pakistan has not stopped its support for the Taliban. Pakistan intentionally followed policies toward the militants that shows its unwillingness to launch a military operation into North Waziristan to dislodge the Afghan Taliban are there, despite years of intense U.S. pressure. In 2014, Pakistan military allowed the Taliban and Haqqanis to escape from North Waziristan military operation, blaming the United States and Afghanistan for their inability to secure the border and capture the fleeing insurgents. Indeed, some anti-Pakistani militants also escaped into eastern Afghanistan where the writ of the Afghan state is particularly weak, establishing sanctuaries there.

Many rural Afghans have come to trust the Taliban's extensive judicial net-works over government courts to "solve disputes in a fair war, without tribal or ethnic bias, or more commonly, without having to pay bribes," says Graeme Smith, a Kabul-based senior analyst at the International Crisis Group.[27]

Afghanistan has repeatedly been a prime theatre for Indian and Pakistani rivalries. More than a decade after 9-11, Pakistan's military-intelligence establishment remains preoccupied with India's ascendance at a time of Pakistan's own stagnation and atrophy. Fearing encirclement by India, Pakistan has been greatly reluctant to suppress Afghan militant groups using Pakistan for sanctuary, networking, their insurgent and criminal activities and many forms of smuggling. Pakistan's continuing support for these groups, despite pressure from the United States and NATO, reflects the persistent view of the Pakistani military-intelligence establishment that the jihadi groups are critical assets in preventing threats on Pakistan's western flank from an India-friendly regime in Kabul and in securing access to Central Asia's trade routes. Another reason for Pakistan's unwillingness to cease its support for the Taliban, are its uncertainties and internal limitations. Pakistan does not have anything approaching total control over the various militant groups that operate from its territory, including the Afghan Taliban. Nor does it have adequate control of the border areas.

Finally, Pakistan's willingness to accommodate anti-Afghanistan militant groups is also motivated by fear of provoking them to start violence in Punjab and threaten the core of the Pakistani state, instead of focusing externally.[28]

Pakistan has been pursuing its own agenda in Afghanistan. Pakistan remains a central node in global terrorism. Osama Bin Laden was killed deep inside Pakistan in an area that raises deep suspicion about what Pakistani intelligence, senior military officers and government officials who did not know about his presence?

Peace Process

Peace-making efforts in Afghanistan range from high-level political negotiations by international negotiators to locally initiated peace missions, conferences/workshops, direct and indirect peacebuilding attempts by humanitarian aid organisations. Although the Geneva Accords of 1988 marked an important achievement of the UN during the Cold-war, the subsequent efforts of the UN and other actors as well as Afghanistan have been suffered and have not produced tangible results neither in reduction of violence nor in the context of conflict. Withdrawal of the Soviet forces did not prevent Afghanistan from descending into further violence and destruction. The talks were held in the absence of the main party (Mujahideen) and the United States who was supporters of Mujahideen did not actively participate in process. Instead the Geneva Accords was indirectly negotiated and signed by Pakistan and Kabul government. The Geneva Accords failed to address the power-struggle between various groups that constitutes one of the root causes of war in Afghanistan. The Geneva negotiations was mainly to prevent further East-West confrontation but it failed to produce a comprehensive settlement for Afghanistan. Although termination of external interference was part of the accord but external supporters continued to flood the Afghan government and the Mujahidden with weapon and means of violence and destruction soon after the Accords was signed. Regional co-operation for a permanent termination of hostilities in Afghanistan was also non-existent during the Geneva talks and with the collapse of Soviet Union, the situation became worst. The UN peace initiatives in 1991-1992 to transfer the power from Najibhullah met severe setbacks due to the disintegration of the USSR and disengagement of the US. Both superpowers during the last round of Geneva negotiations had agreed to use their influence to ensure a political settlement under the auspices of the United Nations. The Mujahedeen leaders were also suspected the UN plan for the establishment of an impartial transition mechanism feeling as attempts to marginalize them.

The peace process between the NUG backing up the ANSF and the insurgent groups are limited and continued with ambiguity. Although there have been a series of informal direct discussions between the Taliban and the NUG, yet there has been no sign of any real desire to work for a negotiation to end the conflict. Some semi-governmental and independent initiatives for peace have taken but not in a very consistent or centralised manner. These efforts may or may not gain momentum, depending on the situation on ground and the quality of the initiatives. Former President Barack Obama tried multiple times to negotiate peace with the Taliban, to no avail.

In September 2016 a Peace Agreement was signed between Afghanistan National Unity Government and Hezb-e-Islami militant group. The militant group agreed to renounce violence and accept the constitution while in return the government promised to free Hezb prisoners, incorporating insurgents into security forces and resettle thousands of refugees living in Hezb affiliated camps inside Pakistan.[29] The agreement paved the way for Hezb-e-Islami leader Gulbuddin Hekmatyar to return to Kabul after twenty years in exile.

US President Donald Trump's announced its new "South Asia strategy" on August 22, 2017. The US Airforce increased the airstrikes targeting Taliban and other terrorist groups in various parts of the country. The number of airstrikes in 2017 was twice the cumulative strikes carried out over the preceding two years – 2015 and 2016. Further, as part of the US Administration's broader efforts to disrupt terrorist fundraising in February 8, 2018, the US Department of the Treasury imposed sanctions against three individuals, Rahman Zeb Faqir Muhammad, Hizb Ullah Astam Khan and Dilawar Khan Nadir Khan, for allegedly having connections with Pakistan-based terror outfits operating in Afghanistan.

The Trump Administration has been eager to end the US role in a war that has cost 2400 American lives and billions of dollars and wants to withdraw its 14,000 troops. Under pressure from a stepped-up Trump administration military campaign, Taliban ready for peaceful dialogue but President Trump rejected the possibility of early talks with the Taliban, following a series of deadly attacks in Kabul and other parts of the country. Trump stated,

"I don't see any talking taking place. I don't think we're prepared to talk right now. It's a whole different fight over there. They're killing people left and right. Innocent people are being killed left and right. Bombing in the middle of children, in the middle of families — bombing, killing all over Afghanistan. So, we don't want to talk with the Taliban. There may be a time, but it's going to be a long time. We're all out, and that's taking place right now, and it's a whole new front. And it's a whole new set of principles that we're being governed by."[30]

Significantly, President Ashraf Ghani and Chief Executive Abdullah Abdullah re-started the Kabul Peace Process in June 2017. The principal purpose of the process is to ensure an Afghan-led and Afghan-owned, inclusive peace process to address the multiple dimensions of ongoing war and violence in Afghanistan. But this is impossible without regional and international cooperation. In this peace process, on January 14, 2018, a 15-member delegation of the United Nations Security Council (UNSC) held talks with the Afghan Government leadership, where they reportedly discussed a wide range of issues, including security and ongoing developments on the political front.

On November 9, 2018, Russia has hosted an international meeting aimed to restart peace talks on Afghanistan after decades of war in Moscow. Members of Afghanistan's High Peace Council, which did not represent the Afghan government, attended the meeting. Though Taliban militants emphasised that they would only hold direct talks with the US - not the Kabul government, also attended this meeting. Despite reservations by some countries, 11 countries invited by Moscow attended the meeting. China, Pakistan, Iran India and Central Asian States also participated in the meeting, The US had observer status.[32] Western officials and the Afghan government view the Moscow talks with some suspicion - some fear it could derail other efforts at negotiations. However, no significant breakthroughs were expected but bringing all the relevant players under one roof is a huge success for Russian diplomacy. It also signifies Russia's return to the diplomatic forefront in Afghan affairs. It was a significant fact that the Taliban were in the same room as Afghan delegates with the US. On the other hand, although Russia and the Taliban are historic foes, the US took part.

To pave the ground for official talks between the two sides on January 14, 2018, Afghan Government representatives held the third round of unofficial talks with five Taliban members in Turkey. The first and second rounds of Government-Taliban negotiations were held in Turkey in 2017. Humayun Jarir, a representative of the Afghan Government in the talks, disclosed that the Taliban members represented the Quetta Shura, Haqqani network and other factions of the Taliban. Meanwhile, Mawlawi Abdul Rauf, the Taliban leader who headed the peace talks delegation in Turkey, announced that “We represent the overall Taliban of the Islamic Emirate except some of individuals who are not willing to opt for intra-Afghan peace talks and who want to talk through Americans. The Taliban sent a five-member delegation from its political office based in Qatar. It emerged in July 2018 that Taliban officials secretly met a senior US diplomat in Qatar and another round of talks was held.

After the long period of halting peace efforts, Taliban insurgents and the United states officials had a six days long, 20-26 January 2019, meeting and negotiation in Qatar to reach a peace deal that could results 17 years long war. American envoy Khalilzad and the Taliban delegation led by Mullah Abdul Ghani Baradar have agreed to the framework of the deal.[33] Taliban demanded the trump administration to lay out the time table for the withdrawal of the US forces while the US officials asked the Taliban to guarantee that other militias will not be allowed such as ISISI and al-Qaida to use the Afghanistan as a base for attacking western interests. However, the meeting was productive and has made progress on the vital issues but a number of issues are still remaining to work out. Taliban have not been agreed to ceasefire. They have said that they will not stop attacking Afghan and foreign targets until all the US troops have been ordered to leave. There are sign of change in Taliban’s attitude. Until now, Taliban’s official refused to talk with the Afghan authorities and government charging that they are not the country’s true leaders and the Afghan government is an American puppet. The United states official agreed to withdraw its forces but only after Taliban insurgents talks with the Afghan government and ready to cease fire as the term to finalize the peace deal. According to US website the Daily Beast, the Taliban negotiators have shown willingness to compromise on the longstanding demand to evict all foreign troops before any negotiations with the Afghan government. The report claimed that the Taliban could even countenance a remaining US force in the country so long as it was involved in the political process that reached such an agreement.

However, there are numbers of issues that have to be sort out and there is no overall agreement on ceasefire including dialogue with the Afghan government. Nothing is agreed until everything is agreed.

The Question why the Taliban insurgency and terrorists’ organizations have brought the country for such a long and difficult period of continuing internal crisis and war need to be consider from various aspects since 1990s. Afghanistan has been widely supported by the international community. Many important countries interested in the continued cooperation to develop and progress a new democratic and secure Afghanistan. However there many hurdles. One such hurdle is the Afghan police and army are unprepared for security responsibility, as reported by the International Crisis Group (ICG). These reports are based on an analysis of the capabilities and the equipment that the internal Afghan security forces have, but also on some information provided by Afghan politicians. In this way, the international support for the Afghan community is very important and the efforts made in these 20 years should continue at economic level, providing aid and support for the country in an attempt to build a secure nation. On the other hand, worst case scenario may turn back in time with the possible collapse of system under a new internal crisis for power and under a weak leadership. The Taliban could rise again to power. Or may lose the position as other terrorist organisations like ISISI. But at present Afghanistan is in a stage of unstable peace and may remain so in the near future.

Notes

1. http://www.crf.org/religion/islam-governing-under-sharia/p8034.
2. Shoaib Shariff and Loise Adamou, Taliban Affected 70% of Afghanistan, BBC Report Study, BBC world Service, January 31,2018.
3. http://www.pbs.org/newshours/indepth_coverage/asia/afghanistan/map flash.html.
4. Key Afghans tied ta Mass Killings in 90s civil.
   war>http://www.nytimes.com/2012/07/23/world/asia-key-afghans-tied-to-mass-killings-in90s-civil-war.html.
5. Qari Salahuddin Ayubi, an ethnic Uzbek, was the Taliban's shadow governor for Faryab until he was killed in a NATO air strike on October 6, 2015. And his predecessor, an ethnic Uzbek known as Yar Mohammad, was killed in 2012. Mohammad ranked so high in the Taliban hierarchy that the militant group, which rarely confirms casualties, issued a statement to commemorate his death.
6. http://tribune.com.pk/story/1023238/afghan-tliban-expel-two-disssenting-leadres.
7. http://www.longwarjournal.org/archives/2012/12/isaf_kills_imutaliba.php.
8. Frud Bezhan, Ethnic Minorities are Fuelling the Taliban's Expansion in Afghanistan, Foreign Policy, the South Asia Channel, July 15,2016.
9. Rubin, Barnett R., *The Fragmentation of Afghanistan: State Formation and Collapse in The International System*. 2nd Edition Vanguard Books Pvt. Ltd Pakistan,1996, p.82.
10. General A. Liakhvosky, civil war in Afghanistan, National Security and the Future 1(1)2000, pp 186.(185-212).
11. BBC Study, Afghanistan Timeline profile, January 31, 2018.
12. Chris Massaro, Fifteen Years After 9/11, Afghan War Has No End In Sight, The Epoch Times Asia Pacific, September 13, 2016.
13. Draft Special Report-Afghanistan DSC 2017, NATO Parliamentary Assembly, Defence and Security Committee, October 7, 2017>www.nato-pa-int.
14. Patricia Grossman, Afghanistan's Civilian Causalities Hit Record High in 2016, Human Rights watch, February 6,2017
15. Mashal Mujib; Rahim, Najim, A Shortage of Coffins After Talibans Slaughters Unarmed Soldiers, the New York Times, April 22, 2017.

16. Civilian Death From Afghan Conflictin 2018 at the Highest Recorded level- Un Assistance Mission in Afghanistan February 24, 2019.
17. http://www.unhcr.org/cgi-bin/texis/vix/search&docid=3ae6b81cfo&query=retun to Afghanistan.
18. Afghanistan: Growing Challenges, the international Crisis group, watch List 2017, 30 April 2017.
19. Global Report on Internal Displacement 2017; Khalid Koser, Afghanistan 2014 : A Crisis of Internal Displacements, Bookings , August 30,2013.
20. UN Office For Coordination of Humanitarian Affairs, July Bulletin UNAMA, August 13, 2013.
21. Civilian Death Fron Afghan Conflict in 2018 at the Highest Recorded Level, UN Report, United Nations Assistance Mission in Afghanistan (UNAMA)February 24, 2019.
22. Mirwais Khan and Lynne O' Donnell, ISIS EXPANDS PRESENCE IN RESTIVE SOUTH AFGHANISTAN; Afghanistan: Taliban's Insurgency, Pioneer, 27 August 11, 2016.
23. Mirwais Khan, ISIS in Afghanistan grows Presence Near Pakistan Borders, Army Times August 14,2016>https://www.armytimes.con/news/your-arm/2016/08/14.
24. BBC Report, January 31,2018.
25. http://www.thenational.ae/world/asia/afghan-security-forces-shrink-as-insurgent-groups-gain-control-1.726482.
26. Con Coughlin, Afghanistan presents a perfect location for ISIS to regroup and continue its bloodshed,The National Opinion, May 3, 2018.
27. Zachary Laub, The Taliban's in Afghanistan, Council on Foreign Relations, July 4, 2014.
28. Ibid.
29. Cassy Garret Johnson, The Political deal with Heze-be-Islami, the united institute for Peace, July 6, 2018.
30. Bart Jansen, The US Today,January , 29,2018.
31. According to a survey entitled 'Peace Stalemate and Solutions' conducted in six Provinces including Kabul, Herat, Kandahar, Balkh and Kunduz, by the Center for Strategic and Regional Studies (CSRS), most Afghans see an Afghan-led peace process as the only solution. The survey result released on December 2, 2017, revealed that 90.2 per cent of the respondents believe that an Afghan-lead peace process can bring peace the country.
32. Dawood Azami, Afghanistan War: Taliban Attend the Landmark peace talks in Russia, BBC World Service, Nov.9,2018.
33. Pamela Constable and Paul Sonne,U.S.-Taliban talks appear closer to pact after marathon negotiations in Qatar, Washington Post , Asia- Pacific, January 26, 2019; Vivek Katju, Towards An Afghan Ceasefire, The Times of India, New Delhi, January 29 ,2019; Memphis Barker and Shami Yousufzai, Taliban hails 'helpful' US talks as boost to Afghan peace process, BBC, August.13,2018.

Appendix - 5

Who are the Talibans

- The hardline Islamic Taliban movement swept to power in Afghanistan in 1996 after the civil war which followed the Soviet-Afghan war, and were ousted by the US-led invasion five years.
- In power, they imposed a brutal version of Sharia law, such as public executions and amputations, and banned women from public life.
- Men had to grow beards and women to wear the all-covering burka; television, music and cinema were banned.
- They sheltered al-Qaeda leaders before and after being ousted - since then they have fought a bloody insurgency which continues today.
- In 2016, Afghan civilian casualties hit a new high - a rise attributed by the UN largely to the Taliban.

Appendix - 6

Afghanistan-Chronology of Events

1838-42 - British forces invade, install King Shah Shujah. He is assassinated in 1842. British and Indian troops are massacred during retreat from Kabul.

1878-80 - Second Anglo-Afghan War. A treaty gives Britain control of Afghan foreign affairs.

1919 - Emir Amanullah Khan declares independence from British influence.

1926-29 - Amanullah tries to introduce social reforms, which however stir civil unrest. He flees.

1933 - Zahir Shah becomes king and Afghanistan remains a monarchy for next four decades.

1953 - General Mohammed Daud becomes prime minister. Turns to Soviet Union for economic and military assistance. Introduces social reforms, such as abolition of purdah (practice of secluding women from public view).

1963 - Mohammed Daud forced to resign as prime minister.

1964 - Constitutional monarchy introduced - but leads to political polarisation and power struggles.

1973 - Mohammed Daud seizes power in a coup and declares a republic. Tries to play off USSR against Western powers.

1978 - General Daud is overthrown and killed in a pro-Soviet coup. The People's Democratic Party comes to power but is paralysed by violent infighting and faces opposition by US-backed mujahideen groups.

Soviet intervention

1979 December - Soviet Army invades and props up communist government.

1980 - Babrak Karmal installed as ruler, backed by Soviet troops. But opposition intensifies with various mujahideen groups fighting Soviet forces. US, Pakistan, China, Iran and Saudi Arabia supply money and arms to the mujahideen.

1985 - Mujahideen come together in Pakistan to form alliance against Soviet forces. Half of Afghan population now estimated to be displaced by war, with many fleeing to neighbouring Iran or Pakistan.

1986 - US begins supplying mujahideen with Stinger missiles, enabling them to shoot down Soviet helicopter gunships. Babrak Karmal replaced by Najibullah as head of Soviet-backed regime.

1988 - Afghanistan, USSR, the US and Pakistan sign peace accords and Soviet Union begins pulling out troops.

Red Army quits

1989 - Last Soviet troops leave, but civil war continues as mujahideen push to overthrow Najibullah.

1992 - Najibullah's government toppled, but a devastating civil war follows.

1996 - Taliban seize control of Kabul and introduce hard-line version of Islam, banning women from work, and introducing Islamic punishments, which include stoning to death and amputations.

1997 - Taliban recognised as legitimate rulers by Pakistan and Saudi Arabia. They now control about two-thirds of country.

1998 - US launches missile strikes at suspected bases of militant Osama bin Laden, accused of bombing US embassies in Africa.

1999 - UN imposes an air embargo and financial sanctions to force Afghanistan to hand over Osama bin Laden for trial.

2001 September - Ahmad Shah Masood, leader of the main opposition to the Taliban - the Northern Alliance - is assassinated.

US-led invasion

2001 October - US-led bombing of Afghanistan begins following the September 11 attacks on the United States. Anti-Taliban Northern Alliance forces enter Kabul shortly afterwards.

2001 December - Afghan groups agree deal in Bonn, Germany for interim government.

Hamid Karzai is sworn in as head of an interim power-sharing government.

2002 January - Deployment of first contingent of foreign peacekeepers- the Nato-led International Security Assistance Force (ISAF) - marking the start of a protracted fight against the Taliban.

2002 April - Former king Zahir Shah returns, but makes no claim to the throne and dies in 2007.

2002 June - Loya Jirga, or grand council, elects Hamid Karzai as interim head of state. Karzai picks members of his administration which is to serve until 2004.

2003 August - NATO takes control of security in Kabul, its first-ever operational commitment outside Europe.

Elections

2004 January - Loya Jirga adopts new constitution which provides for strong presidency.

2004 October-November - Presidential elections. Hamid Karzai is declared winner.

2005 September - Afghans vote in first parliamentary elections in more than 30 years.

2005 December - Parliament opens with warlords and strongmen in most of the seats.

2006 October - Nato assumes responsibility for security across the whole of Afghanistan, taking command in the east from a US-led coalition force.

2007 August - Opium production has soared to a record high, the UN reports.

2008 June - President Karzai warns that Afghanistan will send troops into Pakistan to fight militants if Islamabad fails to take action against them.

2008 July - Suicide bomb attack on Indian embassy in Kabul kills more than 50.

2008 September - US President George Bush sends an extra 4,500 US troops to Afghanistan, in a move he described as a "quiet surge".

2009 January - US Defence Secretary Robert Gates tells Congress that Afghanistan is new US administration's "greatest test".

2009 February - NATO countries pledge to increase military and other commitments in Afghanistan after US announces dispatch of 17,000 extra troops.

New US approach

2009 March - US President Barack Obama unveils new strategy for Afghanistan and Pakistan. An extra 4,000 US personnel will train and bolster the Afghan army and police and there will be support for civilian development.

2009 August - Presidential and provincial elections are marred by widespread Taliban attacks, patchy turnout and claims of serious fraud.

2009 October - Mr Karzai declared winner of August presidential election, after second-placed opponent Abdullah Abdullah pulls out before the second round.

2009 December - US President Obama decides to boost US troop numbers in Afghanistan by 30,000, bringing total to 100,000. He says US will begin withdrawing its forces by 2011.An Al-Qaeda double agent kills seven CIA agents in a suicide attack on a US base in Khost.

2010 February - Nato-led forces launch major offensive, Operation Moshtarak, in bid to secure government control of southern Helmand province.

2010 July - Whistleblowing website Wikileaks publishes thousands of classified US military documents relating to Afghanistan.General David Petraeus takes command of US, ISAF forces.

2010 August - Dutch troops quit.Karzai says private security firms - accused of operating with impunity - must cease operations. He subsequently waters down the decree.

2010 September - Parliamentary polls marred by Taliban violence, widespread fraud and a long delay in announcing results.

2010 November - NATO - at summit in Lisbon - agrees plan to hand control of security to Afghan forces by end of 2014.

2011 January - President Karzai makes first official state visit to Russia by an Afghan leader since the end of the Soviet invasion in 1989.

2011 February - Number of civilians killed since the 2001 invasion hit record levels in 2010, Afghanistan Rights Monitor reports.

2011 April - Burning of Koran by a US pastor prompts country-wide protests in which foreign UN workers and several Afghans are killed.Some 500 mostly Taliban prisoners break out of prison in Kandahar.

2011 July - President's half-brother and Kandahar governor Ahmad Wali Karzai is killed in Taliban campaign against prominent figures.

2011 September - Ex-president Burhanuddin Rabbani - a go-between in talks with the Taliban - is assassinated.

2011 October - As relations with Pakistan worsen after a series of attacks, Afghanistan and India sign a strategic partnership to expand co-operation in security and development.

Military pact

2011 November - President Karzai wins the endorsement of tribal elders to negotiate a 10-year military partnership with the US at a loya jirga traditional assembly. The proposed pact will see US troops remain after 2014, when foreign troops are due to leave the country.

2011 December - At least 58 people are killed in twin attacks at a Shia shrine in Kabul and a Shia mosque in Mazar-i-Sharif.Pakistan and the Taleban boycott the scheduled Bonn Conference on Afghanistan. Pakistan refuses to attend after a NATO air strike killed Pakistani soldiers on the Afghan border.

2012 January - Taliban agree to open office in Dubai as a move towards peace talks with the US and the Afghan government.

2012 February - At least 30 people are killed in protests about the burning of copies of the Koran at the US Bagram airbase. US officials believed Taliban prisoners were using the books to pass messages, and that they were extremist texts not Korans. Two soldiers are also killed in reprisal attacks.

2012 March - US Army Sgt Robert Bales is accused of killing 16 civilians in an armed rampage in the Panjwai district of Kandahar.

2012 April - Taliban announce "spring offensive" with audacious attack on the diplomatic quarter of Kabul. The government blamed the Haqqani Network. Security forces kill 38 militants.

NATO withdrawal plan

2012 May - NATO summit endorses the plan to withdraw foreign combat troops by the end of 2014.

New French President Francois Hollande says France will withdraw its combat mission by the end of 2012 - a year earlier than planned.

Arsala Rahmani of the High Peace Council is shot dead in Kabul. A former Taliban minister, he was crucial in reaching out to rebel commanders. The Taliban deny responsibility.

2012 July - Tokyo donor conference pledges $16bn in civilian aid to Afghanistan up to 2016, with US, Japan, Germany and UK supplying bulk of funds. Afghanistan agrees to new conditions to counter corruption.

2012 August - The US military discipline six soldiers for accidentally burning copies of the Koran and other religious texts in Afghanistan. They will not face criminal prosecution. Three US Marines are also disciplined for a video in which the bodies of dead Taliban fighters were urinated on.

2012 September - US hands over Bagram high-security jail to the Afghan government, although it retains control over some foreign prisoners until March 2013.The US also suspends training new police recruits in order to carry out checks on possible ties to Taliban following series of attacks on foreign troops by apparent police and Afghan soldiers.

2013 February - President Karzai and Pakistan's Asif Ali Zardari agree to work for an Afghan peace deal within six months after talks hosted by Britain's Prime Minister David Cameron. They back the opening of an Afghan office in Doha and urge the Taliban to do the same for talks to take place.

2013 March - Two former Kabul Bank chiefs, Sherkhan Farnood and Khalilullah Ferozi, are jailed for the multi-million dollar fraud that almost led to its collapse and that of the entire Afghan banking system in 2010.

2013 June - Afghan army takes command of all military and security operations from Nato forces.

President Karzai suspends security talks with the US after Washington announces it plans to hold direct talks with the Taliban. Afghanistan insists on conducting the talks with the Taliban in Qatar itself.

2014 January - Taliban suicide squad hits a restaurant in Kabul's diplomatic quarter, the worst attack on foreign civilians since 2001. The 13 foreign victims include IMF country head.

2014 April - The presidential election produces an inconclusive result and goes on to a second round between Abdullah Abdullah and Ashraf Ghani.

2014 June - Second round of presidential election is held, with more than 50 reported killed in various incidents during the vote.

2014 July - Election officials begin recount of all votes cast in June's presidential run-off, as part of a US-mediated deal to end dispute between candidates over widespread claims of fraud.

Election deal

2014 September - The two rivals for the Afghan presidency, Ashraf Ghani and Abdullah Abdullah, sign a power-sharing agreement, following a two-month audit of disputed election results. Ashraf Ghani is sworn in as president.

2014 October - The US and Britain end their combat operations in Afghanistan.

Opium poppy cultivation in Afghanistan reaches an all-time high, according to a US report.

2014 December - NATO formally ends its 13-year combat mission in Afghanistan, handing over to Afghan forces. Despite the official end to Isaf's combat role, violence persists across much of the country, with 2014 said to be the bloodiest year in Afghanistan since 2001.

2015 January - NATO-led follow-on mission "Resolute Support" gets underway, with some 12,000 personnel to provide further training and support for Afghan security forces.

Islamic State (IS) group emerges in eastern Afghanistan and within a few months captures a large swathe of Taliban-controlled areas in Nangarhar province.

2015 March - US President Barack Obama announces that his country will delay its troop withdrawal from Afghanistan, following a request from President Ashraf Ghani.

The lynching of a woman wrongly accused of burning a Koran in Kabul provokes widespread revulsion and criticism of hard-line clerics. Police face accusations of doing too little to save her. The incident leads to widespread protests against the treatment of women. Four men are later convicted of murder.

Taliban offensives

2015 May - Taliban representatives and Afghan officials hold informal peace talks in Qatar. Both sides agree to continue the talks at a later date, though the Taliban insist they will not stop fighting until all foreign troops leave the country.

2015 July - Taliban admits that reclusive founder, Mullah Omar, died a few years ago, and appoints Mullah Akhter Mansour as his replacement.

2015 September - Taliban briefly capture major northern city of Kunduz in their most significant advance since being forced from power in 2001.

2015 October - Powerful earthquake kills more than 80 people in northeast of country.

2015 October - US President Barack Obama announces that 9,800 US troops will remain in Afghanistan until the end of 2016, backtracking on an earlier pledge to pull all but 1,000 troops from the country.

2015 November - A new Taliban splinter group, headed by Mullah Rasool, announces its presence in southern Afghanistan. However, the group is totally crushed by the mainstream Taliban by spring 2016.

2015 December - Taliban make bid to capture Sangin, a town and district in Helmand Province. US warplanes deploy in support of Afghan security forces' attempt to repel insurgents.

2015 December - NATO extends its "Resolute Support" follow-on mission by 12 months to the end of 2016.

2016 - Over one million Afghans are on the go during the year, either due to internal displacement because of the war, or are forced to repatriate by Pakistan, Iran and the European Union, according to the United Nations.Heavy US air strikes reverse Islamic State's gains in the east, and the group is cornered in a few districts in Nangarhar.

2016 May - New Taliban leader Mullah Mansour is killed in a US drone attack in Pakistan's Baluchestan province.

2016 July - US President Barack Obama says 8,400 US troops will remain in Afghanistan into 2017 in light of the "precarious security situation". NATO also agrees to maintain troop numbers and reiterates a funding pledge for local security forces until 2020.

2016 August to October - Taliban advance to the outskirts of Lashkar Gah, the capital of Helmand, and to the northern city of Kunduz. The group has brought much of the two provinces under its control since the bulk of NATO forces withdrew by end of 2014.

2016 September - The Afghan government signs a peace agreement with the militant group Hezb-e-Islami and grants immunity to the group's leader, Gulbuddin Hekmatyar.

2017 January - A bomb attack in Kandahar kills six UAE diplomats.

2017 February - Rise in Islamic State activities reported in a number of northern and southern provinces.

2017 March - Thirty people are killed and more than 50 wounded in an attack by so-called Islamic State on a military hospital in Kabul.

2017 June - Islamic State militants capture the mountainous region of Tora Bora in Nangarhar province, which was formerly used as a base by the late al-Qaeda leader Osama Bin Laden.

2017 August - US President Donald Trump says he's sending more troops to fight a resurgent Taliban.

2018 January - Bomb-laden ambulance explodes in Kabul, killing more than 100 people. It is one of ongoing attacks attributed to the Taliban.

2018 August -The Taliban launched a brazen attack on the strategic Afghan city of Ghazni, south of the capital Kabul, seizing key buildings and trading fire with security forces. At least 16 people were killed and 40 injured, the majority of them Afghan security forces.

Appendix - 7

Ethnic groups in Afghanistan

Afghanistan has a wide variety of ethnic groups with each having different linguistic, religious and ethnic identities.

Afghanistan's topography has contributed to keeping people and communities isolated from each other. During the course of the 20th century, contact between different groups increased, with development of the country's communication and road system and consolidation of state power. This contact continued after the Soviet invasion, although the country's development stagnated and violence erupted.

Politicised overestimation

Estimates of the numbers of different ethnic groups have to be taken with a grain of salt. There has not been a census in Afghanistan for decades, and all figures are based on estimates. In addition, various ethnic groups often exaggerate their own population size for political reasons. This text, including all statistics, is based on the book Afghanistan: A Cultural and Political History by Thomas Barfield, which is generally regarded as a good and balanced reference on Afghanistan.

Pashtuns

Pashtuns are Afghanistan's largest ethnic group and are estimated to make up around 40% of the Afghan population. The majority follow the Sunni Muslim doctrine. Pashtuns are the world's largest remaining tribal community. They have held the reins of power in Afghanistan since the 18th century.

The majority of rural Pashtuns are farmers, while a minority are trading nomads. Their language, Pashto, is an Indo-European language of eastern Iraqi origin. Pashtuns believe they have a common ancestor, Qais Abdur Rashid (575–661 A.C.), the traditionally renowned and perhaps mythical founding father of the Pashtun nation. Pashtuns can trace their lineage back to four of Qais's sons and their family lines: Abdali (later known as Durrani), Gharghasht, Kalanai and Ghilzai. These in turn divide into clans and tribes.

The concept of Pashtunwali is important in the Pashtun culture. It reflects loyalty to a maxim where honour is central as well as independence, courage, self-respect and respect for others. However, many Pashtuns who have lived for generations in the Dari-speaking cities, no longer relate to Pashtunwali, nor do they speak Pashto.

There are significant internal rivalries between the branches and clans of Pashtuns, such as the long-standing political rivalry between the Durrani and the Ghilzai. President Hamid Karzai is a Durrani, while the opposition to his government has been led mainly by Mullah Omar, Gulbuddin Hekmatyar and the Haqqanis, all belonging to the Ghilzai tribe. One of the main grievances of the Ghilzai tribe is the fact that they are underrepresented in the Afghan leadership, which motivates many to continue the insurgency.

Tajiks

Tajiks are also mostly Sunni Muslims, but they speak Dari and group cohesion is non-tribal. They constitute the second largest ethnic group in Afghanistan, an estimated 30%. They have long been more urbanised than other groups. The majority, however, still live scattered in the mountainous north and north-eastern areas, such as Badakhshan, and parts of Herat province along the western border with Iran. They have relatively little internal cohesion as an ethnic group and the majority identify themselves primarily with the region or cities they come from, rather than by ethnicity.

While government leaders and key ministers have had Pashtun origin, the bureaucracy has been traditionally dominated by the Tajik. This is partly because of their Dari language skills, which the public administration historically has used at the regional level.

Like Pashtuns, a clear majority of Tajiks follow the Sunni Muslim doctrine, while about 5% are Shia Muslims, Twelver and Ismaili Shia, concentrated in scattered pockets. Many times, these two Shia minorities have been the victims of discrimination. Rural Tajik live mainly on agriculture, handicrafts and trade while urban Tajiks have been prominent traders, officials and religious scholars.

Hazaras

Hazaras account for about 15% of the population and are the third largest ethnic group. The majority of Hazaras are located in Hazarajat, an area in the central highlands of Afghanistan that they controlled autonomously until the end of the 19thcentury. The majority of the Hazara belong to the Twelvers, a branch of the Shia Muslim doctrine, while only a small minority belongs to the Sunni doctrine.

Hazaras speak Hazaragi, a dialect very close to Dari that uses many Turkish and Mongolian expressions. Ethnically, they originate from the central Asian region and are popularly claimed to be descendants of the Mongol Army that invaded Afghanistan in the 13th century under the command of Genghis Khan. Most Hazaras are farmers, often living at higher altitudes.

Historically, Hazaras have often been victims of discrimination and persecution by other ethnic groups for religious and racial reasons. They have been systematically excluded from government positions and education and have struggled to achieve social mobility. The Taliban regime was particularly brutal in its persecution of Hazaras. However, in the constitution ratified in 2004, Hazaras were given equal rights to other ethnic groups.

Since the late 19th century, many Hazaras migrated to Kabul, Herat and Mazar-e Sharif, often as a result of systematic discrimination by Afghanistan's rulers. By the 1970s they made up one third of the population in the capital.

Uzbeks and Turkmen

The Uzbek and Turkmen minorities in Afghanistan make up about 10% of the population. They are Sunni Muslim and originate historically from nomadic tribes that arrived in waves from Central Asia. Their languages belong to the Turkic language family.

They are traditionally associated with the areas northwest of the Hindu Kush mountain range, near the borders of Uzbekistan and Turkmenistan. Uzbeks live off agriculture, crafts and trade, while the Turkmen herd goats, horses and/or camels. This lifestyle has traditionally given them a relatively good economic basis, but also made them highly vulnerable to war and drought. Both Turkmen and Uzbeks are known for their craftsmanship of hand-woven carpets and sheep pelt export. In Kabul and other northern cities, Turkmen are known for trade.

Aimaqs

Aimaqs are the smallest of the main ethnic groups and probably account for around 5%. They are Sunni Muslims, and their primary language is Dari with many loan words from Turkish. They are tribes that historically settled around the western parts of the Hindu Kush, that is, east of Herat and west of the Hazarajat. Under persecution by the central government at the end of the 19th century, many were displaced to northern Afghanistan. Aimaqs are either settlers, nomads, or a combination of both.

Other minorities

Farsiwan are settled in western Afghanistan, near the border with Iran. They speak a Persian dialect that is close to Dari and they belong to Twelver branch of Shia Muslim in Afghanistan.

Nuristani people are settled in the eastern Afghan mountains where they make their living from agriculture and livestock. They are Sunni Muslims and speak a language that is considered to be very old, with features from both Persian and Hindi. Living in isolated valleys and rough terrain, Nuristanis had a distinct culture and a polytheistic religion, but were conquered and forcibly converted to Islam in the end of the 19th century.

Kyrgyz are Turkic-speaking, and before the war they lived mostly in the Pamir Wakhan Corridor, the long and thin strip of Afghan territory that stretches northeast from Badakshan province to form a narrow border with China. They herd Yak-oxen, goats and camels. There are only few Kyrgyz living in Afghanistan today. Most of them fled to Turkey, China, Pakistan or other countries during the Soviet occupation.

Among other smaller ethnic groups are Arabs, Pashayi, Baloch, Pamiris, Brahuis, Mongols, Qizilbash, Hindus, Kohistani, Gujars and Sikhs.

Chapter - 6

Bangladesh: Ethnic Violence and Islamic Extremism

In recent years, the rise of Islamic extremism and ethnic violence against minorities in Bangladesh is a deep concern of world community. Bangladesh has undergone many fundamental social and political changes since independence. A new brand of nationalism with an Islamic flavor has gradually replaced secular Bengali Nationalism as the basis of nationhood. It is the only country in subcontinent that can claim to be a nation state with one dominant people, one language and one religion. The Bengali Muslim population see Islam both as the idea of the nation and as an integral part of their identity. The Islamists and political leaders want to create a polity guided solely and solely by Islam. Political parties and political leaders too have risen to prominence that have been implicated in violence not only against Hindu minority but also Muslims minorities, Christians and other minorities. This Islamic extremism, a new fabric of Bangladesh society, has ruined the secular texture and has been posing threat to the democratic forms of state.

Bangladesh became an Islamic state in 1982 and has been strengthening its Islamic identity over the years by making it clear that only religion in Bangladesh means only Islam. In 1947, when the British divided India and created the Pakistan, it had two regions-East and West. East Pakistan was ethnically homogenous, dominated by a Bengali ethnic majority, and nearly a quarter of the population were Hindu. In contrast, West Pakistan was ethnically diverse but had less religious diversity. West Pakistan deployed Islam politically to suppress ethnic aspirations in both regions of the emerging state. After enduring decades of economically extractive and discriminatory policies, Bengalis in the east Pakistan launched a civil war to gain an independent state. Pakistan's government used Islamist militias under the control of the Jamaat-e-Islami (JeI) as well as the armed forces to suppress Bengali agitation. On 16 December 1971, the Bengali freedom fighters Mukti Bahini under the leadership of Sheikh Mujibur Rahman gained independence on 16th December 1971 and Bangladesh became full-fledged state with the assistance of India.

Chronology of violence and Bloodshed Against Hindus

The unfolding fate of Hindus in Bangladesh rarely makes headlines but the numbers tell the story. In 1872, 53% of the population were Hindus. In 1900, it was 32.7%, and by 1947, it decreased to 22%. According to the Bangladesh Census, Hindus who were 22 per cent, the numbers came down to 14 percent in 1974. As per the 1991 Census, while the Muslim population increased by 219%, Hindu population increased only 4.5%, in fact, the usual rate of increase of Hindu population was much less. In 2001, the size of Hindu population was further declined and only 1.7 million population was added yielding a 0.6% annual average growth rate. By contrast, the Muslim population almost doubled from 61 million to 111 million and the annual average growth rate was 2.2% during the same period. The last 2011 census suggests that Hindu consists of only 8.4 per cent of the population.[1]

At present, Bangladesh has one of the world's largest Muslim populations approximately 141 million Muslims now if compared to the combined population of Iran (82 million) Afghanistan's 34 million and 29 million of Saudi Arabia. Ever since the birth of Bangladesh, the Hindu population grew only marginally and their relative share in the total population declined considerably. The Hindu population declined to 8.2 percent in the country with annual growth rate coming down to 0.05 percent between 2001 to 2011 and it is projected that in 2051 the share of Hindu population will decline to 3.7 percent and Bangladesh will have achieved the status of Pakistan with no significant Hindu population.

Table 19: Demographic Changes by Religion

Census year	*Muslims*	*Hindu*
1901	66.1	33.0
1911	67.2	31.5
1921	68.1	30.6
1931	69.5	29.4
1941	70.3	28.0
1951	76.9	22.0
1961	80.4	18.5
1974	85.4	13.5

(*Contd...*)

1981	88.3	10.5
2001	89.6	09.3
2011	90.0	08.5

Source: BBS Population Report, 1991, Ct from, Shishir Moral, Rights of Religious Minorities, in Hameeda Hossain (ed). Human Rights Bangladesh, 2000, Dhaka, Ain 'O Salish Kendro, 2001, pp. 160. and Bangladesh Bureau of Statistics (BBS) Literacy Assessment Survey 2011, May 2013, Statistics and Informatics Division (SID) Ministry of Planning.

Forced Migration and Conversion

The migration of Hindus and other minorities from Bangladesh have been progressively increased since independence. Around 11.3 million Hindus have left Bangladesh due to religious persecution and discrimination. Today, on average, 632 Hindus are migrating from Bangladesh each day to India. The minorities groups- Hindu, Buddhist and Christians have been met with unprecedented violence from the Muslims majority. Amnesty International released a report on attacks on members of the Bangladesh's religious minorities, which stated that Hindus-who make up less than 10% of Bangladesh population of 130 million have come under attack. Hindu places of worship have been ransacked village destroyed and scores of Hindu women are reported to have been raped. The Society for Environment and Human Development, a NGO quote a local report that says that non-Muslims minorities have suffered as a result of the recent changes.

According to an estimation, 475 persons belonging to the minority community are migrating from Bangladesh daily.

The religious minority platform disclosed the report on repression against religious minorities in the country at a press conference at Dhaka Reporters' Unity. It said, in 2017 at least 610 Hindus were forced to leave the country, 107 were killed, 25 were raped, 31 went missing, 775 were injured and 4,011 others were tortured. At least 23 Hindus were forced to convert to Islam and 172 others were forced to leave the country in 2017, claimed the report of Bangladesh Jatiya Hindu Mohajote. It stated that all incidents of religious conversion from Sanatan dharma to Islam were forceful. The converts occurred mostly at Shibaloy of Manikganj, Nasirnagar of Brahmanbaria, Kotwali of Chittagong, Cox's Bazar and Faridpur. Beside these, at least 456 incidents of looting, arson, and attack took place alongside 6,474 other incidents of various forms of repressions in 2017.In addition, at least 235 temples were attacked or the idols were damaged last year.[2] Report also mentioned that there were powerful political leaders behind the incidents aimed at grabbing the lands and properties of the religious minorities. The repressive situation of religious minorities, especially of the Hindus, had made them believe that they were 'second-class citizens' in Bangladesh. No Hindus will be left in Bangladesh 30 years from now if the current rate of exodus continues.

Bangladesh government declared 'Vision 2021' by which time the country would be a digital nation. Where will religious minorities stand then? In 2021, Bangladesh will be 50 years old. With the growth of the country, will minorities also grow? If the trend of last 38 years continues and the Enemy Property Act continues, minorities will have no hope. So how does the Enemy Property Act fit in with a Digital Bangladesh?

Today's, Hindus are historically religious minority in Bangladesh. Genocide against Hindus on the basis of religion was exemplary earlier in Pakistan and then in Bangladesh and it is a continuous phenomenon. There were riots in East Pakistan almost every year, and severe killings in 1944, 1947, 1950, 1954, 1958, 1960 and 1963.[3] The unaccountable incidence of atrocities against Hindus like killing, rape, slaughter, forcible annexation of properties, burning of houses and abduction were took place and in considerable number of cases. In course of Bangladesh Independence war 1971, a large number of Hindus were targeted for extermination by the Islamists Pakistani government and their Bengali collaborators. Nearly, 20 million Hindus were put to permanent rest in mass grave in unknown places or mass cremated anonymously or their dead bodies thrown into rivers. Many of them were forcefully converted to Islam or either forces exodus to neighbouring country India. Women were brutally raped and forced to prostitution. According to estimates, at the time of Bangladesh Liberation War, almost 3,000,000 Hindus were butchered in one of the biggest genocides of the century. An article in 'Time' magazine dated 2 August 1971, stated "The Hindus, who account for three-fourths of the refugees and a majority of the dead, have borne the brunt of the Muslim military hatred. According to BBC (9 March 2013) "Official estimates say more than three million were killed and tens of thousands of women raped during the Bangladesh war of independence. The minority Hindu community suffered disproportionately because some Pakistanis blamed them for Bangladesh's secession".[4]

Hindus in Bangladesh are passing through the same fate and all types of violence, attacks, forced migration and conversion, rape till now. Following the destruction of Babri Masjid in Ayodhya in 1992, dozens of Hindus were killed in riots across Bangladesh and approximately 3,000 temples were damaged or destroyed.[5] Hindu community leaders say the attacks are systematic and have been going on for years. They say they are not only carried out by hardliner Islamists but also by supporters of other mainstream political parties, including the Awami League and the main opposition Bangladesh Nationalist Party.[6]

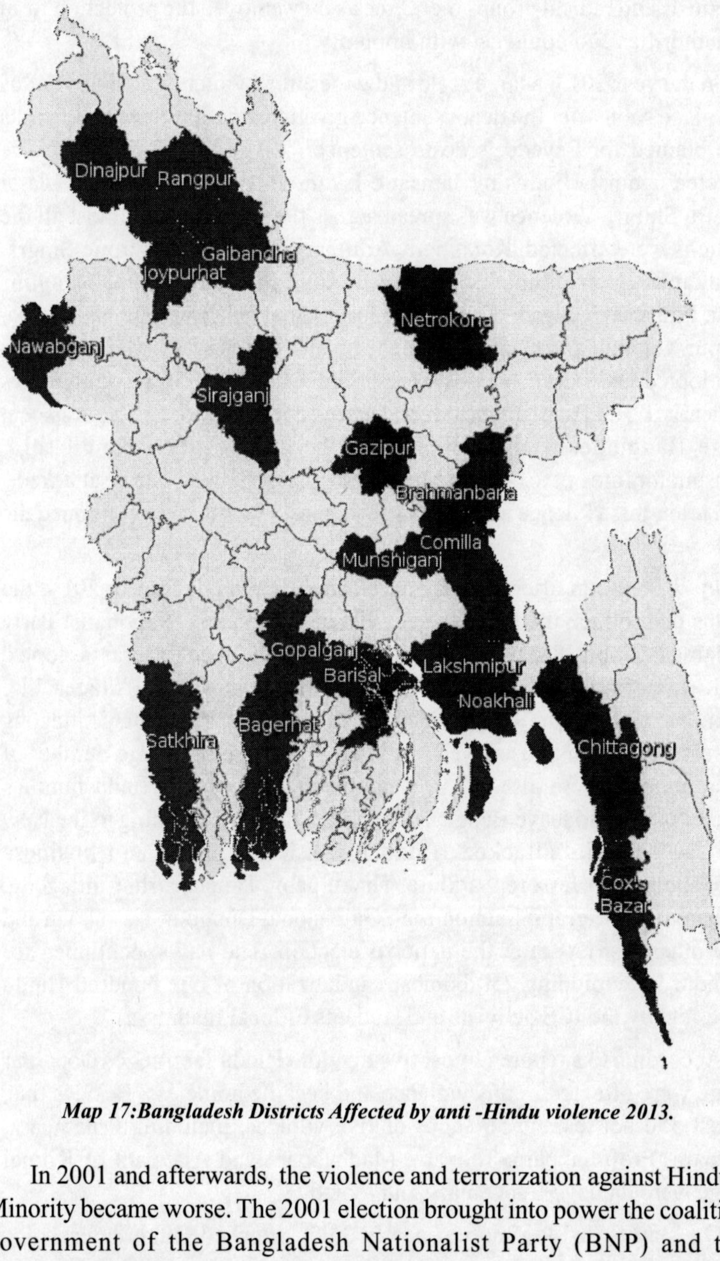

Map 17:Bangladesh Districts Affected by anti -Hindu violence 2013.

In 2001 and afterwards, the violence and terrorization against Hindu's Minority became worse. The 2001 election brought into power the coalition government of the Bangladesh Nationalist Party (BNP) and the fundamentalist Jamaate-e-Islami. Immediately after election, the BNP led Coalition began to punish Hindus who voted for Awami League. The inclusion of Jamaate-e-Islami into the government made the Islamist extremists and radical groups more free as they enjoyed the protection from the authorities and could act with impunity.

In the year 2013, a large scale and widespread violence against Hindus took place soon after the death sentence given to Hossain Sayeedi. Hindus were blamed for Sayedee's death sentence. All forms of violence were activated against Hindus by Jamaat-e-Islami and its student wing Islami Chhatra Shibir. Violence was spread across the country and almost all the divisions were affected. Kotalipara, Aditmari, Satkania, Wazirpur, Singra, Daudkandi, Netrokona, Bamna, Burhanuddin, Sirjdikhan, Rangpur Sadar, Fulbaria, Kaliganj, Kotalipara, Juri, Patuakhali, Sherpur, Netrokona, Sreepur, Gatibali and Gazipur were the most affected areas. Major temples were looted and burnt; Hindus were killed. More than 50 Hindu temples and nearly 1,500 Hindu homes were destroyed in 20 districts. The President of the Bangladesh Hindu Buddhist Christian Unity Council said, "Conspirators are out to create a situation so that the Hindus can be attacked." Even after, this violence and the attacks against Hindus were continued the whole year.[7]

In 2014, Soon after the general election in Bangladesh in 2014, the Hindus had to face the ire of the activist of Bangladesh Nationalist Party and Jamaat-Shibir. The ICS activists and students of local madrassas looted Hindu houses, shops, vandalised and burned in several places like Thakurgaon, Dinajpur, Rangpur, Bogra, Lalmonirhat, Rajshahi, Chittagong and Jessore. Hindu housewives were sexually abused;[8] a large number of Hindu temples were also burnt, vandalized and looted.[9] Hindu families were threatened to leave Bangladesh immediately.[10] According to the New Age, "Miscreants attacked Hindu localities, temples and business establishments in Jessore, Satkhira, Thakurgaon, Panchagarh, Chittagong, Nilphamari, Kurigram, Lalmonirhat, Gaibandha, Dinajpur, Netrakona and some other districts after the national election. The havoc continued for two-hour by exploding 250 bombs, vandalization of one hundred Hindu houses etc by the ICS activists and students of local madrassas"[11]

According to a report, almost five hundred Hindu families of Gopalpur village were affected in this violence and became homeless. Besides this, at least 350 houses and 50 shops of five villages, including Pritampara, Sahapara, Profullahpara, Telipara, Madhabpara and Ajaypara of Kornai village were damaged, set ablaze and looted.[12]

On May 5, 2014, a mob of nearly 3,000 attacked Hindu households and a temple in eastern Bangladesh after two youths from the community allegedly insulted the Prophet Muhammad on Facebook at Homna in Comilla district, about 100 km south east of Dhaka.[13] According to the

Editor of Hindu Existence, Hindus are attacked again and again in Bangladesh on false rumours of defaming Muhammad on Face Book. It is an established fact that some Muslim perpetrators like to use the social media face book to upload objectionable comments and pictures against Islam and Muhammad in a very motivated way. After spreading the rumours of blasphemy or the defamation of Muhammad, the Islamic hoodlums attacked Hindu-households, temples and specially the women folk.

Table-20: Bangladesh Fatalities 2005-2018.

Year	*Civilians*	*SFs*	*Terrorists*	*Total*
2005	37	3	172	212
2006	34	5	145	184
2007	9	0	79	88
2008	4	1	53	58
2009	6	0	81	87
2010	4	3	49	56
2011	0	0	24	24
2012	1	0	17	18
2013	232	18	154	404
2014	29	9	38	76
2015	23	2	48	73
2016	43	4	92	139
2017	9	4	67	80
2018	0	0	4	4
Total*	431	49	1023	1503

*Data till April 1, 2018.
Source: Figures are compiled from news reports and are provisional.

On October 30, 2016, over the allegation of disrespect shown to Islam on Face Book, a group of the demonstrators, armed with local weapons, attacked and looted the houses of the Hindu families and set on fire Hindu houses in central Brahman Barhia district's Nasirnagar. A rumour circulated that a 27-year-old Hindu man edited a photograph superimposing the Hindu God Shiva onto an image of the Kaaba (the holiest site in Islam) and posted it on his Facebook page. Within hours of the post, he was caught by local Muslims and handed over to the police. He pleaded his innocence and apologizing Muslims. Yet the uproar of the Muslim community was not appeased. On October 30, 2016, shortly after the early morning prayer, Muslims, in the name of "hurting Muslims' feelings," called on fellow Muslims, using loudspeakers from the neighbouring mosques, to come out to retaliate. The local administration and police had a nonchalant attitude and did not intervene to protect the Hindu community. Unrest spread across the Bangladesh and many Hindu areas attacked. Muslim fundamentalists vandalized idols, set fire to Hindu temples in several districts and also looted the valuables from temples. They also vandalised the temples at Duttubarhi, Namashudraparha and Ghoshparha, and Jagannath Temple and Goura Temple. Several priests were injured in the attack.[14]

Table 21: Fatalities-Islamist Terrorism 2005 - 2018.

Year	*Civilians*	*SFs*	*Terrorists*	*Total*
2005	26	0	9	35
2006	6	0	6	12
2007	1	0	7	8
2008	1	0	0	1
2009	0	0	0	0
2010	3	0	3	6
2011	0	0	0	0
2012	1	0	2	3
2013	228	18	133	379
2014	29	9	22	60
2015	23	2	31	56
2016	43	4	74	121
2017	9	4	52	65
2018	0	0	3	3
Total*	370	37	342	749

*Data till April 8, 2018.

Muslims, led by two Islamic organizations -- the Tawheedi Janata ("Faithful People") and Ahle Sunnat Wal-Jamaat --vandalized more than 15 temples and 200 houses belonging to Hindus. Violence continued and a few days later, on November 5, Islamists repeated similar attacks in the same area despite police "vigilance." This had been the biggest assault on the Hindu's culture since the 2001 as in Afghanistan where the twin Buddha statue by destructed at the Taliban in Bamiyan.

Minority Rights Group International summarizes the escalating acrimony: "Since 2013, Bangladesh has experienced a series of violent attacks by extremists. The victims have included besides atheists, secular bloggers, liberals and foreigners -- many Buddhists, Christians and Hindus as well as Ahmadis and Shia Muslims. A large number of the attacks targeting religious minorities have been claimed by... Islamic State (IS) – a claim vigorously denied by the Bangladeshi government, which has attributed the attacks to domestic militant groups. Regardless...the authorities have visibly failed to ensure the protection of those targeted. Besides the rising death toll, including civilians killed indiscriminately in bombings or individually selected by armed assailants with machetes in premeditated attacks, the... insecurity has diminished the ability of civil society to operate freely... Communal violence -- long a problem for religious minorities -- continues to take place on a regular basis, driven by political rivalries, expropriation and the apparent impunity enjoyed by perpetrators."[15]

The most important militant group, the Harkat-ul-jihad-al-Islami(Hujji or the Movement of Islamic Holy War). Bangladeshi Hindus and moderate Muslims held them responsible for many of the recent attacks against religious minorities, secular intellectuals and journalists. The US State department in 2001, Huji is described as a terrorist organization with ties to Islamic militants in Pakistan.

Therefore, one can say that Bangladesh is on her way to Talibanization and the State religion Islam is helping the process by killing and displacing minorities. By introducing Islamic Madrasas education in the country, it has been producing the radical militant and fundamentalists groups. Islamic extremists have already formed the shadow government in Bangladesh. Roads of Bangladesh are shacked with slogan "We are Taliban and Bangla will be Afghan".[16]

A wave of targeted violence in Bangladesh since 2013 has given observers reason to believe that the country might be the next victim of the Islamic State (also known as ISISI). In a little over two years, Islamist extremists have killed dozens of bloggers, secular activists, members of minority Muslim sects, Hindus, and even a Buddhist monk in Bangladesh. The victims are tied together by their diversity and their subsequent existential challenge to monolithic, orthodox visions of political Islam.

Western governments fear that these attacks mark the spread of ISISI in Bangladesh[17] withlocal Islamist terrorist group having coalesced around the Islamic State's flag. But William B. Milam, a former U.S. ambassador to Bangladesh and Pakistan, stated that "the recent string of vicious killings in Bangladesh is less a terrorism issue than a governance issue: It is the ruling Awami League's onslaught against its political opponents, which began in earnest after the last election in January 2014, that has unleashed extremists in Bangladesh."[19] It's true that the Awami League has harshly targeted its opponents; this is nothing new in Bangladesh where politics is usually a winner-takes-all game. Yet the Awami League is not to blame for the recent surge in extremism, which began long before the party took power in 2009.

Two Islamist extremist groups are mostly involved in attacks since 2013. One of these extremist groups—the Jamaat-ul-Mujahideen Bangladesh (JMB), which is now affiliated with ISIS—has been active as far back as 2005, when the Nationalist Party Bangladesh (BNP) ruled the country. In fact, the JMB was behind a streak of violence, which culminated in a wave of bombings. Extremists have not only killed secularists in the streets, they have created an opposing movement known as Hefazat-e-Islam. It carried in hundreds of thousands of people to Dhaka to demand sharia law, bans on contact with members of the opposite sex in public, and death sentences for atheists.

Rise of Islamic Extremism and Violence

There are many significant factors responsible for the violence against the Hindus and the rise of Islamic extremism or militancy in Bangladesh. In late 1970s, a new school of Islam from Saudi Arabia entered in South Asia that transformed South Asia's religious scenario. Wahhabism, a fundamental Sunni school of Islam originating in Saudi Arabia with public and private Saudi funding had steadily gained influence among Muslim countries throughout the region. As a result, the nature of South Asian Islam has significantly changed in the last three decades and caused for increasing in Islamist violence in India, Pakistan, Bangladesh, Afghanistan, Maldives and Sri Lanka.[20]

After independence, Sheikh Mujibur Rahman and his party the Awami League declared to establish a secular state but subsequently and gradually, the growing importance of Bangladeshis' personal identity as Muslim made it difficult for the government to maintain its commitment to secularism. While secularism allowed citizens to separate their identities as Bangladeshis and did not eliminate the importance of personal faith. The role of Islam deepened as Mujib sought to secure the support of other Muslim countries to rebuild the war-torn country and burnish his legitimacy. Most of the Muslim countries blamed Awami League for creation of Bangladesh as a means to destroy Pakistan and divide the Muslim world. Suspicion of losing the financial aid from the Islamic bloc, Mujib's government avoided criticizing Islamist influence and became more permissive of Islamist movements. In 1973, Mujib mustered considerable efforts during a meeting of the Non-Aligned movement in Algiers to obtain formal recognition and eventual support of Muslim Arab countries.

Despite the efforts of some Bangladeshi politicians to firmly embed secularism in Bangladeshi society and systems of education, Bangladeshis increasingly equated secularism with dishonouring Islam and tantamount to dependence upon India. Bangladesh has been creeping Islamism and continue to enjoy popular support.[21] The Muslim intellectuals, scholars and secular politician deliberately promoted the view and made the common Bangladesh Muslims to believe that the ethnic minorities are migrants and not Bhumiputra (Son of soil). Religious schools, the media, and the ubiquity of Islam in family and social life subsequently contributed to a growing consensus in support of Islam and away from secularism. As scepticism towards secularism grew, Mujib Rahman was assassinated in a military coup in August 1975.

After the death of Mujibur Rahaman, Bangladesh Government made crucial constitutional amendments. In 1977, Gen. Ziaur's Government made constitutional changes to establish more productive ties with Muslim states and to woo Saudi Arabia. He inserted a clause into Article 25 of the 1972 constitution that formally stated Bangladesh's solidarity with other Muslim countries. He amended the secular orientation of the country by removing the reference of secularism from the preamble of constitution and declared "the absolute trust and faith in the Almighty Allah." In 1978, Ziaur founded the Bangladesh Nationalist Party (BNP) as an alternative to the Awami League and promoted Bangladeshi nationalism, which was "explicitly Islamic in Character" instead of the Awami League's secular Bengali nationalism. During the period 1976 and 1979, he also legalized religious political parties and allowed the Islamists to participate in the government. Bangladesh Jamaat-e-Islami which was banned by the Mujib government for its War crimes committed against Bengalis during war of independence[22] publicly re-join Bangladeshi politics in 1979. By the time Ziaur was assassinated in 1981, reliance on Islam to build nationalism and supporting the government's legitimacy were common.

Constitutional and Legal Provisions

Violence against Hindu Minorities has been supported by the Constitutional provisions and apparatus of state and the government. Bangladeshi government remains vehemently in a state of denial, which means that it is not going to do anything to stop the spread of extremism, fanaticism and the attacks on the country's religious and ethnic minorities. Instead of protecting the Minorities, the government has always tried to hide the whole gamut of torture, rape and murder incidents behind a fabric of lies. The Bangladesh government failed to maintain secular fabric of society. The Constitution of 1972 pronounced secularism as a fundamental principle of state policy. Article 41 guaranteed freedom of religion and Article 12 provided an interpretation of the principal of secularism that made Bangladesh a multi-religious society and maintain separation between state and religion. This Article was discarded in 1977 and subsequent constitutional changes gave rise to religion based politics. The 5th Constitutional amendment changed the principle of secularism and the replaced by the Faith in "The Almighty Allah"(Article 8(1)). Article 8.1(a) states the absolute trust and faith in the Almighty Allah should be the basis of all actions.[23]

General Hossain Mohammad Irshad, Bangladesh's second military dictator (1982-1990) continued consolidating Bangladesh's ties with Muslim countries and extended Ziaur's project of embedding Islam in the governance of country. In 1982, General H. M. Ershad declared Islam as the State Religion by the 8th Constitutional amendment and made the starting of the constitution with Bismillah ar-rahman-ar-rahim, hence, Bangladesh converted into an Islamic state. He also revivified BJeI as a legitimate political actor and appointed two B-JeI war criminals in his cabinet.

Articles 27-29 of Bangladesh constitution provide equality of opportunities and no discrimination on the grounds of religion, creed and castes. Art. 44 equally guarantees the fundamental rights, and section 295-298 of Penal code give protection from offences against religious places but in practice it is totally different.[24] Several thousand Hindu temples have already been destroyed. Jamaate-e-Islami leader Delwar Hossain Sayedee announced that all statutes except those of Muslim worshipers should be destroyed.[25] The Sanskrit and Hindu university which were in operation before independence, closed and its land and assets were confiscated by the government of Bangladesh in a bid to wipe out Hindu Educational system whereas the government spending lots of money on the development of Madrassas.[26] Islamic extremists often targeted temples, churches, libraries and schools of Minorities in an effort to eradicate their cultural memory.

Hindu Minorities face discrimination and oppression in everyday life. The Home Ministry had instructed the Commercial Banks to control substantial cash money against account holders of Hindu Community and to stop disbursement of business loans to the Hindus.[27] It is an unwritten law in Bangladesh, that the religious minorities cannot be given higher post like the Head of the state, Chief of Armed forces, governor of Bangladesh, Bank, Ambassador in Bangladesh Mission, or secretary in the ministry of Defence, Home, Foreign Affairs and Finance. Minorities are deliberately discriminated in recruitment in the civil and military Jobs business and trade, bank loans and credit.[28] The political parties whether in power or opposition also cannot accept that their leader could be from Hindus or minorities.

Minorities are not properly represented in the Parliament. Minority groups though formed 12% of total population, their representation is only 4.24% in Parliament. Political parties despite their electoral promises failed to stand for the cause of Hindus and other minorities.

The Bangladeshi government officially encourages forced conversion to Islam by giving incentives (B.D. Govt. Religious Ministry Circular no. 2/a-7/91-92, dated 28 November 1991), the new Muslims are paid cash doles through budgetary allocations in the name of so-called rehabilitation.

Muslim cadres of Awami League forced Hindu families either to give ransom or confess Islam or leave Bangladesh by keeping them captive. Many such kind of cases have been reported by the newspapers. Hindu families including more than 40 girls and women with 25 children have captive by the Bangladesh's Awami League ruling party cadres (JIMMI) in the village Kankunipara in the Southern District of BD, Patuakhali. Awami League cadres have been torturing these families with creating problems for supply of food and water, physical assault, child labour, molestation of girls and women and demanding Rs 3,00,000 to 5,00,000 (Bangladesh Taka) each family as Jizya tax.[29] Expert in Bangladesh for minority matters said that it is would a more critical situation for the Bangladesh Hindu minorities in the ruling of Awami League Govt. even worse than the regime of communal BNP Govt. The Islamic face of PM Sheikh Hasina of present government may be more dangerous than the face of Khaleda Zia (Ex PM of BD) in the line of Hindu cleansing in Bangladesh.

It is difficult to control Islamic fanaticism in Bangladesh for any party unless 'Islam State Religion' is not repealed for its Constitution, adopted later (Eighth Amendment, 1988) defying the its original principle of "nationalism, socialism, democracy and secularity" as enshrined in 1971.

Bangladesh's Enemy Property or Vested Property Act of 1965(VAP) is a discriminatory and an instrument only in the persecution of the Hindu minority community.[30] This Act was enacted originally by the Pakistani military regime in 1965 empowered the government to declare the Hindu property and possession as enemy property and confiscate them. It was adopted by the Bangladesh government after independence and changed its title but content remained same. Each successive government since then has not only continued this repressive law in one form or another but using it for benefits of Muslims community.

Under this act, they have annexed massive Hindu owned lands. According to a study, 1.2 million Hindu families or 44 percent of all Hindu households were affected by this act. Hindus were displaced of more than two million acres of land, comprising 5.5 percent of Bangladesh's total land mass and 45 percent of all land owned by Hindus in the country. The law, thus, was used not only to dispossess the land properties of the Hindu minority, but also doomed hundreds of thousands of Hindu households to remain in poverty. The law served as a pernicious instrument by callous politicians and land-grabbers to evict the Hindu minorities from their ancestral lands and perpetuate an environment of communal tensions in the country. The seized property under this act have benefited every major political party in Bangladesh. 45% of the spoils went to the BNP, 31 % to the Awami League, 15 % to the Islamist Party and rest to the Jatiya and others.[31] More than 3 million acres of land have been taken over from the Hindus under VPA.[32] The Hindu families destitute and many of them were forced to migrate to India. This is an oppressive act to religious minorities, especially the Hindu population violating the human rights. It has resulted in the widespread economic marginalisation and disenfranchisement of the Hindu community.

The enactment of the Restoration Act 2001 has done little to alleviate the suffering of the Hindu community. In October 2002, the Bangladesh government passed an amendment to that VPA bill, which virtually shelved the return of the confiscated properties to the real owners. They continue to be subjected to ongoing land encroachments by government officials from across the political spectrum as a result of the loopholes in the Act.[33] New incidents of land encroachments continue unabated. These incidents were especially high between 2001 and 2006 when the Bangladesh National Party was in power. In 2009, the government again tried to reform the law, but the Hindu and other minorities demanded to repeal the law. ALRD, a NGO , mobilized both print and online media, and engaged civil society members to raise public awareness on the issues related with the Vested Property (Return) Act. Finally, in 2011, the government passed the Vested Property Return (Amendment) Act which established Tribunals and District Committees in 61 districts. About half a million applications seeking legal redress were submitted by the victims. A Vested Property Return Act Implementation Monitoring Cell supported and facilitated the process, with a round-the-clock hotline to its secretariat, within ALRD's premises. The victims could call to seek legal counselling, as well as to offer their support and advice. Afterwards, the government issued additional administrative rules to clarify the implementation of the new law and from 2011 to 2013 it passed four amendments, the last being the Vested Property Return Bill (Second amendment), which annulled the Schedule-B of the Act and paved the way for regaining the access to about half a million acres of land.[34] This latest amendment literally wiped out a quarter of a million cases from the legal register, significantly reducing the judiciary burden.

Bangladesh's two mainstream political parties are known more for their rivalry, corruption, and incompetence than for governance. Despite these troubling signs, security professionals and analysts have neglected Bangladesh.[35]

The rise of Islamic extremist's violence has not been a direct result of political repression by the government rather a perennial strategy of appeasement toward extremist groups. Political Parties and leaders competed with each other to be tune with the society and its rulers, thus strengthening Islam as a factor in the power struggle in Bangladesh. Since 2001, the political climate in Bangladesh has become worse for minorities. Hostilities between the Awami League and Bangladesh Nationalist Party (BNP) have enhanced the ability of Islamist groups to pursue their agenda without repercussion. The Islamists have gained political power as the Jamaat-e-Islami Bangladesh, the most influential Islamists group, formed a strategic alliance with the ruling Bangladesh Nationalist Party despite ideological differences in 2001. The nationalist felt that they need the Islamist as coalition partner in order to establish a dominant presence in national politics. The BNP, in turn, had blindly accepted them as coalition partners in order to gain state power. Unfortunately, both political parties, Awami League and the BNP-instead of insisting that Islamists Parties embrace democratic values, have assumed that they do not pose a threat to their own dominance in government. Other Islamist political parties include Harkat and Islamic Oikko Jole too have been implicated in the use of ethnic and religious violence for political aims. Though membership of these organizations comprises only fractions of the overall population but their aggressive tactics make them formidable foes of secularist intellectuals and NGO.

In 1990 democracy returned with a BNP electoral victory. The chasm between the religious Bangladeshi nationalism propounded by the BNP and the secular Bengali nationalism espoused by the AL widened in subsequent years. Both parties boycotted parliament at different times to undermine the elected government of the competition and, when out of power, have used total strikes across the country which impose enormous economic costs and often turn violent to destabilize the other in power. Since 1990, Bangladesh's civil societies and political actors have struggled to define the role of Islam within the polity and the state, with proponents of secularism pitted against those who want to see greater formalization of Islam in state and society. Critically, with the country nearly split in its support for two parties, neither party can win an election without coalitions. This has made BJeI an important kingmaker that can extort political gains in change for its coalition support. Electoral politics have thus empowered the BJeI as both parties tried to align with it to augment their own political power.

Unfortunately, the Sheikh Hasina government has bumbled in handling this emerging threat. Rather than addressing the actual international terrorist organizations in Bangladesh, Hasina has remained steadfastly interested in clinging to power at all costs. Bangladesh Prime Minister, Sheik Hasina, said in New York that Bangladesh Hindus "have one foot in India, and the other in Bangladesh" and asked, given this divided loyalty." She has used "terrorism" as an excuse to crack down on political rivals and to render the country an autocracy dominated by her and her political party Awami League.

The marked increase in numbers of attacks on Hindu population appears to have been prompted by a desire to build a state free from minorities as well as motivated by political revenge. More worrisome is that Bangladesh is increasingly the site of Islamist terrorist violence. Between January 2005 and December 2017, some 746 people have died in Islamist terrorist attacks, including 339 alleged terrorists; of those attacks, 91 percent have taken place since 2013. That the Islamic state (IS) and al-Qaeda Indian Sub-continent (AQIS) claim many recent attacks casts a pall over Bangladesh's ostensible success.

There are three complex international developments responsible for the Islamists violence in Bangladesh.

First: during the 1980s, some Bangladeshis participated—and more importantly, learned to fight—in the "jihad" to oust the Soviets from Afghanistan. Returning militants brought with them their new knowledge of insurgent warfare and jihadist ideology to Bangladesh.

Second, in the early 1980s, Muslim ethnic Rohingyas formed the Rohingya Solidarity Organization (RSO) in the wake of a massive military operation waged by the Myanmar military that drove some 200,000 Rohingya into Bangladesh. The RSO enjoyed explicit support from the BJeI. While the size of this organization remains debated, analysts assess that "small numbers" of Rohingya militants continued to train in remote bases in Bangladesh opposite Myanmar's Maungdaw district until the 1990s. In very limited numbers, Rohingyas became sources of recruitment for different Islamist militant groups, including the Afghan Taliban and al-Qaeda.

Third, Bangladesh became one of the regional hubs which Pakistan has used to train hide, and dispatch Islamist terror groups into India for over a decade.[36]

There are many socio-economic and political reasons

First, rise of Islamic fundamentalism and extremism which gave birth to numerous Islamic terrorist organisation want the ethnic cleansing of minorities especially Hindus and to rule the country through Islamic laws.

Second, Bangladesh is a poor country and its economy is agriculture based.[37] The larger objective of these kinds of violence and attack is to grab the land of Hindus. As a result, many Hindus are fleeing to India to escape harassment, intimidation and violence. According to Jyotrimoy Barua, a Supreme Court lawyer in Dhaka, "When we say it's just political, it legitimizes the violence, Most of the people's houses they are burning are poor. If you burn their house, they will leave the country, and you get their land. The Vested Property Act allows the government to expropriate "enemy" (in practice, Hindu) lands. Once the land is acquired, the influential and political people used to grab those lands and most of the Hindu families in Bangladesh is affected by this law. The Vested Properties Return (Amendment) Bills of 2011 and 2012 which obligate the government to publish lists of returnable vested property but in practical these return act has not been enforced properly.[38] According to Barkat, in most of the cases, the beneficiary of these vested properties are the influential political people of different areas across political parties.

Third, Hindu are not significant voters for political parties to gain power hence they are not providing any protection or support to the Hindus minorities.[39] Violence against Hindus in various areas was also erupted due to the refusal by Hindus to boycott the the 2014 election on call of Jamaat Shibir activists.

Most of the newspapers reported that almost all the violence and attacks on Hindus in 2014 were initiated by the activists or members of Jamat-e-Islami and its student wing and Bangladesh National Party.

Finally, Opportunistic leaders have been accused of using divisive communal sentiments to enrich themselves. In some constituencies, all the parties are tussling from the same group of voters if anyone loses, he blames the Hindus.[40]

The violence against Hindus in Bangladesh is a part and result of wider religious intolerance spread against Hindus in the country is not the only cause to be believed. The economic and political aspect of violence in a wider prospect of neighbour-hood studies is required to understand the phenomena of Hindu subjugation in the country. There is a great possibility and chances of under reporting or un-reporting of actual intensity of the violence and oppression in the prevailing situation in Bangladesh over the last 42 years. It is clear that almost all the political parties of Bangladesh are trying to derive political mileage from the plight of Hindus. Besides, draconian laws like vested property act is a useful instrument to grab Hindu land holdings by in the hands of the majority Muslim community grab Hindu's properties. In the absence of any major economic opportunities, agricultural land is the only economic resource for which there is a lot of competition to grab and successive governments played an instrumental role in grabbing Hindu land to satisfy the majority influential community. Most of the Hindus hold the view that land is the major reason for which they have been attacked historically. Being one of the influential countries in the South Asian region, India should try to influence Bangladeshi authorities to save the minorities Hindus. Hindus in rest of the world need to intensify their campaign for safeguarding of minority rights in Bangladesh.

Main Islamist Groups in Bangladesh

Jamaat-e-Islami (JeI) Bangladesh: was founded in undivided India in 1941 by Maulana Abul Ala Mauddudi. It drew its inspiration from the Deobandi school of Islam which promotes religious extremism in several countries of South Asia. With the partition of India, Jamaate-e-Islami was subsequently established in both Pakistan and Bangladesh (then East Pakistan). JeI has a long history of radicalism and violence aim to create an Islamic theocratic and Taliban style regime in Bangladesh and have consistently utilized violent tactics to achieve their religio-political goals, including bombings, political assassinations, targeted killings, and attacks on security personnel. It focused on creating chaos and instability in order to undermine Bangladesh's democracyby killing secular activistsand minorities.

Jamaat has engaged in anti-minority violence since the 1971 War, when their members joined paramilitary militias and collaborated with the Pakistani army in committing mass human rights violations against the Hindu minority. Subsequently, they carried out large-scale attacks on minorities in 2001, which led to the exodus of an estimated 500,000 Hindus from the country.[41]

Moreover, JeI and its supporters have carried out large-scale orchestrated attacks on the homes, businesses, and places of worship of Hindu minorities, as well as engaging in the abductions and forced conversions of Hindu girls.

JeI is the most powerful Islamist group in the country and has been the ideological center and has extensive links with the wider Islamist militant network not only in Banglaadesh but in whole South Asia. It has extensive links with the terrorist groups such as Lashkar-e-Taiba (LeT), the Taliban, and al-Qaeda. During the Taliban's reign in Afghanistan, a large number of its student wing' activists were sent to fight under Osama bin Laden's leadership. It is a recruiting base for domestic militant and terrorist groups, including Harkat-ul-Jihad-al-Islami Bangladesh (HuJI-B)and Jama'atul Mujahideen Bangladesh (JMB), Hizb-ur-Tahrir and IslamiOikyoJote (IOJ) and they all carry out their activities with its assistance. Jamaat-e-Islami has been involved in laundering money for the groups associated with it and reportedly receive funding and support from Pakistan's ISI spy agency and from Saudi Arabia.

Harkat ul Jihad al Islami Bangladesh (HuJI-B)

The Harkat-ul-Jihad-al Islami Bangladesh (HuJI-B) was established in 1992 but it became active in 1996 when the Awami League (AL) came to power. Its purpose is to establish Islamic Rule by waging war and killing progressive intellectuals. They were inspired by Osama and erstwhile Taliban regime of Afghanistan and want to convert Bangladesh into an Islamic state with the help of Taliban and Osama bin Laden's International Islamic Front (IIF). The HuJI-B had reportedly maintaining active links with Al Qaeda network and remnants of the Taliban militia.

The HuJI-B was banned by the Bangladesh Nationalist Party (BNP)-led coalition Government on October 17, 2005.

The principal area of activity of the HuJI-B is the coastal area stretching from the port city of Chittagong south through Cox's Bazaar to the Myanmar's border having cadre strength of around 15,000. Its cadres are trained in the use of weapons in training camps in Chittagong and near Cox's Bazar. Many hundred recruits were reportedly trained at various training camps in Afghanistan, primarily during the reign of the Taliban. Myanmar are a significant source of cadres. The Madrassas are essential tools in recruiting and imparting religious training to the cadres. It is reported that many HuJI-B activists have seen in the Indian State of Jammu and Kashmir, Chechnya and Afghanistan.

The HuJI-B have external links with Pakistan ISI, the Jaish-e-Mohammed (JeM), Lashkar-e-Toiba (LeT) and terrorist groups operating in India's Northeast, including with the United Liberation Front of Asom (ULFA). It has been managing some of ULFA's camps situated in the Chittagong Hill Tracts in Bangladesh along the border with the Indian State of Tripuraand frequentlyinfiltrate into the eastern corridor of India to maintain contacts with terrorist and subversive outfits of the region. It has been responsible for a number of terrorist attacks in India.

In Bangladesh, the HuJI-B have the patronage of mainstream political parties such as the Bangladesh Nationalist Party (BNP) and the Jamaat-e-Islami and another Islamist extremist outfit, the Asif Reza Commando Force (ARCF). A large number of HuJI activists returned to Bangladesh during the BNP regime of Begum Khaleda Zia (1991-96) and are now spearheading the fundamentalist movement in the country.

The HuJI-B reportedly receives financial assistance from Pakistan and Pakistan ISI, Saudi Arabia and Afghanistan through Muslim Non-Governmental Organisations in Bangladesh, including the Adarsa Kutir, Al Faruk Islamic Foundation and Hataddin.

Jagrata Muslim Janata Bangladesh

The Jagrata Muslim Janata Bangladesh (JMJB), an Islamist organization is an extension of Jama'atul Mujahideen Bangladesh, also consider a youth front of the HuJI-B. Its longterm goal is to build the society based on Islamic model Holy Quran-Hadith. The JMJB follows the ideals of the Taliban militia and propagates a movement based on Jihad. Another purpose of the JMJB is to neutralize the activities of left-wing extremist groups especially cadres of the Purba Banglar Communist Party (PBCP). As per its senior leader, who is also the chief of JMB, the group was founded by Maulana Abdur Rahman in 1998 however it came to limelight on April 1, 2004. It was also known by other names like Mujahidin Alliance Council, Islami Jalsha andMuslim Raksha Mujahideen Oikya Parishad.

The JMJB has very strong bases mostly in northwest Bangladesh, in the districts of Rajshahi, Satkhira, Naogaon, Bagerhat, Jessore, Chittagong, Joypurhat, Natore, Rangpur, Bogra, Chittagong, and Khulna and has committee in each village. It has allegedly spread its network through the Madrassas and other educational institutions in these districts. This organization has commands the strength of 300000 activists, about 10,000 full-time activists and at least 100,000 part-time activists in the whole country and established training camps in several districts.[42]

The JMJB is supported by certain members of the ruling Bangladesh National Party (BNP) and certain section of administrative and police officials.[43] The JMJB has external linkages and received funds from Saudi Arabia, Pakistan and Afghanistan. The JMJB activists are reported to have carried out over 100 vigilante operations in different regions, including murders and attacks on people who they believe have committed crimes. Apart from these activities, the JMJB cadres have also been accused of extorting protection money from traders and forcing people to follow a certain variant of Islam. The activities of the outfit appeared to have stopped completely by mid-2005.

Jama'atul Mujahideen Bangladesh (JMB)

A party of Mujahadeen formed in 1998. It is also said to be an extension of JMJB. It aims at establishing the rule of Islam in Bangladesh through an armed struggle and opposed the establishment of democracy and calls for the conduct of government under Islamic law. One of the objectives of JMB is to free the Muslims from the influence of 'anti-Islam forces' and practices that brought women out of their houses to cultural functions, cinema halls, shrines and NGOs.

The Bangladesh National Party-led coalition Government under Prime Minister Khaleda Zia supported this group. The JMB is maintaining about

10,000 fulltime and 100,000 part-time cadres. It is also reported that there are approximately 10 lakh trainees of the outfit. Many of its members are cadres of the Islami Chhatra Shibir (ICS) and Jamaate-e-Islami. Such collaborative linkages with the Jamaat-e-Islami have helped it in terms of unhindered growth but also protecting them from official action. The JMB has been promoted the building of mosques and Madrassas which have used as the training centres for the radical mobilisation. The JMB is active in the Dinajpur, Joypurhat, Jamalpur and Bagerhat districts. It's terrorist campaign is based in the North Bengal region. This group has training camps in 57 districts in Northern and some southern districts.

Many countries like Kuwait, the UAE, Bahrain, Pakistan, Saudi Arabia and Libya individually as well as several international Islamic NGOs of these countries funded this organisation.[44] The JMB is also collected money through Hundi (money laundering) and collect tolls. Its leaders are reported to have invested in a large number of shrimp farms and cold storages in the south-western region of Bangladesh.

The JMB is having its links with the militant groups in Pakistan, Myanmar, Thailand, India and China provide them training, arms and explosives. Militants of the JMB are known to receive extensive training in the explosive making. The JMB's involvement in the August 2005 serial blast in 63 districts countywide is also a proof of its expertise in explosive making and planting. The JMB was banned by the Government on February 23, 2005 following the incident of February 13, 2005. The JMB is reported to have carried out seven bomb explosions in the Chhoto Gurgola area of Dinajpur town in which three persons were wounded. Following this incident international pressure grew on the government forcing it to take actions against the outfit.

Purba Banglar Communist Party (PBCP)

The Purba Banglar Communist Party (PBCP) is a fragmentation of Bangladesh Communist Party founded in 1968. The PBCP has a revolutionary agenda of capturing state power through armed struggle. Its draws inspiration from the Chinese revolution though ideologically it is closer to the Marxists-Leninists groups of India.The PBCP is strongly opposed to the presence of feudal elements in Bangladesh. Its areas of activity is mainly in south-west Bangladesh, bordering the Indian State of West Bengal. Its presence can be noticed in districts suchas Khulna, Satkhira, Bagerhat, Magura, Meherpur, Narail, Kushtia, Jessore, Jhenidah, Chuadanga and Pirojpur. There has been a spurt in the activities of the PBCP since the beginning of the year 2002, in a reversal of trend.

PBCP cadres have been involved in acts of murder, robbery, extortion, land grabbing and abduction for ransom. They primarily target landowners and contractors and extorts money from them. The outlaws are alleged to be indulging in settling land disputes in rural areas and collecting money through their strong-arm tactics from both the parties to a dispute. The PBCP levies a 'tax' on civil contractors involving in constructions of roads, bridges, schools etc. Between 1998 and 2002 April, PBCP cadres have killed 18 political activists belonging to rival groups.

Islami Chhatra Shibir (ICS)

Islamic Chhatra Shibir (ICS) is the strongest student wing of the Jamaat-e-Islami Bangladesh, which came into existence in 1941. Its significant aim is to establish an Afghanistan-Taliban type Islamist regime in Bangladesh and to oppose to forces of modernization, secularism and democracy. They also want to change the existing system of education on the basis of Islamic values, to inspire students to acquire Islamic knowledge and to prepare them to take part in the struggle for establishing Islamic way of life. The ICS is also part of a larger Islamist extremist network of the HUJI, Jamaat-e-Islami, and Islami Oikyo Jote.

The ICS is one of the strongest student fronts in the Universities of Chittagong, Dhaka, Rajshahi and Jahangirnagar and also emerging as a dominant group in the Khulna and Sylhet Universities. It is the largest Islamist student organisations in South Asia maintaining close relationship with various Islamist fundamentalist organisations of different countries of South Asia - Pakistan and Afghanistan. In 1979, the ICS secured membership of International Islamic Federation of Student Organisation (IIFSO). The ICS is maintaining close links with the Pakistan's Inter Services which support their Islamist subversive agenda in many regions in India, particularly in areas bordering Bangladesh. The ISI is also reportedly providing substantial amount of funds to the ICS. Other Islamic countries, particularly Saudi Arabia, have provided a major proportion of its financial resources. Islami Chhatra Shibir (ICS) or Jamaat-Shibir, has also been involved in numerous terrorist attacks against Hindu and other minorities in 2005 attacks.

In addition to these Bangladesh's Islamist Extremist groups, Rohingyas migrants from Myanmar are also closely related it. Arakan Rohingya National Organisation (ARNO 1998) and Rohingya Solidarity Organisation (RSO1999-2000) are political groups based in Bangladesh Chittagong Cox's Bazar area and claim to be fighting for an autonomous Muslims region in Burma's Arakan (Rakhine) state. HuJI-B, JMB and Jamaate-e-Islami recruited migrants Rohingyas, trained them in terrorist activities as in making and detonate bombs.[45]

Besides, the Pakistan's Lashkar-e-Taiba (LeT) and Al-Qaeda, the Islamic State (IS) have increased their activity in Bangladesh in recent years. IS has taken responsibility for attacks and murders of foreigners, Shia, Ahmadis, Sufis, and other religious minorities including secular writers and bloggers in particular.

Some of these murders were committed by Ansarullah Bangla Team (ABT), a banned Bangladeshi Islamist group that first gained attention in 2013, on behalf of AQIS. ABT, which has also called itself Ansar al-Islam and Ansar Bangla 7, is affiliated with al-Qaeda. AQIS has launched its own efforts to focus on Bangladesh and other parts of South Asia.

Despite these claims by IS and AQIS, Bangladesh's government has insisted that these groups do not have a presence in the country. Prime Minister Sheikh Hasina denies the presence of AQIS and IS on Bangladeshi soil and instead alleges that the BNP and BJeI are conducting these attacks "to destabilize the country." Despite Hasina's ostensibly secular reputation, she has demurred from explicitly condemning the killing of secular activists and minorities and has even blamed the victims for provoking the terrorists with their controversial speech.

Table -22 : Bangladesh Extremist and Terror Groups

	Name	*Year*	*Activity*	*Area*	*External links*
1.	Jamaate-e-Islami (JeI)	1941	Supported Pakistan again Bangladesh in 1971, turned into a political party in 2001 1971 partner in coalition government.	The whole country.	Wider Islamists network in South Asia, Pakistan'ISI, Let, al-Qaeda, Taliban as well as internal links withHuJI, JMB and Hizb-ur-Tahrir.
2	Islami chhatra Shibir (ICS)	1941	Student wings opposed democracy modernisation and secularism, aim to establish Taliban's regime, many attacks on Hindus.	University of area Chittagong, Dhaka, Rajshahi and Jahangir Nagar.	Afghan'sand Pakistan Taliban and Terrorist groups, Middle East saudi Arabia, ISISI, Malaysia, Indonesia.
3	Harkat-ul-Jihad-al Islami(HuJI-B)	1992	Establish Islamic rule and waging war against progressive intellectual and secularists.	Coastal area from Chittagong to Cox's Bazar to Myanmar border.	Pakistan's ISI,Al-Qaeda Let, JeM, Afghan's Taliban, India's ULFA. BNP also supported.
4	Jagrata Muslim Janata Bangladesh(JMJB)	1998	Youth wing of HuJI-B also an extension of JMB, propogate Islamic movement Jihad and work to neutralise the Left-wing extremism of PBCP.	North west-Bengal Region	Afghanistan, Pakistan and Saudi Arabia, Bangladesh Nationalist Party and a section of police officials also supported.
5	Jama'atul Mujahideen Bangladesh (JMB)	1998	Rule of Islam through armed struggle and free Bangladesh from anti-Muslim forces. Promoted Madrassas and building of Mosques for training the radicals.	North-Bengal region and some of the southern districts having training camps in 57 districts.	Aghanistan, Pakistan and Kuwait, the UAE, Bahrain, Saudi Arabia and Libya and international Islamic Groups, Myanmar, Thailand China and India.

(*Contd...*)

6	Purba Bangladesh communists Party(PBCP)	1998	Revolutionary agenda capturing power through arms struggle inspired by Chinese Revolution.	South -west Bangladesh bordering the Indian states of West Bengal.	----------------------------- --
7	Arakan Rohingya National Organisation (1998) Rohingyas Solidary Organisations (RSO)	1998 1999-2000	Migrants of Myanmar based in Bangladesh , fighting for an autonomous Muslim regions in Burma's Rakhine state.	Near Burmese border .	With ICS , HuJI-B, Jamate-e-Islami .

Rohingya Crisis

For over a decade, Bangladesh has been facing the refugee crisis of Rohingyas. Rohingyas are predominantly Muslim ethnic group living in the Rakhine State of Myanmar and are considered to be a most oppressed ethnic community in the world. The Rohingyas in Myanmar have been prosecuted and suffered legal and social discrimination for decades so badly that forces them the mass exodus into neighbouring borders countries specially Bangladesh.

As per the estimate of the World Bank, Rohingyas constitute only 1.1 million of total Myanmar population while the Buddhist constitutes 80 percent population. Rohingya's have been living in Arakan region since time immemorial but Myanmar people called them as "illegal immigrants" from Bangladesh. They argued that they are not the natives of Myanmar but they are the local Bengalis. They claimed that those people came to the Rakhine state of Myanmar following its annexation by the British in 1826.[46] During more than 100 years of British rule (1824-1948), many labours migrated to Myanmar from India under British rule that is now Bangladesh. Under the British administration, Myanmar was a province of India. Such migration was considered to be internal. According to Human Rights Watch,[47] Myanmar government have not even included them in the list of 135 officially recognised ethnic groups of Myanmar. In 1982, they were denied citizenship. Rohingya are now the stateless peoples refused by the Myanmar's government to accept them as citizens living as refugees in parts of Bangladesh, India and other south Asian countries.

Violent attacks on the Rohingyas was common during the military junta rule in Myanmar. the Myanmar's army and Buddhist mobs have been massacring the Rohingyas while Rohingyas have been attacking on the Myanmar police, military posts and the common people under the leadership of Arakan Rohingya salvation Army(ARSA), an armed and terrorist outfit of Rohingyas in Myanmar. Violent attacks were intensified following an incident on 24 August 2017 in which the ARSA allegedly attacked border checkpoints and killed nine officers and nearly 400 people.[48] Myanmar army had launched a counter offensive. Myanmar military's helicopters fired on civilians, executed the women and children and burned the entire villages. In fact, it was a Clearance Operations in Rakhine villages, forcing, hundreds of thousands of Rohingyas to leave Myanmar and enter into neighbouring countries by land or boat to save their life.[49] It was one of the largest refugee influxes into Bangladesh. A newspaper report quoted that the number of refugees those crossed the country were nearly about half a million since the beginning of the crisis from 24 August 2017.The United Nations High Commissioner for Human Rights (UNHCR) called this situation a "textbook example of ethnic cleansing."

Rise of the Buddhist Nationalists campaign called "969" is in fact a campaign that gave rise to anti-Muslims rhetoric targeting Rohingyas Muslim population by an organisation called Ma Ba Tha. This campaign designed to reincarnate a form of religious nationalism that is different from peaceful image of Buddhism. The Ma Ba Tha is an Association for the Protection of Race and Religion led by the two Buddhist monks Ashin Wirathu and Ashin Wimala who claim that Muslim are plotting to take over the country and accused Muslims of marrying and converting Buddhist women. These extremist narratives led campaigns that triggered the anti-Muslim drive responsible for the Rohingya's mass exodus.

The initial influx of Rohingya to Bangladesh was started in 1978 and further influx of large numbers in 1991-1992 and now in 2017. Bangladesh is the most affected country as nearly 800,000 people have crossed over the Myanmar border and taken refuge there throughout the decade. Rohingya refugees have been still coming to Bangladesh and their number is ever increasing. Myanmar government has been very reluctant to take back the Rohingyas either on one pretext or other. Such a large influx has been putting pressure on the social, economic and political environment and posing a number of challenges for Bangladesh for the short as well as longer terms. The challenges are range from human security to non-traditional security threats-internal, external as well as transnational security threats like smuggling, militancy and terrorism also.

The social environment is being adversely affected by the Rohingya as they are the trapped people. They do not have enough food, shelter and clothing. They are also living a miserable life, and many have become involved in smuggling, robbery, and piracy. Some have built small houses. There is concern about the risk of such groups merging with the local population and posing threats to local communities in the districts sheltering the refugees. Refugees have been exerted enormous pressure on local civic resources and basic amenities of life like food, shelter, healthcare now and also for the rest of the period so long the Rohingyas stay in this country.

There are violent clashes with the local peoples which has been breeding mistrust between Bangladeshi people and refugees. They are vulnerable people in dire need of a living and are likely to be involved in petty crimes for their survival. Criminal groups will also exploit these migrants coming over the borders. Their prolonged stay will cause deterioration in the country social environment and clashes for providing them with other services essential for continuing their lives in this country. The government as well as a substantial segment of civil society are concerned about the vulnerability of the destitute Rohingyas to the attractions offered by terrorist groups.

It has been the experience of different countries that hosted refugees during many humanitarian crises, finances reduce over time if the refugee crises persist. In this kind of situations, the ultimate financial burden of humanitarian assistance falls on the host country. Bangladesh has also experienced similar situation. About half a million Rohingya refugees are already there who came to Bangladesh at different points of time in the last decade or so and are not repatriated by the Myanmar government. Different forms of assistances to Rohingya refugees are already putting pressures on Bangladesh government's exchequer. Over the past year, the Rohingya problem has resulted in the diversion of a substantial portion of current revenue on immediate refugee relief activities and rehabilitation such as the setting up of camps and investment towards capital expenditure on the development of a barren marshy island known as `Thengar Char` off the Noakhali coast in the Bay of Bengal estuarine area. Each day the government of Bangladesh has to spend the $ 1 million on their relief and rehabilitation activities. According to an estimate, 200 million US dollars is needed to support the current numbers of refugees for a period of six month but with the further influx of Rohingyas, there is all possibilities of overrunning of the estimated costs for supporting them in the short run.

The Bangladesh military has been tasked to organize some of the relief infrastructure for the Rohingya refugees in the affected districts. The objective is to erect more than 14,000 refugee shelters in Cox`s Bazaar, temporarily rehabilitate the refugees and separate them from the local population as well as harmful political and anti-social elements, and obviate local tension and repercussions. The military's involvement is intended to supplement the efforts of the civil machinery on relief administration as well as monitor the refugees and the environment from the perspectives of internal security and counter-terrorism.

The Rohingya crisis is also fetching the internal political domain and influencing political equations in Bangladesh. The Awami League and its allied political parties are facing strong competition-cum-opposition from the BNP and its allies who have been out of power for more than eight years. the Rohingya issue has provided the opposition political parties a tool that may serve their interests and promote a more contentious factor in Bangladesh's power politics. The failure of Sheikh Hasina government to pass a resolution in UN Security Council on the Rohingya situation demanding to condemn the Myanmar government for failure to protect the Rohingyas, to censure the Myanmar government and stop atrocities against them, accept responsibility for their eventual repatriation and, in the interim, share responsibility for providing succour to the refugees in Bangladesh. The 20 opposition political parties combine led by Khaleda Zia`s Bangladesh Nationalist Party (BNP) has criticized Hasina for her government's "failure" to obtain a resolution.[50] Bangladeshi Buddhist groups called the Buddhist Nagarik Oikya (Buddhist Citizens` Alliance) have also joined the BNP and its political allies in condemning the Rohingya-related developments in Bangladesh. The Buddhist community is also developing rapport with the BNP and keep their options open for an alignment if a new ruling configuration of the BNP emerge. It is possible that the extremist communal elements, foreign terror groups and the some of the subverted Rohingyas aligning with the Anti-Awami League political parties in the coming general election of 2018. That will be detrimental to the peace and stability of the country.

Security problem

The massive exodus of Rohingya refugee has been posing both internal and external trans-national security problems to Bangladesh. Internally, it is having severe negative impacts on the law and order situation of the country. Rohingya are mostly been sheltered in the Teknaf-Cox's Bazar areas of Bangladesh adjacent or very close to the settlements of the local citizens. Many untoward incidences have occurred between them causing law and order situations. Public sentiments and emotions are running high on the Rohingya issues in Bangladesh. The continuous atrocities on Rohingya Muslims population in Myanmar by the militant Buddhists nationalist has given rise to strong resentment among the Bangladeshi Muslims population. It may cause counterattacks on the Buddhist minority population in Bangladesh and there is every possibility of increasing such incidences that aggravate the local social harmony and give rise to violence against Buddhists and Hindus minorities.

As regards the transitional security threats, Bangladesh geographical proximity with the golden triangle and golden crescent makes it a viable route for drug smuggling. The international drug mafia groups and arms smugglers are exploiting the refugee as curriers for the drugs and small arms smuggling. This has greatly jeopardizing the security situation in

Bangladesh, as more drug cartels and criminal gangs has been mushrooming near the border areas. The prevalence of illicit drugs and arms smuggling would not only risk the local law and order situation, terror organisations would also benefit from this situation as this would help them to fuel their activities.

Terror groups linkage with Rohingya refugee has been posing threats to Bangladesh internal and external border security. It has been reported in various news media that many local and international terror organisations are trying to make inroads among the Rohingya refugees. These refugees can be easily swayed by the extremist groups by giving funds and money, then there will be serious terrorist threats not only to Bangladesh but to all neighbouring countries especially India. They may join hands with the already existing terrorist outfits in the country like Jammate-e-Islami and HUJI. There is also the possibility of committing terrorist acts in the international arena as many of them have already been relocated in different countries of the world. The terror networks could also bring them to their folds.

The prolonged ethnic conflict in Myanmar has created a hotbed of terror as many militant and terrorist groups set eyes on the region and have called for jihad against the Myanmar atrocities. Stories of thousands of Rohingya victims float around internet. A video was uploaded by Islamist groups released on September 3, 2017, titled "Anak Pengungsi Rohingya Siap Balik ke Myanmar Untuk Berjihad – dari Aceh" (Children of Rohingya in Aceh Ready to Return to Myanmar for Jihad). It shows a group of uniformed personnel from Aceh undergoing physical training without weapons in preparation for their self-proclaimed jihad in Myanmar. Another video, "Laskar FPI Berangkat ke Myanmar" (Soldiers of FPI Departing to Myanmar) demonstrates the attempt by Indonesia's right-wing Islamist organisation, Front Pembela Islam (FPI). FPI has opened registration for mujahideen volunteers to join jihad in Myanmar. Likely, al Qaeda in Indian Subcontinent (AQIS) and Islamic state (IS) both threaten to attack on Myanmar. The situation in the Rakhine state triggered interest of ISISI, the region already declared by the leader Abu Bakr al-Baghdadi as where jihad is to be conducted. The security dilemma comes at a time when IS responding to setbacks in Syria and Iraq and is planning on expanding operations beyond the Middle East.

The prolonged refugee crisis in Myanmar is making Bangladesh, India and Nepal borders vulnerable and unstable. Bangladesh-Myanmar border is unsecure risking the internal security of the states. In 1980s, Bangladesh had encountered a border incursion by Myanmar armed forces. In November 2008, there was a maritime boundary dispute between the two states and intrusion of ships of Myanmar in Bangladesh water for oil rigs establishment that almost brought the two countries to a naval conflict. Given such history, Bangladesh has to be vigilant as the possibility of border conflict cannot be ruled out. There has been report of violation of air space of Bangladesh by the Myanmar air forces also. It is impossible to completely seal off Bangladesh and Myanmar borders due to its porous nature.

Human Trafficking

Human trafficking of the Rohingya refugees is another great problem. It has been reported that international human trafficking gangs are actively looking at this situation to exploit the vulnerability of the Rohingya for profiteering. Many Rohingya families arriving in Bangladesh are without any male family members hence, many young women and children are falling victims of the trafficking gangs and end up in international markets for prostitution and slave labour.

Food Insecurity

There is gross food insecurity for refugee population causing malnutrition and many other allied problems. The country has the food grains for its population consumption but the influx of the refugees that is keeping pouring over the borders will face the shortage of food. If the number of refugees arriving in Bangladesh increases, the country will face shortage of food; price hike in the local market and create instability in the local food grain market. The lack of food grain would create numbers of complex problem.

Health Security

The health security of the refugees is also a cause of concern. Rohingya's arriving in the camps in Bangladesh are living in subhuman conditions densely packed camps without access to adequate hygienic facilities. The health conditions of thousands of migrants in the camps are not documented. Many of the arriving refugees are already carrying a number of diseases, including TB, skin diseases and HIV/AIDS etc. These epidemic diseases could overwhelm the health service resources in the refugee camps, also poses a risk of spreading among the general population within Bangladesh as refugees continue to move from one place to another for work. Any contagious diseases that rely on the human host has the potential to become an epidemic.

Employment and Jobs

The labour market revolves around dynamics of demand and supply. The stability of the market is achieved through constant balance between the availability of work and the workforces. The presence of Rohingya in Bangladesh is also destabilising the labour market as they are in search of jobs. Though, Bangladesh unemployment rate remains static 4.35 in 2017 but it could disrupt the cohesion in the society and more problems would arise if the Bangladeshi jobless people and refugee will seek jobs whatever means necessary to make their living. It will cause resistance from the local community.

Environmental Security

Bangladesh is globally recognised as an environmentally vulnerable country and now is facing a new threat from human induced degradation of the environment. Due to the large influx of the Rohingya, many refugees failed to find accommodation within the camps. They have spread out in the nearby hills causing widespread deforestation and severe degradation of the locality. Clearing of forest land, over exploitation of natural resources to support the livelihoods of the refugees can have long term impact on environmental security and serious consequences on the local environment.

International Response

The influx of the Rohingya refugees from Myanmar need serious consideration by the international community. These are some of the most genuine challenges for Bangladesh caused due to Rohingya refugee crisis. Bangladesh cannot alone face these challenges. The International community needs to come forward to solve this problem permanently by putting pressure on the Myanmar government to take back its citizens and creating a safe and secured environment in its own country. Otherwise, it will be an uphill task for Bangladesh to shelter the Rohingya refugees for an uncertain period of time keeping in mind its limited resources. These pressures might also derail Bangladesh's development initiatives aimed for the betterment of their citizens.

The positions taken by various global and regional powers are very critical, unresponsive and failed to impose pressure on Myanmar and to take back the Rohingya refugees. The responses of all China, the United and other Western Powers and Russia are not satisfactory. Western powers, despite stern rhetoric, have so far stopped short of reviving or imposing new sanctions on Myanmar. The problem of Rohingya minority in Myanmar is creating severe rifts with the country's newly won friends in Washington and London. At the end of November, Pope Francis visited Myanmar and left without uttering the name "Rohingya" publicly. The pontiff's deference to Myanmar's sensitivities perfectly reflects a world in moral retreat. Bangladesh, generous in hosting the refugees, has also signed a repatriation deal with Myanmar which makes no mention of the name "Rohingya."

Bangladesh key allies China realign its position and supported the Myanmar government. China has huge geo-political, strategic and economic interests in Myanmar. China, a close ally of Naypyitaw, initially stated the Myanmar attitude on Rohingyas is an "internal affair"[51] but later on changed its statement due to Bangladesh government and people resentments. It still does not acknowledge that crimes against humanity have transpired, but it reportedly played a behind-the-scenes role leading to the recently inked repatriation deal between Bangladesh and Myanmar. Myanmar is an autocratic state like China and has a deep historic bond with it, albeit as a client state, the force of that affinity has influenced China's decision as much as any tactical calculations. In 1988 following the massacre of pro-democracy demonstrators in Myanmar, the United States, the European Union and Japan imposed sanctions on Myanmar, China then stepped in with trade agreements, bilateral aid and military sales. Now, China is backing Myanmar attitude towards the Rohingya as it has extensive development plans in Rakhine state including access to a strategically critical port. Myanmar is of utmost strategic importance to China for providing access to the Indian Ocean. Oil and gas pipelines from the Bay of Bengal through Myanmar to Yunnan province is the shortest supply routes from the Middle East which allowing China to avoid the potentially vulnerable chokepoint of the Strait of Malacca.

The Western Media strongly criticised Aung San Suu Kyi, the Myanmar State Counsellor and Noble laureate for not opposing the army's actions against Rohingyas. In fact, Aung San Suu Kyi has no power over the army which, according to the country's military-drafted 2008 constitution stipulates that it takes orders only from its commander-in-chief. Aung San Suu Kyi has gained popularity with Chinese netizens, who praised her defiance against 'outside pressure while safe-guarding the people's interest.' During her visit to China in September 2017 , the Chinese social media went on to say that Suu Kyi, who "had long been seen as a proxy of the West…has won cheers…from Chinese online communities who are routinely indignant over Western pressure on developing countries over issues concerning national security."[52] China's official news agency Xinhua quoted that she appreciated China's recognition that the problems facing Myanmar are extremely complex and cannot be solved overnight. When asked about China's ambitious Belt and Road development initiative, she stressed that "it has great potential to create better economic and social environment for all the countries and regions concerned."[53] "The Rakhine state issue is in essence an issue between Myanmar and Bangladesh. China does not approve of complicating, expanding or internationalising this issue,"[54] Wang said, according to a Chinese foreign ministry.

Russia has also taken a stand to support Myanmar on the Rohingya's issue. Russia is also having strategic interests wants to increase its presence and enhancing its capacity in the south East Asia region while denying strategic interests of others. Therefore, a new game of power realignment is taking place in this region which is detrimental to the interest of the Rohingya. Thailand also refrained from criticizing Myanmar, pledging to work with the Association of Southeast Asian Nations, ASEAN, to promote peace and provide humanitarian assistance to the conflict's victims.

After Bangladesh if any country that is affected most by the Rohingyas is India which has 1,643-km long border with Myanmar. The number of the Rohingya refugees in India is estimated nearly 40,000. According to the India-Myanmar agreement of the Free Movement Regime between the two countries, the people living up to 16 km on either side of the Indo-Myanmar border have been allowed to travel visa-free in each other's territory up to 72 hours.[54] Taking undue advantage from the porous border, many of the Rohingyas enter into India. Besides, there are around 140 vulnerable spots along the Indo-Bangladesh border, which are also used by the Rohingyas to cross over to India. India, which is one of the victims of terrorism, is gradually becoming more sensitive towards the influx of Rohingyas. It is suspected that some of them are influenced by the international terrorist organizations and have linkage with the Pakistani and local Islamists terror outfits. This is one of the reasons why the country is gearing up its efforts to expel them. Raj Nath Singh, India's Home Minister, said that he does not find any reason why he should not deport them as they are living in this country illegally. He said, "Rohingyas are not refugees, nor have they taken asylum. They are illegal immigrants." Since India is not a signatory to the UN Refugees Convention 1951, it is not committed to any binding for not deporting the Rohingyas.[55] However, the United Nations High Commissioner for Human Rights Zeid Ra'ad al-Hussein, apart from the civil rights activists is highly critical of India. It is perceived that the deportation issue is humanitarian in character and as such the government should think about it more seriously before initiating any action towards deportation.

India's soft attitude towards Myanmar in concern of Rohingya refugee is also a compulsion of its Act East Policy. India is having strategic and economic interests and as a part of it, she wants to improve relations with Myanmar. Prime Minister Narendra Modi, during his visit to Myanmar in September 2017, although expressed concern over "extremist violence" in Rakhine State but Suu Kyi thanked India for its stand on terror threats confronting Myanmar, saying that "both countries should cooperate to tackle terrorism." India and Myanmar also signed several agreements on maritime security cooperation and sharing shipping information — which could be seen as an attempt by India to keep an eye on its rival power China and to secure its interests in the Indian Ocean.

Nepal that is at the distance of 1,391 kilometres and they do not have a common border. Nepal and Myanmar are separated by India and/or Bangladesh. It is estimated that there are nearly 500 Rohingyas in Nepal. They are living in temporary sheds on private land at Kapan in Kathmandu and are provided food by the UN Commission for Refugees. It is feared that many of them might have mixed up with Muslim communities in different parts of the country, particularly in the Terai region, to avoid any attention from the government authorities. Until recently, not even the government of Nepal was conscious of the influx of Rohingyas in the country. Therefore, they have neither been recognised as refugees nor are they prosecuted by the law of the land.

Nepal, which has been many facing crisis since so many years, is preventing now the entry of the Rohingyas in the country. The spokesperson of the Ministry of Home Affairs in Nepal, Ram Krishna stated that, "Nepal has increased surveillance at its border to stop more Rohingyas from entering the country after the Rohingyas crisis in Myanmar because we cannot bear any more crises."[56] Experts feel that Nepal should immediately deport the Rohingyas as they are a potential threat to the security of the country. Former Home Secretary Govind Kusum fears that they might have been influenced by Islamic State and as such they could be a threat to the security to the country. So, he warned the authorities concerned against giving them refugee status as granted by the Government of Nepal to the Tibetan and Bhutani refugees.As the Rohingyas crises deepen, on 11 September 2017, the Muslim community in the Nepalgunj municipality of the Banke district, in western part of the Terai region, took out a rally and submitted a memorandum to the Chief District Officer Ramesh K.C. They wanted the Nepal government to exert pressure on the Myanmar government to stop the atrocities against the Rohingyas.

What is a silver lining is that the Myanmar government has given an indication that it has no problem in taking back those Rohingyas who are its nationals? Myanmar Counsellor Aung San Suu Kyi said that the Rohingyas could return to their homeland through the proper verification process. Since India and Bangladesh are affected by the influx of the Rohingyas, they must adopt common stand to find the solution to the crisis. In this context, Bangladesh's Prime Minister Sheikh Hasina has suggested to set up 'safe zones' in Myanmar itself under UN supervision to ensure the safe return of the Rohingyas. It seems to be a practical suggestion but it is not known as to how the Rohingyas could be deported to their country and how they will secure where they fear annihilation. It is essential for India and Bangladesh to strengthen their border vigilance to see that the unwanted elements do not enter into their territories. But more than that they must use their diplomatic efforts to influence Myanmar government to take back the Rohingyas and make them re-settle on their land peacefully for which it will also be important to improve their living conditions.

Bangladesh is also fraught with other consequences because of the presence of Rohingya's refugee population. The Sheikh Hasina government has dealt with Bangladesh's basic developmental issues, investment needs and matters pertaining to equitable growth and employment with a reasonable measure of success. In 2016, the country's GDP grew by 6.8 per cent and the rate of inflation stood at less than seven per cent. However, the manner in which the international community supports the Hasina government's efforts to reverse the refugee influx as well as its outcome will determine the extent of the fallout on the country's domestic political milieu. The actions taken by countries like India and China are silent in this regard considering their capacity to contribute to the mitigation of the crisis to an extent.

A planned elimination of the Rohingyas by the Myanmar government is noteworthy not only in its scale and thoroughness, but also in the world's disposition to abet what amount to an expurgation of identity. Since 2012, the Rohingya face a unique dilemma then and now whether to surrender their identity for the right to return home. The Rohingya crisis is unique because there is no national or security interest driving the violence against a defenceless community. The sole purpose is to cause indescribable misery which forced the peoples oust from their homeland. States are rapidly leaving behind a world order based on rights and rules and heading toward an older formation of interests and alliances. One can easily find this transition to many numbers of events; the American invasion of Iraq, the world's passive response to Syria's use of chemical weapons, or Russia's violent intervention in Ukraine, in Afghanistan, Pakistan, Sri Lanka or Nepal. In fact, Bangladesh's security forces and Islamic extremists' groups have been involving in violence, murder and accused of numerous human rights violations and ethnic cleansing of its Hindu and other Minorities population, then whom to blame?

Notes

1. Bangladesh population grew by over 1 percent in a year: Report, Press Trust India, June 23, 2016.
2. New age Bangladesh April 7, 2018; Hindu Mahajote, Jan. 7, 2018.
3. States *SK Bhattacharyya in Genocide in East Pakistan/Bangladesh.*

4. BBC News, 9 March 2013.
5. Dr. Nimchandra Bhoumik, A Bleak Future for Bangladesh Hindu, The Hinduism today, Feb. 2000.
6. The Daily Star, November 3, 2013; Gatestone Institute, November 21, 2013.
7. Bangladesh News 24, January 10, 2014;International Business Times, February 19, 2014.
8. New Age, January 11, 2014; The Hindu, January 8, 2014.
9. Satkhira Correspondent, published in Hindu Existence, January 29, 2014.
10. Dhaka Tribune Correspondent, January 29, 2014.
11. The Daily Star, January 7, 2014.
12. Hindu Existence, May 7, 2014.
13. Indian Express, November 5, 2016.
14. The Hindu, October 31, 2016.
15. Humanity Assassinated: Ethnic Cleansing of Minorities in Islamic Bangladesh, July12,2009 www.islam-watch.org/index.php?view.
16. Sidharthya Roy, Bangladesh's New Generation Militants, the Diplomates, January 29, 2018.
17. http://www.nytimes.com2016/05/20/0pinion the real source of terror in Bangladesh.
18. Joseph Allchin, The rise of extremism in Bangladesh: who is responsible for Killings?Foreign Affairs, June 9, 2016.
19. Georgetown Security Studies Review, 2014.
20. Islamism that continues to enjoy popular support.the resurgent importance of Banglades his' personal identity as Muslim made it difficult for the government to maintain its commitment to secularism. It did not eliminate the importance of personal faith, and openly criticizing Islam was politically unpopular.
21. Bangladesh Prime Minister Sheikh Hasina is fulfilling a long-standing promise to prosecute B JeI activists, among others, in a Controversial War Crimes Tribunal controversial war crimes tribunal. Her government has carried out several death sentences accordingly.
22. Shakhawat Liton, the Depth Of 5th Amendment, the Daily Star, March 17, 2019.
23. The Bangladesh Constitution Part III related with Fundamental Rights, Khan and Mahmod, P. 16; Gobinda Mandal, Rights of the Minorities: the Case of Bangladesh. www.academic.edu/839004/.
24. Ruth Baldwin, the Talibanization of Bangladesh, the Nation Magzine, May 17, 2002.
25. Amarendra Roy, Minorities and Right to education, a report submitted at Forum on Minorities Issues, Conference in the United Nations, Geneva Switzerland, 2008.
26. Saleem Samad, State of Minorities in Bangladesh, 1998: http://www.mukto-mona.com.
27. Shaha 1998, p. 5.
28. Private BD News Dainik Jugasankha.
29. Sections of Bangladesh Constitution- Article 11: Democracy and human rights, Article 13: Principles of ownership, Article.
30. Richard Benkin, Root of Ethnic Cleansing in A Quiet Case of Ethnic Cleansing in Bangladesh, http://www.inetrfaithstrength.com/collusion.html.
31. Barkat A Zaman, Vested Property Act: Political nad Economic Consequences,German Research Trust, Dhaka, 1998. US States department statistics.

32. Srabasti Sarker, Hindu enemies of Bangladesh, Institute of Asia and Pacific, university of Nottingham. March 21, 2018.
33. Advocacy for Implementation of vested return property Act, case study Bangladesh, international Land Coalition, united for land rights and ALRD. 2013; Sitangshu Guha, Bangladesh Enemy Property Act: 1965-2010: How long must we bear this burden? Nov.17 2010.http://www.ipetitions.com/petition/repealenemypropertyactnow/.
34. C. Christine fair, Political Islam and Islamists terrorism in Bangladesh, what you need to know? The Lawfare Institute in Cooperation with Brookings, January 28, 2018.
35. Pakistani Militants Expand Abroad starting in Bangladesh:

    https://www.csmonitor.com/world/asia-south-centarl/2016/0805.
36. BBC, 9 March 2014.
37. AZAD S., Status 0f Minority Communities In Bangladesh; htpp://www2.ohchr.org; http://www.google.co.in/url? sa = t&rct = j&q = &esrc = s&source = web&cd = 1&cad = rja...
38. The Daily Star, January 2, 2014; New Age, January 11, 2014; The daily Ittefaq, 29 January 2014.
39. Time, January 14, 2014.
40. Jamaat-e-Islami Bangladesh: A Nexus of Terror.
41. JMJB 10 camps in Atrai and Raninagar in the Naogaon district, Bagmara in Rajshahi district, and Naldanga and Singra in Natore district.
42. Daily Star on May 5, 2004.
43. International NGOs of these count such as the Kuwait-based Revival of Islamic Heritage and Doulatul Kuwait, UAE-based Al Fuzaira, Khairul Ansar Al Khairia, Bahrain-based Doulatul Bahrain and the Saudi Arabia-based Al Haramaine Islamic Institute have provided, over the years, a generous amount of funding to the outfit.
44. Many Rohingyas also closely collaborated with and even trained HuJI-B members in the 1990s. HuJI-B recruited members from Rohingya communities in southeastern Bangladesh, assigning them to perform the riskiest fighting jobs, doing tasks such as carrying equipment or removing mines.
45. https://www.orfonline.org/expert-speaks/dealing-rohingya-crisis-nepal-bangladesh-india/.
46. Human Rights Watch, Myanmar: Events of 2018, Report 2019.
47. Al Jazeera Network, "Myanmar: Who are the Rohingya?" September 28, 2017.
48. Ibid.,
49. In her address to the 76th United Nation General Assembly session, Prime Minister Sheikh Hasina of Bangladesh wanted the UN to set up 'safe zones' under international supervision for the Rohingya in Myanmar territory itself to address the refugee problem effectively. She also wanted Rohingya to return back from Bangladesh to Rakhine of Myanmar under secure conditions.
50. China's Role in Myanmar's Internal Conflicts, USIP China Myanmar Senior Study Group Report, September 14, 2018.
51. The Global Times , September 18, 2017,a televised speech on September 19, 2017,
52. Ibid.
53. China Says Rohingya Issue should Not be Internationalised, Reuters world News, September 28, 2018.

54. Chauhan, Neeraj, "Rohingya exodus from Myanmar: Centre reviews Free Movement Regime at Indo-Myanmar border," The Times of India, September 25, 2017.
55. Ibid.
56. "Fleeing violence at home, Rohingya Muslims face difficulties in India, Nepal, Bangladesh," September 17, 2017, in http://www.presstv.com/Detail/2017/09/17/535440/Rohingya-difficulties-India-Nepal-Bangladesh.

Appendix-8

The Enemy Property Act

1965: Government of Pakistan passed an executive order titled "Enemy Property (Custody and Regulation) Order II of 1965" under the provisions of Emergency powers and the "Defense of Pakistan Rules" on Sept. 9, 1965.

1968: The Supreme Court of Pakistan considered it a pure political issue asked the Government of Pakistan to explain viewpoint on the said Act in 1968 [21 DLR (SC) page 20].

1969: Government of Pakistan promulgated a new Ordinance, the Enemy Property (Continuance of Emergency Provision) Ordinance 1969 (Ordinance No. I of 1969). Field Marshall Ayub Khan handed over power to Pakistan Army Chief General Yahya Khan who promulgated Martial Law on 25 March 1969 and cancelled the then constitution of Pakistan on April 1, 1969. Notwithstanding cancellation of the constitution, to continue the Enemy Property Ordinance, a new Ordinance was incorporated retro-effective from March 25, 1969, which kept alive the most discriminatory law against Hindus till the formal declaration of Bangladesh on March 26, 1971, when the war of liberation ended.

1971: Independence was declared on March 26, 1971, and the proclamation of independence and formation of a provisional government of Bangladesh took place on April 10, 1971 in Mujibnagar, the temporary capital of the new country. The same day, the "Laws of Continuance Enforcement Order, 1971" was promulgated to keep in force all Pakistani laws in force in the then East Pakistan till March 25, 1971. Thus, Ordinance No. I of 1969, which was inconsistent with the spirit of the proclamation of independence of Bangladesh, remained alive in the new-born nation.

1972: Immediately after the war was over, the Government of Bangladesh on March 26, 1972 enforced the "Vesting of Property and Assets Order, 1972" through Order No. 29 of 1972.

1974: This order brought together the properties left behind by Pakistanis in Bangladesh and the erstwhile enemy properties of Pakistan in a single category. Then, on March 23, 1974, the Government of Bangladesh passed the Enemy Property (Continuance of) Emergency Provisions (Repeal) Act, Act XLV of 1974, repealing Ordinance I of 1969. But despite repealing Ordinance I of 1969, all enemy properties and firms vested with the Custodian of Enemy Property in the then East Pakistan remained vested in the Government of Bangladesh as "vested property." At the same time, the Government of Bangladesh enacted the "Vested and Non-resident Property (Administration) Act" (Act XLVI of 1974).

1976: To help plots to grab Hindu lands by Muslims, in November 1976 the Government of Bangladesh repealed previous Act No. XLVI of 1974 by Ordinance XCII of 1976 with retrospective effect from the date of the enactment amended of Act XCIII of 1976.

1977-1990: Military dictator Gen. Zia-ur Rahman and later Gen. H.M. Ershad made the situation worse. Although Gen. Ershad declared that no new property would be declared as vested property and that properties already enlisted as vested would no longer be disposed off, the opposite happened. During these two Generals' tenure, the abuse of this law made hundreds of thousands of Hindus homeless; they were forced to migrate to India, causing a major decline of minority population in Bangladesh.

1991: Bangladesh Nationalist Party won the election of 1991 and throughout its tenure until mid-1996 did not touch the Vested Property Act, which remained on the statute book till the Ershad regime.

2001: The Government led by the Awami League took five years to place and pass a bill in parliament on April 11, 2001, the "Restoration of Vested Property Act, 2001" (Act No. 16 of 2001) near the end of its tenure. But the Act did not much help provide solutions to affected Hindus, and made some issues more complicated because of inherent defects.

2002: In the October 2001 election, the Bangladesh Nationalist Party (BNP) led 4-party coalition formed the government, including Islamist elements. This government passed an amendment bill in parliament to the "Restoration of Vested Property Act 2001" on Nov. 26, 2002, which virtually shelved the return of confiscated properties to Hindus. This amendment allows Government unlimited time to return vested properties which are to remain under the control of Deputy Commissioners until a tribunal settles ownership. The amendment gives Deputy Commissioners the right to lease such properties until they are returned to their owners.

2009: The present democratic government is trying to reform the law, but the victim religious minorities want the law repealed.

Chapter - 7

NEPAL: New Constitution and Madhesi Crisis

Nepal is an immensely diverse country by all measures including geography, ethnicity, language, religion and castes. Nepal a beautiful Himalayan kingdom engulfs into political instability and various problems since many decades starting from the monarchical absolutism and Maoist armed rebellion to the present ethnic crisis over the new constitution. Promulgation of Nepal New Constitution on 20th September 2015 ended the decade old constitutional deadlock which began shortly after the end of Maoists insurgency in 2006 but gave birth to a new violent crisis. While many people welcomed new Constitution, some were deeply unhappy for varying reasons. The country was widely polarized in support and against the new constitution. Ruling political parties Nepali Congress and CPN-UML favoured but the Madhesi political parties and Tharuhat Struggle Committee observed it as a black day. Madhesi leaders burnt the new constitution. Major Madhesi political parties did not sign the new Constitution, alleged that it has failed to satisfy the 70% of Madhesi and Tharus population of Terai. The Madhesi and Tharus were sidelined in the entire constitution making process due to prevailing distrust towards them among the main stream political parties. The Madhesi Janaadhikar Forum-Democratic was initially involved in the Constitution drafting process but later it had quitted as its point of view was not considered. Shivaji Yadav of the Federal Socialist Forum said that the big parties have tried to crush the minority groups and pushed the Nation into Chaos. A former National Election Commissioner also criticized the constitution, commented that the constitution was leading to conflict and the state must immediately address the grievances of those opposing it, the country's future depends on it.

Historical Background

To understand the present crisis in Nepal one must look back to the complex and exhaustive history of Nepal. Political history of Nepal has passed through uncertainty and controversies. From 18th century to the 20th century, Nepal was monarchical state ruled by the king Mahendra. In 1959 king Mahendra tried to set up democracy and election was held in which B.P.Koirala became the Prime Minister. But the democratically elected government was ended within the 18th months. King Mahendra used his emergency power to take the charge of government and blamed the Nepali Congress for fostering corruption, promoted party above the national interests, failed to maintain law and order and encouraged anti national elements.

Political parties were banned and all prominent figures including the Prime Minister were put behind the bars. Civil liberties were curtailed and press freedom muzzled. In 1962, King Mahindra declared new constitution and introduced party-less Panchayat system guided by democracy in which people could elect representatives while real power remained in the hands of monarch. The panchayat system was promulgated after overthrowing the democratically elected government and dissolving the Parliament. Political Parties were declared illegal. The Nepal Congress leadership demonstrated a non-violent struggle against the new order and formed alliances with several political parties. The Panchayat polity emphasized decentralization while class coordination was to be implemented through active and dynamic leadership. The panchayat political legacy has had a long-lasting impact on Nepal's history. This was a calculated move which granted control to the Monarchy under disguise of being better suited for the will of the people.

In 1979, King Birendra, the successor of King Mahindra maintained power but due to the anti-regime protests, he promised to held national referendum to decide the nature of the Nepal government whether to continue the Panchayat system with democratic reforms or to established multi-party system. The people of Nepal voted in favour of Panchayat System and allowed the King to maintain his autocratic powers and control over the Parliamentary System. King Birendra introduced the selection of the Prime Minister by the Rashtriya Panchayat. Many people believed that the decision had been rigged against the demand of multiparty system.

In 1987, there was widespread feeling among the masses against the king being non-representative and due to political scandals and misappropriation of funds; and souring trade relations with India. The Nepali congress and Left-wings parties blamed government for perpetuating crisis and not taking serious measures to solve it. In December 1989, the Nepal Congress launched a people awareness programme. The Left-Wing Alliance United Left Front (ULF) extended its support to the Nepal Congress in its campaign for a party system. In 1990, the Nepali Congress held a conference attended by members and leaders of various countries-India, Germany, Spain Finland and the United States. Inspired by the international support and the democratic movement occurring throughout the world after disintegration of the Soviet Union, the Nepal Congress and The ULF launched a non-violent mass Movement -Jan Andolan- in February 1990 to end the Panchayat regime and to established multi-party democracy. In order to stall the movement, the government arrested national and districts level leaders of both political parties, banned all opposition newspapers. Police fired on the demonstration in Bhaktapur killed 12 people. Movement became increasingly large and dangerous as thousands of students marched against police and hundreds were arrested and injured. The movement called for bandhs and spread across the country and escalated from the countryside until they reached the capital Kathmandu. The movement gathered 2,00,000 peoples who marched in protest against Monarchy.[1] Police shot and killed dozens of protesters. Protesters blocked the streets and surrounded the government officials' buildings to force the king to accept the demand. On 8th April 1990, the king removed ban from the political parties and on 16th April 1990, Royal proclamation was issued which dissolve the National Panchayat, the panchayat policy, the evaluation committee and the class organizations. The proclamation declared functioning of the political parties and maintained that all political parties will always keep the national interests uppermost in organizing themselves according their political ideology. In May 1991, national elections were held in Nepal Congress party won 205 seats and formed the government.

Nepal who struggled so valiantly against the tyrannical rule of the royal generation soon led to a worst political and deadly crisis- the Maoist Arms Insurgency 1996-2006. In 1996 the leftist party, the Communist party of Nepal began an armed rebellion against the government seeking to destroy constitutional monarchy and aiming to establish a Maoist people's democracy. The Maoist modelled after the Peruvian guerrilla group the "Shinning Path" had declared war against the Monarch using many tactics to aggravate their movement. Political analysts believe the rise of Maoism in Nepal was directly connected with the fall of absolute Monarchy in 1990 and the subsequent introduction of parliamentary democracy. In fact, the Maoist insurgency was firstly appeared in 1949 and then in 1970 but failed to gain the ground. In 1996 people from other castes particularly untouchable and Jan-Jatis (tribals) joined it in larger numbers. Actually earlier, these movements were basically the movement against Brahmin, Chhetri and Newar (BCN) ruling elite v/s the non-ruling elite hence could not succeeded. In 1996, the scenario was changed in view of the broader participation of person from other castes particularly. The untouchable (such as Kami, Sarki, Damai, etc.) and janjatya (Rai, Limbu, Gurung, Magar, Tamang, etc.) joined the Maoist insurgency in the hope that they will be emancipative from the clutches of BNC.

Within a decade, the insurgency expanded across the country shaken the whole population and parliamentary constituencies affected the lives of the 24 million peoples of Nepal and killed 13,000 people.[2] In the name of war, insurgents along with the national security forces have committed the acts of kidnapping, bombing killings, torture, intimidations and other means of threats. State failed to control Maoists insurgent activities. Since the start of insurgency, all the successive government had treated the Maoist insurgency as a law and order problem and followed authoritarian policies in order to suppress it but without addressing the basic inequalities of its society. The police operations have applied the policy of encircle and kill-a policy similar to China's Chiang-Kai-shek's extermination of Communists campaign in 1930s. The failures of government's operations, the Maoist insurgency took momentum with substantial popular support giving sanctuaries to insurgents. Independent observers argue that the government suffers from political instability and rampant corruption. While the king of Nepal suspended several provisions of the constitution including freedom of press, speech and expression, peaceful assembly, the right to privacy and the right against preventive detention. But Nepal's strategic planners failed to find a way in which people would stop giving sanctions to insurgents.

On June 1, 2001 ten members of Royal family including King Birendra of Nepal were killed by Prince Dipendra during a dinner party of Royal family. Prince Dipendra was proclaimed King while in coma he died after three day, hence Gyanendra, brother of Nepal King Birendra, became the King. In 2005, king Gyanendra sacked the government, dissolve the parliament and took absolute power trying to instigate his own democratic norms and values. The Mass movement of April 2006 ended the Maoist insurgency and sought to restore Parliamentary democratic process. The event also marked willingness of the communist party of Nepal –Maoists (CPN-M) to join the democratic mainstream and initiate peace process. The Comprehensive Peace Agreement (CPA-12 Points) between the CPN-Maoist and Seven Party Alliance (SPA) provided the restoration of Peace in the country.

For long time, Nepal had witnessed the constitutional deadlock and political disturbances. There was political panics in the initial phase intended to make a constitution to achieve a number of objectives including promotion of perpetual peace and state restructuring inclusive democracy. The Interim constitution, 2007 underlined the basic concept of political parties as the guiding principle but soon after the election of the Constitution Assembly (CA), the political parties remained involved in numerical game concentrating on the formation of the government or capturing political power. The political parties represented in the Constituent Assembly failed to demonstrate friendly environment by developing political consensus to frame constitution within the stipulated time. There were still differences among the parties. The UPCN and Maoist wants first to form the government under its leadership, before moving ahead with the drafting of new constitution. On the other hand, the parties supporting the government want the UPCN and Maoists to fulfil its commitments made under various agreements and understanding in the peace process. The present government is ready to accommodate legitimate demands of the Maoists, which were set with the support of the Maoists themselves.

The agreement among the political parties that they would take all major decision through consensus, did not worked. Consensus democracy is considered as one of the best tools to address the democratic objectives. It is not a mere rhetoric tool but a fundamental value for a better democratic practice. But in Nepal, it was failed due to negative role of political parties particularly the Communist Party; mutual disrespect between political parties and actors and indecisiveness in Politics? Before practices of consensus democracy get matured, indeterminate traits of Consensus democracy was overshadowed and dominated by undefined political behaviour. The Maoists emerged as the largest party though without an absolute majority in the constituent Assembly election. The Maoists led government resigned after ten months when President Ram Baran Yadav vetoed the dismissal of the army chief by PM Prachanda. The CPN-M saw this move of the president as affront to the principle of civilian supremacy.Again, the government led by Madhav in Nepal, which they called it illegitimate, forced to dismiss. A political deadlock created for the past so many yearswas the Maoist inflexibility and rigid attitude and a space for agitation. Lack of political understanding between major political parties, the Maoists, Nepali Congress and CPN-UML and allegations and counter-allegations between the government and the Maoists blocked the process.

Nepal's Ethnic and Social structure

Nepal's provisional population, according to Census-2011, is 26.62 million comprising of 103 recognized ethno-demographic groups. The largest ones are Chhetri about 16%, Brahmin 13.6% Magar 7.5%, Tharu

7.1% Tamang 5.7% Newar 5.7% Muslim 4.2% Kami 4% and Yadav 3.2%. Smaller ethnic groups like Gurung, Chhepa, Limbu, Rai, Raute, Sherpa, Thakali etc. and marginalised lower castes groups constitute about 35-40% of the population.[3] Actually, there is no majority ethnic community in Nepal; each minority group is dominant in some parts; many have social and economic relationship and shared culture with other groups as is common in any multi ethnic nations around the world. Newars are natives of mid-Himalayan region astute business. Tamang, Tharu and Kami are tribes. However, from the religious perspective 80.6% are Hindu, 10.7% Buddhists, 4.2% Muslim and 4.5% follow other religion making Nepal Hindu dominate state and it has remained so since hoary antiquity. The Tarai region (the area contiguous to Northern Indian Plains) is home to predominantly Hindu and comprises of 50.2% total population. The 103 ethnic minorities are spread across all 75 districts.

Table 23: Composition of each proposed six states and the Ethnic Groups.

The table below shows 10 largest ethnic groups in each of the proposed six federal states in Nepal.

10 Largest Ethnic Groups in Proposed Six Federal States in Nepal						
S.N.	*State 1*	*State 2*	*State 3*	*State 4*	*State 5*	*State 6*
1	Chhetree	Yadav	Tamang	Brahman – Hill	Chhetree	Chhetree
2	Brahman – Hill	Musalman	Brahman – Hill	Magar	Magar	Brahman – Hill
3	Rai	Tharu	Chhetree	Chhetree	Tharu	Tharu
4	Limbu	Teli	Newar	Gurung	Brahman – Hill	Kami
5	Tamang	Koiri/Kushwaha	Magar	Kami	Musalman	Thakuri
6	Magar	Chamar/Harijan/ Ram	Kami	Newar	Kami	Magar
7	Tharu	Dhanuk	Gurung	Tharu	Yadav	Damai/Dholi
8	Newar	Musahar	Tharu	Sarki	Damai/Dholi	Dalit Others
9	Musalman	Kurmi	Rai	Damai/Dholi	Sarki	Sarki
10	Kami	Dusadh/Pasawan /Pasi	Damai/Dholi	Tamang	Chamar/Harijan /Ram	Dashnami/Sanyasi

The table below shows which of the 10 major ethnic groups have a clear majority and a majority in the six proposed federal states. In this analysis, a clear majority refers to a condition in which the noted ethnic group has the largest population in the given state. A majority refers to a condition in which the noted ethnic group is among the three largest ethnic groups in the given state.

Table-24: Major ethnic groups majority in the proposed six states.

10 Largest Ethnic Groups Have Majorities in Proposed Federal States					
S.N.	***10 Largest Ethnic Groups in Nepal***	***Clear Majority* (Yes/No)***	***State(s)****	***Majority*** (Yes/No)***	***State(s)*******
1	Chhetree	Yes	State 1, State 5, State 6	Yes	State 1, State 3, State 5, State 6
2	Brahman – Hill	Yes	State 4	Yes	State 1, State 3, State 4, State 6
3	Magar	No		Yes	State 4, 5
4	Tharu	No		Yes	State 2, 5, 6
5	Tamang	Yes	State 3	Yes	State 3
6	Newar	No		No	
7	Kami	No		No	
8	Musalman	No		Yes	State 2
9	Yadav	Yes	State 2	Yes	State 2
10	Rai	No		Yes	State 1
	* Where The Ethnic Group Is The Largest in The State				
	*** Where The Ethnic Group Is Among The Three Largest Ethnic Groups				

Sources: Nepal's Central Bureau of statistics.

Nepal population are ethnically geographically divided into high v/s low caste, Nepali speaking v/s speakers of indigenous languages, hills ethnicities v/s low land ethnicities and gender divisions. Near about 100 languages are speaking by the Nepali people. Nepal's society is deeply polarised and ethnically delineated.

Many traditionally marginalised groups are fearing that the new constitution will not protect their interests and it will be dominated by the high castes. It has been especially very tense in the Terai region in the southern and western low lands where tensions between highlanders and lowlanders have been seen from many years. In the western Terai, other indigenous group "Tharus" are also opposing at the division of their area in two and prospects of sharing its province with the hill districts. They fear predominance by hills highlands groups. In the eastern Terai, Madhesi communities also feel the same fear as have always faced discrimination and lack of acceptance by the Nepalese state. Women are also discriminated between Nepalese women and others women.

Madhesi Problems

Madhesi and Tharus are non-Nepali speaking people residing in the Terai region of Nepal who are culturally distinct from the hill people. Geographically, the word "Madhesi" referred to the entire Terai region within the Nepal territory sharing border with India. The word Madhes has originated from the Sanskrit term Madhyadesh which means middle country and the land between the Himalaya and the plains. It is the part of ancient kingdom of Videha and Shakya whose minor part is now the part of Nepal while major part is in India. The Middle country including Awadh is now in India and partially in Nepalgunj and Tulsipur Dang region of Nepal. The total land area of the Terai region is less than 34109 square kilometer comprises of 20 districts that account 23% of Nepal total area.

The Madhesi's communities have long been complained about being treated unfairly. They have been suffered, discriminated and exploited by the dominant Hill castes groups (Pahadis) and politically marginalized by appearing to be more Indian than Nepalese. The common mass of the Madhesi and Tharus have always been humiliated ever since central and eastern part of Terai was gifted by the British East India Company to Nepal partly after the Sugauli Tearty of 1816 and partly after the Sepoy Mutiny in 1860.[4] A feeling of discrimination and deprivation made the Madhesi region a hub of pro-democratic movement since 1950s. Nepalese considered them as the Indian agents and perceived as anti-establishment to claim the Terai region as India's territory. Their loyalties towards the Nepal state was always suspected by the Hills elites. This distrust towards the Madhesi's people provided the Nepal government ample ground to adopt stringent and discriminated policies.

- The first such policy was the Citizenship Act of 1964 and the constitution of 1990 under which Madhesi's were debarred from citizenship certificates due to which they could neither acquire land ownership nor could avail government benefits. In 2006, though the Citizenship Act was amended and allowed Madhesi people born before 1990 and those residing permanently there to acquire citizenship. But many Madhesi and Dalits people are still deprived of citizenship.
- Second, until 1954, the Madhesi and Tharus formed 94% of the total population in Terai but since 1970s, the Monarchical rulers in the name of land reforms, land belonging to Mdhaesi's people were given to Hills peoples. Hundred off thousands of hill migrants were settled in Terai mostly by clearing the thick forest lands. In 1980s, A Commission on Internal and International

migration, constituted in 1980s, recommended to clear the remaining forests along the east and west side Highway with a view to settle the Hill migrants. For this, resettlement companies were set up but none of the Madhesi's people got any piece of land even though landlessness is common problem of Terai peoples. Big chunk of land was gifted to civil servants, army, and family members of ruling class. Madhesi, Tharus, Rajbanshis and Satars were suffered most due to state sponsored migration of population in Terai region. Land of many of those people were confiscated; many were forced to migrate to India and those who stayed at region were forced to work as Kamiyas (Paupers)whose only means of survival was to work as slaves in the house of Hill migrants.

- A policy was adopted by the ruling class of Nepal not to employ the Madhesi people in civil services, judiciary security agencies and other higher administrative post. Even in the private corporate sectors and industries their presence was minimal.
- Until 1950, the Madhesi had to received visa from the government to enter into the capital city Kathmandu.
- In Political field, no the Political Parties were not interested to give Tickets to Madhesi people to contest elections from any of the hill constituencies though they placed several hill elites as candidates in Terai.[5]

The type of discriminations and deprivation of migrated Indian population and several tribal groups led to the emergence of resentments and identity-based movement in Madheshi. In the 1950, Nepal Terai Congress gave a call for federal state for Terai region but the movement did not gain much support as the party lost general election in 1959. In 1990, when the multi-party democracy was adopted, Nepal Sadbhavna Party demanded federal state and the Communist Party of Nepal also demanded federal state. Historically, it has been the Bahun, Chettri and Newari groups in Kathmandu who have held political power and cultural sway over the national narrative of Nepal. Traditional associations of the Nepali-speaking hill Brahmin represented Nepali national – at the cost of half the country's diverse population who live in the Terai-Madhes, speak various languages such as Hindi, Maithili, Urdu and Bhojpuri, and have deep cultural continuities with Bihar and Uttar Pradesh –

The 2006 people's movement that overthrew the monarchy and ensured a 'safe landing' for the Maoists to come over ground and join parliamentary politics. The Comprehensive Peace Agreement of 2006 that had put to an end a decade-long civil war. As a part of that agreement, all the involved parties, even when they didn't directly refer to federalism, made an overarching commitment to end the "unitary centralised" state structure of political governance in Nepal. A chief consequence of that centralised monopoly of power and resources has been the collective dispossession of a people based on class, caste and ethnicity – a history that had been the vector on which various revolutionary mobilisations had taken place. An important agreement, on the Comprehensive Peace Accord reached between the former combatants in November 2006 was that the structure of the state would be drastically reformed, with the intent that Nepal would become a federal state. The future federal structure of Nepal was enshrined in the Interim Constitution of 2007, which sets as a directive principle for the restructuring of it says the state. "the state shall be made inclusive and restructured into a progressive, democratic federal system" in order to "bring an end to discrimination based on class, caste, language, gender, culture, religion and region by eliminating the centralized and unitary form of the state." (Article 138).

In 2007, there was major Terai uprising which demanded formation of single autonomous Madhesi Pradesh with the Right to Self-Determination. In April 2006, a 21 day long mass movement participated by large number of the Madhesi population – was an unprecedented event parallel to Janandolan II. In the post-Janandolan II transitional government granted some benefits to Janjatis, women, and Dalits, but they granted nothing in the case of the Madhesi. Thus, the Madhesi movement was a natural outcome of the Madhesi's resentment against the Nepali state for its long ignorance and negligence to their grievances. It was so powerful and effective that Girija Prasad Koirala, the Prime Minister of the eight-party coalition government was forced to proclaim twice within a single week that federalism would be instituted and that the number of constituencies in the Tarai would be increased. Accordingly, the Interim Constitution was amended twice within less than three months of its promulgation in January 2007. The Madhesi uprising, thus, has to its credit the achievement of federalism and redistribution and increment of electoral constituencies in favor of Tarai, both being important and substantial steps towards more inclusive democracy.

Protest to New Constitution

On 20th September 2015, Nepal new constitution was promulgated and ended the constitutional deadlock which began shortly after the end of Maoists War in 2006 but on the other hand gave birth to new crisis and faced violent demonstration and protests which killed nearly 40 people in clashes against the new constitution. While many people were happy but some were deeply unhappy for varying reasons. Ruling political parties including Nepali Congress, CPN-UML welcome the new Constitution but Madhesi and Tharuhat Struggle Committee observed it as a black day. Copies of new constitution were burnt by Madhesi's leaders. Shivaji Yadav of Federal Socialists Forum alleged that 'the big parties have tried to crush the minority groups and pushed the nation into chaos'. When the New Constitution of Nepal was promulgated on Jan 2015, Upendra Yadav, then the leader of Madhesi-centred activist group Madhesi Jana Adhikar Forum, burned a copy of the document at the Maitighar Mandala, an area close to the government complex in Kathmandu.

One of the main reasons of the conflict is the argument that the new constitution has highly centralized the powers and resources of government and failed to serve the needs of the people. As a result, protest was started by the Madhesi leader and it sparked all over the country when Maoist activists reportedly shot dead a Madhesi who was among a group trying to enforce a transportation strike to protest the new constitution. Eight people died, hundreds have been injured. Strike crippled the economic lifelines from the plains to the capital Kathmandu from central hills and remote mountain regions in the country.[6]

The Terai region was under curfew with violent clashes between the protestors and the police killing 35 civilian and nine policemen. Following the passage of the constitution, asix-month long blockade ensued that affected the country's economic and social life all the way to Kathmandu and polarised its polity. Famously, the atmosphere of Kathmandu has tended to be at odds with the anger and discontent in the plains. While a majority of residents in Nepal believed the blockade as unwanted Indian interference in the sovereign decisions of the nation-state, Nepalis in the Terai carry a profound sense of ownership over the movement. However, he blockade ended on February 5, 2016, and some of stability was restored.

Madhesi people's aspiration for autonomy is among one of the long-standing struggles in the Nepal history. They are not immigrants they are living from centuries so want to be treated like a Nepalese. They demanded the inclusion of the word 'federalism' which was an abiding promise of Comprehensive Peace Agreement towards state restructuring and that would take into account ethnic identity; provides proportional representation for Madhesi in the parliament. And indeed, the inclusion of the word federalism was included in the interim constitution, guaranteeing Nepal a federal structure. In fact, Federalism had been articulated as an instrument that would not only devolve power to the future states but also correct the course of history in which Madhesi and indigenous janjati groups were left out of power sharing and remained structurally marginalised. Many members of traditionally marginalised groups fear that the new constitution will work against them as it has been framed hasty by established political parties specially the Maoists and it will be dominated by the high castes mostly male.

In context of new constitution, major demands[7] of Madhesi are:

- Current constitution allocates parliamentary seats on basis of geographical area and as a result, Madhesi who represent 50% of population, will get just 39% of parliamentary seats (65 out of 165). So, Madhesi's demand the representation on basis of population.
- Similarly, geographical spread and not population is also a precondition for other benefits and rights like - representation in National Assembly. Such provisions should also be amended.
- There is also a clause that only persons who are by 'descent' Nepalis shall be able to occupy high constitutional posts like President, Prime Minister, Security heads, Speaker of assembly and so on. This will exclude lakhs of Madhesi who have acquired citizenship on the basis of birth or naturalization.
- Madhesi and some ethnic communities are unhappy at the proposed boundaries of the new provinces, although these may be subject to change. The formation of seven federal province as per the constitution are grossly unfair to them. Seven new provinces that have been formed are gerrymandered in such a manner that they work against Madhesi population. Only eight districts in the terai region from Saptari in the east to Parsa in the west, have been given the status of province (see Map, state-18). The remaining 14 districts are to be joined with the hill dsitricts with the sole purpose of converting the local people into minority. Provinces have to be redrawn to club Madhesi populations together. Some Madhesi want to add Jhapa, Morang, Sunsari and create only madhesi province with no Hills while some others want to add Hill districts like Udaypur or Makwanpur so that province 2 becomes more viable economically. This unrest has been especially intense in the Terai - Nepal's long southern lowland strip bordering India, where recent years have seen tensions between lowlanders and highlanders who have migrated there over recent decades. In the western Terai, one lowland group, the indigenous Tharus, are unhappy at the prospect of being split in two and forced to share their provinces with hill districts that they fear will predominate.

Nepal's draft provincial boundaries

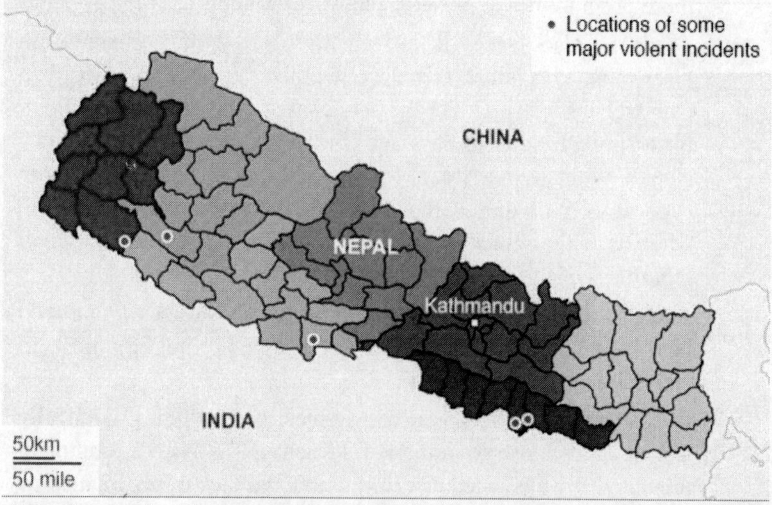

Note: Colours show the proposed boundaries for seven federal provinces BBC

- The constitution has delimitation exercise (re-adjustment of the electoral boundaries) after 20 years, but Madhesi wanted it to be done in 10 years. Further, the earlier draft outline of constitution also had the same provision, but has changed in final constitution.
- The prime demands are rooted in perceived historical injustice, poor representation in government jobs and power centres and apparent ethnic discrimination as Madhesi and many other Janjatis look more like ethnic Indians in plains, rather than like the 'true blooded Nepalis' which Pahari people claim themselves to be. Madhesi also demand adequate representation in Nepal' state institutions like bureaucracy, security forces, in Parliament among others. This is a legitimate demand, as the representation of not only Madhesi but also janajatis is fairly low as compared to Nepali population.
- Like every Nepali, Madhesi also demands jobs, development, good education, affordable healthcare, ability to feed and care for their children and basic human needs. In this regard, Nepal government has failed not only for Madhesi but virtually for every Nepali, it's very important.
- Madhesi's also want their language, culture, traditions preserved and also promoted in some aspects. It's another legitimate demand and the current constitution provides use of languages in Madhesi

like Maithli or Bhojuri in Provincial Government, and there may be more programmes to preserve culture of Madhesi as time goes by.

- There is also issue of citizenship in the new constitution discriminates against Nepalese women in what is already a patriarchal society. Under the new constitution, it will be difficult for a single mother to pass her citizenship to her child. And if a Nepali woman marries a foreign man, their children cannot become Nepali unless the man first takes Nepali citizenship; whereas if the father is Nepali, his children can also be Nepali regardless of the wife's nationality.

  There is also a debate about whether those Indian women who later become Nepalis should be given rights to hold top posts in Nepal like President or PM.

  In eastern Terai, the so-called Madhesi communities, ethnically and socially close to Indians just across the border, complain they have always faced discrimination and lack of acceptance by the Nepalese state. They say the above citizenship measures will disproportionately affect them because there are many cross-border marriages.

- There is also a huge problem of discrimination and issue of land reform of Madhesi, these demands are essential for the poor and lower caste Madhesi like Madhesi Dalits who in some cases are discriminated even badly than in Hills. Some few upper castes, Madhesi also hold large amount of land causing big problem of landlessness among lower caste and poor Madhesi. This also needs to be sorted out.

Madhesi Outfits

The emergence of identity-based outfits in Madhesi Pradesh were started with the formation of two groups: the Nepal Terai Congress led by Vedanta Jha in 1951 and the Madhesi Mukti Andolan led by Raghunath Thakur in 1956. At present, numerous political parties and non-state actors are involved in the Madhesi cause. In this context, examples of Madhesi Janadhikar Forum (MJF), Terai Madhesh Loktantrik Party (TMLP), etc., are significant. There also exist a number of major armed groups in the Terai region, such as the Janatantrik Terai Mukti Morcha (JTMM), Terai Cobra, Nepal Defence Army (NDA), Nepal Janatantrik Party (NJP), and Chure Bhawar Ekta Samaj (CBES). Although all these forces are involved in armed revolution in Nepal, there seems to be a divergence in the goals which each of them aspires to achieve. While JTMM demands the establishment of an autonomous Terai region; and Terai Cobra aspires to launch an armed separatist struggle for a sovereign Terai state; the objective of NDA is to form a Hindu army with suicide bombers to fight against religious extremism, conversion, as well as Maoists. Similarly, while as a royalist outfit, the NJP aspires to retain constitutional monarchy and multiparty democracy in Nepal, the CBES basically demands the establishment of a federal region in Terai and is opposed to 'one Madhesi one Pradesh' demand.

One of the most important factors is that no one political party or group represents the views of all the Madhesi despite the overwhelming size of all the Madhesi and Tharus in the Nepal. Neither Madhesi are not a homogenous group with the same demands. It is very diverse community from Muslims to upper castes Madhesi to Dalits among other speaking several languages with different culture therefore all of their demands may not be similar. This is the reason why the Madhesi political parties could not got more than 10 % seats in the 601 members Constituent Assembly (CA-2) elections in December 2013. Many of the Madhesi leaders were defeated in the CA-2 beacaue they failed to address their people's problems. Out of the lust for money and power they did not hesitate to fragment the parties. During the Constituent Assembly election in 2008, only three Madhesi parties had contested election and they had a substantial presence in the Constituent assembly though the vote percentage in both the CA-1 and CA-2 was almost same about 12 %. Madhesi political leaders lost the election because their vote was divided and making it convenient for the non-Madhesi political parties to win. The Madhesi based political parties did not learn any lesson from the election debacle and they could not unite to protect their interests. The three major political parties including the NC-CPN-UML and UCPM- Maoists took advantage. The Madhesi and Tharus were sidelined in the entire constitution making process due to prevailing distrusts towards them among the main stream political parties. Bijay Kumar Gachhada involved in the constitution drafting process but later on, it also had no option but to quit the alliance as it point of view was not considered.

First Constitution Amendment

The New constitution of Nepal was amended for the first time within 126 days of its promulgation on January 23, 2016 to address the demands of the agitating United Democratic Madhesi Front (UDMF). Although the amendment did incorporate issues ensuring proportional inclusion of the backward communities including the Madhesi in the state bodies and delineating electoral constituencies on the basis of population as raised by the UDMF. The amendment has failed to appease the agitating parties. Nepal's Madhesi Front refused to back the Amendment Bill saying it is not acceptable in its current discriminated form and it did not address the demands of indigenous nationalities Tharus, Khas, Muslims, women, Dalits and Madhesi.[8] The United Democratic Front and Federal Socialist Forum-Nepal (FSF-N) and Terai Madhesh Democratic Party and Terai Madhesh Sadbhavna Party-Nepal also refused the Amendment Bill. However, the amendment bill registered in the parliament by the government despite opposition from CPN-UML. The UDF and FSF-N stated that we cannot accept the amendment bill because it does not address the issues raised by the Madhesi, janjatis and deprived communities.

Map-19

The provincial autonomy and 10 province model were still being treated as disputed issues and the concern over the five Terai districts Jhapa, Morang, Sunsari, Kailali and Kanchanpur were yet to be addressed. On the crucial issue of federal demarcation, the proposed amendment seems to have recognized indigenous Thaur people's demand for autonomy by carving a province that includes six districts with demographic advantage but the proponents have left out Kailali and Kanchanpur districts which have a major Tharu population to suit the political interests of few leaders of the NC Party.

The constitutional bill did not mention proportional representation on the basis of the population of the ethnic groups and recognition of national identity. Upendra Yadav, leader of UDMF comments that the federal Alliance has been demanding representation based on population. If the constitution amended as per the bill's proposal, Madhesi would never be in Majority in the upper house. Other issues of concern were the recognition of all mother tongues and the issue of naturalized citizenship. The amendment Bill did not endorse the rights of equal citizenship denying more than the half of the population. Nepali women can not pass down citizenship rights to their children without declaring the citizenship status of the man who fathers the child. They argued that women who acquire naturalized citizenship on the basis of matrimony should be treated as citizen by the descent but the bill applied that these women would never hold top constitutional posts. Such a provision is deeply humiliating and discriminating for women who want to exercise their rights to be treated equally by the constitution and it violates the several provisions under international law including the convention on the elimination of all forms of Discrimination against women and universal declarations of human rights.

The Madhsi outfits rejected the bill and warned that they will continue their protests that includes an indefinite general strike in the southern plains and sit-in at the border points. In a way, the amendment has missed its purpose for the time being. No doubt, the internal dynamics of the three major parties played a role in the way the amendment was made without securing an agreement from the agitating UDMF. As the NC was holding its national congress within a few months, and the party found it very difficult to carry out the party's district level congresses in the Terai district, the amendment was important to pacify its district leaders and cadres. Nepali Congress senior leader Ram Chandra Poudel slammed the leaders of Madhesi based political parties for distorting facts saying the Nepali Congress party has always favoured the inclusion, citizenship rights, development and welfare of the Madhesi people. The Madhesi Parties which are demanding more representation and re-demarcation of state are opposing local body elections.

Nepal has lived through a decade of bloody conflict and another decade of painful transition but the country is not yet at peace with its own people and their liberated political aspirations. The new constitution has violated fundamental principles of democracy-liberty, equality and justice. Nepal has been held hostage of the dictate of incompetent and greedy political leaders forcing the country into a dangerous political course. In order to promote democracy and ensure a long-term peace and stability in the country, it is essential to amend the constitution if not re-write. The constitution is the only way to accommodate the aspirations of marginalised Madhesi people and other ethnic minorities people. If the demands of these people are not accommodating within the framework of the constitution, the Madhesi movement may turn into an ethno-nationalist separatist movement.

Political structure should take into account the diversity of its country, inclusion of minority rights and accommodation of dissent through peaceful means.

Notes

1. Nepal Politics 1990-2008, Global Security. org.
2. Dr.Chitra K.Tiwari, Maoist Insurgency in Nepal: Internal dimensions, paper no.187, South Asia Analysis Group, 2001.
3. Nepal's Population Census - 2011.
4. Hari Bans Jha, Nepal's New Constitution : An Analysis From Madheshi Parspective, Aljazeera, September 24, 2015.
5. Nihar R. Nayak, Madhesi Movement in Nepal: Implications for India, IDSA, May 28, 2010.
6. Charles Haviland,Why is Nepal'sNew Constitution Controversial?BBC News, 19 Sept. 2015.
7. Pooja Sen, What Are Nepal Madhesi Fighting for? The Wire, July 21, 2016.
8. Constitutional Bill Fails in Nepal, Hindustan Times, August 21, 2017.

Appendix - 9

A chronology of key events of Nepal

1768 - Gurkha ruler Prithvi Narayan Shah conquers Kathmandu and lays foundations for unified kingdom.

1792 - Nepalese expansion halted by defeat at hands of Chinese in Tibet.

1814-16 - Anglo-Nepalese War; culminates in treaty which establishes Nepal's current boundaries.

1846 - Nepal falls under sway of hereditary chief ministers known as Ranas, who dominate the monarchy and cut off country from outside world.

1923 - Treaty with Britain affirms Nepal's sovereignty.

Absolute monarchy

1950 - Anti-Rana forces based in India form alliance with monarch.

1951 - End of Rana rule. Sovereignty of crown restored and anti-Rana rebels in Nepalese Congress Party form government.

1953 New Zealander Edmund Hillary and Nepal's Sherpa Tenzing Norgay become the first climbers to reach the summit of Mount Everest.

1955 - Nepal joins the United Nations.

Image copyrightPAImage caption First to the top of Everest: Sherpa Tenzing Norgay and Edmund Hillary

1955 - King Tribhuwan dies, King Mahendra ascends throne.

1959 - Multi-party constitution adopted.

1960 - King Mahendra seizes control and suspends parliament, constitution and party politics after Nepali Congress Party (NCP) wins elections with B. P. Koirala as premier.

1962 - New constitution provides for non-party system of councils known as "panchayat" under which king exercises sole power. First elections to Rastrya Panchayat held in 1963.

1972 - King Mahendra dies, succeeded by Birendra.

Multi-party politics

1980 - Constitutional referendum follows agitation for reform. Small majority favours keeping existing panchayat system. King agrees to allow direct elections to national assembly-but on a non-party basis.

Image copyright AFP Image caption A Nepalese woman spins a prayer wheel, in a country where religion plays a major role.

1985 - NCP begins civil disobedience campaign for restoration of multi-party system.

1986 - New elections boycotted by NCP.

1989 - Trade and transit dispute with India leads to border blockade by Delhi resulting in worsening economic situation.

1990 - Pro-democracy agitation co-ordinated by NCP and leftist groups. Street protests suppressed by security forces resulting in deaths and mass arrests. King Birendra eventually bows to pressure and agrees to new democratic constitution.

1991 - Nepali Congress Party wins first democratic elections. Girija Prasad Koirala becomes prime minister.

Political instability

1994 - Koirala's government defeated in no-confidence motion. New elections lead to formation of Communist government.

1995 - Communist government dissolved.

Image copyright AFP Image caption Maoists waged a bloody war against the monarchy.

1995 - Start of Maoist revolt which drags on for more than a decade and kills thousands. The rebels want the monarchy to be abolished.

1997 - Prime Minister Sher Bahadur Deuba loses no-confidence vote, ushering in period of increased political instability, with frequent changes of prime minister.

2000 - GP Koirala returns as prime minister, heading the ninth government in 10 years.

Palace massacre

2001 1 June - Crown Prince Dipendra kills King Birendra, Queen Aishwarya and several members of the royal family, before shooting himself. The king's brother, Gyanendra is crowned king.

Image copyright AFP Image caption Nepalese mourn the royal family slain in a shooting spree

2001 July - Maoist rebels step up campaign of violence. Prime Minister GP Koirala quits over the violence; succeeded by Sher Bahadur Deuba.

2001 November - Maoists end four-month old truce with government, declare peace talks with government failed. Launch coordinated attacks on army and police posts.

Emergency

2001 November - State of emergency declared after more than 100 people are killed in four days of violence. King Gyanendra orders army to crush the Maoist rebels. Many hundreds are killed in rebel and government operations in the following months.

2002 May - Parliament dissolved, fresh elections called amid political confrontation over extending the state of emergency. Sher Bahadur Deuba heads interim government, renews emergency.

2002 October - King Gyanendra dismisses Deuba and indefinitely puts off elections set for November.

2003 January - Rebels, government declare ceasefire.

End of truce

2003 August - Rebels pull out of peace talks with government and end seven-month truce. The following months see resurgence of violence and frequent clashes between students/activists and police.

2004 April - Nepal joins the World Trade Organisation (WTO).

2004 May - Street protests by opposition groups demanding a return to democracy. Royalist Prime Minister Surya Bahadur Thapa quits.

Absolute monarchy restored

2005 February - King Gyanendra dismisses the government, restores an absolute monarchy and declares a state of emergency, citing the need to defeat Maoist rebels.

2005 April - King Gyanendra bows to international pressure, lifts the state of emergency and reinstates parliament.

2005 November - Maoist rebels and main opposition parties agree on a programme intended to restore democracy.

2006 April - King Gyanendra agrees to reinstate parliament following weeks of violent strikes and protests against direct royal rule. Maoist rebels call a three-month ceasefire.

2006 May - Parliament votes unanimously to curb the king's political powers. The government holds peace talks with the Maoist rebels.

Peace deal

2006 November - The government sign a peace deal with the Maoists - the Comprehensive Peace Agreement (CPA) - formally ending the decade-long insurgency.

2007 January - Maoist leaders enter parliament under the terms of a temporary constitution.

Maoists join government

2007 April - Maoists join an interim government, a move which brings them into the political mainstream.

2007 September - Three bombs hit Kathmandu in the first attack in the capital since the end of the Maoist insurgency.

Maoists quit the interim government, demanding the abolition of the monarchy. November's constituent assembly elections are postponed.

End of monarchy

2007 December - Parliament approves the abolition of monarchy as part of peace deal with Maoists, who agree to rejoin government.

2008 January - A series of bomb blasts kill and injure dozens in the southern Terai plains, where activists have been demanding regional autonomy.

2008 April - Former Maoist rebels win the largest bloc of seats in elections to the new Constituent Assembly (CA), but fail to achieve an outright majority.

2008 May - Nepal becomes a republic.

2008 June - Maoist ministers resign from the cabinet in a row over who should be the next head of state.

2008 July - Ram Baran Yadav becomes Nepal's first president.

2008 August - Maoist leader Pushpa Kamal Dahal aka Prachanda forms coalition government, with Nepali Congress going into opposition.

Maoists leave government

2009 May - Prime Minister Prachanda resigns following a row with President Yadav over the integration of former rebel fighters into the military.

2009 May - Britain announces that Gurkha veterans with at least four years' service in the British army will be allowed to settle in the UK.

2009 December - Four people are killed in clashes triggered by a Maoist-led land grab in the far west, giving rise to fears for peace process.

Impasse over constitution

2010 May - The Constituent Assembly (CA) votes to extend the deadline for drafting the constitution, the first of four extensions.

2011 January - UN ends its peace monitoring mission.

2012 May - The Constituent Assembly (CA) is dissolved after failing to produce a draft constitution.

2013 November - The left-wing Nepali Congress wins the second Constituent Assembly elections, pushing the former ruling Maoists into third place and leaving no party with a majority.

2014 February -Nepali Congress leader Sushil Koirala is elected prime minister after securing parliamentary support.

2014 April - Sixteen Nepalese Sherpa guides die in an avalanche on Mount Everest in the worst recorded accident in the mountain's history.

2014 November - Nepal and India sign a deal to build a $1bn hydro-power plant on Nepal's Arun river to counter crippling energy shortages.

2015 April - A 7.8-magnitude earthquake strikes Kathmandu and its surrounding areas killing more than 8,000 people, causing mass devastation and leaving millions homeless.

Landmark constitution

2015 September - Parliament passes a landmark constitution, which defines Nepal as a secular country, despite calls to delay voting after more than 40 people are killed in protests.

2015 October - K.P. Prasad becomes the first prime minister to be elected under the new constitution.

2016 February - Government lifts fuel rationing after the ethnic minority Madhesi communities, partially backed by India, end a six-month border blockade in protest over the new constitution which they say is discriminatory.

2016 July - Maoist party pulls out of the governing coalition. Prime Minister K.P. Oli resigns ahead of a no-confidence vote in parliament.

2016 August - Parliament elects former communist rebel leader and Maoist party leader Pushpa Kamal Dahal aka Prachanda as prime minister for the second time.

2017 April - Three former soldiers are convicted over the murder of a 15-year-old girl during the civil war, the first time serving or former members of the army have been found guilty of crimes linked to the conflict.

2017 June - Pushpa Kamal Dahal replaced as prime minister by the Congress leader Sher Bahadur Deuba under a rotation agreement reached the previous April and set to last until elections in February 2018.

Sources: BBC News south Asia, Feb. 2018.

Chapter - 8

Sri Lanka: Small State and Big Problems:

Sri Lanka traditionally a democratic parliamentary state adopted the Westminster model a year before its independence in 1947. Its democratic governance was well settled and stable, all peoples got democratic rights. In the first three decades of independence from British rule in 1948, the country developed a model of successful democracy but that model was collapsed due to violent ethnic civil war. A country that hailed in the world one of the successful models for human development forfeited its opportunities to make a progressive government and showed a tendency to move in the direction of authoritarian regime. A major change occurred when an executive presidency was introduced under the second Republican constitution and replaced Westminster model in 1978. Political establishment was also prepared to bend the rules of partisan gain. Political parties and interest groups of all kinds were willing to bend the rules with impunity for short term political gain at the cost of democracy. Political parties divided the country along ethnic lines. Two major political parties, United National Front and Sri Lanka Freedom party (UNP & SLFP) belonged to the Sinhalese majority while Tamils had one major party, first known as the Federal Party and later renamed Tamil United Liberation Front. The Plantation Tamils also have their own political party called the Ceylon Workers Congress and the Muslims were generally seeking political representation through the major political parties but by the mid-1970s they also formed their own political parties called Sri Lanka Muslim Congress.

Most important truth is that the politics of the country began to divide along ethnic lines in the late 1940s and accelerated pace after 1956. The first major event was the disenfranchisement of the plantation Tamils in 1948 on the grounds that they were not legal citizens of the country.

The British colonial policy of divide and rule sowed the seeds of tensions between the Sinhalese and Tamil communities. Tamil although well-educated were given disproportionate numbers of jobs in the civil services by the British.

The beginning of political fighting along the ethnic lines became more bitter after independence. Ethnic divisions along with the linguistic divisive rivalries soon entered into the body politics of this nation and spreaded to other major areas of public policy and governance. In plural-multi-ethnic society, the Neo-liberal political philosophy allows to build a state where all groups irrespective of race, ethnicity and primordial division owe allegiance and the minorities must feel that their rights are protected and the majoritarian dominance by virtue of superior numbers is not allowed to undermine the political institutions and political culture. But, between the early 1950s and the late 1970s, the policies were detrimental to Tamil interests, hence, denial of their rights.

After independence, the Sinhalese majority held sway and its politician sought to redress the balance with populist but discriminatory policies against Tamils. The attitude of the government and the Sinhalese people were not inclined to concede the Tamil minority rights which they claimed for themselves. Therefore, the Tamil insurgency developed against the backdrop of repeated refusal by the political elite of the Sinhalese community to pay attention to the Tamil. In 1970s, the Sri Lanka government compounded the situation by introducing a quota system for admission in education and jobs which were discriminatory. The controversial land colonisation schemes to settle landless small farmers outside the area also changed the ethnic composition of the region. They demanded that they should be allowed to administer the areas in the north and east under a devolved system of government. Therefore, Tamils demands for regional autonomy and self-determination entered a period of mass mobilization during the parliamentary elections in 1977. In 1980s, the Jayewardene government agreed to a system of District Development Councils to devolve power and Tamil United Liberation Front (TULF) agreed to cooperate. But, the then government failed to satisfy Tamil aspirations. In the July 1983 ethnic violence proved to be fatal in Sinhalese- Tamil relations and the country entered in long civil ethnic violence war.

It generated a crisis and formed the background to the ethnic war that began in the early 1980s. The ethnic divide between Tamils and Sinhalese was resulted in the thirty years of bloodiest Tamils insurgency and war in which approximately 22,000 LTTE fighters died and 275000 civilians were displaced. Liberation of Tamil Tigers Eelam (LTTE) demanded a separate homeland for Tamils that eventually turned a full- blown civil war.

The Sri Lanka civil war passed through various phases from July 1983-2009 and several rounds of negotiations and ceasefires. All the efforts by the all succeeding Sri Lankan government as well as regional and international powers to bring the LTTE to negotiations failed. The LTTE refused any political compromise except the establishment of a separate Tamil state. The Rajapaksa government finally took military actions and the three decades old civil war came to an end in 2009.

Anti-Muslims Violence

Sri Lanka's long civil war ended in 2009 with the bloody crushing of the Tamil insurgency. But Sri Lankan state environment has been further deteriorating due to the atrocities and violence occurring against another minority community-Muslims. Sri Lanka has been coming closer to the emergence of Islamist terrorism step by step. Recent violence against Muslim was reportedly sparked by an incident of road rage involving a Sinhalese truck driver and a group of Muslim men in Kandy district of the central highlands on 28 February 2018. A Muslim man assaulted the Sinhalese driver resulted in his death at a hospital a few days later. The day after his death, Sinhalese mobs went on a rampage, attacking Muslims, burning their homes, shops, vehicles and the violence soon spread to other districts. Immediately the Sri Lankan government declared the state-wide emergency

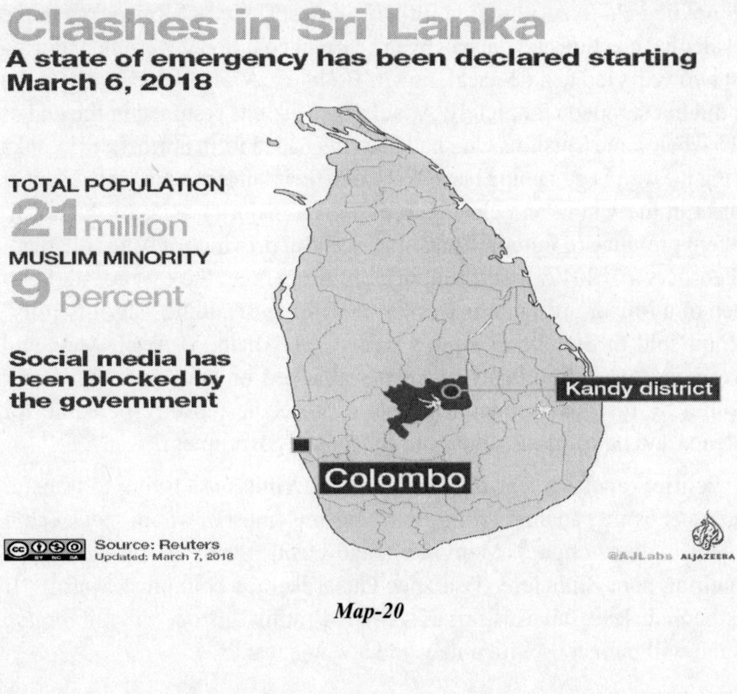

Map-20

on March 6, 2018. Curfew was imposed and the army deployed in the areas affected by the violence. Even then, attacks on Muslims continue and appear to be spreading geographically too. This is for the first time after 2011 the emergency was reimposed. It underlines the new political and ethnic dynamics of violence in Sri Lanka. In a series of violent episodes, this incident is latest targeting the Muslim community that Sri Lanka witnessed in the post-war years.

Earlier in 2012, monks destroyed a mosque in Dambulla, saying it violated a Buddhist religious area. In 2013, the warehouse of a clothes retailer owned by a Muslim businessman was targeted; in 2014, four people were killed and 80 injured in riots in the western seaside district of Kalutara where the Sinhalese and Muslim villages had never seen communal tensions earlier. In between, the Bodu Bala Sena (BBS) ran a campaign against halal certification and burqas. The monks of BBS made incendiary speeches against Muslims, one of which was directly responsible for the riots. The Secretariat for Muslims (SFM), a Muslim civil society organisation, documented 538 anti-Muslim incidents from 2013 to 2015.

The present Sri Lankan government won elections in 2015 on the promise of ending ethnic strife, ensuring accountability for conflict-related crimes, and taking steps towards reconciliation. But all these pledges are stalled, perhaps allowing militant Buddhist groups to believe that they will not be held to accountable for any abuses. Defeat of Rajapaksa in the presidential election and the ban by the current coalition government during first two years led to a de-escalation of Buddhist. Violence against Muslim but did not stopped completely. Attacks on Muslims resumed in the end of 2016 when some Muslims who had been displaced from northern Sri Lanka during the war, began going back to reclaim their lands in villages in Mannar district in the Vanni, and close to the Sinhala majority areas of the north-western province of Puttalam and north-central province of Anuradhapura. In February 26, 2017, mobs rampaged in Ampara on the east coast after a video of a Muslim restaurant-worker confessing to adding "sterility pills" to food sold to Sinhalese women went viral. Again, in April, May, and November 2017, Buddhists militant's attacked on Muslims apparently inspired by the government's failure to prosecute those responsible for violence and hate speech under the Rajapaksa government.[1]

Political analysts fear that Sinhalese extremists are trying to transfer lingering hostility against Tamils onto Muslims (most of whom speak Tamil as their mother tongue). Many are small businessmen, easily painted as exploiting poor Sinhalese. Tisaranee Gunasekara, a columnist, warns, "If we, the Sinhalese, fail Muslims as we failed Tamils, history will not forgive us, and will punish us with a new and a worse war."[2]

Violence against Muslims minority has been emphasised the country's fragility since 2011. Muslims have come under repeated attacks by the Sinhalese community. Such violence is said to be organized and orchestrated by the Buddhist Sinhalese groups and supported by the politicians and parliamentarians. These orchestrating attacks on Muslims is fuelling more and deadlier cycles of violence. The successive governments failed to bring the justice[3] and hardly and rarely any guilty have been punished. In fact, with every incident of violence being unleashed on Muslims, resentments among Muslim youths increasing and the Sri Lankan government's avoiding attitude in reining the Sinhalese extremist groups has been giving Muslims population reasons to pick up arms, if only to defend themselves.

The Buddhist-Muslim riots and violence have surfaced in Sri Lanka nearly a century after. Violence targeting the minorities came to the forefront during the colonial rule. The first Anti-Muslims incidents took place in 1915 when the Sinhala Buddhist revival professed the marginalisation of the community under colonial rule around the country. Sinhalese felt that Christians and Muslims were more benefited from the colonial policies. Muslim domination on the economy also evoked deep resentment among them. In effect, past bitterness, latent anti-Muslim sentiment, hunger for loot and chaos for its own sake collectively caused the 1915 Sinhalese-Muslim riots. In 1915, it was more a senseless destruction of property rather than killings. The riots claimed only three lives but it deepened the sense of alienation among Sri Lanka's Muslims, who have endured periodic episodes of majoritarian violence.

"The Sinhala majority is signalling that their dominance is not to be messed around with," he said. "The moment a minority demonstrates economic success—as with the Muslim community—or struggles for autonomy like the Tamil community, or is accused of conversion like the Christian community, the moment there is some kind of threat to that dominant status, there is a tendency for violence to be used to re-assert that dominance."[4]

For almost six decades, the Sinhalese-Buddhist supremacist project thrived by depicting Tamils as "the enemy." With the end of Tamil civil strife in 2009, Sinhalese extremists needed a new enemy to keep the project relevant. Sinhala-Buddhist extremism treated Muslims a new enemy and the rise of Islamists fundamentalism and terrorism provided a suitable tool to handle and demonise the community. A careful observation and analysis of anti-Muslim violence in Sri Lanka show that it did not occur in vacuum. There is an ideology and a political program behind this violence. It has it's root in historical, demographic, social-cultural, political and economic contexts that needs to be understand if the problem is to be solved.

State Ideology

Sri Lanka state's central ideology rooted in Buddhism and the interests of Sinhala-Buddhists. Though Buddhism is not a state religion in Sri Lanka, it accorded foremost position while allowing people of other faiths to practice. This placed in the constitution has actively empowered Singhalese-Buddhists to pressure politicians to gain concessions and to mobilize population. There was a pressure from liberal groups to change the constitution in order to reflect true secular nature by removing special status for Buddhism. But there was huge opposition from Sinhala-Buddhist forces and politicians. More than 75 prominent monks warned the government not to change the constitution or it would face consequences. The opposition, led by former president Mahinda Rajapaksa, and hard-line Buddhist groups have warned the government of nationwide demonstrations if the government went ahead with changes to the charter.

Since Buddhism is a crucial part of Sinhala-Buddhists ,so the symbol like language and national flag which are the markers of Sinhalese Buddhist hegemony. Flag is one of most important identity markers of the nation which represent multi dynamics of different ethno-religious communities. In the flag, "the lion represents bravery of Sinhalese. The four Bo leaves represent four main concepts of Buddhism-Metta, Karuna, Mudita and Upeksha. The stripes represent the two main minority groups. The saffron stripe represents Tamils and the green stripe represents Muslims, and the maroon background represents the majority Sinhalese. The Gold border around the flag represents the unity of Sri Lankans."[5] The lion, which represents the Sinhala-Buddhists, occupies the majority portion of the flag. The lion with sword not simply represents the Sinhala-Buddhists, but also it is warning both Tamils and Muslims with bloody consequences if they (Tamils and Muslims) would go against the interests of the majoritarian domination. In other words, the lion with sword passes the message to non-Sinhalese communities to "behave" in a way the majority Sinhala-Buddhists want or face the dire consequences.

Another important characteristic of the Sinhalese that has influenced their attitude towards minorities is that they are "a majority with a minority complex", says as noted Sri Lankan anthropologist Stanley Tambiah in his book "Sri Lanka: Ethnic Fratricide and the Dismantling of Democracy." They believe the Sri Lankan Tamils are the part of the larger Tamil community of Tamil Nadu state of India and the Sri Lankan Muslims as part of the Muslim ummah. This "minority complex" has resulted in Sinhalese viewing themselves as victims, who have to act, even violently, to defend the island and Sinhalese-Buddhist culture from being taken over by the asinhala (un-Sinhala) and abaudha (un-Buddhist). These groups are viewed as essentially "foreigners," who are staying on the island due to Sinhalese-Buddhist sufferance. Publications like Sinhala Bauddhaya and Sinhala Jathiya carried articles that were inflammatory in content and are said to have culminated in the anti-Muslim violence in 1915.[6]

Historically, the Revivalists like Anagarika Dharmapala claimed that the "Muslims were alien invaders"[7] who used "Shylockian methods to become prosperous like the Jews." They had become prosperous at the expense of the "sons of the soil," i.e. the Sinhalese, he said. Mahanama's linked the concepts[8] of Sinhadipa (land of the lion race, i.e. of the Sinhalese) with Dhammadipa (the land chosen by Buddha to protect and propagate his Dhamma or teachings) and it has had enormous impact on Sinhalese-Buddhist self-perception. Although the Mahanama's is more myth than the facts, Sinhalese-Buddhists draw on it to justify their claim that the island belongs to them and that they are a people chosen to protect Buddha's teachings. Experiences suggest that Sinhala-Buddhist politicians seek support from Buddhist monks and authorities to win and to consolidate power. In some cases, these forces win concessions from the state and its institutions.

Demographic Factors

Sri Lanka is a multi-ethnic, multi-lingual and multi-religious society. Sinhalese constitute the majority and are mainly Buddhist. The total population of Sri Lankan 20.95 million Population[9] and the ethnic distribution of population in Sri Lanka shows Sinhalese is in majority (74.9%) followed by Tamils (11.2%) and Sri Lanka Moor (Muslims) (9.3%). Other ethnic groups namely Burgher, Malay, Sri Lanka Chetty and Bharatha form 0.5 percent of total population. The highest percentages of Sinhalese, Tamil and Sri Lanka moor population are reported from Southern province (95.0%), Northern province (93.8%) and Eastern province (36.9%) respectively. Almost 70 percent of Sri Lankan population is Buddhist followed by Hindus (12.6%), Islam (9.7%), Roman Catholic (6.2%) and other religions (1.4%).

The statistical interpretation between 1981 and 2012 census shows that the Buddhist and Muslim population increased from 69.30% to 70.19% and from 7.56% to 9.71% respectively while the Hindu and Christian population decreased from 15.48% to 12.61% and 7.62 to 7.45% respectively. Muslim population increased 2% leap forward from 7.62% to 7.45%. Therefore, the Muslim population has increased by 78.60% that is double of the national average growth of 36.48% and more than the increase of the Buddhist population.

Table 25: Ethnic Population of Sri Lanka.

Rank	*Ethnic Groups*	*Percentage of Population*
1	Sinhalese	74.9%
2	Tamils	11.2%
3	Muslims(Moor)	9.3%
4	Indian Tamils	4.1%
5	Sri Lankan Malay	0.2%
6		0.2%
7	OtherGroups	0.1%

According to an estimated projection by the World Population Review that Sri Lanka will become a predominantly Muslim country by 2050. It is calculated by an ineluctable process according to the norms established during the hundred-year period from 1881-1981 Muslim population increases. Izeth Hussain an analyst rejected the projection said, the expectation that Sri Lanka will become a Muslim majority country by 2050 is no more than an expression of racist Islamophobia. The future Muslim population increase would be along the lines indicated by the statistics from 1881 to 1981.Therefore, it would be idle to speculate.[10]

Many Sinhalese believe that the higher birth rate among Muslims poses a threat to the continued demographic supremacy of the Sinhalese. This mistrust is a biggest Faultline in Sri Lankan Society earlier between Tamils and Sinhalese and now with Muslims. Although Sinhalese population increased vastly in terms of numbers than the Tamilians and Muslims even then they feel outnumbered by them. The main accusations of the BBS against the Muslims that they are procreating at a faster rate[11] than the Sinhalese, forcibly converting Buddhists to Islam, and following a culture that is at odds with that of the Sinhalese-Buddhists. This has fuelled fears among the masses that Muslims will soon outnumber the Sinhalese and that Sinhala-Buddhist culture will be wiped out of the island. All the extremist outfits BBS including the Sinhala Ravaya, Sinhale, and Mahason Balaya have been creating fear and insecurities among the Sinhalese people and encouraging them to start violence by spreading these baseless rumours. In the run-up to the current wave of violence, rumours were circulated that Muslims are implementing plans to reduce the Sinhalese population by "adding sterility pills in the food serve to Sinhalese". A video of a Muslim cook of a restaurant confessing the 'adding of sterility pills'[12] to the food served to Sinhalese went viral in social media which resulted in the mob violence; vandalize Muslim homes, mosques, and business establishments.

Currently Buddhist has been following the same pattern and attitude resentment toward Sri Lankan Muslims as elsewhere in the world. The intercommunal violence in Sri Lanka parallels to the crisis throughout the Buddhist world where tensions between Buddhist majority communities and their Muslim minorities have been growing. In Myanmar, Buddhist monks has been carrying out atrocities and repression with the hallmarks of a genocide toward its Rohingya Muslim minority.[13] They are systematically restricted their access to healthcare, education, food, marriages, freedom of movement with a brutal campaign of violence that forced them to flee. Likewise, in southern Thailand, a crisis between the Thai Buddhist and ethnic Malay Muslim minority has led to over 6,000 deaths in both communities and alleged[14] the Thai government for continued human rights abuses.[15] Similarly, Buddhist radicals in Sri Lanka regularly accuses the Muslim community for forced conversions or vandalism of Buddhist holy sites. Meenakshi Gungaly of Human Rights Watch said, "Unfortunately, too many populist leaders around the world are exploiting the fear of terrorist attacks or of immigrants by engaging in hate-mongering against Muslims".[16]

Buddhists Ultra Extremism

The anti-Muslim violence is the result of a concerted nationwide effort of Buddhist ultra-nationalism and the direct fallout of the triumphalism and majoritarianism that took hold in the Sinhala Buddhist majority community after the military defeat of the LTTE. The resurgence of militant Buddhist groups grew in popularity and number of groups has developed hatred and openly professing it for Muslims community. They have used social media to spread their venom against Muslims with the covert support of former Mahinda Rajapaksa's government. Among them are the Bodu Bala Sena, Sinhala Ravaya, Sinhale, and Mahason Balaya. The first and foremost outfit among them is the Bodu Bala Sena (BBS) founded in 2012 by a monk named Galabode Aththe Gnanasara and patronaged by the Rajapaksa clan. Mahinda Rajapaksa, who relies strongly on Sinhalese nationalist support, has enjoyed popularity and his newly founded party won 239 out of 340 seats at local elections in 2018. Though, he denied that the violence was part of a political conspiracy and blamed the government's failure to respond to social tensions on a media comment.

Another factor of anti-Muslim Violence in Sri Lanka, Sinhalese-Buddhist extremists are developing overseas links with Buddhist radical monks and outfits specially Myanmar Buddhists outfits. Sri Lanka's Buddhist extremism has links with an ally in Myanmar's hard-line Buddhist monks. Both countries practise the Theravada variant of Buddhism. In September 2014, ahead of the presidential election, the BBS invited Ashin Wirathu, a monk from Mandalay in Myanmar and the leader of a virulently anti-Muslim group called 969, known for his toxic speeches. At a rally in

Colombo, he said, he would join hands with the BBS to "protect" Buddhists. Though he has not made a return visit since, extremist Buddhists in Sri Lanka have clearly taken inspiration from the anti-Rohingya movement in Myanmar. Coincidence or not, the first clashes against the Rohingya in Myanmar erupted in 2012, around the time that BBS was formed in Sri Lanka.[17]

In 2014, Ashin Wirathu, who has incited violence against Rohingya Muslims, offered to support the BBS[18] in its fight against Muslims, claiming a "serious threat from jihadist groups" in Sri Lanka. There were several incidents through April and May 2017 across Sri Lanka and around the same time, the Buddhist outfits began a campaign against the arrival of a group of Rohingya in Colombo. On September 28, 2016, a monk led an attack on the UN-maintained safehouse for the Rohingya in the Colombo suburb of Mt Lavinia. The Rohingya group had been taken into custody by the Navy after they attempted to land on the Sri Lankan coast, and they were ordered to be kept in the safehouse under UN protection. The group that attacked the safehouse alleged the Rohingya had killed Buddhists in Myanmar. In November, Buddhists and Muslims clashed on the streets of Gintota in Galle.

Buddhist outfits and monks have been active to incite anti-Muslim sentiments and the increase of Islamophobia. Although the Sinhalese Buddhist sangha primarily opposed to violence yet it has not done anything to control the situation. They believe themselves as the guardians of the Sinhalese Buddhist ethno-religious identity and the legitimators of the Sinhalese Buddhist to have a privileged position in the island's affairs.[19] There are vocal groups of monks who whip up the antagonism or hatred to the lay Buddhists toward other communities and even incite them to act violently. There are reasons that prevent them from playing an effective role. Sri Lanka has a history of mobilising ethno-cultural nationalism to justify majoritarian violence. While the civil war is frequently framed as a clash between ethnicities, much of the mobilisation and rhetoric are often religious as well. They still stick to the ideology that Sri Lanka as a modern nation essentially belongs to the Sinhalese Buddhists, while the other residents of the island have perpetual guest status. The Singhalese Buddhist Sangh never condemn the violence forcefully nor they stress strongly in their sermons for inter-communal harmony and respect for other religions. The Sinhalese Buddhist majority has been trained to feel continually disenfranchised. Their sense of aggrievement and insecurity has become a key part of their self-perceived identity and has been mobilised for political purposes since decades.

Rise of anti-Muslims feeling have long been harboured by the Singhalese Buddhists. It is a campaign generating imagined fear and myth that "Buddhism is under threat" and that Muslim are out to take control of the country by pushing the Sinhalese Buddhists into a marginal position. These false campaigns have spread lies about an alleged increase in the Muslim population and rumours that they have a secret plan to make Sri Lanka a Muslim majority country. These misinformation campaigns have also focused on the alleged increase of wealth and influence of the Muslim population. Fundamentalist Buddhist groups such as the Bodu Bala Sena and the Ravana Balaya, which promote the concept of "Sri Lanka for Sinhalese Buddhists", exploit and propagate these myths. Such myth led Sinhalese Buddhists of Ampara to destroy Muslim businesses following a rumour that Muslim eateries were mixing some pill in their food to make their Sinhalese patrons impotent.

Religious- Communal Separatism

The growing influence of Wahabi Islam and the increasing numbers of mosques built with money from Saudi Arabia have resulted in the Muslims being seen as "not one of us", but as "the other". In Sri Lanka, it has eroded the traditional cultural links between Muslims and other religious communities. In the past, Sri Lankan Muslim traders and artisans had specific roles to play in Buddhist religious festivities but these began to be frowned upon by Wahabi purists backed by new Saudi-funded Islamic institutions. Though the rift between the Sinhalese Buddhists and the Muslims began much earlier but with the segregation of schools on the basis of language and religion, it has increased more. Tamils study in Tamil medium schools, the Sinhalese in Sinhalese medium schools and Muslims in Muslim schools to learn Islamic values. So, in a way, the seeds of communal separatism are planted in childhood. During the Tamil separatism in the 1970 and 1980 When the Sinhalese Buddhist were befriended with the Muslims and their interests were promoted to keep them away from the Tamils with whom they had linguistic affinity. The Muslims were co-opted in governmental and political institutions, which enabled their rise as a wealthy and influential business community. The downside was its engendered Sinhalese Buddhist jealousy. The Muslims came to be seen as the "Jews of Sri Lanka", clever, wealthy and influential pursuers of self-interest. The arrival of Wahhabism only widened the gulf by creating a cultural and social divide. The Muslims became the quintessential "other".

Political Supports

After independence, Sri Lankan political leaders and parties garnered Sinhala-Buddhism for three decades starting with SWRD Bandaranaike. Sinhalese political parties contesting with each other to project themselves as the guardians of the Sinhalese-Buddhists. It led to the Sinhalization of the state and its institutions which resulted in political, economic and cultural marginalization of minorities. In 1970s importantly, Tamils and their properties were targeted by Sinhalese mobs, often backed by the state. Tamil alienation with the Sri Lankan state led to the emergence of a powerful ethnic insurgency. Same story is repeating again. Muslims of Sri Lanka found themselves in constantly changing situations. Until 1990, Muslims believed they had common cause with Tamil political aspirations because of the common language and residence. Muslims language is Tamil and the majority of Muslims still live in the East, which was part of the LTTE's Eelam vision. But, that year (1990), LTTE drove out nearly 100,000 Muslims from Jaffna and other parts of northern Sri Lanka under its control. The eviction took place overnight, Muslim people left behind their houses, lands, shops, and possessions, becoming a new set of internally displaced people in Sri Lanka.

Emerging Muslim Political Consciousness

Given the old Sinhalese-Tamil political divide, it was but natural that the Muslims should also seek their own political identity in a communalised political system. The Sri Lanka Muslim Congress was duly established in the late 1980s. Later, many Muslim parties centred around leaders and regions emerged. Led by ambitious, well-endowed leaders, the Muslim parties started branches everywhere and put up candidates in elections. In time, the Muslims, who previously supported multi-ethnic national parties, gravitated towards voting for Muslim parties. The net result was that no Sri Lankan was thinking "nationally" any more, but only as one belonging to this or that ethnic or religious group. As former President Rajapaksa pointed out recently, in such a communally divided society, even a fight between two individuals could be turned into a communal one with mass participation, causing a law and order problem.

Sri Lankan Muslim Congress Party was formed in 1981 by a small study group of local Eastern Province, developed a new political consciousness among and within a decade of its formation. Sri Lanka Muslim Congress was seen by Sinhala political parties as a "kingmaker" party. In the legislative election of 2004,[20] the party won 2.0% of the popular vote and 5 out of 225 legislative seats. Winning seats in Parliament from the predominantly Muslim areas of Ampara; from Batticaloa, where Muslims are the second biggest community after the majority Hindu Tamils; from Trincomalee up the eastern coast, where they are one-third of the population (Tamils and Sinhalese are also one-third each); as well as a few from Kandy and other areas, the community was in the impermeable of national politics. It has always sided with the ruling party, and is even now part of the coalition government.

The current wave of violence against Muslims is really dangerous. Sri Lanka politicians should take punitive measures to ease tensions and to calm fears shared by many quarters of Muslims in the island. Sri Lanka should not open a new path for destruction and instability by pushing Muslims into corner and/or giving birth to new form of protracted tensions and violence. If, the violence being systematically unleashed on Muslims, it will provoke a strong response from Muslim youth. It can have radicalized Muslim youths. One can recall how Sinhalese racists attitude towards the Tamils played role in spawning Tamil militancy and a three-decade long civil war. If this will repeat again, Sri Lanka's path to embrace peace and harmony may have to confront more tensions and violence. Sri Lankan political parties and even the government are reluctant to sever the still nascent links or criticize Sinhalese-Buddhist extremism as they do not want to lose the votes of the Sinhalese hardliners. In such political conditions, ethnic minority groups may also resort to violence and extremism. This is a blueprint for instability and insecurities. If Sri Lanka's political elites want to establish peace and reconciliation, they should demonstrate political willingness to take measures to establish peace.

Notes

1. Mathew Gidin, Sri Lanka struggle to Contain its Violent Buddhist Extremists, Trike Daily News Society and Environment, March 9, 2018.
2. https://srilankatwo.wordpress.com/2018/04/25/Sri-Lankan-Muslim-the New Others.
3. Sri Lanka Hate Speech Impunity Fuel anti-Muslims Violence, Aljazeera News, March 3, 2018.
4. Ibid.
5. Imtiyaz Razak, Why Violence in Sri Lanka: Some Critical Notes on Sinhala-Buddhist Symbols, Colombo telegraph, March 9, 2018.
6. Stanely J. Tambiah, Sinhalese Majority with Minority Complexes, IB Taurus publisher, 1986, Chapter six, pp. 92-113.
7. Sri Lanka Muslims in The Cross Heirs? The Diplomate, Nov. 9, 2013.
8. Ayesha Zuhair, Dynamics of Sinhala Buddhist Ethno Nationalism in Post War Sri Lanka, Centre for Policy Alternatives, Colombo, Sri Lanka, 2016.
9. World population review, department of census and statistic, 2018>world population-review.com/countries/sri-lanka-population/.
10. Izeth Husian, Muslim Population Problem, Sri Lankan Muslims at the cross roads – 17, September 19, 2014.
11. Sri Lanka Firebrand Monk invokes Muslim menaces, http://www.japantimes.co.jp/opinion/2017/06/17.
12. http://www.sundayobeserver.lk/2018/03/04/news/ tension-ampara-after-fakesterlisation-pills%e2%80%99-controversy.
13. http://www.businessinsider.com/2018/02-sun says-Myanmar-treatment-of-Rohingyamuslims- has-the-hallmarks-of-genocide/2018.
14. Thailand activists held incommunicado-http://www.hrw.org/news/2018/2/27.

15. Sri Lanka declare state of emergency after mob attacks on Muslims, the New York times, March 6, 2018 by Mujib Mashal and Darisha Bastians; Anti-Muslim riots in Sri Lanka signal a new social fissure, Sinhalese nationalists may be looking for an enemy, The economist, march 8, 2018.
16. James Shaheen, Tricycle Talks: How Buddhistand Muslim stereotypes conceal the Real history, Trike daily, NY, Feb. 27, 2018.
17. Nirupama.subramanian@expressindia.com.
18. http://www.aljazeera.com/news/southasia/2014/04 buddhist-monk-fight-jihad-threatasia-201498153512953861.html.
19. Ven. Bhikkhu Bodhi, renowned scholar-monk and founder of Buddhist Global Relief, who lived in Sri Lanka for 24 years, told Tricycle.
20. Y. Warnapala, Minority Electoral Politics: A Sri Lankan Case Study, Journal of Asian and African Studies, 40(6), 2016 pp. 439-461.

Chapter - 9

Maldives' Political Crisis: Autocratic Democracy

Maldives, a south Asian country, south west of Sri Lanka in the Arabian Sea. It is the first country of south Asia facing not any socio-religious or ethnic crisis but a political crisis-struggles for power. A severe political crisis erupted on February 5, 2018 when President Yameen Abdul Gayoom declared a state of emergency. Security forces arrested two judges of the supreme court and two members of the opposition and sealed the Parliament. Many opposition leaders were prisoned and others fear arrest. The supreme court Judges were arrested because they declared the actions of President Yameen unconstitutional and ordered the release of imprisoned nine high profile opposition leaders. The supreme Court also ruled out the Yameen government decision to remove the 12 legislators and ordered their reinstatement when they defected from Yameen ruling party in 2017. Allowing them to return to the legislature would deprive him of a majority. The Yameen government justified its actions and purposely declared 15 days emergency so that all powers would be granted to the president and he will be able to uphold its power. He immediately suspended two police chiefs who were implementing the court decisions. He suspended the constitutional rights of the power of the Parliament and the supreme court. Both the parliament and the supreme court have power to impeach the president. The supreme court can impeach the president and has power to issue an arrest warrant if president commits crime and violates the constitution.

The entire episode, in fact, is the struggle for power. Maldives whole opposition was united in a coalition and wanted to remove the Yameen Gayoom. The state of emergency prevented the President from being forcibly removed and gave him power to control the opposition leaders. Although emergency was imposed for 15 day but it could be extended so that the Yameen Gayoom could restore its power. He replaced the remaining judges and reversed the court's order and hold the convictions against the opposition leaders. If the Yameen Gayoom fail to control the opposition and state institutions, it will have great implications for the upcoming presidential elections.

Historical Background

The political history of Maldives has been full of coups, corruption and conspiracies. Maldives is a low-lying island country in the Indian Ocean, 717 km away from Sri Lanka and 430 km from India. In the 5th century BC people from Southern India and Sri Lanka migrated there establishing Hindu culture and followed Buddhism. In the 10th to 12th century Christian era, the sailors from Arabia and East Africa began to settle around the Maldives and brought the Islam with them. By the year 1153, the whole island was converted into Islam and the Buddhist kings of the Maldives became Sultans.

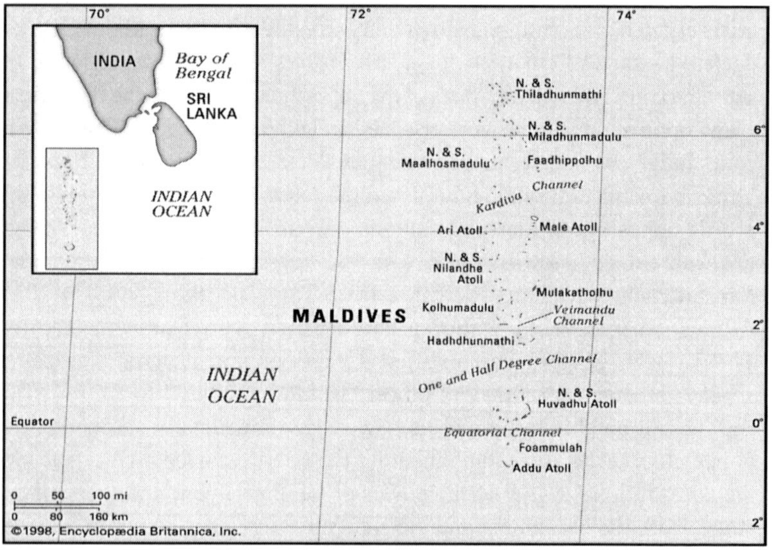

Map-21: Maldives

Maldives was also under the dominance of foreign colonial power in the 16th century because of their rule in Sri Lanka and India. In 1558, Portuguese established a trading post in Maldives which they administered from their main colony Goa but could not sustain for long. the local leaders of Maldives organised a revolt and drove the Portuguese out of the country.

In mid 17th century, the Dutch's established East India Company in Maldives and tried to dominance the country's internal affairs. They were ousted by the Britishers in 1776 and made Maldives a part of British Protectorate. On 16th December 1887, the sultan of Maldives and the British Governor of Ceylon signed a treaty which gave the British government sole power to run the country's diplomatic and foreign affairs and leaving the internal affairs to the Sultan. The British government promised to the military protection and non-interference in local administration of the island. Maldives gained independence in 1965.[1]

During the British era, Maldives continued to be ruled under the succession of Sultan, however, the Britain encouraged the development of a constitutional Monarchy. The first constitution was proclaimed in 1932 but the angry mob publicly torn up the constitution. In 1940s, in a referendum held, Maldives became a Republic and ended the more than 800 years old institution of Sultanate. Mohammed Amin Didi was elected as the first president. But after the death of Amin Didi, the old institution of Sultanate was again reinstated. In a referendum, 98% population of Maldives voted in favour of the restoration of Monarchy. Prince Mohammed Fareed Didi was elected as the Sultan in 1954 and Ehgamngey Ibrahim Didi became the Prime Minister in 1957. The Prime was forced to resign and Velaanagey Ibrahim Nasir was appointed the new Prime Minister.

In 1968, Maldives abolished the Monarchy rule and became Republican state under the presidency of Ibrahim Nasir who had increasingly dominated the political scene. The members of Parliament voted in favour of a Republican state (40 out of 44) and in a national referendum held on the question, 97.16 % of the participated people voted in favour of establishing a republic.[2] Under the new constitution, the member of parliament Majilis indirectly elected Nasir as president for a period of four years and his candidacy was ratified by referendum thus ended the era of Monarchy. Ahmad Zaki was appointed as the new Prime Minister.

In 1972, the Nasir government amended the constitution and the term of presidency was extended four to five year and the election of Prime Minister by the majlis was introduced. In 1973 Nasir was elected president for the second term. Prime Ahmad Zaki was arrested in a bloodless coup because his popularity was posing a threat to the Nasir faction. Nasir popularity was declining due to his authoritarian rule and the methods he adopted against his opponent. Other reasons were the deteriorating economic situation in the country; handling an insurrection of Abdu island and introduction of the Latin alphabets (Male Latin) instead of the local Thaana script. Nasir period of authoritarian rule was ended abruptly in 1978 when he absconded with million dollars from the state treasury.

In 1978, Maumoon Abdul Gayoom became the president who rule the country till 2008. In the second ballot he received majority vote he secured 92.96% of vote. It was seen as the ushering in a new era of Maldives politics and political stability. But Abdul Gayoom period was full of coups and corruption and authoritarian rule. He faced three attempts of coups in 1980, 1983 and 1988. The 1980 and 1983 coups were not very serious but the third coup was alarming.[3] In 1988 Tamil militant outfit PLOTE of armed mercenaries invaded the capital city Male in order to topple the government and succeeded in controlling the many government offices.[4] The Indian military intervened on the request of President Gayoom and saved the government.

Abdul Gayoom served three more presidential term. But he was also alleged for the autocratic rule, corruption and Human Rights abuses. His government did not allow any opposition and employed the terror tactics against the dissidents such as arbitrary arrests and detention without trial employing torture, forced confession and politically motivated killings. He was finally forced out of the office when Mohammad Nasheed won 2008 presidential election.

Demand for Democracy

Maldivians shook off a three-decade-long dictatorship and chose to walk down the path of democracy. An independent political movement was emerged under the leadership of Mohammad Nasheed which demanded democracy and challenged the autocratic rule of the Gayoom. Mohammad Nasheed, a journalist and activist, founded a political party called Maldivian Democratic Party (MDP). Due to civil unrest, several anti-government demonstrations were held and calling for the political reforms, democratic freedom and the end of torture and oppression. In September 2003, violent protest broke out in the capital city of Male when a prisoner was died due to the brutal torture of prisoner staffs.[5] When people came to know the reason of death, riots triggered in the prison and police guard opened fired on the unarmed inmates. It caused the death of three person. Several governments buildings were set on fire during the riot.

In August 2004, another civil demonstration took place on the arrest of Mohammad Nasheed and other political activists. Supporters and members of Maldivian Democratic party demanded the resignation of the President Abdul Gayoom and release of Mohammad Nasheed and the political activists arrested. Protest continued to grow and the demolition of Dhunfini tent complicated the situation and provoking the unrest. Maldivian National security services and National Defence Force used batons and tear gas on the unarmed civilians. President Abdul Gayoom declared the state of emergency to suppress the demonstration and suspended all human rights, banning demonstration and freedom of press.[6] All media and internet social services were curtailed.

The protest movement brought significant change in the political structure and started a new era in the Maldivians politics. A new constitution was ratified in August 2008 paving the way for first time to democratic election for the presidency after two months. Political parties were allowed registration. The Maldivian Democratic Party (MDP), The Dhivehi Raiyythunge Party (DRP), The Islamic Democratic party (IDP) and the Adhaalath Party were registered. The most popular party was MDP headed by Mohammad Nasheed. In October 2008, long-term Maldivian leader Maumoon Abdul Gayoom left power peacefully, after a popular opposition movement challenged his power and forced him to hold the Maldives' first multiparty presidential vote.

In November 2008, Presidential election Abdul Gayoom lost the election in second round in which he received 45.75% of the vote against 54.25% for his opponent presidential candidate Mohammad Nasheed.[7] Mohammad Nasheed emerged victorious carrying with him the badge of the first democratically elected president. Mohammad Waheed Hassan of the Gaumee Itthihaad's party became the Vice-President.

President Nasheed political term though historic in nature but caught up in large amount of trouble since the beginning. Nasheed's government faced many challenges including huge debt left by the Abdul Gayoom government, economic downturn, overspending by means of overprinting local currency Ryfiaa, unemployment, corruption and increasing drugs use. Nasheed carried out numerous reforms like a public ferry transport system and universal health care. But because of no clear majority, his reforms initiatives[8] were frequently delayed and hindered by the opposition. The antagonism between the government and its institutions led to public discontent and dissatisfaction over economic mismanagement. The primary cause was the rising commodity price and poor economic situations in the country. Several Islamic Nationalist outfits also blamed the Nasheed government for planning to destroy the Islam in the country. By the 2011, demonstrations and protests were breaking out demanding the resignation of president Nasheed.In fact, these public demonstrations and protests were organised by the opposition party Dhivehi Rayyinthung under the leadership of Abdul Gayoom. Oppositions blamed Nasheed "talking about democracy but not putting it into practice".

Matter came to head when he ordered the imprisonment of the Chief Justice of the Criminal Court Abdullah Mohammad on the charge of corruption. Nasheed's order was seen as politically motivated by his opponents and protested in the Capital city of Male. Abdul Gayoom called for people for protest. Maldives police also joined the protesters and refused to use force against the protesters. The Maldives Army then clashed with Police and other protesters.[9] The chief Justice was released from the detention and Nasheed resigned on 7 February 2012. Mohammad Waheed Hasan Malik was sworn as president. Eventually he was forced to resign allegedly with a gun held to his head.

In October 2012, Nasheed was arrested on the charge of not to appear before the court in case of his order of arrest of the chief Justice. His detention was politically motivated in order to prevent him from campaigning for the 2013 presidential elections. President Waheed Hassan Manik declared presidential elections to be held in November 2013. Later on, Nasheed was convicted under the country terrorisms laws for ordering the arrest of judge and jailed him for 13 year.[10] Thus, the fall of the Nasheed was a sign of returning of dictatorial rule and breaking down of democracy.

In 2013 presidential election, Mohammad Nasheed won the first-round contrary to the assessment of international election observers, the Supreme Court annulled it on the ground of irregularities. Later on, the opposition combined and gained majority and Abdulla Yameen Gayoom, half-brother of the Maumoon Abdul Gayoom,was appointed the President. The election of the President Yameen was in fact an attempt of Abdul Gayoom to re-impose an autocratic rule. Yameen employed Islam as a tool of identity politics framing religious mobilization as the solution to perceived western attempts to undermine the national sovereignty and public support. Yameen grew increasingly authoritarian smashing out the opponents and former allies. His government suppressed all the peaceful protests, shut down independent media outlets and jailed political opponents on flimsy and feck grounds. Widespread and credible allegations of corruption caused unpopularity of the Yameen Government.

The main reason of Maldives' current crisis is the split of Yameen Progressive People Party which was established by the Abdul Gayoom in 2011. This Progressive Party was the main ruling party of Maldives since 2014. The relationship between Abdul Gayoom and Yameen Gayoom was increasingly deteriorated and there was clashed over a number of key issues. Several members of PPM who were supporters of Abdul Gayoom started leaving and the party was finally splited and Yameen Gayoom ousted Abdul Gayoom from the party. As a result, Yameen's ruling coalition had all but fallen apart. Yameen was hugely opposed by the opposition political parties. All the opposition was united under a common banner with the explicit purpose of dethrone him in the coming presidential elections in 2018. The

Abdul Gayoom faction of PPM also alliance with the opposition, Yameen sense the danger of isolation and insecurity. He felt the danger of losing its power. In local election, opposition showed strong presence.

In 2015, there was an assassination attempts on president Yameen when he was returning from Saudi Arabia haj pilgrimage. In the explosion, Yameen was unharmed while three people including his wife was injured. Maldives Vice-President was arrested for plotting his murder. President Yameen also instituted a plan to crackdown its political opponents. He declared thirty days state of emergency on 4th November 2015 and ordered the arrest of number of political leaders in order to stop the opposition rally headed by former President Nasheed.[11] He arrested Nasheed under the charge of terrorism and later on he was exiled. Vice-President along with 17 of his supporters were also arrested on the charge of Public offences. Vice President Ahmad Adeeb and Colonel Mohammad Naziam and an ex-defence Minister, who were the allies of Yameen, were received long prison sentence. The Maldives Parliament Majilis passed the no-confidence vote for the removal of Vice President with a majority of 61 member voted in favour hence the Vice President was removed. On 10th November 2015, President Yameen revoked the state of emergency declaring that there is no imminent threat to the country.[12]

The Supreme court of Maldives on February 2, 2018, ordered the immediate release of political prisoners including President Nasheed and eight others terming their trials a violation of Constitution and international law. The Supreme Court ordered new trials, deciding the earlier trial of these political leaders "questionably and politically motivated" nature of the trials of the political leaders. Most of the observers including the UNO agreed that trial was intentionally unfair and politically motivated.[13] Nasheed who has been in exile in the United Kingdom wanted to contest presidential election while President Yameen wanted to prevent Nasheed from contesting the upcoming presidential election. Nasheed had sought UN help to restore his political rights. The release of political prisoners twisted the Maldivians politics and the opposition demanded immediate resignation of the President Yameen. The Yameen government challenged the legality of the Supreme court order and claimed that it will threaten public security. He blamed the judiciary to join the political opponents. In a quick action to sustain its power, he immediately imposed emergency and arrested the judges of supreme court. Imposing of emergency was to bruise democracy and prospects of free and fair election and to silent every kind of dissidents.

Over the past years, the country has held regular multiparty elections even now in 2018. In any young democracy, election will be considered an expression of democratic life but in the Maldives, it is an indication of death of its democracy. In Maldives, democracy never existed it was just a myth. In the context of the short history of the Maldives where democracy has been on the shaky grounds ever since it set itself free from the clutches of the British protectorate in 1965. In the 1940s, during the colonial era, it adopted Constitutional Monarchy for a short period but immediately failed and converted back to Authoritarian monarchy. After independence in 1968, it became Republican state under the regime of Nasir who politically dominated the country. Only in 2008-2011, for a short period, it had democratically elected government. Actually, all the regimes in the Maldives fall within the categories of authoritarianism as they did not meet any standard of democracy.

Any democratic country must fulfil the following conditions:

- Open, free and fair elections.
- Separation of powers among legislature (Parliament), Executive and Judiciary.
- Right to vote
- Political and civil rights of the citizens.
- Freedom of Press and Media.
- Independent Judiciary.

These conditions are met by the Maldivian regimes are questionable. The electoral process for the members of executive and legislature in Maldives are non-competitive. The electoral process has been manifested by large scale abuse of power and hallmarks of full-scale authoritarianism where elections are either devoid of any serious competition and are not at all free and fair. The systematic imprisonment of all opposition leaders is a common characteristic in Maldives. Major opposition parties' leaders either threatened or imprisoned as a routine. In 2013 presidential election opposition was totally denied and harassed the opposition leaders and their supporters. At the local level, the electoral process has all but disappeared. In 2013 during the presidential elections, many tricks and tactics were used to draw out the election; judiciary also intervened and eventually Yameen was declared elected. In 2014, the parliament (Majlis) election was also not fair. It was marred by vote-buying, excessive campaign expenditure and abuse of state resources. The supreme court fired the president of the election commission Suo moto on the charge of vote buying and selling. It is clear to see that mere existence of right to vote for virtually all the adults does not ensure the existence of democracy if people are not free to elect candidates of its choice and if the judiciary deeply involve in vote buying and selling, patronage blackmail and corruption.

In the legislative arena, the Majlis is controlled by the ruling majority party where opposition even if occasionally criticize the government. The Majilis is no longer serve as a people's house representing differing opinions and voices. It has become a hallmark of full-scale authoritarianism where conflict between legislature and executive is virtually unthinkable. The entire governance system has been dismantled and elected members and officials of governing body like the Majlis (Parliament) rendered powerless. In the parliament, the ruling party and its allies enjoyed the majority and powers to pass the bill they desire where an absolute majority is need. They used the methods to blackmail, coercion, patronage and usual web of corruption and deceit to engineer the result as they desired. The powers of elected members of parliament were snatched away by two important constitutional amendments. Members of Parliament lost their powers by abolishing the requirements of debates and discussion before passing any bill. Second constitutional amendment has introduced new rules which provided that only PPM members can propose any bill or amendments related to the state finances.

The protection of civil and political rights was also suffered largely. From 2012, it became the norms of the government to quell opposition protest with brutal violence, baton beating, imprisonment from the regime of Muamoon Abdul Gayoom to till now. It has been standard practice that no protester is allowed as in 2015 the Yameen government arrested 200 protesters and they were subsequently détente and mistreated. Their intimidation and imprisonment had effectively put a stop to all opposition rallies and demonstrations. It silenced all the activists and mass protesters, civil society, organisation and other independent institutions to oppose or criticise the government. The independent election Commission, Human Rights Commission was taken away through the Supreme Court instigated Suo moto cases. Other institutions like the Police Integrity Commission rendered powerless by appointing its members loyalists to regime. Many steps were taken against civil society organisation which eliminated the civil and political rights of masses, politicians, opposition leaders, civil society and independent state institutions.[14]

Freedom of press and expression which is the fourth pillar of democracy is non-existence in the country. Spying on dissenting voices, attacks, threats, harassments and imprisonments of journalist and media organisations are common. Maldives has slipped from 51st place in the World Press Freedom Index in 2012 to 120th in 2018.[15] Though media is also often biased.

Judiciary is under the complete control of the executive. Numbers of reports have been published by a whole range of the international organisation from the United Nations to International Court of Justice censuring its lack of independence and corruptions. From the Gayoom to Yameen regime, widespread, corruption, patronage and blackmail prevalent in the judiciary. There is no room for individual judge to express dissenting opinions, several decisions taken by the executive or the Yameen government such as the restructuring of the Supreme Court have destroyed any wiggle room for independent thought or action in the Judiciary. Under the new constitutional amendment in 2013, the supreme court bench was reduced from seven to five judges. While the opposition, senior lawyers, commentators, media and social activists even the lower civil courts opposed the amendment as illegal and unconstitutional but the president bargained the politician to win the majority.

In the absence of a culture of democracy, judiciary and legislature has regularly reduced to whatever the executive decided by hook and crook. Contravention of the constitution especially when breaches were blatantly defended by the supreme court. To win is the ultimate goal of the government in elections as well as litigations.

The Supreme Court in Maldives has politicised and parliament majority with President, an executive dictatorship reigned in the shadow of the Supreme Court. In 2013, Presidential election judiciary repeatedly intervened in the election process often working the graveyard shift and issuing mid-night decrees and directives to control the election. Polls were nullified and voting was repeatedly rescheduled to ensure an election win for Yameen Gayoom. The Supreme Court also facilitated President Yameen's Progressive Party of Maldives in Parliament election removing the Election Commissioner and his deputy in the suo moto case on the allegation of contempt of court and undermining the powers of the supreme court.[16]

Maldives judiciary has also adopted contempt of Court regulation to prohibit media and public criticism and initiate court actions against the Human Rights Commission of Maldives in the Suo moto case charging all members of the Human Rights Commission with high treason for their report of 2014 to Universal Periodic Review for commenting on Supreme Court unduly influences and controls of judiciary.[17]

Maldives failed to meet the minimum requirements to be a democratic country and has been described as a 'weak', 'flawed' or 'diminished democracy'. Democratic transition and the steps taken by the Nasheed's government were totally remained under the grips of the autocratic forces. The legislature and the judiciary remained under the control of opposition acted as a bulwark against the democratic reforms and instigated against the measures taken necessary for democracy. Maldives existing frame work of political system fitted well into the full-scale authoritarian regime. This must change and start freshly learning from the past. It has already begun with the change of regime in the recent presidential election held in September 2018. Ibrahim Mohamed Solih of the Maldivian Democratic Party and joint candidate of the Coalition of opposition parties won the election and became the country's third democratically elected President after 2008 thus ended the 30 years of incumbency.

Notes

1. Maldives: History, the Commonwealth.org.; Encyclopaedia of Britannica> britiannica.com.
2. Maldives, March 15, 1968 , State Reform, database, Direct Democracy http://www/sudd.ch/event.php?
3. Matt Mulberry, the Maldives- From Dictatorship to Democracy, and Back? International Centre on Nonviolent Conflict, July 2012.
4. Vishnu Gopinath, Operation Cactus: the Day India saved the Maldives, the Quint, 2012 (updated 6, 2018).
5. Amnesty International Report 2004- Maldives https://www.refworld.org/docid/40b5a1fbc.html.
6. State of Emergency for Maldives, BBC News, August 14,2004.
7. Maldivians Vote in run-off-election, Miadhu Daily, October 28, 2008 ; Judith Evan, Maldiives Hold Historic Presidential Poll , Reuters , October 9, 2008.
8. Daniel Bosley, A Presidential Power Struggle in Maldives, South Asia Journal, January 2013,: southasiajournal.net/a-presidential-power-struggle-in-Maldives.
9. Jason Burke, Mohammad Nasheed Resigns as Maldives President, the Guardian world News, February 7 2012.
10. Jason Burke and Zaheena Rasheed, Former President Mohammad Nasheed Jailed for 13 Years, the Gaurdian World News, March 14, 2015.
11. President of Maldives Declare of State of Emenrgency, the New York Times, Asia Pacific, November 4, 2015.
12. Maldives revokes state of emergency amid global outcry and tourism worries, the Guardian , November 10, 2015.
13. Meera Srinivasan, Maldives Supreme Court orders release of former President Mohamed Nasheed Eight others, the Hindu, 2 feb. 2018.
14. HRCM Submission to the Universal Periodic Review of the Maldives, April –May 2015 (22nd session) September 2014.
15. Fathmath Shaahunaz, Maldives Again Drops on World Press Index, The Edition, May 3, 2018.
16. Olof Blomquist, Democracy on Brink in Maldives, the Diplomate, February 9, 2018.
17. Aishatha Valezinee, Mutinny of the state: Maldives Gets away with another Coup d'état, Dhivehi site, December 16, 2014. Maldives- 2018, Human Rights Watchhttps://www.hrw.org/world-report/2019/country-chapters/maldives.;

Conclusions and Observations

Internal crisis in South Asia are implicated a large regional and global picture. Diverse political system, ideologies and socio-economic conditions have been posing significant challenges to the security, stability and over all development across the region. South Asia have been increasingly overwhelmed with the traditional ethno-religious-communal-linguistic-nationalistic insurgency and non-traditional terrorism those have been undermining the abilities of the state to manage the internal conflicts or to give the suitable solutions. An analysis of these crisis inclined to focus on how they are contributing directly or indirectly the intra-states and inter-states rivalries whether it is separatists, extremists or fundamentalists insurgencies in India, Pakistan, Afghanistan, Sri Lanka or Maoists movement in India and Nepal, problems of Rohingya or Maldives.

South Asia has higher level of World concern with theses internal crisis or conflicts. South Asian Countries have been not able to develop or create an atmosphere of political and social consciousness and failed to give sufficient strength to eliminate the large-scale use of force and violence by the communities living in a country due to mutual distrust or hate against each other. As a matter of political life, these colonial states' rulers did not restructure these states so that different ethnic-religious and communal groups be allowed to share power with major communities equally. Instead, post-independence ruling elites either supressing, downplaying and appeasing their identities to gain political powers. They have created a syndrome of fear in the mind of the majoritarian ruling class to implement devolution of powers between Centre and their provinces (Federal states) or autonomy to accommodate the diverse interest of diverse population and acknowledge their diverse cultural religious peculiarities as a part of these societies.

The existing culture of violence in the name of jihad or separatist movements demanding separate independent state in name of religion, region or language are causing deaths and injuries to thousands of thousands innocent civilians, security forces, Children and women. Numbers of native people are homeless, internally displaces and forcefully migrated in search of secure life as in case of Afghanistan, Bangladeshi and Pakistani Hindu or Rohingyas etc. women are raped and has been used as a tool for human bombs or suicidal attacks. All these are gravest challenges. Educated and uneducated youth are fascinated by the extremists Islamists ideologies and joining the separatist/ extremist/ insurgent fundamentalist groups in an alarmingly large number. The religious fundamentalist groups are brain washing the mind of highly educated youths and making them to hold bombs and arms. The prevalent culture of Islamic or religious fundamentalist violence is part and parcel of all South Asian states whether it is anti-Muslim violence and Buddhists Fundamentalism of Sri Lanka or Anti-Hindu fundamentalist violence of Bangladesh or both as in India. In Afghanistan, it is the result of militant group-radical Islamists and right wings Taliban who was intended to fight against the USSR and then the United States who created them and thence spilling over from Afghanistan to Pakistan's tribal areas of FATA, Southern Waziristan, NWFP, Punjab, Pakhtunistan, Baluchistan and to Gilgit Baltistan.

The inner weakness and responses to these crises have been encouraging the extremist and insurgent groups up to serious heights and state and its institutions are unable to cope with these crises. The region was marked by assaults on civil society. Journalists, bloggers, activists and others human rights defenders have been vilified and subjected to threats and violence. South Asia also remains one of the most dangerous regions to be a member of a religious minority. Muslims in India and Sri Lanka, Shi'as in Pakistan and Afghanistan, and Hindus in Bangladesh have all come under attack over the past year. In each case, the governments have failed to protect them and even encouraged a climate of hostility.

India over the past decades have been trying to solve their gravest internal crisis but are not successful. The Naxal's crisis has continued to be a grave threat to the security of the states in spite of the comprehensive policy. Over the past year, the centre and states have been tom-tomming massive and multi-pronged approaches and operations in major Maoists affected areas. The problem is that there approaches and strategies are away from ground realities. The entire counter-insurgency discourses in India has remained doctrinaire with almost no reference to a coherent-strategies and how they are to be implemented. It is failed due to the poor implementation of the schemes by the government because of administrative inefficiency, corruption, red-tepism, political interference and political support to Naxalist. The administrative and security establishment in the states have lacked commitment dedication and above all competence to deliver. Development has never been systemically and effectively applied as a Counter-insurgency strategy while military actions used very widely across the affected areas. In spite of the host of development schemes of central and States governments such as a NEREGA, National Rural Health Mission, Serva Siksha Abhiyan, Integrated Child Development Schemes, Sadbhavna, Backward Tribes Initiatives and plethora of legislations, the conditions of Adivasis in Naxal's affected Areas remain terrible.

Despite much hearts and minds rhetoric, the military solution- the use of force- is the only visible counter insurgency in operation. However, the military actions or law and order solution, indeed, comprehends wide spectrum of force dispositions and strategies, tactics, policies and practices, many of them are effective while others are entirely counter-productive. No military action can be effective without reference to detail realities on ground, including the character and stage of the insurgency, forces, structure, leadership, capacities deployment, motivation and topography of the areas. An old, ill-trained and ill-equipped forces in the hit areas and states having no orientation to deal with a full-blown insurgency is another major reason for failures. Manpower deficits are substantially compounded by extreme shortfalls in technical, technological and training variables; irrational and wasteful deployment of forces, and persistently imprudent political interventions. The outcome is that current capacities of police force in the afflicted states are simply insufficient to design an effective response to the Maoist challenge. However, in the long run use of force is not the solution.

One cannot support the arguments given by the Maoists as an explanation for the insurgency. The conventional theories of grievances, rural economic conditions, redistributive economic programme and proxy access to justice do not provide ground for augmenting violence in India. The reality is that the Maoist ideology and strategy find fertile ground in the security, administrative and political vacuum that extends over the vast areas of the country. The entire structure of rural administration in the Naxalite affected areas has been wholly ineffective because of the combination of factors including primarily the incompetence, corruption and criminalization of the political leadership deteriorated to the point of paralysis.

The problem of terrorism or insurgency cannot be addressed through arms or use of force but must be resolved through the implementation of a range of programmes for poverty alleviation, the empowerment of disadvantaged groups, the redressal of grievances and delivery on wider development goal to undercut the recruitment pool of terrorist and violent political groups. However, the states' capacities to deliver an acceptable level of development to populations in the problem areas are themselves limited by demographics and available natural and financial resources based on the structural infirmities. The development solution has progressively become an alibi for persistent failures to address immediate tasks of response. The time frames of counter- terrorism and developmental policy cannot be reconciled. The counter-terrorism demands immediate responses; development is by definition, a long- drawn out process.

For internal security situation, India will have a well thought policies and measurement to counter insurgency and thwart the adverse forces to destabilize the country. The main concern should be to revive the legitimacy and credibility of the state and its institutions and for that, it will follow a pragmatic and transparent approach. People wants real empowerment and participation in decision making, therefore, diverse interests of the society need to be given self-rule and autonomy in their local affairs and their cultural and social identities will be recognized by adoption of indigenous models suited to their genius and traditions. Structural changes will be required to ensure independent functioning of law enforcing agencies coordinating at the Centre, state and lower levels based on consensus and people oriented. At last, it requires political will most of all. Security as well as development has to run hand in hand to counter the Naxal problem.

The Kashmir conflict is not a security issue alone; it is a political problem that needs a political solution. The prolongation of the armed conflict in Kashmir has resulted in unspeakable sufferings for the Kashmiris as well as the security personnel posted in that extremely volatile region. Besides diverting scarce resources from much-needed development projects to an extraordinary arms build-up in the region, an entire generation has grown up in Kashmir for whom killings are a routine affair. The Kashmiri people's sense of alienation from India remains as strong as ever. The peace initiatives like the Operation Sadbhavna to win the heart and mind of the Kashmiri people is also failed. But despite widespread anti-India feeling, the general Kashmiri perception is that joining Pakistan is not the best option for Kashmir. Thus, Modi government's strategic vision for Kashmir should place less emphasis on hard tools, tipping the balance toward a political resolution of the seemingly intractable conflict. The need is to bring peace not politics back into Kashmir.

Indian government must re-evaluate its counter-insurgency strategy because all military options have been exhausted and the Indian army is under stress since it is fighting a prolonged insurgency again and again without producing different outcome on the ground and that threatening army to professionalism.

Kashmiri youths are becoming easy tools of radicalization by Jihadist ideology that draws immediate inspiration from the militants and terrorist groups inside Pakistan state. A military-focused kinetic approach to fight jihadist-inspired radicalization is proving insufficient; the battle must be fought ideologically. In absence of concrete proposal, large numbers of Kashmiri youths have become hostile to the Indian state. The year of social unrest, instability and incoherent. The Central and State governments should stridently engage the local Kashmir youth in education, provide jobs and invest largely in those industrial and economic sectors which have abundance resources.

The normalization or acceptance of armed militants professing jihad against the Indian state will seriously undermine India's national security. It will be deadly for the state to reduce its military forces in the valley but clearly separate the roles of its police and army, reformulate its military laws, and develop a robust political strategy that grants Kashmiris more autonomy and favours engagement over detachment. The problematic sections of Armed Forces Special Powers Act (AFSPA) must be amended to ameliorate for the military, government and Kashmiris. Indian government should develop a plan that neutralise the allure of jihadist-inspired radicalization. Counter radicalisation must be part of counter-terrorism strategy.

On a much broader level, Indian government will have to fight the dangerously noxious propaganda of Pakistan-based terrorist groups pressure and alliances with the countries who are facing the same problems as the US. Working with the United States to combat terrorism cannot be the only strategy. A realistic counter-terrorism approach demands that India take the terrorism issue on a wider level. Instead of provoking Pakistan, India should build global lead in developing effective counter-terrorism tools.

There must be a concerted effort to clamp down on Financing of terrorist groups to dismantle their structures. The National Investigation Agency (NIA) arrested seven Kashmiri separatist leaders, including Hurriyat chief Syed Ali Shah Geelani's son-in-law Altaf Ahmed Shah, in a probe linked to terrorist funding. The NIA is investigated that huge inflow and outflow of funds coming in from Pakistan and have been used to fuel unrest in the Kashmir Valley. Tehreek-e-Hurriyat's Ayaz Akbar and Mehrajuddin Kalwal, Shahid-ul-Islam, who is from the Mirwaiz faction of the Hurriyat, Nayeem Khan of the Jammu Kashmir National Front and Peer Saifullah were arrested in Srinagar. Farooq Ahmed Dar aka Bitta Karatay was taken into custody in New Delhi. the NIA raided places across Kashmir, New Delhi and Haryana looking for evidence of separatist leaders and businessmen receiving funds from Hafiz Saeed, who heads the Jamaat-ud-Dawa group, and other Pakistan-based militant outfits.

Problem has become more complex, as Kashmir's internal politics has worked against decentralization of power at the grassroots level, with local state parties interested in their own agendas.[1] The BJP government and political administrations must preserve Article 370 because India is not going to give up its territorial claims to Kashmir in anyway. But any attempt to repeal it would only exacerbate a political crisis in Kashmir. The government give priorities to wipe-out the insurgency and win the heart of the people and then make constitutional change in Article 370 to maintain territorial integrity and sovereignty of the country.

These suggestions are simply meant to bring Kashmir in the path of normalcy and to compel India's military and political leadership to demonstrate clarity in principle and action. A military sceptical of achieving progress in Kashmir should be a red flag for any political administration. And if Kashmir is indeed an integral part of India, the commitment to it must be higher. Engagement is the only way to stabilize Kashmir and combat Pakistan's proxy war.

The creation of Pakistan was a movement by the Indian Muslim Leadership to have a state for Muslim, a Muslim way of life and greater social and economic opportunities were the motive behind it not an Islamic blueprint. The loose Islamic identity of a Muslim state changed into an Islamic state under the regime of Zia-ul-Haq with its nexus with Mullah and military and has been continuing till now. Every political ruler of Pakistan has given it a new dimension and new heights not only to Islamic radicalization but to seek political powers from Gen. Parvez Musharraf to Imran Khan.

In Pakistan, Islamic fundamentalism and terrorism have developed because of the long-standing support from state and Military Intelligent service (ISI). The gradual destruction and diminution of the constitution and all state institutions- legislature, judiciary, bureaucracy and even governance has trans-glorified the military. The Army has been growing in strength stunning the growth of state political system the parliamentary democracy and has filled the State's political vacuum. The army has superseded the administrative governance and has established a patron-clientele relationship with the bureaucracy and terrorist insurgent groups Like Taliban, Jaishe-e-Mohammad, Al-Qaida etc. in its efforts to fight internal populist leaders as well as externally with its neighbours India by fuelling insurgency in Jammu and Kashmir.

To sum up, the ethnic crisis of Gilgit-Baltistan, Baluchistan, Pakhtunistan and Sindh, all are the outcome of the colonial policies and inefficiency and manipulative attitude of post-colonial rulers to control these provinces without keeping in mind the cultural identity and necessities of their population. All were forcefully occupied after the Britishers left which generated the separatist impulses among the leaders of these provinces of Pakistan. Hence the most effective step to manage the secessionist impulses in the South Asian countries is to reconstitute the state in such a way that different ethnic groups be allowed to share state power along with the majority community. It requires political and economic restructuring in order to accommodate diverse population and radical shifts in value orientation so as to acknowledge that diverse culture-religious categories are part of the public space in these societies. The rulers in Pakistan needs to realize that over-emphasizing 'Pakistani-Islamic' identity, while suppressing and downplaying ethno-regional identities, and also keeping the constituent groups out of economic and political set-up will not serve any purpose. Instead it will prove counter-productive. After all it is a failure of state-formation that led to the disintegration of the country in 1971. Religion has proved to be too fragile to keep the country united, though it has been fundamental in the creation of the country. Ethnic linguistic and regional identities should be given due recognition for nation-formation and the constituent groups should be given due political share for appropriate state-building.

The ethnic caldron in Gilgit Baltistan, Baluchistan, Pakhutinistan and Sindh are political problems and should be solved accordingly. While devising any solution to these crises in the provinces, it needs to be recognized that even though the migrants might not constitute a homogeneous cultural or even linguistic group but the sense of community with others should not be underestimated. Also, the law and order situation in the provinces should not be tackled militarily.

To conclude, Pakistan is in free fall, a state which is collapsing with every passing day and is bound to degenerate into theocratic murderous chaos. For Pakistanis and their ruler whose fictional threat is from India and not from Jihad, are seemingly callousness about the prevailing state of affairs. If the civilian and politician both fail to pay heed to the changes around them, then the rising tide of Jihad may transform the radical Islamists wave that will sweep both the civil society and the Pakistan army into embrace, with result that what not Pakistan nor its neighbours and friends desire.

It is essential that the state machinery will provide effective governance, demonstrate fairness and is indifferent to ethnic origins. More important, given the dominant role of the army and ISI in Pakistan's polity, if Pakistan is to mature, thrive, and survive as a successful state and a nation, the army needs to take a back seat and allow politician and civil society and other to lead their lives without fear of the radical forces of Islam that are vying for power today.

Keeping the militant Islamists at bay remains a daunting task however, need not be used only as a scary scenario to gain western support for military in Pakistan. A progressive and pluralistic Pakistan needs to provide opportunities for its citizens important element of society to function unfettered. These are challenges that both the army and civil society in Pakistan must surmount through a return to democratic norms so they can fulfil their promise to the country and win long war against in this age of terror. Although religion will remain an important part of Pakistan's social reality for the foreseeable future, it must seek new roots lying within the country's social reality rather than religion.

Tacking the situation in Afghanistan, it is very complicated and complex for any negotiable solution. Afghanistan civil crisis has many antagonistic actors liberal- illiberal, national, regional and international and the brutal local militant tribal groups. All these groups are politically adversial and competing actors and all have been trying to occupy the space. On the one side of this crisis is the United States and its European powers who intervened in the Afghanistan to defeat the Osama-bin-laden and Taliban to bring peace and security. On the other side is Pakistan who is continuously supporting its afghan proxies allowing them to recruit, fundraising as well as planning to conduct terrorist attacks and operations from inside Pakistan. Pakistan most notably remain unwilling to facilitate talks between Taliban and Kabul Government since her relations with Afghanistan has been strained. There are further many complicating regional factors. Recently Russia's involvement in reaching out to Taliban and proposing to lead the peace process could not be welcomed by the United States and will further complicate the Afghan's problem. India's close ties and initiative in restructuring and resettlement of Afghanistan are also viewed as provocative by the Pakistan and China. Iran has also been suspects of providing military help-arms and ammunitions to some Taliban factions intended by its acrimony to the United States.

Still, the United States is the most powerful and influential player in Afghanistan civil crisis. While Trump Administration was dubious on the Afghan policy, but it is now in progress. The United States will maintain its presence in Afghanistan and will continue its military forces. In fact, the United states declination will give invitation to Soviet Russia that could be endanger the US interests in the region and its absence would be detrimental to the Afghanistan peace process.

The over-all situation in Afghanistan has been putting enormous cost to the human life. The recent negotiation with Taliban is a new shift in US Afghan policy but the absence of Afghan' government and major Taliban's local tribal factions, it will not provide any solution and would be a serious challenge. Taliban is despised by many local stake holders and for peace talks to be durable, every stake holders of the Afghanistan conflict should be involved. Otherwise, it would again deepen the ethnic division and would kick off to another sectarian war.

Taliban's main strategy is to resist the foreign forces occupying the country and confronting with Afghan's present Government. They are only demanding a fixed and rigid timetable for withdrawal of all foreign troops. The chaotic state of the government is another fundamental problem. The intra-governmental division and corruption, nepotism and factionalism in the Afghan's National army and National police and at the Afghanistan state apparatus at all level are playing dysfunctional role in the advancement of Taliban. It requires internal consensus and political partnership among the Afghan's factions those backing and opposing the government to pursue a negotiated peace rather continued conflict. Any meaningful solution is to accept the present constitution as a guarantor to all the stake holders and Taliban, though highly hypothetical. Accepting Taliban to be a part of the government would give clear message to the world that the bullets are more effective than ballots.

Like Pakistan, Islam is playing an even more important role in shaping the future identity of Bangladesh as it is evident from the increased role of Islamic fundamentalists. Islamic fundamentalism has been promoted by the desire of majoritarian to build minority free especially Hindu free nation as well as motivated by a political revenge. The Islamic extremist groups along with the political parties are pursuing this agenda. The Jamaate-e-Islami and Hirkutul-Jihade-islami and other affiliated outfits have assumed political powers and have established dominant pressure in national politics either with BNP or Awami League. The Islamic Extremists have already formed the shadow government in Bangladesh and present state's government is in a state of denial, it is not going to do anything to stop the spread of violence attacks and killing of Hindu communities. Because the political party in power has blindly accepted them as coalition partner in order to gain power. Bangladesh is also on the way to produce radical Islamists militant. A new emerging Bangladesh can give rise to Talibani militants for whom religious fanaticism is equals to national pride. Therefore, there is every reason for international society to watch developments in Bangladesh carefully as its government is not going to do anything to stop it.

The Rohingya crisis is unique because there is no national or security interest driving the violence against a defenceless community. The sole purpose is to cause indescribable misery which forced the peoples oust from their homeland. States are rapidly leaving behind a world order based on rights and rules and heading toward an older formation of interests and alliances. One can easily find this transition to many numbers of events; the American invasion of Iraq, the world's passive response to Syria's use of chemical weapons, or Russia's violent intervention in Ukraine, in Afghanistan, Pakistan, Sri Lanka or Nepal. In fact, Bangladesh's security forces and Islamic extremists' groups have been involving in violence, murder and accused of numerous human rights violations and ethnic cleansing of its Hindu and other Minorities population, then whom to blame?

Nepal has lived through a decade of bloody conflict and a decade of painful transition; it is not yet at peace with its own people and their liberated political aspirations. Political history of Nepal has passed through uncertainty and controversies. After the end of Maoist Insurgency 2006 a mismanaged transition, a constitutional deadlock and political disturbances failed to establish peace in the country. The political instability, intra and inter party conflicts and their unhealthy competition for sharing power and their less priority in government formation and constitution making had turned Nepal into a civil unrest.

Nepal is still in fragile phase. The promulgation of New Constitution after a decade failed to satisfy the demands of Madhesi /Terai region. The formation of federal structure according to the ethnic identity and proportional representation in the parliament was the abiding promise of the Comprehensive Peace Agreement (CPA 2007) between the CPN Maoist and seven Party Alliance. Madhesi protests against the new constitution is in fact a long fight against the century old discrimination and fair representation in the state as the Madhesi and Tharus have been treated unfairly by the dominant hill castes groups the demand for federal autonomy has become a contentious issue. Madhesi are demanding an autonomous province with a demographic advantage. The formation of seven federal provinces and only Eight districts are connected with the Madhesi region while remaining 14 districts have clubbed with hill states intentionally to marginalized and converting them into minority. In fact, the protest to the new constitution is genuine because the Nepal government was agreed in 2008 for the formation of single undivided Madhesi province.

The New constitution has divided this tiny hill state and pushed further in instability and violence. It has deeply polarized the state. The new constitution is discriminatory and has serious flaws. It seems that there were extensive manipulations in the constitution framing process which has not accommodated the demands of Madhesi people. It has compromised the political representation by reduces the share of proportional representation for the excluded groups, diluted the principles of reservation and affirmative actions, federalism and citizenship provisions. Unequal distribution of parliamentary constituencies and restrictions on the rights of women to pass citizenship to their children will turn them a second-class citizens.

The border acceptance of the constitution is a minimum requirement to ensure it, but the new constitution as well as the Amendment Bill failed to guarantee it. The impact of ongoing Madhesi agitation in Nepal as a whole in general and in the Terai region in particular is quite severe but the government and the main political parties are not serious to the needs of their own people and the security challenges. Blaming India for the crisis would only create troubles for the Nepal, they must take initiative to solve the crisis. Ruling Political Parties should accept the problems of Nepalese people of all ethnicities especially Madhesi and Tharus and develop a sense of ownership in the new constitution. A forward-looking constitution must take adequate care to accommodate the genuine aspiration and expectation of a substantial cross sections of the people. Although, the opposition parties are no less responsible for the present plight of the people, the UDMF's strike has given them an excuse. The UDMF should change the form of protest so that they can win the hearts of a larger section of the society.

Any long drawn out political stalemate will push the Nepalese people to the brink and further delay in the democratic process. Therefore, the political parties must have to demonstrate strong political will and dedication according to people's mandate otherwise they will lose public faith and recognition. All this will also have spill-over effects in the South Asia. The cost of failure will not be confined to Nepal but also to a large extent to India as India have a much bigger stake to save the peace process in Nepal. The unstable Nepal can provide avenues both China and Pakistan to encourage anti- India elements there.

Anti-Muslim violence in Sri-Lanka is on the rise and feeding Buddhism. In the recent anti- Muslim violence, the government of Sri Lanka failed to respond effectively and adequately. Sri Lankan citizens and international observers were also disappointed at the lack of actions taken by the government. The ruling and other political parties who relies strongly on Sinhalese backing have been supporting the radical Buddhist outfits to remain in power. The country leaders have struggled to rein the nationalist fervour of the Sinhalese Buddhism. The propaganda of Bodu Bela Sena (BBS) and its agenda to cause violence on the false ground can not be ignore. The BBS false propaganda of increasing Muslim Population and

Muslim Population plan to reduce the Sinhalese population is misinformative campaign just to target the Muslim community. The rise of aggressive Buddhist Nationalism collided with Islamophobia that Buddhism is under threat, is a corollary of rising aggressive Buddhism in South East Asian Nations. Buddhism which is a peaceful religion since centuries has surprisingly turn into violence is as problematic as Islamic Terrorism. A country that endured a brutal civil war are not aware of peace, unity and respect for its citizen instead promoting hate, prejudice and discrimination is very strange.

Sri Lanka which has already faced a long ethnic civil war between Tamil and Sinhalese cannot afford another ethnic crisis between Muslims and Sinhalese. The government of Sri Lanka must take actions before any event spiral out of control. It is crucial that attacks on minority communities must be stop in order to prevent further escalations of violence. The government of Sri Lanka must take responsibility and accountability to protect all its citizens honour and their dignity. It is time for Sri Lankan government to step up and fulfil the promises made to diverse minorities in the country. Otherwise Sri Lanka will just be another example of Buddhist Majority lead discriminations and crimes against Muslims citizens as in Myanmar and Thailand. It is the time to take actions against those who commits crime against humanity and peace. Time will tell whether Sri Lanka will respond effectively to the new surge of violent Buddhist nationalism or slide back into a state of conflict.

Maldives' political crisis is culmination of its political trends and it has to be evaluated in the context of history where democracy has never been existed. Maldives' transmitted monarchy to republican democracy by deposing the last Sultan Ibrahim Nasir but soon turn into autocracy with the assuming of powers by Abdul Gyoom. Gayoom autocratic rule continued for 30 years and survived even after three coups and an assassination attempt. But the emergence of the Maldivian Democratic Party and Constitutional reforms, for the first time, Mohammad Nasheed was democratically elected president of Maldives.

Dictatorship can not die even if the dictator leaves office is a harsh reality of Maldivian politics. Revolution, powerful networks of regime loyalists can attempt to strangle their nascent democracies. The lack of clear majority in the government, the antagonism between government and other state actors; the Islamic plank of destroying Islam forced the President Nasheed to resign forcefully at the gun point was a sign of dictatorial autocracy to breakdown the democracy. Democracy was flawed. Despite interest of the international community, efforts to democratize the Maldives defeated.

Democracy in Maldives is flawed, it is simply a power struggle between competing political forces. Seizure of powers were the efforts to reconsolidate control by the former dictators and their associates. The Gayoom allies deposed Nasheed because of his commitment against corruption and authoritarianism. Election were held regularly but full of massive fraud; members of opposition were jailed exiled or assaulted or murdered. Maldivian polity is totally unfamiliar with the concept of rule of law. Contravention of the constitution when breaches were blatantly defended by the Supreme court. In the absence of a Culture of democracy, it was often reducing to whatever majority decided by hook or crook. To win was the ultimate goal in elections as well as litigations. Supreme court was politicized and executive dictatorship reigned under its' shadow of the supreme court. Parliament majority along with the president was on path of ruining the constitutional rights and safeguards.

Maldives failed to meet the minimum requirements to be a democratic country and has been described as a 'weak', 'flawed' or 'diminished democracy'. Democratic transition and the steps taken by the Nasheed's government were remained under the grips of the autocratic forces. The legislature and the judiciary remained under the control of opposition acting as a bulwark against the democratic reforms, unable and instigated against the actions necessary for democracy. Maldives existing frame work of political system fitted well into the full-scale authoritarian regime. This must change and learn from the past. It has already started with the change of regime in 2018 presidential election Ibrahim Mohamed Solih of the Maldivian Democratic Party and joint candidate of the Coalition of opposition parties became democratically elected President after 2008.

South Asia has a higher level of concern with domestically generated threats to the security. The inner weakness and instability have encouraged external threats and posing serious challenges to national security. An analysis of the security implications of South Asian states, internal crises tend to focus on the inter-states rivalries which have been contributing directly or indirectly to each other's and because the states are sponsoring violence due to cross-border connections in different ethnic and religious communities in the region. The States boundaries cannot be closed. While the states have responded adequately to the external threats, its responses to internal challenges have been very inadequate.

The defining feature of regional security of South Asia is that it is Indo-centric followed by the mutual distrust and enmity between India and other south Asian states- Pakistan, Bangladesh, Nepal ad Sri Lanka. There has been a spill-over of political turmoil in each country across the borders, involving India in most of the cases. In all India's neighbouring states, the sectarian and undemocratic regimes have often been propelled by their sense of insecurity to arouse anti-India nationalism for their survival. This is one of the reasons that all states are involved in blame game. Bangladesh accuses India for philanthropic shelter and arms to Bangladeshi insurgents. The ethnic crisis between Tamils and Sinhalese has created bottlenecks between India and Sri Lanka. In relation to broaden our horizons, sub-continent ethnic groups sometime create domestic crisis which has stern impacts in other countries of the region. This enmity between India and all neighbours provide justification for the states to spend huge budgets on defence.

In case of Pakistan, when the host of social problems continues to plague the nation state, instead of concentrating and solving the problem, Pakistan is building-up of conventional and nuclear weapons to combat India.The disparities between India and the other states has also created the psychological problem for the smaller countries. The geographical factors such sharing of common borders and water resources, territorial disputes have continued to cloud the relationship specifically between India-Pakistan and India-Bangladesh etc. The asymmetry in size, population and economic resources has influenced the perception and attitudes of the neighbour's countries and apprehensions about the India 's political and economic domination.

India is also facing an uncertain political situation virtually because of its every South Asian neighbour. Ruling elites in Pakistan, Bangladesh, Nepal and Sri Lanka have a stake in whipping up fears of alleged Indian hegemony. India's situation in South Asia is most perplexing. While outlining relations with neighbours, one should not fail to acknowledge that India itself faces many challenges within its body politics, problem arising from poor governance coupled with rampant corruption and criminalization of politics. It is not that in these circumstances, neighbours like Pakistan and Bangladesh may not take advantage of religious and ethnic faultiness within India. Recent, terrorist strikes have been carried out by deriving inspiration, motivation, support and substance from across Indian borders.

South Asian regional security and stability has been troubled by the absence of an institutionalized security mechanism. Neutral and non-partisan bodies-international or regional organization within the region have far greater difficulty in proposing methods to manage these sorts of conflicts.

Notes

1. How Omar Failed the Panchayat System Source: http://www.tehlka.com/2012/10.

Index

B

C

D

I

J

Q

R

S

Y

Y

Z